Anglistik

International Journal
of English Studies

Volume 27 · Issue 1 · March 2016

Edited by
RÜDIGER AHRENS
HEINZ ANTOR

Focus on
Comic Representations in Post-Millennial British and Irish Fiction

Focus editor
BARBARA PUSCHMANN-NALENZ

Universitätsverlag
WINTER
Heidelberg

TABLE OF CONTENTS

FOCUS ON COMIC REPRESENTATIONS IN POST-MILLENNIAL BRITISH AND IRISH FICTION

ARTICLES

FOCUS ON COMIC REPRESENTATIONS IN POST-MILLENNIAL BRITISH AND IRISH FICTION

BARBARA PUSCHMANN-NALENZ

Introduction

The 20th century, regardless of – or because of – its repeated catastrophes, paid considerable theoretical and artistic attention to the investigation of the comic in cultural life and literature. In 1905 Sigmund Freud analyzed humour and joke as essentially connected to the human unconscious. Dating from the 1940s, first published in the 60s, Mikhail Bakhtin's theories on the carnivalesque and the influence of folklore on culture put laughter centre stage as liberating and possibly subversive. For the post-World-War-II era Samuel Beckett especially emphasized the ambiguous nature of comedy as intertwined with the tragic in a conjunction of opposites in the literary representations of drama as well as fiction.[1] Even though the comic remained an area of interdisciplinary research as well, with philosophy, communication science and psychology as probably the most strongly involved academic fields, the study of literature with its various manifestations of the comic has been considered especially rewarding because of the arts' hyperbolic expressiveness regarding cultural shifts and tensions. To perceive and discuss post-millennium developments of comic representation in British and Irish fiction is the objective of this special issue.

Research on the comedic has often been focused on categorizations of its more or less distinct varieties – a venture this introduction does not engage in, since "we immediately become entangled in a cat's-cradle of conflicting definitions" (Cavaliero 2000, ix). Cavaliero distinguishes seven types of the fictionalized comic: "celebration, parody, satire, farce, irony, burlesque and wit" (x). Each of them, he states, unfolds in the process of narration and is illustrated by a number of novels. As the title of the epilogue and subtitle of his book indicates, the narrative undergoes and stimulates "the alchemy of the comedic process" (238). That his survey ends in about 1960 is explained as resulting from the faultlines in society and culture which became effective then and diverged from traditional thinking and perception (x). Very recently, the British writer Jonathan Coe in his discussion of the comic novel (2013) pinpointed the same moment in time as precipitating great cultural change.

For this introduction I initially wish to draw attention to some observations by living anglophone fiction writers on the issue of the comic in narrative literature. "The novel, at a certain basic level, is a comic form" John Banville plainly claims (Anon. n.d., "Amazon Q&A"), and therein agrees with Cavaliero (2000, ix), who regards the novelistic genre's hybridity of origin and history as the main cause for the evident incongruities which produce comedy. The Irish writer equally identifies comedy in

1 For a brief explanation of comedy theories see Niederhoff (2014, esp. 28-35). Beckett as a postmodern writer and audience laughter are explored by Tönnies (1996).

narratives as a generic characteristic which leads to "the history of laughter" (Pfister 2002) in Britain and Ireland. The reason for Banville's generalizing statement, I presume, partly lies in the English novel's pronounced societal concern and impact since its beginnings with Fielding and Sterne in the 18th century. Towards the end of the 20th century the subversive nature of laughter was stretched by revolutionary scientific and social innovations which by then had become central in Western society so that Margaret Drabble described the intellectual-artistic situation of the 1990s in a novelistic portrayal as separated by a cultural watershed from previous ages when science was by most contemporaries regarded as deterministic, space was still clearly defined and the notion of linear time unshakeable. Compartmentalizations and borderlines were apparently breaking down or perceived as dysfunctional, if not illusionary. Established concepts of man and the structure of the world have been recognized as undergoing a constant change at an ever faster pace so that we find ourselves caught in an interminable process of restless revision and bereaved of all absolutes. Drabble's narrator believes – irrespective of the Death of the Author – that we can only respond with laughter even when we become the object of ridicule:

> [...] that other time extends forever, and nothing comes back but a thin cosmic giggle. We got over Copernicus, we got over Galileo, we got over Darwin, we have survived Einstein and the Death of God and the Death of the Family and the Death of the Novel, and what can we do now but laugh? Can the joke save us? (Drabble 1993, 440)

The inducement and target of the "cosmic giggle" is humanity's unavoidable pressure for an incessant updating, which ostentatiously reveals the limitations of the mindscape of *homo sapiens* and mocks his fervour for absolute truths. This exposure to ridicule fulfils one of the basic functions of the comic: to point out the shortcomings of individuals or the species, on account of which we may indeed feel compromised (cf. Peters in this focus section, 85-86). The contemporary challenge to revise theories of the world and of man is obviously as old as these theories themselves and occasionally became a necessity that caused anxieties instead of curiosity, to which persons as well as institutions often responded with fierce resistance. Another English fiction writer's *dictum* published twenty years after Drabble's *The Gates of Ivory* reads like a thoughtful albeit contradictory reply to the final question whether we can be saved by joking: "I think jokes are a good way of being serious. Often the best way" (Barnes 2011, 83). To laugh can prove releasing, liberate tensions or aggression, even though the sort of joke which the postmodern condition evokes may at times not be very far from cynicism because of the apparent circumscription of our nature.

Any 'post' condition obviously stimulates writers to respond with a special mode of gaiety, such as black humour, satire, comic relief, or witticisms, all of which are meant to provoke hilarity by revealing and addressing the comical aspects in the serious or grave. Thus the second fundamental purpose of laughter becomes evident, which is the opposite of the first, namely to signify that a transgression of otherwise respected boundaries is feasible:[2] post-disaster novels such as Kurt Vonnegut's *Slaughterhouse-Five*, Joseph Heller's *Catch-22* or the musical *Oh! What a Lovely War*, anti-war fictions produced in the 1960s with a moderate temporal distance from

2 Laughter and the comic as the essential manifestations of the two contrasting varieties of human borderline experience – limitation and transgression – are defined e.g. by Helmut Bachmaier (2005, 9; 123-24).

the experience of World War II, use non-mimetic yet relational narrativization including surrealist and fantasy elements to represent the unspeakable and absurd, often without words. As their pictorial and graphic signifiers also symbolically indicate, the exposure of farcical elements in tragedies and a comically distorting treatment of the catastrophe imply a transposition of the signified from the ethical level, which may include empathy, to the aesthetic – often with the result that by seemingly ostracizing the moral sphere from the fiction its banishment from both the signifier and the signified is embarrassingly conspicuous. To thematize or foreground the comic when confronting the disastrous presupposes a sometimes radically distancing view, which satire, whose purpose aims at moral criticism, does not establish in the same way. For such works of black humour an American critic coined the term "comic apocalypses" (Schulz 1973, 66). Schulz's concept of "the aesthetics of anxiety," on the other hand, signals how narrative representations dating from the early stages of postmodern fiction in the United States, which subvert a sense of 'stable reality' and blatantly epitomize the notion of 'anything goes' on the layer of diegesis, can, as in Drabble's later quotation, be imbued with black humour in view of "*A Pluralistic Definition of Man and His World*" (Schulz).

In British late 20th-century literature the different kinds of the comic are manifest as a response to the changing state of affairs on the threshold to the third millennium. After the turn of last century the representation of the post-human in narrative fiction has additionally been observed to result in "bleak comedy" (John Mullan 2009, 112 on Kazuo Ishiguro's *Never Let Me Go*). Several films produced in other European countries, e.g. *Life is Beautiful!* (*La vita è bella!*, 1997) or *Good Bye, Lenin!* (2003), present tragicomedies as a response to historic landmarks perceived as deeply disturbing by many contemporaries.[3]

Even though laughter has been convincingly traced as a permanent feature of English literature and claimed as typical of the novel in particular the present collection of essays, informed by published criticism on late 20th-century British narrative fiction and culture, was first instigated not by the discourse on the comic but by the literary treatment of loss and mourning, which is antithetically linked to the renewed topicality of narrative comedy. The present volume focuses on the intricacy of perceived comical crosscurrents countering British 'Millennial Melancholia'[4] and the "rhetoric of loss" which has been observed as permeating international literary theory at least since 1990 (Schiesari 1992, 1). The incidence of successive melancholia and comedy, which is visible in a large number of post-2000 narratives in English, inspired this study of a wide selection of recently published fictions and of the theoretical implications inherent in the paradoxical and disquieting combination of 'melancholy comedy.' To choose the narrative representation of the comic – instead of its social occurrence – for a scholarly investigation proves relevant and well founded, as Manfred Pfister explains in the *History of English Laughter*: "we believe that the representations of

3 *Extremely Loud and Incredibly Close*, the 2005 novel by American author Jonathan Safran Foer that deals with the terrorist attacks of 9/11, has strong comic elemnets due to the narrator/protagonist's point-of-view reminiscient of the hero of *The Tin Drum* by Günther Grass.

4 British cultural and social melancholia are the topics of articles by Vermeulen (2011) and by Gilroy (2011). Cf. also the volume *Narrating Loss* (Glaser and Puschmann-Nalenz 2014).

laughter reveal the faultlines of the anxieties and the social pressures at work at a given historical moment more distinctly than actual laughter does" (2002, vii). Yet up to now contemporary comic fiction has nearly always been explored in the campus novel or feminist women's writing and hardly in connection with the melancholic mood fed by the political and historical impact of loss and change, which is widespread in literature from 1990 on.

Jonathan Coe (2013), whose article incidentally reproaches Germans for not perceiving the jokes in his fiction, has the modern English comic novel start with Kingsley Amis's *Lucky Jim* (1954), of which he rightly claims that it is not so very different in its social comedy from *Joseph Andrews* or *Tom Jones*. The impression persists – and I agree here with Coe – that the palpable caesura in the development of the modern British novel arrived after *Lucky Jim*. Coe himself allegedly doubts that the comic novel can survive in face of imminent dangers and recent catastrophes. Yet ironically both his own recent book *Expo 58* and David Lodge's *Deaf Sentence*, which he quotes as indicative of the death of the comic English novel, are presented as examples of its resurrection in two essays in this volume. The first decade of the new millennium and the beginning of the second decade turned out to be a "historical moment" which continually produced "*Contemporary Crisis Fictions*" (Horton 2014), but where, on the other hand, the imaginative reaction to extremities also resulted in comic prose celebrating "humour, the handmaid of sorrow and fear" (Flann O'Brien, qtd. in Coe 2013). Writers who are known to have become involved in today's burning issues and weighty ethical questions, e.g. climate change, demographic developments, genetic engineering, migration, spying, or crime construct a universe, plots and characters that contain strong farcical overtones as well as humorous and satirical features. The articles in this collection of essays strive to pinpoint the particularly comic qualities of British narratives in a period of accelerated crucial change to which many of the writers discussed here have also paid tribute in 'serious' fiction and nonfiction, and yet for all critical efforts the statement remains valid that "it is impossible to retrieve the phenomenon of the comic as mediated by poetic imagination through systematic description."[5] The narrative comic and its equivalent reception, laughter, defined by Pfister as typical of English literature through the ages (2002, viii), take on a peculiar shape and tone which may be labelled as "*Seriously Funny: from the Ridiculous to the Sublime*" (Jacobson 1997) in an era gloomily aware of oppressive communal problems. Much to the surprise of some of his readers, Ian McEwan said in an interview that fiction at the end of the first decade was "[m]ore fun in lots of ways" compared to the 1970s, but also "more vulgar, a little more trashy" (Anon. 2010).

To propagate the end or impossibility of the literary comic today proves illusionary in view of Jonathan Coe's following observation:

> Jim Dixon ["Lucky Jim"] may have had the cold war to worry about, but in other respects he seems to have been living in a fool's paradise, a bubble of provincial ignorance which today's novelists are simply not permitted to share. Where are the laughs in massacre, famine and climate change, exactly? What's so funny about the Middle East, North Korea and Afghanistan? Who's going to chuckle when they pick up the London Review of Books and find John Lanchester arguing, effectively as always,

5 "Die Erscheinung des Komischen im Medium der poetischen Imagination ist durch systematische Beschreibung nicht einzuholen" (Stierle 1976, 268; my translation).

> that the banking habits of the British people pose a greater threat to their own security than terrorism? (2013)

Jim Dixon may have been lucky and the "bubble" in which he lived may have remained intact due to the limited reach of the media, but we are facing new horrors today, a fact which raises the question how fiction responds to these challenges. We may be oppressed by the above list of disastrous situations to which many more could be added, but Jean Paul's statement from more than 200 years ago still holds: "[...] the comic, like the sublime, never resides in the object, but in the subject."[6] The different forms of comedy in narrative representations supply and provoke varied responses to distressing conditions or events, and they do not aim at excluding highly topical problems from fictional texts.

In the attempt to contextualize contemporary narratives and the poetics of laughter and the fictional(ized) comic a recent monograph has to be mentioned which presents new insights into mostly anglophone novels published before 1975: James Wood's *The Irresponsible Self* (2004). Wood distinguishes between "a kind of tragicomic stoicism which might best be called the comedy of forgiveness" (6) and the more traditional type of "the comedy of correction" (6), whose links to religion, to notions of a stratified society and socially shared moral stances are made evident. While in incidents of the comedy of correction we laugh *at* something or – more often – someone, we laugh *with* somebody in cases of the comedy of forgiveness which hides and obscures human faults instead of censoriously exposing them. Pretense and hypocrisy, according to Wood, are most frequently stimuli for the "monolithic" – that is immovably normative – comedy of correction. A subset of the contrasting comedy of forgiveness, according to Wood, is the "irresponsibility" of the self. He defines this concept as coterminous with unreliability – in a reliably unreliable or unreliably unreliable narration (10). The terminology reveals this concept's special closeness to late 20th-century narrative theory and postmodernism's influence; it also betrays an affinity to the narrator's adoption of a pose, his/her invading of consciousnesses and assuming of diverse voices. Wood emphasizes, however, that clear dividing demarcations between the two types of comedy or straight evolutionary lines from one to the other are impossible to draw. The prime characteristic of the comedy of forgiveness as the result of an "irresponsible self" and the main reason why readers increasingly find it in (post)modern fiction is, according to Wood, the mingling of emotions – laughing and tears. Freud's term "broken humour," also qualifying a frequently displayed self-irony, aptly expresses the human condition shown in many narratives of the early 21st century (15). That this "irresponsibility" of the "comedy of forgiveness" is a highly charged issue has quite lately become evident. In January 2015 the French satirical magazine *Charlie Hebdo* exhibited the resolution to respond with 'tearful mockery' to the Islamist terrorist attacks on its editorial office in Paris: the front cover of 14 January 2015 showed a weeping Mohammed who has already forgiven the killing of eleven members of the staff (and, as the caption implies, of eight more innocent people in a supermarket). In the caricaturist mode the drawing mourns the victims as well as the

---

6 Jean Paul (Johann Paul Friedrich Richter), *Vorschule der Aesthetik* (1804): "so dass also das Komische, wie das Erhabene, nie im Objekte wohnt, sondern im Subjekte" (qtd. in Bachmaier 2005, 31; my translation).

Muslim perpetrators and their deed.[7] By resuming their assignment in February the survivors demonstrated that "kind of tragicomic stoicism" James Wood had diagnosed as characteristic of laughter in the novel and whose future Jonathan Coe incredulously doubted when he gruffly asked "[w]hat's so funny about [present disasters]?" (2013). The editors of *Charlie Hebdo* contended through the pictorial and verbal form of their protest that they consider cartoons, polemics and jokes to be a necessity for maintaining a freedom of expression, which can itself become a social and political problem. The question arises, then, whether in current British narrative fiction the recent turns of the comic will be temporary and fleeting – possibly because of the gravity of the situation; in other words whether we can continue to 'make fun of' the seriousness of the present global and regional conditions. The following short introduction to the individual essays will try to summarize the responses by writers of fiction and their respective literary critics.

At the turn of the millennium Cavaliero argued that the comedic faces a new challenge. The reason, according to him, is the continual social and moral accommodation of individual consciousnesses and a pluralistic improvisation, which began in the 18th century and has meanwhile reached our "itemized, instinctual, fragmentary world" (2000, 241). Cavaliero's conclusive statement is based on his argument that "[c]omedy is a vehicle of communication [that could lead] into an acceptance of differing beliefs and attitudes, and into a recognition of the inevitable relativity of every human aspiration to finality and truth" (239). This assessment supports Margaret Drabble's above-mentioned observation and turns her question into a rhetorical one: if we cannot anticipate whether the joke can save us at the beginning of the 21st century, fiction writers and critics, like journalists, equally advocate that the often controversial turn to the comic will prove supportive when we want to meet present challenges. Certainly humour will not be the only answer, and the comic turn, which reached its peak at the end of the first decade, may grow – or dwindle – into 'turns' of a varying kind and intensity.

The contributions to this focus section have been arranged in four different groups, a structure which my brief presentation of the individual articles follows. However, the division has to be regarded, if not as provisional, at least in terms of a working hypothesis. A writer like Martin Amis – to choose a prominent example – who speaks of himself as a comic writer, may after some dissension also be classified as one of those who created one or two totally funny digressions inside his production of more unambiguously serious narrative works – and is therefore rightly placed with *Lionel Asbo* in Section II.

The first part of the focus section discusses new turns of the comic in novels by British writers who are known for inscribing their fictional narratives with different kinds of comedy, humour and satire; in some cases, I wish to anticipate, the comic had already become the object of contrasting analyses.

In his article on Jonathan Coe's *Expo 58* (2013) Jean-Michel Ganteau takes as his starting point statements by Laurent Mellet published the same year on the responsibility of satire in recent British fictions. Ganteau shows how Coe's novels of the early years of the third millennium provide comic state-of–the-nation narratives strong on

7 For the cover illustration see: "*Charlie Hebdo*. Issue No. 1178." *Wikipedia*. 14 January 2015. Web. 26 February 2015.

issues from the 1970s, 80s and 90s, which also gave rise to comments about this author's realism or his commitment to political topics. *Expo 58* is no exception in this respect, and it also confirms Coe's status as a writer of humorous and satirical fiction, with Evelyn Waugh as his forerunner. However, Ganteau argues that in this instance Coe 'fails' to fulfill generic criteria and instead achieves something new that does not smoothly fit in either category: the article contends that he engages with issues of failure and limitedness instead of deriding them as modern satire does (20). The title of *Expo 58* indicates its historical character and refers to the novelty of an international public event and to its multinational audience in the 1950s. The protagonist, an average person and stranger in a foreign country – Belgium –, is sent to supervise the cultural representation of the supposed quintessence of a popularized version of Britishness: the pub 'Britannia' in the British pavilion in Brussels. This becomes the source of hilarity in the narrative and is analyzed by Ganteau with reference to Henry Fielding's explanation of the comic epic in the preface to *Joseph Andrews*. Coe also finds in human frailty and its concomitant errors abundant material for shaping the narrative in terms of an empathetic "ethical – as opposed to moral – orientation of the contemporary comic novel" (22). Ganteau designates *Expo 58* as approaching Wood's concept of the Comedy of Forgiveness. Comedy as a 'democratizing genre' and a means of introducing and admonishing the toleration, even protection, of difference(s) celebrates values such as relationality and forbearance in *Expo 58* (27-28).

Andrew Tate's article, which deals with Nick Hornby's melancholic comedies and focuses on *A Long Way Down* (2005), the failed-suicide story of four Londoners, analyzes the tragicomic novels that this writer has produced since the early 1990s. Hornby's combination of the funny and the sad, itself already part of a tradition of humorous and comic writing, leads to playing with the "happy ending" convention.[8] In Tate's exploration of style and structure in Hornby's work seriousness emerges as one of the main effects of the comic which is frequently informed by loss, vulnerability or anger. The comic in *A Long Way Down* also results from attempts at incorporating failure and loss into one's life (narrative). To make life livable it is insufficient for the characters to accept a few life lessons; in his recent novels Hornby rejects 'smooth' closures in the tradition of romanticizing comedy. His comic turn after the millennium displays an "equivocally merciful attitude to his richly flawed characters" in *A Long Way Down* (page 11), who at the end solemnly and with ambivalence consider the god-like perspective from 'their' high-rise once more. Apart from contextualizing *A Long Way Down* in Hornby's oeuvre, Tate delineates the problems which arise from the attempt to diachronically and hierarchically classify it as coming "after ladlit" or between popular and the high-culture novel, respectively. The critical reception of these strands of fiction is considered, and among current theories of the comic James Wood's concept of "the comedy of forgiveness" stands out, the application of which on a metafictional level also reveals the novelist's generosity towards the despisers of the comic who deny its seriousness. Tate's statement that "contemporary Britain has an uneasy relationship with comedy and comic fiction, in particular" (42), summarizes his evaluation of Hornby's work in the national culture.

8 This ambiguity is also manifest in the fact that the volume *Narrating Loss: Mourning, Melancholia and Nostalgia in Contemporary Anglophone Fictions* (Glaser and Puschmann-Nalenz 2014) could also comprise an article on Hornby's *How to Be Good*.

Whether *The Finkler Question* by Howard Jacobson is more humorous or sad has been debated ever since its appearance in 2010 and particularly after its nomination for the Man Booker Prize, regardless of the fact that the author calls himself a comic writer without specifying this. As Andrew Tate underlines in his essay (cf. 33, note 3) the reception of Jacobson's novel marks the first time in more than twenty years that a truly comic novel has been taken seriously enough to receive the Booker Prize. Christoph Houswitschka analyzes Jacobson's novel and in particular the kind of humour – British or Jewish? – used or ridiculed in it by applying a narratological approach which distinguishes between different internal focalizers, the shifting narrators and the implied reader. Thereby it becomes possible to show how tensions between the diverging figural views and deviating images of the other, prejudice included, create humour. The main character, Julian Treslove, a Gentile who wishes to be considered a Jew, keeps asking himself how others see him or how he wants to be seen, and invents himself accordingly. Tensions thus arise between focalization and narration and this is then correlated to (self)images or stereotypes the implied and the flesh-and-blood readers may hold about Jewishness. This may create funny incongruities between observation, perception and narration and subvert opinionated stances (47). Jacobson thereby certainly evades a definition of Jewishness (51) and "achieves humour and comedy mainly by shifting focalization" (57). "[C]hallenging our routine sympathies and valuations" (51) may be effected by humour, as Jacobson also stated in an interview. It is interesting how Houswitschka explains the author's self-characterization as "a Jewish Jane Austen:" analogous to Austen's comedic female portrayals and comments, which she directs in her fictionalizations of a male-dominated society to readers living in such a one, Jacobson's narrative accommodates Jewishness and its past in contemporary British society. This procedure, which does not deny the diasporic and endangered situation of Jews, uncovers its ludicrous elements by the distance achieved and makes the whole social mesh a comedy of manners.

Heinrich Versteegen's essay interprets David Lodge's 2008 "off-campus novel" (70) *Deaf Sentence* as a new turn of the comic screw differing from the author's earlier works, because the "level of darkness and woefulness" (62) is much higher here and deeply imbued with the awareness of saddening issues. Again, as was emphasized for Hornby's and Jacobson's narratives, the funny and the grievous are intertwined, so that they evoke laughter and tears. Therefor, *Deaf Sentence* does not fall into neatly divided gloomy and comic parts, but integrates the two moods into each other to achieve a narrative fluidity corresponding to the characters' 'mixed feelings' and the novel's tragicomic situations. Versteegen argues that on the one hand this mixture can be phenomenologically observed (69, footnote 17) and that, on the other hand, the representations of grievous situations and the comic responses to them are not opposed to each other in the novel, "but that both are ambivalent and fluid modes of storytelling which complement each other" (62). The differing perspectives of the unreliable homodiegetic focalizer/narrator and a heterodiegetic observer – the reader – produce "Lodge's unstable comedy about decrepitude and disability" (68; cf. 63). Society's tendency towards a pathos, which was prescribed in order not to offend proper reverence for death and assisted suicide, is subverted by the depiction of the protagonist's relief. Although it cannot be called funny this portrayal does not oppose the humorous mode. "Both the comic and the serious parts jointly explore the fluid modes with which contemporary culture handles aging and dying" (68). Versteegen claims. Conclusively, he contends that in the early 21st century established patterns and rites surrounding old age and death have largely lost their meaning, together with the discourse available for these topics – a situation Lodge pays tribute to in his novel.

The following articles address exceptional comic works in the oeuvre of well-established seriously committed writers. Ian McEwan, Martin Amis and John Banville have become known as authors concerned with contemporary problematic issues or disquieting emotional conditions and have a reputation for often writing in a thoughtful and dark, even melancholic, mode.

Peter Childs regards Ian McEwan's novels *Solar* (2010) and *Sweet Tooth* (2012) as an effort to connect representations of humour and politics in a comic way (73). In *Solar* human frailty, Childs maintains, is exposed as the reason why theoretically successful solutions for grave situations like climate change fail spectacularly. The protagonist Beard, egotistic and undisciplined, represents the members of the Arctic expedition and human kind in an emblematic way, as Childs shows: selfishness and thoughtlessness reign supreme. Discrepancies and incongruity abound in related events and relationships, which implicitly describes the characters as blankly irresponsible in putting short-term gain over long-term charges, and consequently even more intensely demands from the reader an ethical attitude towards serious problems instead of a head-in-the-sand policy. The way of portraying the negligent and careless – because convenient – behaviour of the protagonist (who resembles a grotesque postmodern Falstaff) in his environment is above all funny, and if it makes him a comic character we can indeed feel ourselves addressed. Tackling a serious, politically relevant problem is exposed as subverted by everyday stupidity as a result of ordinary human flaws rather than evil intents or downright badness, thereby revealing the absurdity of humanity's stances in threatening situations. The novelist thus approaches James Wood's comedy type of the irresponsible self, yet the question still arises whether we wish to forgive this protagonist and thus want to forgive ourselves (80).

Sweet Tooth is considered by Childs to be "a very different example of comic writing, deceptive and manipulative" (80). Concealed identities and secrets invoke and parody the pattern of the spy novel, toying with surfaces and distortions, lies, intrigues and frauds. Neither irresponsibility nor forgiveness are earnestly addressed, in "a devious turn to a furtive amusement" (83) that contrasts with McEwan's more serious fictions before and – I wish to add – after.

Martin Amis's "State-of-England" novel *Lionel Asbo*, published in 2013, certainly justifies the author's reputation as satirist. Susanne Peters discusses whether it is a humorous novel and in what way the comedy is displayed. Discrepancies between the two main characters, Desmond and his uncle Lionel, are one source of the comedic, and the narrative's insistence on the emblematic degradation of the eponymous hero's habits, presented as entropy, gains a ludicrous speed. On a metafictional level the more romantic reader expectations in regard to generic characteristics are disappointed to a degree which turns the effect into the hilarious: neither does the end bring poetic justice with punishment of crime and/or reward of virtue nor does it reconcile, relax or recompense the reader. Indeed, Amis's is a very "peculiar kind of humour" (88). As in the essays on Hornby, Lodge or Jacobson, in Peters's article it is also emphasized that the related events and circumstances are not at all comic in themselves, but become comic to the reader by the distancing mode of telling. Amis's narrative includes incidents and a style reminiscent of the tabloids, but presented to the educated reader of 'highbrow' contemporary fiction. The similarity with Dickens is unmistakable. "Comically juxtaposed discrepancies" (94), the topicality of excessiveness, and vernacular as well as the incongruent imagery unfold the comedic in this novel's discourse on the anti-social in society. Finally aggression and mock-aggression, already named by Sigmund Freud as the prime cause of joking and laughter, are identified in the narrative and shown contribute to the author's dark variety of humour, which includes menace by social pressure and the ensuing feelings of anxiety and fear. That we are dealing with a kind of gallows humour is perhaps verified by the author's escape from (his image of) the country that he allegorizes in *Lionel Asbo*.

The article by Barbara Puschmann-Nalenz on John Banville's *The Infinities* (2009) considers this narrativization of mortality and death as opposed to his preceding novel *The Sea*. Whereas melancholia also characterized the memories of the protagonists in his third trilogy, which includes *Ancient Light* (2012), *The Infinities* presents human death and love as a divine comedy. Similarly to Ian McEwan's 'comic swerve' (see Peter Childs's article), Banville's *The Infinities* stands out among his production of serious narrativizations of often saddening issues. The manner of producing comedy through the representation of a grievous subject hinges on the perspective of an ancient Greek god, Hermes the messenger. The divine point-of-view and the depiction of the world as theatre with human life as spectacle make the events appear as relative and limited, because of the anthropomorphous way of "constructing" the world. The humorous, the bucolic and the grotesque dominate the portrayal of a celebrity's illness and dying and the accompanying family reunion, which is duplicated on the Olympian level in a reenactment of the Amphitryon myth. Zeus, Hermes (both invisible) and Pan (in human disguise) have come to Arden House to seek pleasure and offer comfort and guidance at this hour, but only Rex the Dog on account of his animal nature is able to see the gods. Humour spreads far into this unusual discourse on love and death: in the telling names of characters and places, through the youthful vernacular of Hermes commenting on the erotic adventures of the different agents, and in the discrepancies of their perception which is highlighted by shifting focalization. Forgiveness and benevolence, dispensed by the gods, turn suffering and grief into a harmonious ending in Arcadia, so that death appears as a possible transfiguration and life as romantic – tongue-in-cheek of course, because as god is the author of the events and their representation so is the author unmistakably god in the text's universe.

The next two articles about acculturation experience and retrospect opens with an article by Merle Tönnies about memoirs by British Asians born/raised in Britain – a genre that is selling well at the moment. The comic potential of Pakistani and Muslim immigrant experience can more easily become visible in memoirs written from a distance and situated between fiction and biography than in the Black British Bildungsroman whose emphasis lies on the hardships of generating a social identity. Different narrative techniques are used in a memoir to heighten this potential in similar conflicting encounters with racism and divided loyalties. Merle Tönnies scrutinizes memoirs of male and female authors by comparing the representations of specific experiences in five texts, such as moving in Britain from the margins to the social and spatial centres, coping with cultural and religious disparities at home and in school, and reaching an individual balance between belonging and distancing within the family. It is precisely these divergences that provoke comedy, not least because the reader's position can frequently approach that of the narrator who is no longer completely part of the other (non-British) culture. This convergence of narrator and reader is also facilitated as the first person of the memoir often discloses criticism of his/her own former positions and distinguishes sharply between the narrating and the narrated self. Self-irony makes it easy for the reader to laugh at some of these experiences, since in the memoirs perspective prevails over the seriousness of objective fact. The generational gap between immigrant parents and British-born youths with their corresponding cultural disparateness remembered years later can thus equally provoke mirth in both focalizer and recipient. Laughter expresses the discrepancies, and the humour of the narrating I can manipulate the reader's laughter or – more rarely – outrage, even where Islam is mocked.

Stephan Karschay and Joanna Rostek interpret Bernadine Evaristo's *Mr Loverman* (2013) as a "demonstrat[ion of] how we fashion ourselves and are perceived by others through a range of markers that dissect identity into separate categories, such as class, race, age, gender [...]" (125), so that we consider the novel's protagonist, an aging, black, married man of Caribbean origin, and, in addition, a (formerly closeted) homosexual as its epitome. The article aims at an analysis of the function of the main character's humour in the painful process of revealing his sexual orientation to himself and others. As a basis for the close reading of the novel the authors discuss especially gender theory and the connection between sex and laughter as it has been investigated by Sigmund Freud and recently explained by Gaby Pailer or Manfred Pfister. Humour is discovered as versatile and multifunctional, and this is how Barry, the protagonist, uses it; the essay applies psychological categories to reveal the central character's disposition in considering his existence humorously (128). The argument additionally relies on Thomas Hobbes' writings, where humour also expresses a (real or feigned) sense of superiority. On the level of the story, Barry needs this attitude to mask his insecurity about being a homosexual from a homophobic patriarchal culture in a heterosexually normative society. From linguistic and rhetorical details to gender or class markers the narrative unveils the fluidity of borderlines, which Barry also gradually discovers while constructing for himself and eventually others his 'new' – long denied – very individual identity. At last the marker 'aging' or 'old' is – not least by the help of humour – equally viewed as socially constructed and fluid. Barry can be seen as the exponent of developments of the last decades which "add up to a joint effort to move these categories away from the realm of 'nature' and situate them closer to the domain of 'culture'" (132).

In the final two articles of this focus section other forms beside the novel are encompassed in the research on fiction and humour: e.g. film, tv and short stories, which equally employ the comic as an instrument of narration. As Marion Gymnich shows in her article on Sebastian Faulks's satirical novel *A Week in December* (2006), films and TV shows are thematically and diegetically linked to the comic novel. Faulks "addresses a remarkable range of problems British society has to face at the beginning of the new millennium, including for instance the fear of terrorism, challenges in the field of health care as well as the increasing lack of trust in the international financial and banking system" (137). Faulks's type of Condition-of-England novel reflects the 19th-century novel of social criticism by Dickens and Elizabeth Gaskell, while its narration is informed by different comic traditions. In the several plot strands, which are held together by the narrative device of the preparations for a dinner party, Faulks draws upon the stereotypes of romantic comedy epitomized in contemporary film as in pornography (139), but most of all refers to the tradition of satire. Its main targets are the entertainment industry such as 'reality tv' with its cynical exposure and exploitation of contestants with psychological or health problems, the cliché of the evil banker prospering on the financial crisis, and the fear of terrorism viewed from the terrorist's angle – a narrative procedure which seems to go back to Jonathan Swift's *Modest Proposal* (145). The failure of another planned terrorist attack in London causes convulsive laughter in the Islamist perpetrator – and, quite incongruously, – instant conversion from his previous convictions. Marion Gymnich contends that the reference to the romantic comedy as the structuring force is important even for this plot strand. This is diegetically expressed by the characters' numerous smiles and laughter, and the narrative ends on an optimistic note, demonstrating that the traditions of romantic comedy and satire are not irreconcilable and that the novel's hybridity is its asset.

Ulrike Zimmermann states that the comic after the turn of the millennium is increasingly to be found in all fictional genres and in connection with every possible topic, even the most serious ones. On the other hand, acceptance of the comic is hesitant, especially when it is applied to grave issues. After a brief survey of Immanuel Kant's, Sigmund Freud's and Henri Bergson's theories of the comic the author emphasizes that comedy has an impact on a text's meaning and must not be conceived of as a mere decoration or way of expression. The short stories she chooses for her analysis "have the comic as part of their innermost structure" (150). Muriel Spark and Fay Weldon, from whose work her first examples are taken, both demonstrate incongruity as the source of the comic, in Weldon's story "Site" also with a subversive effect mainly directed against the encrusted way of thinking in public institutions, in Sparks's as a juxtaposition of the protagonist's fantastic self-image and the narrator's portrayal deflating it/him. Zimmermann's more extensive interpretation of Marina Lewycka's "The Importance of Having Warm Feet" emphasizes the structuring effect of humour on the narrative and its message, which is achieved by juxtaposing death, first of an army and then of a much-loved mother, with the hilarious performance of a nativity play. In all incidents woolen socks and the lack of warm footwear play an important role. The discrepancy between the everyday object and its significance in the grievous or supposedly festive situation results in a sense of the humorous and produces a conciliatory and composed attitude in the first-person narrator. Finally, in the reading of a short story by Jackie Kay the reader follows the experience of Maggie Lockhart who comes to terms with her 'fate' of resembling the Queen in achieving to laugh about it and even gain some gratification from her looks.

Works Cited

Anon. "You Ask … Ian McEwan." *Waterstone's Books Quarterly.* March 2010. Web. 31 May 2010.

Anon. "Q&A with Author John Banville." The Infinities Amazon Editorial Reviews. *Amazon.com Review*. n.d. Web. 20 January 2016.

Bachmaier, Helmut, ed. *Texte zur Theorie der Komik*. Stuttgart: Reclam, 2005.

Barnes, Julian. *Pulse*. London: Vintage, 2011.

Cavaliero, Glen. *The Alchemy of Laughter: Comedy in English Fiction*. Houndmills: Macmillan, 2000.

"*Charlie Hebdo*. Issue No. 1178." (14 January 2015). *Wikipedia*. Web. 26 February 2015.

Coe, Jonathan. "What's so Funny about Comic Novels?" *The Guardian*. 7 September 2013. Web. 14 February 2015.

Drabble, Margaret. *The Gates of Ivory*. [1991]. New York: Penguin, 1993.

Gilroy, Paul. "The Closed Circle of Britain's Postcolonial Melancholia." *The Literature of Melancholia. Early Modern to Postmodern*. Eds. Martin Middeke and Christina Wald. London: Palgrave Macmillan, 2011. 187-204.

Glaser, Brigitte Johanna and Barbara Puschmann-Nalenz, eds. *Narrating Loss: Mourning, Melancholia and Nostalgia in Contemporary Anglophone Fictions*. Trier: WVT, 2014.

Horton, Emily. *Contemporary Crisis Fictions: Affect and Ethics in the Modern British Novel*. London: Palgrave Macmillan, 2014.

Jacobson, Howard. *Seriously Funny: From the Ridiculous to the Sublime*. London: Viking, 1997.

Mullan, John. "On First Reading Kazuo Ishiguro's *Never Let Me Go*." *Kazuo Ishiguro: Contemporary Critical Perspectives*. Eds. Sean Matthews and Sebastian Groes. London: Continuum, 2009. 104-13.

Niederhoff, Burkhard. *Die englische Komödie. Eine Einführung*. Berlin: Schmidt, 2014.

Pfister, Manfred. "Beckett, Barker, and Other Grim Laughers." *A History of English Laughter: Laughter from Beowulf to Beckett and Beyond*. Ed. Manfred Pfister. Amsterdam: Rodopi, 2002. 175-89.

—. "Introduction: A History of English Laughter?" *A History of English Laughter: Laughter from Beowulf to Beckett and Beyond*. Ed. Manfred Pfister. Amsterdam: Rodopi, 2002. v-x.

Schiesari, Juliana. *The Gendering of Melancholia: Feminism, Psychoanalysis, and the Symbolics of Loss in Renaissance Literature*. Ithaca, NY: Cornell University Press, 1992.

Schulz, Max F. *Black Humor Fiction of the Sixties: A Pluralistic Definition of Man and His World*. Athens, OH: Ohio University Press, 1973.

Stierle, Karlheinz. "Komik der Handlung, Komik der Sprachhandlung, Komik der Komödie." *Das Komische*. Eds. Wolfgang Preisendanz and Rainer Warning. München: Fink, 1976. 237-68.

Tönnies, Merle. *Samuel Beckett's Dramatic Strategy: Audience Laughter and the Postmodernist Debate*. Trier: WVT, 1996.

Vermeulen, Pieter. "The Novel after Melancholia: On Tom McCarthy's Remainder and David Mitchell's Ghostwritten." *The Literature of Melancholia. Early Modern to Postmodern*. Eds. Martin Middeke and Christina Wald. London: Palgrave Macmillan, 2011. 254-67.

Wood, James. *The Irresponsible Self: On Laughter and the Novel*. New York: Farrar, Strauss and Giroux, 2004.

JEAN-MICHEL GANTEAU

Innocent Abroad: Jonathan Coe's *Expo 58* and the Comedy of Forgiveness

In an article on the evolution of the satirical novel in Britain from E. M. Forster to the present, Laurent Mellet draws our attention to the function of contemporary satire (with special reference to Martin Amis and Jonathan Coe):

> Satire should now reject the deontic and, through metafictional confrontations, define the task to confront us with amoral or not moral fiction as the new responsibility of literature. In other words, to widen the gap and create new forms of dissensus, to question our spontaneity towards literary satire, to play with our expectations so that literature can still be the other eventually responsible for us – ethically responsible or politically humanistic. (Mellet 2013, 179-80)

In his view, satirical fiction has gone through various phases during the last century, taking its distance from the humanist stance perceptible in Forster's work, before coming back to a more humanist practice. Such a move is supposed to be attuned to a Levinasian-based ethics predicated on openness and tentativeness as opposed to an earlier, deontic moral inspiration. What Mellet confronts us with, then, is a paradoxical vision of literary satire geared to an explicit, direct expression of humanism as opposed to an earlier one in which the loss of humanist values was deplored in a more prescriptive way. Said differently, he sees the new type of satire as essentially based on ethical openness, i.e. some form of humbled satire conscious of its own vulnerabilities and considering vulnerability not merely as a failure or a sin to be castigated, but as a state worthy of our less distant, more benevolent attention.

In describing such an evolution, Mellet may well be thinking of some of Coe's early novels, like *What A Carve Up!* (1994), in which an uncompromising satire of the effects of liberalism on the working and middle classes in the 1980s is mixed up with a sympathetic consideration of the suffering individual taken in his or her singularity – as is the case with Fiona –, and with a metafictional, parodic playfulness that may be felt to tone down or problematize the stark political message.[1] It must be said that most of Coe's most recent production has tended to confirm such a diagnosis. What I have in mind is the satire that runs through *The Rotters' Club* (2001) or *The Closed Circle* (2004), two narratives intent on providing a radioscopy of the nation from the 1970s to the late 1990s, concentrating on social and political issues, and elaborating on the secular tradition of the state-of-the-nation subgenre (Mellet 2015, 6). In such narratives, which provide an up-to-date, at times euphemized version of the committed novel, political concerns come high on the author's agenda and are conversant with a commitment of another type, as they engage with the evocation of

1 On politics and the representation of individual or intimate helplessness or vulnerability in Coe's *oeuvre*, see Mellet's *Jonathan Coe. Les politiques de l'intime*, and more specifically his analysis of *The Rain before It Falls* (2015, 13). Vanessa Guignery addresses the relations between playfulness and satire in her "'Colonel Mustard, in the Billiard Room, with the Revolver': Jonathan Coe's *What A Carve Up!* as a Postmodern Whodunit" (Guignery 2011).

individual destinies and private affects, even while relying on comedy (5).[2] The mixture of satire, in its euphemized form, humour and comedic structures or *topoi* has become one of the hallmarks of Coe's production, and his 2013 novel, *Expo 58*, comes as no surprise to the reader in this respect.

As underlined by most commentators, *Expo 58* works in the realist tradition even while flaunting its parodic dimension by building on the type of spy novel popularized by Ian Fleming (complete with clearly signposted references on pages 130 and 140, for instance), and by borrowing some characters from the world of Belgian artist Hergé (the two improbable, twin-like agents have been identified as imported from the world of the *Tintin* series and as latter-day avatars of the Tomson and Thompson couple [Guignery 2014; Lasdun 2013]). What is often emphasized is the "lightness of touch" (Carty 2013) and the "delightfully funny" (Connolly 2013) dimension of the narrative, which contributes to a vision of the novel as an exercise in light comedy, as underscored by references to the influence of Ealing comedies of yesteryear (Leith 2013). Still, several critics underlined its polytonal aspect, as it blends "frivolous comedy" with "bone-dry history" (Robson 2013), and Coe's "unusual ability to counterpoint the comic and the poignant [that sets] his writing apart" (Carty 2013). The mildness of tone that emerges from the narratives may well be one of the effects of the mingling of the satirical and the comedic, of the humorous and the seriously historical, of distance from and engagement with the subject at hand. This is why I shall argue that *Expo 58* contributes to the creation of new forms of dissensus (Mellet 2013, 180) by producing a comic novel that is not so comic, a satire that is not quite a satire, and a comedy that is full of *gravitas*. More precisely, my point will be that what characterizes *Expo 58*, as emblematic of a great part of Coe's production, is an engagement with the central issues of failure, fallibility and limits that canonical satire and comedy are used to deriding. What I find singular in Coe's novel, then, is that it addresses human fallibility not as a vice or fault, but as a complex of situations and emotions to be paid attention to. This it does by turning its back on the "comedy of correction" to adopt the aesthetic and ethical choices of the "comedy of forgiveness" (Wood 2004, 4), which implies eroding the emotional distance inherent in satire and humour and casting human frailties in a sympathetic light. *Expo 58* thus performs an emotional and ethical inversion by promoting a move from traditional satire to grave comedy. To demonstrate this, I shall first concentrate on *Expo 58* as updating the comic novel. I shall then address the way in which it recuperates and distorts satire by providing a parody of such canonical antecedents as Evelyn Waugh's *Scoop* (1938). I shall conclude on the text's adoption of the idiom and ambitions of the comedy of forgiveness, which will lead me to argue that it is primarily concerned with time.

A Comic Novel ... But Not Quite

As suggested in the brief survey presented above, *Expo 58* is generally taken to be "tremendously good fun" (Connolly 2013), and thereby meets the basic criterion of the comic novel. Besides, in conformity with its metafictional vein, it introduces elements of self-reflection on its use of humour. This is the case in all parodic passages – but more about this later – and above all in one of the comments on the essence of Englishness or, rather Britishness, with which the novel is rife. I should state at this point that the novel is concerned with a few months in the life of Thomas

2 For an overview of the reception of Coe's novels, see the introduction to Mellet's monograph (Mellet 2015, 3-14).

Foley, an unexceptional, unassuming young man working in the Central Office of Information in London, living with his young wife Sylvia and their baby girl in Tooting, who is selected to overlook the replica of a traditional British pub, the Britannia, the jewel in the crown of the British pavilion at the 1958 Brussels Universal Exposition. Such a choice is motivated, ludicrously enough, by the double fact that his mother is Belgian and his father used to be a publican. Britishness, or rather quintessential Britishness, or rather its popular representation, fuels one of the thematic strands of a novel that uses the pretext of an international event staged in what is still considered the post-war period to bring together people of various nationalities, in a spirit of dialogue that does not exclude the appraisal and confrontation of differences. This provides the opportunity to present the reader with a series of types: the loud American, the scheming Russian, the provincial Belgian, and the eccentric Briton and the innocent abroad who, given the opportunity of a holiday from his humdrum family life, discovers a new world that he in many ways fails to come to terms with. Britishness, then, is said to be best emblematized by humour, as indicated by one of the characters, towards the end: "Odd, isn't it? All that science, and technology, and culture, and history, and it's the good old British sense of humour that sees us through in the end" (Coe 2013a, 208). Even while evoking the parochial, not too technologically advanced state of a nation that Coe at times nostalgically reconstitutes in *Expo 58*, such a metafictional wink certainly aims at sounding the theme of a nation very much attached to its traditions. One step further, the reader who is cognizant of the fact that Coe wrote his MA dissertation on the works of Henry Fielding (Coe 2013c) cannot but spot an allusion to Fielding's practice of the comic novel and definition of the subgenre in the preface to *Joseph Andrews*.

Overall, *Expo 58* abides by the conventions of realism, a realism at times problematized by some metafictional and hypertextual games, though not to the same extent as what is to be found in *What A Carve Up!* From this point of view, Fielding's 1742 prescriptions as to the comic novel's faithfulness to reality, where "every thing is copied from the book of nature" (Fielding 1977, 30), are respected. And even though the novel introduces some amount of what the 18th-century master called "burlesque" through the parody of the spy novel – which is reminiscent of the parody of the novel of detection in *What A Carve Up!* –, this component is not prominent and does not manage to jeopardize the realistic framework. Besides, on top of the realistic mode, the narrative boasts the ingredients that Fielding defined as constitutive of the comic novel. For one thing, it introduces ordinary characters who may be said to be hyperbolically ordinary at times, as is the case with Thomas, the main protagonist, reported to be "'a decent sort' and 'the unassuming, dependable type'" (Coe 2013a, 2). This is also true of the main female characters, his continental friends Anneke and Clara, but also of most people he meets within the capsule of privilege and extraordinariness that the expo provides. *Expo 58* follows Fielding's rules not only in introducing "persons of inferiour rank, and consequently of inferiour manners," but also people ordinary in "sentiments and diction" by privileging the ludicrous and "a certain drollery in style" (Fielding 1977, 26).

Indeed, *Expo 58* resonates with jokes and puns. In its revisiting of post-war Europe, it takes pains to use what to the contemporary reader sound like anachronistic words, or uses, as is the case with the officials' insistence on the presentation of "Gay Belgium," the adjective being used in a meaning altogether different from what the contemporary reader has in mind. Even while this helps measure the passing of time and assert the pastness of the past, the practice of *double entendre* solicits the reader's alertness to the presence of two distinct messages, thus introducing the intellectual perception and above all the emotional distance necessary for humour to emerge. Similarly, one of the running jokes is based on the pun-*cum*-antanaclasis associated with the name of the pub waitress, Shirley Knott, a sequence that is almost homophonous with "Surely not!," as ostentatiously indicated on pages 85 and 242. The same vein of lightness or "drollery" is extended in passages when verbal humour leaves room for situational humour, as when, in a parodic revision of one of the spy-novel *topoi*, Thomas is taken away in a car that is too small to welcome him and his kidnapper comfortably (Coe 2013a, 133), or whenever Radford and Wayne, the avatars of Hergé's Thomson and Thompson, reappear in incongruous circumstances and indulge in a patter based on absurd paraphrase and reminiscent of music-hall pieces (33, 152, 237, 244). Now, even if they do not necessarily make the reader laugh out loud, such devices are characteristic of the diction of the comic novel, in that they do privilege the ludicrous over the sublime, to take up Fielding's categories and definitions (Fielding 1977, 26), and the reliance on such passages contributes to building up the atmosphere of lightness and mildness accommodated by the realistic idiom.

There are moments when Coe gives Fielding's definitions a berth, though, in his observation of the ridiculous, which is the province of the comic novel, according to the author of *Joseph Andrews* (28). What is supposed to generate the ridiculous is affectation, in the shape of the twin vices of vanity and hypocrisy (28). Now, even though Thomas Foley may at times dissemble (throughout the narrative, he never manages to tell his Belgian sweetheart, Anneke, that he is a married man, and the reader is led to infer that he never tells his wife of his 'affair' with Anneke either), and even though the opening of the novel warns the reader that there may be a touch of "self-assurance, bordering on arrogance" in the man (Coe 2013a, 2), the portrait that emerges from the novel as a whole is that of an ordinary, innocent individual, some sort of an *homme moyen sensuel* whose limitations are exposed by the circumstances into which he is plunged. In other words, in *Expo 58* the source of the ridiculous is not so much the wish to correct hypocrisy and affectation – the mainsprings of the comic novel – as the desire to bank on the secondary source of the ridiculous as defined by Fielding, i.e. "the accidental consequences of some human frailty, or foible" (Fielding 1977, 30).

My point is that what fuels the *vis comica* of *Expo 58* is not so much the moral evocation of vice as the representation of human frailty or vulnerability or, in Fielding's terms, "the affectations of nature" (29). That Thomas Foley represents the *homme moyen sensuel* as characterized by a whole array of limitations is emblematic of Coe's personal take on the form and of the ethical – as opposed to moral – orientation of the contemporary comic novel. For instance, in his use of the error that leads Thomas to misinterpret the presence of a corn cushion in his connubial bed (he thinks that it belongs to his neighbour, even while it has been left there by his wife [Coe 2013a, 180]), Coe underlines the character's limitations and his tendency to err as opposed to sin.[3] What we are presented with, ultimately, is the main protagonist's benign errors (even if an appendix-like paragraph, on page 250, underlines his responsibilities) and his repeated humiliations when, in epiphanic moments or instants when *anagnorisis* triumphs, he realizes that he was wrong, that he has failed, thus signposting vulnerability's sway. If we take up Northrop Frye's categorizations, and his distinction between *eiron*, *alazon*, *agroikos* and buffoon (Frye 1990, 172) as emblematic comic

3 For a thoroughly convincing treatment of error as opposed to mistake in Coe's novels, see Mellet 2015, 71-76.

characters, what appears is that Thomas is certainly not so much an *alazon*, or impostor, or a self-deprecating *eiron*, as an *agroikos*, or gull (admittedly, he falls short of being a buffoon). And from this point of view, *Expo 58* stresses the democratic element of comedy, always concerned with the "inferiour" and the ordinary, certainly no supermen but fallible individuals briefly thrown into visibility as their own little life-stories are allowed to puncture the backdrop of official history (Le Blanc 2014, 16).

A Satire ... But Not Quite

Among the various reviewers that reported on the novel, Toby Lichtig was quick to spot a resemblance to a specific hypotext, as he mentioned that "much like the hapless William Boot in Evelyn Waugh's *Scoop*, the young man [Thomas] is sent off dumbly on his mission" (Lichtig 2013). True enough, both novels' plots share many traits: in *Scoop*, William Boot, a humble columnist working for the broadsheet *The Beast*, is sent on a mission to the African republic of Ishmaelia. Rumour that a war is impending there has spurred Western press magnates to send reporters to the place, where in fact nothing much happens by way of political incident, so much so that news have to be invented and manufactured. Boot himself is the picture of the innocent abroad and a figure of ridicule, not so much for his boasting or self-deprecation (to take up Frye's categories again) as for his blissful absence of any grasp on and even of the situation. The fact that he should be the heir of a family living ensconced in Boot Magna, far away in the provinces (this is the pretext for an eccentric gallery of portraits and the occasion for a ludicrous episode when Salter, *The Beast*'s editor, is confronted with the to him altogether foreign world of the countryside), confirms his affinity with the *agroikos* type. This allows for dramatic irony to inform the novel as a whole, Boot being in many ways a descendant of Gulliver. Still, in Waugh's third-person narrative, a fairly intrusive narrator consistently underlines the character's limitations with a ruthless distance leaving very little room for empathy. The structure of *Expo 58* closely echoes that of *Scoop*, as Thomas is sent away on his mission to the continent, a less exotic expedition than the one attempted by William Boot some twenty years earlier so that he can come back more easily to Britain and his family home at the end of the narrative. In *Scoop*, the character ultimately acquires some three-dimensionality, as he refuses the offers of the tycoon who owns *The Beast* who himself, deluded to the end, constitutes the real butt of the satire), in the same way as Thomas gains in psychological complexity and emotional depth as the novel unfolds. Other structural similarities clinch the hypertextual connection between the two novels: of course, both protagonists meet a woman while they are abroad, and a great deal of misunderstanding takes place, which is partly resolved by a letter from each female protagonist, Kätchen and Anneke, sent to the innocent heroes at the end of the narrative (Waugh 2000, 221-22; Coe 2013a, 234).

Yet, even though the plot lines run roughly parallel to one another – thereby reactivating the etymology of the term 'parody' –, some modifications and inversion are at work in Coe's novel, making his characters more complex in various ways (Lasdun has remarked on Thomas's evolution from "cartoon character" to more engaged protagonist [Lasdun 2013]). For instance, whereas William Boot is the victim of Kätchen's shameless, cynical wiles, Anneke in *Expo 58* is the one who is ill-treated by Thomas, as the bulk of the narrative suggests, and the end confirms that she falls very much in love with him while her feelings are only partly requited for various reasons. Still, this is not so much meant to make Thomas appear as a heartless seducer (despite his looking like a cross between Cary Grant and Dirk Bogarde, as we are informed from the outset) as to dramatize his fallibility: he is not able to make his wife Sylvia happy, "condemn[ing] her, through vacillation, to a lifetime of unrest" (Coe 2013a, 250),[4] and neither does he rise to the occasion of loving and committing himself to Anneke before being called back to London and leaving Brussels. Such a refusal to choose or to privilege either option when confronted with a dilemma refers to the desire not to exclude, according to Mellet (2015, 123), an ethical complexity that is nowhere at work in Waugh's novel. One of the effects of such adaptations is of course to paradoxically use the parody of a Modernist satire to extenuate its violence and reduce the reader's distance from the characters. From this perspective, Coe introduces *dissensus* into the canonical form of satire (Mellet 2013, 180) through the means of affects.

However, the revisiting of Waugh's canonical text is made inescapable through a series of complementary devices, namely the pastiche of the characters' discourse. That Lord Copper, the tycoon in *Scoop*, has been replaced by Mr Cooke, who is in charge of the COI, and that Salter, Boot's superior, has been replaced by Swaine in Coe's novel is already indicated by the strict correspondence in initials. Both pairs fulfil the same narrative function and have the same influence on the main protagonists in the two texts. Still, it is their language that seems to echo, which introduces yet another temporal and stylistic dimension into *Expo 58*. In fact, several commentators have remarked on Coe's ear for the English of the late 1950s and have acclaimed (with a certain number of reservations) his resort to linguistic realism, the "Gay Belgium" mentioned above being a case in point. Many dialogues are peppered with such outdated tags as "old boy," and some characters find themselves saying things like "What a pip" (Coe 2013a, 48), yet another way of building up a strong sense of the past – both its pastness and presence, in fact, as such phrases are accommodated by a vocabulary and register shared with contemporary English, which helps perform a link with the not too distant past, as will be underlined in the next part. One step further, the early chapters are characterized by a resort to an even more outdated use of English, in the dialogues conducted among Cooke, Swaine and Thomas. This is perhaps nowhere more apparent than in the "We're all excited about Brussels" chapter, in which the syntax, vocabulary and what may sound like the mature characters' idiosyncrasies build up a pocket of slightly archaic language at the heart of the novel (8-11), in slight though unmistakable contrast with the English of the late 1950s and the narrator's contemporary English. In all such passages, homage to the past is compounded by reference to the British tradition of satire, while updating it and making it more benign through playful pastiche and by renouncing any strictly defined and unique target.

This is perhaps not very surprising if we consider Coe's own vision of satire that, like what he calls "anti-establishment comedy" (Coe 2013b), fails to bring social or political change (Coe 2013c). That Coe believes that neither comedy nor satire have any real political leverage is confirmed in his belief that laughter implies some loss of political agency as it has become "a substitute for thought" (Coe 2013b). This is perceptible in the novel's reluctance to castigate or lampoon, as if it were caught between the temptation to tap the tradition of satire even while being at a loss as to its targets and orientations. True, British parochialism, the prevalence of simulacra in the British pavilion, the persistence of racial or imperialist prejudice among the Belgians who build up a native village, complete with coloured natives who are stared at by visitors, all those cultural flaws are addressed and criticized. And of course, the double-

4 Coe has indicated that *Expo 58* is part of a larger project provisionally entitled *Unrest* (Coe 2014, 102), and the rump-like paragraph annexed to the end of the "Unrest" chapter opens up possibilities for future novelistic developments, as do the last two chapters.

dealing, scheming characters in the Expo's nest of spies, even while the event is supposed to foster international dialogue and friendship, is certainly a way to expose – as the title playfully seems to suggest – affectation and hypocrisy in international relationships. But the satire is never biting, and its diffraction makes it even more tenuous. This may correspond to what Glen Cavaliero has seen as the end of "the monolithic pretension of the hubristic individual self" (Cavaliero 2000, 241), since the chief protagonist is certainly not the locus of undiluted *hubris*, but rather characterized by his gentleness and humility as an *homme moyen sensuel*, as indicated above. And Lisa Colletta casts similar light on the subject when she shows that satire requires a context marked by moral stability to be effective. In her analysis of dark humour and satire in the modern British novel, and especially in some of its most notorious representatives, like Waugh's narratives, she suggests that "the post-Enlightenment assumptions about the rational, scientific ordering of the self and the world are viewed as ridiculous [..., so that] the grotesque and the absurd become the moral standards" (Colletta 2003, 5). In other words, she considers the type of satire that Waugh performs in *Scoop* to have little power to change society and to have an essentially protective, consolatory (as opposed to corrective) function (6-7), despite its apparently cynical orientation. The dark, absurdist tone in *Scoop* would thus channel the expression of a sense of hopelessness, banking on the protective, pleasurable potential of humour: behind the bleakness of the satire lies a sense of extreme vulnerability and a consciousness of ineffectuality. I would then argue that Coe's parody of satire is a sympathetic one, in which despite appearances the values of the original text are expanded on, updated and adapted to the contemporary situation: the world of the late 50s provides a mirror to the contemporary situation in which moral standards have lost their stability and appeal, a situation that finds its origins in the modernist period. In the move from a moral to an ethical age, *Expo 58* shows how the comic turn and the ethical turn meet. The dissensus introduced in modernist satire would then be effected not so much through rupture or inversion as through the means of the selection and intensification of its more humanistic traits: protection replaces correction and vice is superseded by vulnerability.

A Comedy of Forgiveness, Possibly

In his *The Irresponsible Self. Laughter and the Novel*, James Wood distinguishes between what he calls the "comedy of correction" or "religious comedy" and the "comedy of forgiveness," which he defines in the following terms: "a kind of tragicomic stoicism which might best be called the comedy of forgiveness. This comedy can be distinguished – if a little roughly – from the comedy of correction. The latter is a way of laughing at; the former a way of laughing with" (Wood 2004, 4).

In the comedy of forgiveness, then, correction and derision leave room for an understanding of human frailties and errors. Vulnerability is accommodated in the world of the novel and considered in a favourable light instead of being lampooned. Such a situation may be said to apply only partly to a satire like *Scoop*, since the main protagonist is submitted to the worst treatments at the hands of all the other characters while the butt of the satire lies elsewhere than in his own personality and actions. But if only implicit in *Scoop*, the benevolent consideration of vulnerability is given pride of place in Coe's novels – and particularly so in *Expo 58*.

Now, if in a comic novel, let alone in a satire, the characters' weakness and foibles are seen from a distance and never or rarely allowed to trigger empathy, the comedy of forgiveness brings along a measure of *gravitas* germane with emotional involvement. This is what Carty (2013) underscores when describing *Expo 58* as welcoming a mixture of the humorous and the poignant. The two tones and attitudes towards the various characters and actions are fairly evenly distributed throughout the narrative, and I would say that they are never as efficiently thrown together as with the motif of the cigarette that can be bad for smokers' health. This is introduced early in the narrative, when Thomas informs the incredulous Mr Cooke and Mr Swaine that "[a] recent study has shown [...] that there may be a link between smoking and lung cancer" (Coe 2013a, 10). To the contemporary reader, of course, a great deal of irony lies in the use of the modal, and such tentativeness has an immediate function, i.e. that of situating the passage within a definite historical context, thus enhancing historical realism. Another effect consists in triggering a fair amount of dramatic irony as the reader benevolently and from the vantage point of the present assesses the characters' innocence and emotionally relates to them. What is received as a joke by the character's interlocutors (10) is taken with gravity by the reader, making the two tones interact without one totally neutralizing the other. Still, things change towards the end of the narrative as the subject is broached once again when we learn that Thomas, on coming back to England to Sylvia, has given up smoking "[a]lthough, as a concession, he had agreed that she could smoke while she was pregnant. It was a stressful time for a woman, after all, and smoking did help her to relax" (238). With the second occurrence, derision is certainly no longer in order, and the dramatic irony heightens, intensifying the characters' innocence, need for protection, hence vulnerability. In such passages, we feel as if the consolidation of historical realism were not the chief aim of the remark. What seems to be at stake is a vision of the protagonists who, instead of being corrected, should be protected: the basic components of vulnerability as the capacity to be wounded – i.e. exposure and passivity – are promoted, so much so that the shift towards the comedy of forgiveness is neatly clinched. Instead of derision and rejection, an attitude more particularly associated with attentiveness and care (as taking care of and care-taking) is solicited.

One step further, I would like to argue that what is at the heart of *Expo 58* is a reflection on time as *the* element which has a necessary effect on the body, thereby allowing for vulnerability and putting biopolitics right at the heart of the novel. I would say that time may be one of the main themes and concerns of the novel, as one of the greatest tricks that *Expo 58* plays on its reader is that of unexpected acceleration, in the last two chapters. This is all the more striking as, from pages 251 to 254, we are given a series of dates corresponding to events relating to the destiny of the Atomium and the Britannia pub, right up to the destruction of the latter in 2011. The next paragraph resumes Thomas's story at a more sedate pace, taking up the thread of his life in 2009, fifty years after the events narrated in the previous chapters. Of course, the ellipsis concerning the main protagonist's life is very partially filled with the series of events sketched over the five previous pages, so much so that the central character becomes elderly overnight. He now benefits from care and ministrations provided by Gill, who used to be baby Gill just a few pages earlier, making story time and narrative time collide. With the last chapters, then, and with the list-form adaptation of what may be identified as a Victorian winding up, time becomes compacted and is shown to be in crisis. The text plays the same type of trick upon the reader as at the beginning of *The Rotters' Club*, when the children of the characters whose destinies throughout the 1970s the novel is about to evoke are seen from the perspective of 2003. As in the earlier novel, then, a strong sense of hindsight is provided through the embedding of temporal strata:[5] time is no longer seen as a continuum, and chronological order as the succession of episodes is considered as less important than the flinging together of separate moments that emphasize their interdependence and relationality. The temporal configuration of *Expo 58* privileges the linked time of *kairos* to the linear one of *chronos*. Thus, it signposts the idea that no instant is autonomous and that moments and actions are linked. What may be inferred from such a choice is that no moment is an island and, as a matter of course, that no man is an island unto himself: each action has consequences and is entangled in a web of occurrences in the same way as each individual is responsible for his/her own actions. By underlining the inescapable reality of interconnectedness and interdependence, the temporal setup of *Expo 58* may be interpreted in ethical terms, and as a relational, hence ethical apparatus. In other words, what originally passes off as a way to promote dramatic irony within the framework of a comic novel that addresses the mishaps of a contemporary gull shifts focus and tone and veers towards *gravitas*.

From this perspective, *Expo 58* plays with the conventions of the comedy of forgiveness in more ways than one: instead of laughing at the protagonist, the novel smiles with him, as Thomas, in conformity with the *nostos* convention that characterizes narratives of departure, not only comes back home at the end, but performs a double *nostos* and returns to Brussels on Clara's invitation. There he learns that Anneke is dead, that she loved him, and that their unique sexual congress on Thomas's last night in Brussels, in the summer of 1958, most probably materialized into a daughter, about the same age as Thomas's second child. In such moments when the unjustly separated are neatly re-united – or, precisely, *fail* to be re-united – *in extremis* (even though the reader cannot but feel that the reunion will have literary consequences within the *Unrest* sequence), the comedy of forgiveness edges towards melodrama, and pathos is ushered in to bring dissensus into the world not only of satire but also of comedy. What the reader is ultimately left with is a sense of lateness, as if the real theme of the novel were missed opportunities: Thomas realizes too late that he could have had a genuine, generous relationship with either Anneke or his wife, but that he failed in both cases. This is what Sam Leith suggests in his review of *Expo 58*, which opens with the paradoxical sentence: "Nothing dates like the future" (Leith 2013). And of course, when reading the last two chapters, the readers are led to reminisce about some of the novel's epiphanic moments, when, in the long "Pastorale d'Eté" chapter, Thomas is confronted with a confident, glowing vision of the future that they now know has never materialized and will never turn up (Coe 2013a, 204). The impression that we are left with is that the future is always already beyond reach, but instead of the sour irony that might have been used to evoke such a reality within the context of satire, the forgiving, integrating, healing powers of comedy are solicited. The summer pastoral gives an illusion of temporal stasis and protection, but does not preclude the flow of time or the sway of lateness as two of the chief modalities of vulnerability.

In "What's so Funny about Comic Novels?" Coe ponders on the evolution of the genre, over the last few decades and concludes that, in a post-9/11, post-2008 world, the aspirations of the more traditional comic novel (he has in mind Kingsley Amis's *Lucky Jim*) cannot be fulfilled as they used to not such a long time ago. He wonders: "is it time for novelists to jettison comedy altogether, like Desmond Bastes in *Deaf Sentence*, and finally get serious?" (Coe 1013c). I find the reference to one of David Lodge's most recent productions of interest as, when reading *Expo 58*, the reader

5 On hindsight in Coe, see Tew (2004, 80) and Mellet (2015, 124).

cannot but be reminded of the mixture of realism and humour, of the mild satire and of the *gravitas* that inform Lodge's fiction. Indeed, homage is paid to Lodge in one of the funniest parts, the epistolary chapter, when we learn about the couple's estrangement through innuendoes and pointed remarks, thus taking up one of the most obvious formal experiments performed by Lodge's *Changing Places*. Still, I would say that Coe's more obvious debt is to an earlier text by the same author, *Out of the Shelter*, certainly no comic novel but a *Bildungsroman* whose central protagonist, Timothy Young, just like Thomas Foley (yet another typographical and onomastic link), is sent on a holiday to occupied Germany and learns about life and love, in a mood of *gravitas* that culminates in the *explicit.* I would argue that *Expo 58*'s darker passages, when Thomas's mother tells him about the circumstances in which the German soldiers executed her father and brothers during World War 1 (Coe 2013a, 174, 202) or when Clara evokes her East Canton origins (259), all reverberate with the sense of historical catastrophe that rumbles through Lodge's fourth novel. One step further, it is perhaps Lodge's *How Far Can You Go?* that may provide one of the most pointed echoes, with its mixing up of satire and empathy, as apparent in the use of the winding up that closes the narrative, takes stock of the situation, promotes a sense of hindsight and lateness, and makes what has hitherto been a satirical novel veer towards the themes, techniques and tone of the comedy of forgiveness. In all these novels, as in *Expo 58*, I would argue ultimately that what is at stake is the use of comedy not only to evoke but to *relate* to human frailty. With Coe's version of comedy, we are told that ethical responsibility is based on "an anthropology of incompleteness and vulnerability" (Maillard 2011, 336) that fiction embraces and engages with in its singularity.

Works Cited

Carty, Peter. "Review: *Expo 58*, By Jonathan Coe. Back to the Future, only in Belgium." 8 September 2013. *The Independent*. Web. 23 January 2015.

Cavaliero, Glen. *The Alchemy of Laughter. Comedy in English Fiction*. Houndmills, Basingstoke: Palgrave, 2000.

Coe, Jonathan. *What A Carve Up!* 1994. Harmondsworth: Penguin, 1995.

—. *The Rotters' Club*. 2001. London: Vintage, 2003.

—. *The Closed Circle*. 2004. London: Penguin, 2005.

—. *Expo 58*. London: Viking, 2013a.

—. "Sinking Giggling into the Sea." *The London Review of Books* 35.14. 18 July 2013b. Web. 23 January 2015.

—. *Loggerheads and Other Stories*. London: Penguin. Ebook. 2014.

—. "What's so Funny about Comic Novels?" *The Guardian*. 7 September 2013c. Web. 23 January 2015.

Colletta, Lisa. *Dark Humour and Social Satire in the Modern British Novel*. Houndmills, Basingstoke: Palgrave Macmillan, 2003.

Connolly, Cressida. "*Expo 58*, by Jonathan Coe – Review." 21 September 2013. *The Spectator*. Web. 23 January 2015.

Fielding, Henry. *Joseph Andrews*. Ed. R.F. Brissenden. 1742. Harmondsworth: Penguin, 1977.

Frye, Northrop. *Anatomy of Criticism. Four Essays*. 1957. Harmondsworth: Penguin, 1990.

Guignery, Vanessa. "'Colonel Mustard, in the Billiard Room, with the Revolver:' Jonathan Coe's *What a Carve Up!* as a Postmodern Whodunit." *Études anglaises* 64.4 (2011): 427-438.

—. "Experimentation and Tradition: Adam Thirlwell and Jonathan Coe." *Etudes britanniques contemporaines* 47. December 2014. Web. 23 January 2015

Lasdun, James. "*Expo 58* by Jonathan Coe – Review." 19 September 2013. *The Guardian*. Web. 23 January 2015.

Le Blanc, Guillaume. *L'insurrection des vies minuscules*. Montreuil: Bayard, 2014.

Leith, Sam. "Double Jamesian." 6 September 2013. *The Times Literary Supplement*. Web. 23 January 2015.

Lichtig, Leo. "*Expo 58*, by Jonathan Coe, review." 27 September 2013. *The Telegraph*. Web. 23 January 2015.

Lodge, David. *Out of the Shelter*. 1970. Harmondsworth: Penguin, 1985.

—. *Changing Places. A Tale of Two Campuses*. 1975. Harmondsworth: Penguin, 1978.

—. *How Far Can You Go?* 1980. Harmondsworth: Penguin, 1981.

Maillard, Nathalie. *La Vulnérabilité. Une nouvelle catégorie morale?* Genève: Labor et Fides, 2011.

Mellet, Laurent. "Moral Questions and Ethical Answers: On some Responsibilities of British Satire in the 20th and 21st Centuries." *Ethics of Alterity, Confrontation and Responsibility in 19th- to 21st-Century British Literature*. Eds Christine Reynier and Jean-Michel Ganteau. Montpellier: PULM, 2013. 169-180.

—. *Jonathan Coe. Les Politiques de l'intime*. Paris: PUPS, 2015.

Robson, Leo. "*Expo 58* by Jonathan Coe." 31 August 2013. *The Times*. Web. 23 January 2015.

Tew, Philip. *The Contemporary British Novel*. London and New York: Continuum, 2004.

Waugh, Evelyn. *Scoop*. 1938. London: Penguin, 2000.

Wood, James. *The Irresponsible Self. Laughter and the Novel*. London: Jonathan Cape, 2004.

HILGENDORF, ERIC
MARSCHELKE, JAN-CHRISTOPH
SEKORA, KARIN (Eds.)

Slavery as a Global and Regional Phenomenon

2015. V, 176 Seiten,
6 Abbildungen. (Anglistische Forschungen, Band 449)
Geb. € 32,–
ISBN 978-3-8253-6393-2

Slavery is a phenomenon that can be traced back to antiquity. Until the middle of the 19th century, it was socially accepted in many parts of the world. Today it is universally outlawed. The Rome Statute (2002) of the International Criminal Court lists slavery as a crime against humanity. Nevertheless, slavery still exists in many countries – in which human beings continue to be treated as mere goods. Unfortunately, our knowledge of slavery is still fragmentary. Gaps exist both with regard to certain historical periods as well as to regionally specific features of its emergence, forms and abolition. To this day, the traces slavery has left are not only visible, but its impact can still be felt around the world.

In this work, international scholars examine the concept and history of slavery, its regional forms in the Caribbean and Latin America, and its contemporary guises. Our twin goals have been both to highlight the diverse features of slavery as well as to elucidate its universal structures. This collection includes a contribution by the 1986 Nobel laureate Wole Soyinka.

D-69051 Heidelberg · Postfach 10 61 40 · Tel. (49) 62 21/77 02 60 · Fax (49) 62 21/77 02 69
Mehr Information unter www.winter-verlag.de · E-mail: info@winter-verlag.de

ANDREW TATE

Nick Hornby's Melancholy Comedy

> [M]elancholy animals that we are, human beings are also the most cheerful. We smile and find ourselves ridiculous. Our wretchedness is our greatness. (Critchley 2002, 111)

Four strangers, each depressed enough to seek a swift, violent end to their lives, fortuitously meet on New Year's eve on the roof of a north London tower block callously nicknamed Toppers' House, a dwelling notorious for its high-rise suicides. This collision of disparate (and desperate) individuals, united only by their shared desire to die, might be either the starting point of a very sick joke or the culmination of poignant melodrama. Yet Nick Hornby's *A Long Way Down* (2005a) does not quite belong to the capacious family of genres labeled "tragic" nor is it a taboo-transgressing satire about the contingencies of precarious mental health. Hornby's fourth novel is a story of loss, anomie, isolation, loneliness, disappointment, failure, and disastrous ethical choices – all signifiers of tragedy, to be sure – but it is also, despite the bleak subject matter, full of laughter, diffident wit, chronic non-self-awareness, farce, incongruous friendships, ill-advised holidays with virtual strangers, awkward family reunions, creative swearing and other tropes of comic fiction.

Martin, a shamed former breakfast television presenter, and the only member of this unlikely quartet of thwarted suicidal narrators to be recognized by his new acquaintances, reflects on the odd (at least temporarily) salvific outcome of that evening: "I'm not sitting here now because I suddenly saw sense. [... T]hat night turned into as much of a mess as everything else. I couldn't even jump off a fucking tower block without fucking it up" (Hornby 2005a, 11). The three others that he meets have very different reasons for despairing: Maureen has lived as a single-parent for twenty years to a son, Matty, who is so severely disabled he is unable to respond to her; teenage Jess is angry and confused about almost everything; JJ, a struggling musician, has lost his sense of purpose and self-worth. All of these protagonists are privately ashamed of their motivation, though Martin, who has recently served a prison sentence for sleeping with a fifteen-year old girl, in his pursuit of a swift end to a life that he has wrecked, is initially the most single-minded member of the new desolate fraternity.

The non-event of the New Year's eve suicide – a relief to readers but not a source of immediate, life-affirming joy to Hornby's characters – is transformed by a pact not to die, at least not deliberately and not before 14 February, Valentine's Day, the next significant calendar date of compulsory happiness. Martin is grimly funny about his despairing state of mind and, foreshadowing a major theme of Hornby's novel, he also dismisses the cultural expectation that sorrow results in the sufferer's moral improvement characterized by deeper wisdom and the discovery of new reserves of compassion. Indeed, the novel as a whole simultaneously resists and is tempted by traditional comic "happy" resolutions. One does not need to be an aficionado of black comedy to find the luckless protagonists' initial meeting, a kind of literal *anti*-catastrophe in which nobody falls, funny as well as sad. To laugh even when faced with the joyfully absurd outcome of such a distressing situation is, unsurprisingly, deeply uncomfortable but it is also a reminder that many strands of comedy are informed by loss and hurt as vivid and inescapable as that experienced by characters in more austere narratives.

***Anglistik: International Journal of English Studies* 27.1 (March 2016): 31-44.**

In his study of "laughter and the novel," *The Irresponsible Self* (2004), James Wood makes a consciously imprecise distinction between two principal comic styles in fiction: the first he describes as "tragi-comic stoicism which might best be called the comedy of forgiveness"; the second is "the comedy of correction." This latter form is "a way of laughing at; the former a way of laughing with" (Wood 2005, 4). Both comic modes, however, involve a painful transformation of perspective. Comedy and suffering, as Eric Bentley argues in *The Life of the Drama* (1964), are not entirely separate phenomena. Tragedy, he concedes, citing Philip Sidney, "openeth the greatest wounds" and may be a more legible way of encountering grief but the comic mode frequently depends on pain, both physical and emotional. Slapstick, farce and social comedy all rely on humiliation. "The plain man," claims Bentley, "goes wrong only if he assumes that comedy has nothing to do with pain at all" (Bentley 1992, 138).[1] And Bentley's description of the stage comedies of Shakespeare and Molière as "sweetly melancholy, and at moments overwhelmingly sad," might also be an apt description of many of Hornby's novels (137).

Can Hornby's characteristic narrative form – described by Dominic Head as "serio-comic" (2008, 18) – represent such grave subject matter as attempted suicide without trivializing it? This article explores the style and structure of Hornby's melancholic comedies. It places *A Long Way Down* in the wider context of his writing, with particular reference to *High Fidelity* (1995), *About a Boy* (1998), *How to Be Good* (2001), *Juliet, Naked* (2010) and *Funny Girl* (2014). The article argues that Hornby's fiction belongs to the tradition Wood names "the comedy of forgiveness" (2005, 4).[2] The article will address the ways in which Hornby's realist mode engages with ideas of human agency, the capacity for change at a personal and shared level. Is Hornby's comedy cruel? Does it rely on the ritual humiliation of its characters? The article will draw on theorists of humour including Simon Critchley and Peter Berger and argue that melancholia, depression and different kinds of sadness run through Hornby's comic fictions of the contemporary self.

1. After "Ladlit:" Genre, Gender and Criticism

Hornby is frequently read as a social realist whose bestselling novels and memoir reflect rather than refract popular debates regarding gender, class and social belonging. McCombe, for example, locates Hornby's fiction "squarely within the tradition of Dickensian comic realism" and argues that the writer's typical "hero eventually reconciles his own values with those of the larger community in which he lives" (2014, 166). This is the classic move towards conformity or social integration of the *Bildungsroman*. Later work, including Hornby's only novel written primarily for a 'young adult' readership, *Slam* (2007), and the apocalyptically-inclined short story "Otherwise Pandemonium" (2005), draw on the magical realist tropes of time-travel and enchanted technologies. Such experiments with genre quietly subvert aspects of the traditional rites-of-passage plot; the comic-visionary elements of both of these contemporary fables, narrated by teenage boys, undermine the idea of a

---

1 Bel Mooney cites a different passage from Bentley's *The Life of the Drama* in her defence of *A Long Way Down* (2006).

2 Hornby is not, I should stress, one of the subjects of Wood's study. Indeed, in his review of DBC Pierre's *Vernon God Little*, Wood made an acerbic comparison between Hornby's *How to be Good* and J.M. Coetzee's *Elizabeth Costello* in a withering reference to the opinion of John Carey, former Oxford Professor, sometime Booker Prize judge, and noted high-culture sceptic. Carey had indicated his enthusiasm for Hornby's novel as an example of a book worthy of the literary award (Wood 2003, 25).

happily achievable future, a time of stability that will reward the hero after years of uncertainty and struggle.

The critical reception of Hornby's writing, based primarily on his thematically-connected first two books, *Fever Pitch* (1992) and *High Fidelity*, has focused on his ambivalent, witty representation of contemporary masculinity (Bentley 2008; Falk 2007; Keskinen 2005). Head, for example, describes him as the originator of a peculiarly 1990s phenomenon and the male counterpart of Helen Fielding whose *Bridget Jones's Diary* (1996) shares both Hornby's confessional style and emphasis on "the tribulations of urban twenty- and thirty-somethings faced with changing heterosexual mores and the pursuit of a desired lifestyle" (2002, 248). The most marketable examples of "Ladlit" and "Chick Lit" – the latter tag, in particular, popularized in the British press, is so sexist it seems bizarre that the soubriquet was ever used without irony or anger by literary critics – typically focus on the misadventures of straight, middle-class "post-youth" men and women, faced with romantic and professional disappointment, finding, for the most part, traditionally happy, romantic resolutions.

Head suggests that both Fielding's and Hornby's bestsellers "reveal something more interesting about the social function of the novel than the generic straightjacket was soon to allow" (2002, 248-49). However, even this acknowledgement of nuance and aesthetic value is indicative of a certain critical condescension towards popular fiction in general and comic-romantic narratives in particular. Indeed, in a later study of the "state of the novel," Head uses Hornby as an example of a writer who occupies a difficult middle position between popular and literary-critical success. For Head, Hornby "is one of those writers who seems to flirt with seriousness" but "as a popular comic author he clearly does not belong to the elite group of contemporary novelists" (2008, 13-14).

Why do the adjectives "comic" and "popular" make it clear that a writer may not belong to an elite rank of contemporary authors?[3] Head restates the views of critics such as Sean O'Brien who were sceptical about Hornby's endeavour in *A Long Way Down* "to graft a philosophical treatment of misery on to his familiar comic style;" according to this view, a comic writer's struggle with solemnity "exposed the limitations of his method, the seriousness undermined by formulaic devices and tics" (Head 2008, 18, 16; O'Brien 2005, 20; see also Mars-Jones 2005). One reviewer of *A Long Way Down* notes that he feels defensive of the writer because "there's an insinuation in even the positive reviews that Hornby's work is, at best, a guilty pleasure;" he wishes to "make a case for Hornby as a serious writer, producing serious literature – it's just a shame I have to feel so furtive about it" (Coake 2005, 17). Hornby, Head notes, has located himself on one side of the hypothetical divide in making the claim that he could not write literary fiction (Hornby 2006, 28, qtd. in Head 2008, 13). The critic does not mention, however, that this disavowal of literary fiction appears as a glib aside in an entry in Hornby's collection on his (mis)adventures in reading, *The Complete Polysyllabic Spree*, in which a passage in Paula Fox's *Desperate Creatures*

3 Literary culture, in particular, is bad at recognizing the value of humour: for example, Howard Jacobson's *The Finkler Question* (2010) was the first outwardly "comic" novel – albeit one marked with much sadness – to win the Man Booker Prize since DBC Pierre's tragic-comic *Vernon God Little* (2003) and, indeed since this narrative of scapegoating after a high-school shooting is particularly bleak, we might look back as far as 1986 to Kingsley Amis' *The Old Devils* for the triumph of a "true" comic novel, if such a thing exists. Hornby has never been shortlisted for the prize, though in 2001 *How to be Good* appeared on the first-ever published long list for the prize.

(1970) causes him to realize "with some regret that not only could I never write a literary novel, but I couldn't even be a character in a literary novel" (2006, 28). This kind of self-deprecation might say something about Hornby's relationship with high culture but more revealing still is the difficulty that critics have in taking fiction that is popular and comic seriously.

The terrain of literary lad culture is the subject of an influential article by Elaine Showalter who argues that the genre was not, in fact, a new phenomenon but, by the time of the millennium, one that was on the brink of extinction. "Ladlit," argues Showalter, thrived, in multiple fashionable and "high end" iterations, from Kingsley Amis' 1950s comedy to the era of his son Martin and, more widely, of "developmentally arrested good ol' boys of 1990s popular culture" (2002, 60). For Showalter, the latter days of the genre were eclectic enough to embrace "the addicts and petty criminals" of Irvine Welsh's ecstatically soiled iteration of magical realism, "the postmodern urban picaresques of Martin Amis, Will Self and Hanif Kureishi" alongside "the underemployed thirtysomething heroes of Nick Hornby and Tony Parsons" (61). Hornby is frequently – if unfairly – placed side-by-side with writers such as Parsons as well as Tim Lott, John O'Farrell, David Baddiel and, in the words of Joseph Brooker, "a congeries of former stand-up comics" (2006, 7). Martin Amis' *Money: a Suicide Note* (1984), with its grotesque but, for Showalter at least, "intensely likable" narrator, John Self, is sometimes read as the unholy scripture that accidentally invented a subgenre of men-in-crisis narratives. Brooker, in an echo of blokeish antagonism, suggests that as stylists none of the authors who feature in Showalter's list "are fit to light Amis' cigarettes" (6). One of the differences that Showalter identifies between the 1990s generation of "male coming-of-age" storytellers is that they were "no longer able to blame" outside forces – class or their father, for example – for personal struggles. Narrators like Rob in *High Fidelity*, she suggests, recognize that "their problems are their own fault" and they are "the most introspective of all the lads, constantly self-monitoring and monologic" (2002, 73).

The bestseller status of many of these writers might, as Peter Childs has suggested, be a result of their appeal to "a readership that had found little reflection of itself in fiction before 1990" (2012, 255). This may well cause other readers, surprised to be told that middle-class white men have been under-represented in popular narrative, to raise an eyebrow. Hornby's early books bear superficial comparison with some of the popular titles that followed his success: for example, John O'Farrell's memoir of his love-hate relationship with the Labour Party, *Things Can Only Get Better* (1998), echoes the self-deprecating wit and rite-of-passage structure of *Fever Pitch*; and Tony Parsons' *Man and Boy* (1999), like *High Fidelity*, is about a no-longer-very-young man facing up to responsibility, uncertain about how to belong in the modern world. However, reading Hornby's near 25-year career as a whole, another contemporary novelist might more fittingly be regarded as his true peer: Roddy Doyle. Like Hornby, Doyle has written fiction, screenplays and creative non-fiction and has a comparable aptitude for melancholic comedy and the rhythms of everyday speech; he has also contributed to two collections edited by Hornby, *My Favourite Year* (1993) and *Speaking With the Angel* (2000).

Doyle's *Barrytown* quartet, set in a fictional, working class area of North Dublin – *The Commitments* (1987), *The Snapper* (1990), *The Van* (1991) and *The Guts* (2013) – connect a fascination with community, character and popular culture also visible in Hornby's novels of middle-class north London. The sequence is a comic iteration of the family saga and, though the novels are full of wry wit they are also frequently permeated with a sense of sadness about the reality of love, family loyalties and friendship as it plays out over time, particularly in the life of Jimmy Rabbitte Jr, an entrepreneurial, loudmouth teenager in the first novel and a 47-year-old family man awakening to the rude fact of his mortality in *The Guts*.

Hornby is both celebrated and disparaged for the way in which he weaves together pop culture and men who define themselves by their obsessions with football, music and television. Mikko Keskinen, for example, observes that *High Fidelity* "epitomizes the British author's oeuvre, which is populated by male monomaniacs, perennial bachelors, or early-middle-aged adolescents" (2005, 3). In Keskinen's view "the football enthusiast in *Fever Pitch*, the commitment-avoiding womanizer in *About a Boy*, and the seemingly saintly men in *How to be Good* can be read as versions of Rob Fleming, the protagonist and narrator of *High Fidelity*" (2005, 3). *High Fidelity* certainly anticipates a twenty-year focus on masculine embarrassment and personal failings. However, Hornby's fiction after *About a Boy* has shifted from singular masculine perspectives to something more diverse in narrative terms: *How to be Good* is narrated by Katie Carr, a GP on the verge of leaving her husband ("The Angriest Man in Holloway," [Hornby 2001, 4]); *A Long Way Down* has multiple narrators – two women, two men – rather than just a middle-aged man in crisis. His more recent fiction shifts to third person narration: *Juliet, Naked* shares the pop culture territory of *High Fidelity* but focuses on a woman whose long-term relationship with her selfish partner is coming to an end; *Funny Girl* is focalized via a young, working-class northern woman, a gay man and his (possibly) bi-sexual writing partner.

High Fidelity created a kind of comic *chiaroscuro* style that many of his subsequent novels have followed, focusing on genial (if sometimes secretly melancholy) characters in moments of loss or grief. As the novel opens, its narrator, Rob Fleming, has been ditched by Laura, his long-term partner, a successful lawyer. Rob runs Championship Vinyl, a specialist music shop, the kind of place that was able to exist, once upon a time, in an era before internet shopping, "because of the people who make a special effort – young men, always young men, with John Lennon specs and carrier bags […] young men who seem to spend a disproportionate amount of time looking for deleted Smiths singles" (Hornby 1996, 38). Rob Fleming is more confident and self-aware than Dick and Barry, his colleagues and fellow vinyl enthusiasts; in many ways they are conventional comic sidekicks (Dick is shy and tongue-tied; Barry assertive and continually rude to customers). However, Rob is not Hornby's mouthpiece for enlightened contemporary masculinity. Indeed, for Daniel Lea and Berthold Schoene, Rob and his colleagues "seem like tragic casualties of a not-yet-quite-post-patriarchal age" whose competitive best-ever-band-and-song list-making compensates for personal failures (2003, 13). These are bewildered men – confident about the minutiae of pop culture but emotionally inarticulate – who frequently "relapse into anachronistic and blatantly inadequate behavior" (Lea and Schoene 2003, 13).

Rob's laconic reflection on obsessive collectors ("as close to being mad as makes no difference" (1996, 39)) is ironized by his own compulsive nature; he lists records and romantic catastrophes with corresponding intensity. The most significant of these bruising losses he describes in terms of cinematic narrative and consumption: "I lost the plot for a while then. And I lost the subplot, the script, the soundtrack, the intermission, my popcorn, the credits and the exit sign" (Hornby 1996, 25). Rob is the first of a number of Hornby's protagonists to see the world through a pop cultural haze. In *A Long Way Down*, Maureen describes the rapid rhythm of her three new friends as "[l]ike people in a soap opera, bang bang bang" (38). This perspective on her garrulous cohort shaped by the grammar of television drama is rather different from the kinds of social isolation that many of Hornby's other characters achieve via the media. For example, Will Freeman in *About a Boy* is able to escape ordinary commitments – work, love, the messy awkwardness of long-term friendship – because he lives on the royalties of a bestselling Christmas song that his father wrote more than 50 years earlier. "Santa's Super Sleigh" is an expedient narrative conceit that allows Will's comically extreme selfishness to thrive but it also implies an undercurrent of pathos about the commercial exploitation of creativity. Pop music, in particular, recurs in Hornby's writing as a powerful mode of expression and shared memory; a great piece of pop, as the essays in Hornby's *31 Songs* (2003) suggest, can crystallize a moment and exceed its status as an ephemeral, cheap form of culture. In *About a Boy,* the festive favourite might be a link between the tragically immature Will and his father but, instead, the unearned wealth that it brings is represented as a source of rather dreary corruption. A comic counterpoint to this cynical use of pop music is the communal singing of Joni Mitchell's "Both Sides Now" by Will's teenage friend, Marcus, and his bohemian mother, Fiona. Hornby intensifies the comedy of discomfort in relation to such public expression of emotion: Will is deeply embarrassed by the "sincerity" of their singing – with eyes closed – in part because it reminds him of his lack of engagement with the world (Hornby 1998, 97-98).

In *Juliet, Naked*, Duncan, who is neither as affluent nor as self-assured as Will, is similarly dependent on music as a kind of displacement; Duncan's romantic life is circumscribed by his obsessive, quasi-academic focus on Tucker Crowe, an American singer-songwriter whose cult status is perpetuated by his mysterious withdrawal from public life.

The novel begins, comically enough, with an English man in a toilet: Duncan and his preternaturally patient lover, Annie, are on a road trip of the United States but instead of visiting the Empire State Building, Disneyland or the Grand Canyon, they are on a "Tucker Crowe pilgrimage" (Hornby 2009, 5). This "dank, dark, smelly and entirely unremarkable" toilet in an unprepossessing Minneapolis club has aura for Hornby's infatuated protagonist only because it was the last place Tucker visited before abruptly cancelling his last ever tour and shunning life as a musician. This mildly scatological opening – a kind of mischievous homage to English toilet humour – parodies overzealous enthusiasm for creativity that is a mirror-image of Will Freeman's dread of authenticity. Indeed, Duncan might have been one of the fanatical young men who spent too much of their time in Championship Vinyl, looked at with a mixture of empathy and scorn by Rob and his colleagues. *Juliet, Naked* features a tragi-comic twist; Annie, disappointed and eventually betrayed by Duncan, following a series of social-media-governed connections, ends up in a relationship with a revitalized Tucker. It is not entirely clear whether Duncan is, finally, more jealous of his former partner or of the enigmatic musician.

Popular narrative as a kind of alternative for conventional forms of intimacy is a trope that persists in Hornby's recent fiction. In *Funny Girl*, for example, an affectionate but unsentimental revisiting of 1960s British television comedy, Tony and Bill, who later become a kind of Lennon and McCartney of sitcom scriptwriting, are initially bound by a shared secret, something that they "may or may not have in common" (Hornby 2014, 53) and which they never discuss. In December 1959, during the final days of their National Service, Tony and Bill meet in a holding cell of a police station in Aldershot. They have been arrested, two hours apart, in a gentlemen's public lavatory at a time when gay men were criminalized. They are not prosecuted but forge their friendship during the boredom of their brief incarceration. They bond over their "mutual passion" for Ray Galton and Alan Simpson, the writers of *Hancock's Half Hour*. Instead of sharing their hopes and fears, they repeat, near word-perfect, scenes from the famous "Blood Donor" episode of the series. In a moment when two men are faced with "humiliation and possible ruin," Hornby's characters find a way of addressing their situation obliquely by finding solace and connection in the words written for a famously melancholic comedian (52). Their lifelong friendship frequently involves evasion and social disconnection – Tony marries and leads a suburban, conventional lifestyle; Bill rejects conformity and embraces his sexuality – but they are always able to talk, and to argue, about comedy and the mechanics of getting a laugh. The conventions of comedy give Bill and Tony a vocabulary for speaking about all those things that they – and, indeed the stars and producer of their show – otherwise cannot articulate. The four series of "*Barbara (and Jim)*" that the pair write in the mid-1960s, watched by millions, tackle differences of class, politics, sexual confidence and, eventually, marital breakup. This might be an oblique comment on Hornby's wider fictional world: melancholy comedy is a way of looking at the world that makes sadness comprehensible, both to ourselves and to others.

2. "We'd formed a nation:" Melancholy versus Superiority

The sad situation in which the four narrators of *A Long Way Down* find themselves at the beginning of the novel is swiftly enmeshed in a bathetic humour. Martin and Maureen are the first characters to meet, the latter stumbling upon the recently disgraced television presenter; attempting to diffuse tension, Martin, formerly famous for his silver-tongued interviewing technique, quips: "I'll give you a shout on the way down" (Hornby 2005a, 18). Maureen, set up by Hornby to play the straight woman role in an unlikely double act, is not amused but her poker-faced reply ("I suppose I'm not in the mood, Mr Sharp.") elicits laughter from her suicidal acquaintance. When Jess and JJ join them on the roof, Martin reflects that "we were in the process of turning a solemn and private moment into a farce with a cast of thousands" (25). What is initially conceived by each of these individuals as a tragic end is transformed by the presence of others into another genre characterized by perfect bad timing, coincidence and comic frustration. Elements of this approach are deployed elsewhere in the novel. When the coincidence of the four characters' non-suicide is discovered, they are interviewed on television with the hope that it will elicit tearful catharsis. In reality, the interview degenerates into recrimination, uncomfortable laughter and another end to Martin's modestly revived career. Similarly, the group's decision to go on a foreign holiday – rather like an overreaching episode of a sitcom produced after other ideas have been exhausted – is not quite the therapeutic, bonding experience that they desire. This plays with readerly expectation: the experienced (or even jaded) student of comedy expects amusing calamity and is rewarded. However, for Maureen, who has never in her adult life been on holiday, the experience is liberating. The friction between these two interpretations of the same mildly chaotic events – drunken arguments and romantic embarrassment, for example – produces a hopeful comedy. For Eric Bentley, the crucial distinction to be made is not between comedy and tragedy but comedy and farce: the latter form, he argues, always refuses to look at the darkness and misery that comedy "has seen; taken note; and has not forgotten" (1992, 137). In Bentley's reading, true comedy is far from an "unfeeling" genre; indeed the "bitterness and sadness that so readily come to the surface constitute our first, best evidence that in comedy feeling is not only present but abundant" (Bentley 1992, 137). Hornby's narrative draws on the conventions of farce but produces something that is closer in shape to the "adult genre" of comedy that takes place "on the other side of despair" (137).

Simon Critchley has argued that humour "views the world awry, bringing us back to the everyday by estranging us from it," a form that offers "an oblique phenomenology of ordinary life" (2002, 65-66). *A Long Way Down* is not only a tragi-comic novel; it is also a narrative about the ways in which humour might transfigure a sense of disconnection. This is emphatically not to argue that Hornby's novel endorses the trite notion that "laughter is the best medicine." Rather, it embodies a critique of comedy as an attitude of cruelty or superiority. In *The Seven Basic Plots*, Christopher Booker presents a version of this theory – the notion that comedy is frequently based on judgement and scorn: "Almost all Comedy intended to make us laugh is […] centred on […] a contrast between the self-regarding delusion of someone who is in some way blinded by egotism, and our capacity to see from outside what [he] is unable to see. We even do it, of course, when we laugh self-deprecatingly at ourselves" (Booker 2004, 2). Such a form of comedy allows spectators to laugh – and to feel morally or intellectually superior – in comparison with the fool on (a figurative or literal) stage (Stott 2005, 131-37; Critchley 2002, 2).

Hornby's fiction resists this model; his narratives do not simply mock the pompous comedic victim as useful scapegoat for shared laughter. In *A Long Way Down*, Martin is closest to embodying that traditional figure associated with both comedy and tragedy, the great man brought low; he is a hypocrite because he vigorously campaigned in the tabloid newspapers against criminals who were guilty of the very thing for which he was imprisoned. Hornby does not, however, exploit this comedy of hypocrisy: Martin is arrogant and not a little self-pitying but he is also ashamed, world-weary and damaged. He even acknowledges that, though the popular press "have been full of shit about me […] every word of the shit was true" (Hornby 2005a, 127). He has almost nothing in common with the three people he meets on New Year's Eve "beyond that one thing" and this is enough to forge a new identity:

> the one thing was enough to make us feel that there wasn't anything else – not money, or class, or education, or age, or cultural interests – that was worth a damn; we'd formed a nation, suddenly, in that couple of hours, and for the time being we wanted only to be with our new compatriots. (57-58)

The life-threatening sorrow of Martin and the "Toppers" House Four with which *A Long Way Down* begins is an extreme version of something that haunted many of Hornby's earlier narratives: in *How to Be Good*, Katie Carr's brother suffers from long-term depression and in *About a Boy*, Fiona attempts suicide following a number of personal losses. Will Freeman insulates himself against too much feeling (being "engaged") and "that he knew would guarantee him a long and depression-free life" (Hornby 1998, 98). Indeed, the reality of Fiona's illness frightens Will back into a flight from maturity or living for anybody other than himself. However, this apparently free man with a plan to avoid any potential emotional pain is far from typical.

Melancholia and anxiety has figured in Hornby's writing since *Fever Pitch*. The bestselling memoir is not only about the twinned agonies and ecstasies of following Arsenal FC and other forms of romance but also candidly addresses "the bouts of vicious, exhausting depression" which the author suffered during the 1980s (1993, 123). Watching his team with unforgiving relentless focus during a losing streak because of, rather than despite, their bad form, Hornby confesses that this was partly inspired by his "latent depression, permanently looking for a way out," but also as an act of faith that the club might prove "that things did not stay bad for ever, that it *was* possible to change patterns, that losing streaks did not last" (162). *Fever Pitch* is also, in part, a narrative of recovery and, though it does not have the teleology of conventional comedy it certainly moves towards a renewed sense of self, one that remembers the experience of depression without fear. Late in the narrative, Hornby reflects that "all I could feel was the place where the ache had been, and that was a pleasurable sensation, just as when you are recovering from food poisoning and eating again, the soreness of the stomach muscles is pleasurable" (184).

In *High Fidelity*, Rob is more circumspect than the narrator of *Fever Pitch,* Hornby as memoirist: Rob alludes to depression in a glib fashion – a kind of joke that, perhaps, reveals more than is intended about his state of mind. He also admits to a suicide attempt, many years ago, after his first major heartbreak ("I took an overdose of valium, and stuck a finger down my throat within a minute") (Hornby 1996, 26). Perhaps more important is Rob's oblique confession that he is not, on the whole, a happy man. That his favourite songs are melancholy classics – "Only Love Can Break Your Heart," "Last Night I Dreamed that Somebody Loved Me" and "I Don't Want to Talk About it," among others – is not unusual. Yet even a man whose life is caught-up with both enjoying and selling music, in its most authentically moving forms, is sceptical about the influence of so much sad music. The comic plot of the novel is partly an awakening to the ambiguous position of melancholy art: Rob learns to live with his sense of yearning and loss.

3. Almost Comic Endings

Hornby's comedy, then, is defined by painful sympathy rather than easy judgment. Readers are made aware of his characters' failures, limitations and self-deceptions, but these shortcomings are not used as a pretext for eventual exclusion from the community. His narratives rarely, if ever, feature a character that might occupy a position similar, for example, to the unrepentant Don John in Shakespeare's *Much Ado About Nothing*, who, in Christopher Booker's words, "remains off stage as the 'unreconciled dark figure', due for punishment" (2004, 119). The protagonists of Hornby's first two novels, Rob Fleming and Will Freeman, are granted the qualified promise of romantic contentment as a kind of reward for their new self-awareness; they have left behind part of their former selves without being required to relinquish every aspect of their egotism. Indeed, Will's cynicism, moderated by his conscience waking up to a wider world, still gets the last word. When his awkward teenage protégé refuses a playful invitation to sing one of his mother's favourite folk-tinged songs (he now professes to "bloody hate Joni Mitchell") Will is assured "beyond any shadow of a doubt, that Marcus would be okay" (Hornby 1998, 286). These are "happy endings" in the traditional comic sense that Showalter identifies as typical of the genre of "popular male confessional literature" also known as "Ladlit" (Showalter, 2002, 60). Indeed, Hornby's initial penchant for emotionally reassuring comedy was gently, but not inaccurately, burlesqued in a parody of *About a Boy* for *Private Eye* magazine; it concludes with a mischievous re-writing of the last line of the novel in which "Will Goodbloke" realizes "beyond any shadow of a doubt, that the reviews were going to be OK" (Taylor 2012, 56). However, few of Hornby's 21st-century novels precisely correspond to the kind of cheerful denouement in which a likable enough everyman can return to a life of insouciance, changed, but only a little, after a few life lessons.

How to be Good is the first of Hornby's novels that explicitly subverts traditional comic resolution in an ending that mixes fragile hope with a foreboding atmosphere. Katie, warily reunited with her husband, reflects on the near biblical downpour that has been flooding the country, the kind of rain that might persuade this committed rationalist to believe in a supernatural reality. "It feels like the end of the world," she observes as the novel draws to a close with a secular sense of imminent judgment: "we are drowning because we abused our planet" (Hornby 2001, 243). During the storm, her husband ineffectually attempts to clear the gutters, precariously clambering onto a windowsill like a 21st-century Harold Lloyd. The final image of this novel of marital disappointment and liberal frustration is tragi-comic:

> Tom and I grab hold of one back pocket each in an attempt to anchor him, while Molly in turn hangs on to us, purposelessly but sweetly. My family, I think, just that. And then, I can do this. I can live this life. I can, I can. It's a spark I want to cherish, a splutter of life in the flat battery; but just at the wrong moment I catch a glimpse of the night sky behind David, and I can see that there's nothing out there at all. (Hornby 2001, 244)

The scene is both one of resolution – a family in crisis finds meaning in mutual support – and of potential disintegration as the group clings together. The final, anti-epiphany is similarly ambiguous: there is "nothing" out in the night sky, suggesting, *pace* Peter Berger's "redeeming laughter," a stark lack of transcendence (Berger, 1997). "The consolations of humour," Simon Critchley claims, "come from acknowledging that this is the only world and, imperfect as it is and we are, it is only here that we can make a difference" (2002, 17). The final line of *How to be Good* resonates with this idea and suggests that the ordinary comedy of everyday, mundane life is sacred. *Juliet, Naked*, by contrast, ends with another female protagonist, Annie, who is expecting a child, refusing to settle for unhappy domestic routine when she rejects the conservative advice of her counsellor: "This is how England spoke, and she couldn't listen to her any more" (2009, 247). She abandons relative security for an uncertain future in America. The ending is one in which agency is asserted: it's clear that ineffectual or overpowering men will no longer prevent Annie from making her own choices.

Hornby's equivocally merciful attitude to his richly flawed characters, many of whom do not *quite* learn their lesson, connects with what James Wood argues is a relatively new kind of comedy, one that emerged only with the advent of the "modern" novel, particularly in the late 19th and early 20th centuries. Earlier forms of the comic, Wood suggests, routinely echo Aristotelian ideas in which "comedy arises from a perceived defect or ugliness that should not be so painful that we feel compassion, since compassion is the enemy of laughter" (Wood 2005, 5). The "comedy of forgiveness," according to Wood, with its greater sense of pathos, comes close to inverting Aristotle's model. "If religious comedy is punishment for those who deserve it," argues Wood, "secular comedy is forgiveness for those who don't" (6). This chiasmatic taxonomy of old and new, religious and secular, upsets traditional understandings of a Christian comic ending as one defined by forgiveness, the visible operation of divine grace in which erring characters are restored to the community. For Wood the older "religious" mode of comedy – exemplified by Molière's plays – favour moral stability, didacticism and "the closure of punishment" (6). The "tragicomedy" made available in the modern novel, however, registers a much more ambiguous relation to the world and "replaces the knowable with the unknowable, transparency with unreliablity" (8).

The four "*un*reliably *un*reliable" narrators – to borrow Wood's phrase – of *A Long Way Down* make reference to their lives as narrative, as a series of events that needs a shape and that will be defined by their end (Wood 2005, 8; 9). JJ is the most self-consciously literary of the quartet ("I read the fuck out of every book I can get my hands on" [Hornby 2005a, 29]), citing Dickens, Faulkner and Vonnegut as favourites, and confessing (to the reader rather than his new friends) that he had considered clutching a copy of Richard Yates' *Revolutionary Road* when he took his own life: "not only because it would have been kinda cool, and would've added a little mystique to my death, but because it might have been a good way of getting more people to read it" (29). This gallows humour is self-deceiving but anticipates the novel's wider focus on the construction of meaning in relation to a conventional teleology, in which a happy end transfigures prior suffering. JJ cautions against reading Yates' novel on "Christmas Day [...] in a city where you don't really know anybody [...] because the ending is a real downer" (29). Maureen, who enjoys escapist romance, has constructed her own mini-narrative of an imagined New Year's Eve get-together in order to justify leaving her son in a care home on the night of her planned suicide: "And I suppose I came to believe in the party a little bit myself, in the way that you come to believe the story in a book" (6). The four even plan to read books by authors who have committed suicide ("They were, like, our people," (207) observes Jess). This experiment in literary therapy is quickly abandoned after a disastrous reading of Virginia Woolf's *To the Lighthouse*. Although Jess is the least literary and literate of the group – indeed, unnecessarily long words make her angry – she is aware of the desire for narrative closure. After talking about her missing (presumed dead) sister, she abruptly warns the future reader not to expect Jen "to pop up later to rescue me [...] forget about that sort of ending. It's not that sort of story" (140). This self-consciousness introduces a metafictional strand to the novel: if this is not the "sort of story" that includes improbable, near miraculous reunions, what kind of story is it? Jess later naïvely attempts to construct a *deus ex machina* that will bring Martin back together with his ex-wife and children. She senses that "our story was sort of coming to an end" and despite her aversion for literature she does have a sense of what constitutes a proper comic resolution: "That's when stories end isn't it? When people show they've learned things, and problems get solved. I've seen loads of films like that [...] we'd meet on the roof after ninety days, and smile, and hug, and know that we had moved on" (248).

The impact of her intervention is, as we might expect, comically disastrous and defers rather than accelerates the denouement: more arguments and public humiliations ensue from Jess's good intentions. For Dominic Head, this "preoccupation with the populist happy ending," with each character thinking about "the cliché of the propitious felicitous outcome," reads "a little bit like Hornby seeking to persuade us that this is not the sentimental book it appears to be, with four strangers [...] finding salvation in a discovered community [...] and, of course, the central idea of the book is to show that they *do* find salvation in a new community" (2008, 17). However, the end, when it comes, is neither as cathartic as Jess might hope nor quite as sentimental as Head implies. In the final pages of the novel, a few things have changed: Maureen and JJ have both achieved modest, but significant, steps forward; Martin's arrogance, meanwhile, though tempered, has not disappeared and Jess remains as frustratingly obtuse as she is insensitive. Yet neither of these endlessly bickering figures is omitted from the final gathering, narrated by Maureen, as the group reconvenes at a pub opposite Toppers' House, to mark progress since their improbable first encounter. The ending of the novel rhymes with the original, almost tragic meeting on the roof; as the conventionally unconventional quartet quarrel and confess ongoing doubts about the future, they gaze out at the iconic monuments of the modern metropolis, a frantically ludic world from which they might feel alienated. The London Eye – a gigantic wheel that affords cheery tourists a similarly elevated view to the mock god-like perspective at the summit of Toppers' House – appears, from a distance, to be static: "We stared at it for a long time, trying to work it out [...]. It didn't look as though it was moving, but it must have been, I suppose" (Hornby 2005a, 332-33). This is a terse way to end any novel and might seem a particularly muted conclusion to such a sequence of garrulous interior monologues. However, it's crucial that this mundane vision is, in an echo of the ambiguous ending of *How to be Good*, a shared moment, this time with a surrogate family: Maureen's laconic summation, qualified by the tentative "I suppose," suggests that life, however decelerated, remains possible in communion with others.

4. Conclusion

For a nation whose self-image is much invested in its gift for irony, satirical impulses and absurd sensibility, contemporary Britain has an uneasy relationship with comedy and comic fiction, in particular. Occasionally, however, a critical voice will capsize orthodox thinking about depth and wit. In a scathing review of Alan Bennett's television play *The Old Crowd*, originally published in *The Observer* on 4 February 1979, Clive James suggested that Lindsay Anderson's direction had cut all of the jokes and that the piece had bought into "the delusion that solemnity equals seriousness" (James 1991, 307). In the review James argues that for a writer "like Bennett the jokes are not decoration but architecture." He offers the most eloquent salute to the comic that I know: "common sense and a sense of humour are the same thing, moving at different speeds. A sense of humour is just common sense, dancing. Those who lack humour are without judgment and should be trusted with nothing" (307).

Hornby's fiction, full of "common sense, dancing," indicates that he takes the business of laughter quite seriously; his novels have little time for those who deride it as a debased form of feeling. A key episode in *Funny Girl* embodies this perspective. Dennis Maxwell-Bishop, the Cambridge-educated, rather unworldly producer-director of "*Barbara (and Jim)*," is required to defend the sitcom on a late night talk-show named "*Pipe Show*" (the kind of programme "in which men with beards and spectacles [...] talked with annoying certainty about God and the H-bomb" (Hornby 2014, 154)). The deadpan comedy of this antiquated homosocial environment is intensified because Dennis' opponent, a snooty aesthete named Vernon Whitfield, has also been having an affair with his wife. Dennis unexpectedly beats the pompous critic, using the man's vanity and temper against him; Whitfield is the kind of man who claims to "love ordinary people individually" but is troubled by them "en masse" (59). The critic's arrogance – and simmering embarrassment regarding his erotic misdemeanor – cause him to swear on air in a still somewhat censorious era. More importantly, Whitfield embodies a kind of flushed, high culture contempt for shared laughter. The episode might be Hornby's fierce apologia for a "comedy of forgiveness" that is generous but not always peaceable in addressing its cultured despisers.

Works Cited

Amis, Martin. *Money: A Suicide Note.* London: Cape, 1984.

Bentley, Eric. "On the Other Side of Despair." [1964]. *Comedy: Developments in Criticism.* Ed. D.J. Palmer. Houndmills: Palgrave, 1992. 135-150.

Bentley, Nick. *Contemporary British Fiction.* Edinburgh: Edinburgh University Press, 2008.

Berger, Peter. L. *Redeeming Laughter: The Comic Dimension of Human Experience.* Berlin: De Gruyter, 1997.

Bergson, Henri. *Laughter: An Essay on the Meaning of the Comic*. Trans. by Cloudesley Brereton and Fred Rothwell. London: Macmillan, 1921.
Booker, Christopher. *The Seven Basic Plots: Why We Tell Stories*. London: Continuum, 2004.
Brooker, Joseph. "The Middle Years of Martin Amis." *British Fiction Today*. Eds. Philip Tew and Rod Mengham. London: Continuum, 2006. 3-14.
Brown, Craig. "Diary – Nick Hornby: Four More Songs." *Private Eye* 1074 (21 February 2003): 24.
Childs, Peter. *Contemporary Novelists: British Fiction Since 1970*. 2nd ed. Houndmills: Palgrave, 2012.
Coake, Christopher. "Subversive Hope" [review of *A Long Way Down*]. *American Book Review* 27.1 (2005): 17-18.
Critchley, Simon. *On Humour*. London: Routledge, 2002.
Falk, Barry. "Love and Lists in Nick Hornby's *High Fidelity*." *Cultural Critique* 66 (2007): 153-76.
Head, Dominic. *The Cambridge Introduction to Modern British Fiction, 1950-2000*. Cambridge: Cambridge University Press, 2002.
—. *The State of the Novel: Britain and Beyond*. Oxford: Blackwell, 2008.
Hornby, Nick. *Fever Pitch*. [1992]. London: Gollancz, 1993.
—, ed. *My Favourite Year: a Collection of New Football Writing*. London: Witherby, 1993.
—. *High Fidelity*. London: Indigo, 1996.
—. *About a Boy*. London: Gollancz, 1998.
—. *Speaking with the Angel*. London: Penguin, 2000.
—. *How to Be Good*. London: Penguin, 2001.
—. *31 Songs*. London: Viking, 2003.
—. *A Long Way Down*. London: Penguin, 2005a. Kindle edition.
—. *Otherwise Pandemonium*. London: Penguin, 2005b.
—. *The Complete Polysyllabic Spree*. London: Penguin, 2006.
—. *Slam*. London: Penguin, 2008.
—. *Juliet, Naked*. London: Penguin, 2009.
—. *Funny Girl*. London: Penguin, 2014.
James, Clive. *On Television: Criticism from The Observer, 1972-1982*. London: Picador, 1991.
Keskinen, Ikko. "Single, Long-Playing, and Compilation: The Formats of Audio and Amorousness in Nick Hornby's *High Fidelity*." *Critique: Studies in Contemporary Fiction* 47.1 (2005): 3-21.
Lea, Daniel and Berthold Schoene. "Masculinity in Transition: An Introduction." *Posting the Male: Masculinities in Post-War and Contemporary British Literature*. Eds. Daniel Lea and Berthold Schoene. Amsterdam: Rodopi, 2003. 7-18.
Mars-Jones, Adam. "Meet the four Toppers." *The Observer*. 1 May 2005. Web. 15 February 2015.
McCombe, John. "'Common People': Realism, Class Difference, and the Male Domestic Sphere in Nick Hornby's Collision with Britpop." *Modern Fiction Studies* 60.1 (2014): 165-84.
Mooney, Bel. "Nick Hornby, *A Long Way Down*." *The Times*. 8 April 2006. Web. 15 February 2015.
O'Brien, Sean. "Toppers' Talk." *The Times Literary Supplement* 5327 (6 May 2005): 20.

O'Farrell, John. *Things Can Only Get Better: Eighteen Miserable Years in The Life of a Labour Supporter, 1979-1997*. London: Doubleday, 1998.
Palmer, D.J., ed. *Comedy: Developments in Criticism*. Houndmills: Palgrave, 1992.
Parsons, Tony. *Man and Boy*. London: HaperCollins, 1999.
Showalter, Elaine. "Ladlit." *On Modern British Fiction*. Ed. Zachary Leader. Oxford: Oxford University Press, 2002. 60-76.
Stott, Andrew. *Comedy*. New York: Routledge, 2005.
Taylor, D.J., ed. *What You Didn't Miss: A Book of Literary Parodies*. London: Constable, 2012.
Wood, James. "The Lie-World." *London Review of Books* 25.22. 20 November 2003. Web. 15 February 2015.
—. *The Irresponsible Self: On Laughter and the Novel*. London: Pimlico, 2005.

CHRISTOPH HOUSWITSCHKA

"Show me a novel that's not comic ...:" Howard Jacobson's *The Finkler Question*

Howard Jacobson's work is funny, but seriously funny.[1] He claims that comic novels should be taken seriously and that the distinction between 'comic novelist' and 'literary novelist' is to be abolished altogether: "Show me a novel that's not comic and I'll show you a novel that's not doing its job," he starts suggesting his discussion of comic novels (Jacobson, 2010b).

In the same article, Jacobson admits that in a period of stand-up comedies some people might argue "that we are laughing too much." Jacobson believes that "we have created a false division between laughter and thought, between comedy and seriousness," but "the exhilaration" of the funniest novels also offers "whatever else it is we now think we want from literature" (2010b). Jacobson regrets the "fear of comedy in the novel today" (qtd. in Díaz Bild 2013, 90). In his novel, he links comedy with the concept of the perfect Jewish joke that "would never finish" (Jacobson 2012). Jacobson regards the Jewish joke above all as

> a strategy for survival. It looks, of necessity, to the future. It anticipates a woe before that woe is visited upon us. It gets in first with the criticism and the cruelty. If anybody is going to knock us around it won't be the Cossacks, it will be ourselves. So that while a Jewish joke appears to be the perfecting of self-denigration, it is actually the opposite. It is the fruit of a perpetual vigilance and in the process demonstrates an intelligence that is, because it has to be, unremitting. (Jacobson 2012)

The Finkler Question (2010)[2] fathoms issues of Jewish self-images in London. Andrew Motion, the former poet Laureate and chairman of the judges who made Howard Jacobson the 2010 winner of the Man Booker Prize, described the novel as "very clever and very funny," but also "a very sad, melancholic book. It is comic, it is laughter – but it is laughter in the dark" (Lyall 2010). Lezard confirms this intertwined reading of the novel: "Although it's true that *The Finkler Question* has its moments of high comedy, it also has moments of heartbreaking sadness [...]. But if there's one thing that everyone can agree on, it's that *The Finkler Question* is about Jewishness" (Lezard 2010). Like all good comedy the novel neither denies that its humour evolves from the tragedy of centuries-old anti-Semitism nor that laughter appears to be the only way to embrace the complexities of all possible perspectives shaping the paradoxes of Jewish self-images in the British diaspora. Jacobson is a Jewish writer,[3] but at the same time he has repeatedly insisted on standing firmly in the tradition of the English novel. Therefore, he suggested that *The Finkler Question* is not really about Jewishness, but love. Both approaches to his novel seem to be true.

1 See the title of his book *Seriously Funny: From the Ridiculous to the Sublime* (1997) and his Channel Four TV series.
2 *The Finkler Question* (Jacobson 2010a) will hereafter be referred to as *FQ*.
3 For this complex term, see Gilbert (2013, 1-19), for Jacobson (8-9) and for Israel in *FQ* (90-92).

Anglistik: International Journal of English Studies 27.1 (March 2016): 45-59.

In the *New York Times*, Howard Jacobson described himself as "an English writer who happens to know about Jews and would like to write like Jane Austen, with a little bit of Yiddish" and he rejected to be called an exclusively humorous author:

> 'To *me*, being a comic novelist is obviously to be serious, too – what else is there to be comic about? [...] But when I hear people call me a comic novelist, I want to scream, because they mean something different. I can call myself a comic novelist, though, because I know what I mean when I say it.' (Lyall 2010)

These are undoubtedly very useful hints to understand how humour in this novel could be approached. It speaks for his self-consciousness as a writer that Howard Jacobson does not tell us what he means when he calls himself a comic novelist, but falls short of being derogatory about his readers' concept of it. In line with this and perhaps part of an explanation, is his insistence on being rather called "the Jewish Jane Austen" than "the English Philip Roth" (Lyall 2010; see also Maslin 2010). Maslin is reminded of Philip Roth or Woody Allen. Jacobson represents male Jewish identity in sexual relationships with (mainly) Gentile women in a very similar fashion.

The wickedness of Jacobson's humour seems deeply rooted in colliding narrative perspectives that split self-images and turn them into self-delusions. This is true not just of an author who has the self-consciousness to take part in all of them and still avoid almost completely any biased point of view. He also takes into account the self-delusions of his readers who might think they recognize one particular obsession among the diverse positions and activities Jacobson's characters cling to while miserably failing. It is human failure and the weaknesses of human nature quite generally speaking which breed instances of wicked humour. This is abstract enough a statement to insist on Jacobson's humour being not about content or any specific truths, but about manners, neither good manners nor bad manners, as Lyall (2010) believes, but the manners that help Jacobson's characters to carry themselves through their lives. His representations of manners, however, – as is always the case in what Jacobson calls "serious" novels – are not meant to be realistic, but rather illusions created by the highly artistic use of narrative conventions. Presenting literary form in such a way that we learn something about the playfulness of social conventions, without ever recognizing more than their witty hypocrisy, became a manifestation of Englishness in the tradition of the novel of manners. In the realm of narrative art, it was Jane Austen who excelled in this highly artistic way of creating texts which escape a realistic representation of the world and embrace literary conventions. This seriousness of literary form presents to us the funny elegance of human nature that evolves from the sophisticated literary illusion of the everyday behaviour of people. It is this artistic tension between literary form and real life that might help the reader not to despair in our world, but rather give up on the self-delusions of literary characters. This tension allows the reader to trace the humour of the text, finding comic relief in the confrontation with the seriousness of human beings' fragile and futile existence. "If we are to be true to the form there will be only 'novels' and they will be effusive with wit and humour," as Jacobson explains in an article for the *Guardian* (2010b).

So when Lyall suggests that Jacobson's "inner Roth did more than his inner Austen to win him" the Man Booker Prize for *The Finkler Question*, she avoids a crucial issue in discussing Jacobson's humour. Should one approach his concept of humour focusing on English literary traditions or Jewish ones? Jacobson responded to this by creating the quite unlikely allegory of a "Jewish Austen" (Lyall 2010).

Familiar concepts of English and Jewish humour will be compared to comic features Jacobson uses. Quite inevitably, these concepts of humour do not only inform

Jacobson's humour, but are also ridiculed by him. More significant is a narratological approach that allows for a thorough analysis of the changing internal focalizers that create diverse perspectives on Jewish self-images. These shifting perspectives of the focalizers manipulate our view on characters and help the narrator to avoid closure.[4]

Concentrating on focalization might also limit our view without defining the way focalization creates various types of self-images based on characters. Since the novel is about the question of what it means to be Jewish, the self-images created are those of Jews living in London – of three aging long-time friends and their wives and lovers, in particular. The anguish of these middle-aged men shows in their relationship to their wives and lovers as much as in their self-images as Jews and Gentiles. The three main characters are "a gentile fascinated by Jews, and his two Jewish friends, one a Zionist comfortable in London, and the other an anti-Zionist comfortable in his outrage," as Anthony Julius phrased it (2010a). The tensions and incongruities between various character-bound focalizations of Jewishness create humour.

Sam Finkler is a member of the ASHamed Jews, who are anti-Zionists coming close to anti-Semitism and self-hatred. They provide the reader with quite a few hilarious scenes in the novel, in the words of Jacobson: "People think they're parodies of Jews who happen to disapprove of Israel. But they're not. They're parodies of Jews who parade their disapproval of Israel" (Lyall 2010). Libor Sevick is of Czech origin. He is the least English character and has a strong sense of his Jewish and Zionist identity, the "whole Jewish *gesheft*. You think it's a short cut to catastrophe. And I'm not going to say you're wrong" (*FQ,* 244-45). In the narrative, he rarely becomes the focalizer and when he does, his humour is Jewish and he tries to characterize Treslove as a Gentile: "Those who can't wait to pitchfork us into the flames want to go down screaming by our side. It's one or the other" (245). He represents a self-image resulting from how other Jews (Sam Finkler) and Gentiles (Julian Treslove) see him as a Jew. This way Libor turns into a tragic-comical character.

As the plot unfolds, both Sam and Libor become widowers. On the level of the story, all three friends generate their self-image as characters through their relationships with women. They either try to escape who they are by falling in love with or being married to their respective opposite, either Jewish or Gentile, or they are thrown back to their original identity, without any chance of manipulating it. This is the case with Libor, who is a widower from the very beginning of the story.[5]

The main character is a Gentile, Julian Treslove. Walton suggests that readers might be quite puzzled by Jacobson's narrative twist: "As it turns out, though, they needn't worry. Julian Treslove may not be Jewish, but in most other respects he's a typical Jacobson protagonist." Even more so, "he's obsessed with Jews and Jewishness" (Walton 2010). The question arising from this narrative arrangement, of course, is whether the narrator is closer to the Jewish writer or the Gentile character.

The narrator often seems to disappear behind Treslove. The internal focalizer creates a self-image that the reader can hardly see as the Jewish self-image of a Gentile, but rather will believe to result from how the narrator perceives Gentiles seeing him.[6]

---

4 The terminology follows Mieke Bal (2009, 145-53).

5 For Libor's attempt to find a new partner and the funny generational problems that emerge from this, see Bayer's interpretation (2012, 178) of Jacobson: "Oh God, [...] she will want me to be against fox hunting" (*FQ,* 36).

6 According to Bal (2009, 17), the implied (Jewish) author belongs to an older terminology coined by Booth (1961). Bal prefers the term "narrator." Her valid points are less important in the context of this novel because the Jewish identity of the author informs an essential issue of the novel. Bal criticized

As Díaz Bild explains, "Treslove, the Gentile, is merely reproducing what Jacobson believes others think of Jews" (2013, 94). Therefore, the latent tension between the narrator and the internal focalizer creates humorous statements based on mute assumptions the author does not have to accept responsibility for. The same could be said about Sam Finkler und Libor Sevick, who perceive Treslove the way they believe he sees them. While the latter tension is one between various self-images on the level of the story, the former Jewish self-image is constructed on the basis of how the narrator is believed to construct Treslove according to what he assumes others see him as. This tension is one between focalization and narration and makes visible what would remain invisible, the implied reader's stereotypes about what they believe to be Jewish. This implied reader, of course, might either be Jewish or Gentile. What both have most likely in common, however, is the belief that a Jewish author must show in the narrator's voice an assumption that is far from necessary in narratological terms.

On the level of the story, Treslove is both a philosemite and an anti-Zionist. On the level of form and focalization, a Gentile internal focalizer (Treslove) is presented by a Jewish narrator, allowing for a more complex diasporic writing of what is invisible or unspeakable in Jewish self-images, projected by Jewish characters and hidden behind Treslove's sometimes foolish attempts to become a Jew. It is needless to say that this generates funny incongruities of perception and observation, as Finkler tells him when they have an argument about the subject:

> 'You can't be us. You shouldn't want to be us.' 'I don't want to be you.' 'Somewhere you do. I don't mean to be cruel but there has always been some part of us you have wanted.' '*Us*? Since when were you and Libor *us*?' 'That's an insensitive question.' (*FQ*, 67)

Brauner explains this complex play of self-images and images of otherness in his wittily entitled chapter "The Gentile Who Mistook Himself for a Jew."[7] In Brauner's assessment of Sartre's *Anti-Semite and Jew* (1946), "Jewishness holds sway: what matters is not whether you perceive yourself to be Jewish, but whether others – specifically anti-Semites – perceive you to be Jewish" (Brauner 2001, 50). In contrast to such a content-based view, the signifiers of Jewishness may be the representation of narrative form rather than any conclusive idea of Jewishness. This also creates a concept of humour that does not fall back on statements about Jewishness or anti-Semitism but rather comments on the form of their presentation, the focalization of Jewish identity.

Humour emerges from dialogues and comments whenever the internal seems to collide with the mute assumptions conveyed by what the reader believes to be a Jewish narrator representing the voice of the (implied) author. Therefore, Jacobson also insists on novels not following standards of religion, morality or political rectitude. He calls this "shrinkage:"

> Thus a novel may be as offensive as it chooses or happens to be – so long, of course, as it is funny or, at the least, enlivening. It may be sexist, misogynistic, homophobic, antisemitic, masculinist, man-hating, misanthropic, etc. And the reader who complains of finding any of those unpalatable is describing his own nervous system, not the novel. (Jacobson 2010b)

---

the concept of the "implied author" because it is "the result of the investigation of the meaning of a text, and not the source of that meaning" (17). The implied author of *The Finkler Question* remains the source of the meaning because the concept of the implied author helps to ridicule the investigation, i.e. the question of Jewish identity.

7 Cf. Oliver Sacks's famous case study, "The Man Who Mistook His Wife for a Hat" (1985).

Treslove represents the voice of the fool who utters unreasonable statements and who takes on "the role of speaking the unspeakable, of revealing through his [...] folly the folly that afflicts all humankind" (Palmer 1994, 48). Treslove turns into a belittled and humorous character by his desire to become someone else and the shrinkage of what he believes to be Jewish generates all the politically incorrect behaviour that ridicules him, particularly in his behaviour to women, both Gentile (Tyler Finkler) and Jewish (Hephzibah Weizenbaum).

Treslove "seems to have walked out of a Woody Allen film with his constant neuroticism, questioning reality, a tendency to overanalyze and overdramatize everyday life situations and fear of a pending catastrophe."[8] This category of humour is "used for egotistical purposes to 'squelch' other people or attributes. Often, of course, the two processes converge, as in the 'ethnic stupidity' jokes" (*FQ,* 103-104). In Jacobson's novel such jokes could also be used to elaborate anti-Semitism on the level of the story, e.g. Gentiles cheering or attacking Jews, a fantasy Treslove pursues to gain his Jewish friends' recognition. Jacobson carefully avoids any such explicit episodes. His humour is built on assumptions and fantasies made about Jewishness or anti-Semitism that are revealed by incongruities between focalizer and narrator. This tension originates from Jacobson's recognition that although stories about life are serious there is no good reason not to laugh about them if you look at them from a detached and borrowed perspective, i.e. if you resort to another focalizer:

> 'Now more than ever I want you to be funny [...] now that you are in the toils and at any moment you're going to die and you are fed up with everything and everybody.' I feel the same with Woody Allen: 'Fine, it was easy before. Joke now.' It's never too serious to laugh. (Jacobs 2008)

Treslove believes to have been exposed to an attack by someone he heard calling him a "Jew." Ethnic discrimination is not turned against Jews, but against Treslove who thinks to have been mistaken for one (*FQ,* 10-11; 72). Ethnic stupidity jokes are thus avoided without denying their existence. Real things remain uncontrollable as Roth claims in *Operation Shylock*: "In the modern world, the Jew has perpetually been on trial; still today the Jew is on trial, in the person of the Israeli – and this modern trial of the Jew, this trial which never ends, begins with the trial of Shylock" (Roth 1993, 274). Jacobson's humour is also not limited to ridiculing Treslove, whose obsession with recognition (without ever actually converting) is far from routinely rejected by his Jewish friends and his Jewish girlfriend. Treslove has conversations exploiting the hidden anguish of not knowing when anti-Semitism will hit again, and he proudly parades his anti-Zionism at the same time.[9] Focalization of characters is not about blaming anybody of anti-Semitism, but rather about scrutinizing its effect on those who can neither control nor predict its re-emergence.

When Treslove has an affair with Tyler, Sam Finkler's wife, this betrayal is not forgiven by Libor who learns about it after Tyler's death. It is not only the betrayal of a friend (*FQ,* 246-47). Treslove does not only claim Sam Finkler's Jewishness, but also undermines his friend's trust in society: "Probably more wrong of you to tell me than to do it. I don't want the burden of the knowledge" (*FQ,* 247). The meaning of sexual relationships is more sophisticated than this. Behind his back, the sexual rela-

---

8 I owe this poignant description to Anna Linetsky (Trier) who gave a talk on Jacobson at the University of Bamberg on June 12, 2013. I would like to thank her for suggestions and comments.

9 In *Trials of the Diaspora*, Julius distinguishes and studies in detail three different types of anti-Zionism: Anglo-Muslim, Anglo-Jewish, and Anglo-Christian (2010, 544-60).

tionship stands for a persistent feeling that he is not safe in the diaspora.[10] Libor recognizes Treslove's mute intentions: "'Are you proud of it because you got one over on Sam?' […] 'Not got one *over*, Libor. I hope not that. More having got *into* his world. Their world.' 'From which you'd felt excluded?'" (*FQ,* 247).

When Treslove learns that Tyler Finkler is not Jewish, he is disappointed: "'Well, your everything is a nothing,' she said. He was bitterly upset. 'Not a Jewess, Tyler?'" (*FQ,* 77). Obviously, a relationship with his friend's Jewish wife was supposed to make him more Jewish. In a similar way, Tyler personifies Sam Finkler's wish not to be Jewish all the time. Therefore he never acknowledged her interest in Jewish culture: "He had at no time been sympathetic to Tyler's Jewish aspirations. He didn't need to be married to a Jew. He was Jew enough at least in his antecedence – for both of them" (*FQ,* 271).

Finkler's Jewish identity is a precarious one. He marries Tyler and joins an anti-Zionist group of the name ASHamed Jews. It is only after his wife's death that Finkler's Jewishness becomes more self-assured and acknowledges anti-Semitism to be a threat no Jew may evade. Treslove's affair with Tyler develops more momentum only later in the novel when Treslove tells Libor about his relationship. Libor is deeply hurt and when he commits suicide the narrator suggests Treslove believes his disappointment to be one of the reasons for his dwindling wish to live: "If Finkler thought that was grandiose, what would he say if he ever found out that Treslove thought Libor had committed suicide because of what he knew about his and Tyler's adultery?" (*FQ,* 285). Treslove's behaviour is not only about friendship and betrayal. Treslove, who entertains a relationship with a Jewish woman at the time he reveals his former affair with Tyler to Libor, is trespassing. The infidelity of his non-Jewish wife with a Gentile, Treslove, carries a vague sense of diasporic vulnerability.

Jacobson finds "God's laughter" in the self-denial and the unfulfilled desires of both Finkler and Treslove. It is the "laughter at the very idea that we can think our way out of the unthinkable. And the nearest we approach to it – in skepticism, in play, and yes, in cruelty – is the novel" (Jacobson 2010b).

This answer to the Jewish question is a cruel one, because a sense of anguish and threat never leaves Finkler. The narration's focalization shifts from Treslove to Sam Finkler towards the end of the novel. Finkler becomes more pessimistic than one would have expected, but he also turns against Treslove's anti-Zionism. The cruelty of the unthinkable, of anti-Semitism and what it means to Jewish life, emerges from Treslove's and Finkler's foolishness, but it is Sam Finkler's Jewishness that prevails.

The Jewish question, however, is answered in many ways, none of which being utterly convincing or conclusive. This is in line with definitions of Jewishness in studies about Jewish literature. David Brauner suggests that the Jewish experience is not only different from all other ethnic and religious identities, but also unique. He quotes George Steiner:

> *Of course there is a Jewish question.* Only cant or a self-deluding investment in normalcy could deny that. The political map, the plethora of ethnic-historical legacies, the patchwork of societies, faiths, communal identifications across our globe teems with unresolved conflicts, with religious-racial enmities, with non-negotiable claims to an empowering past, to sacred grounds. None the less, the Jewish condition differs. Irreducibly, maddeningly, it embodies what modern physics calls a 'singularity,' a construct

10 See Lyall (2010): "Indeed, there is an ominous undercurrent in the book in the form of a growing number of anti-Semitic attacks, mostly offstage, that shatter the complacency of characters who resist the notion of Jews as perpetual victims. Mr. Jacobson says that such incidents worry him too."

> or happening outside the norms, extraterritorial to probability and the findings of common reason. (Steiner 1998, 48, qtd. in Brauner 2001, 2)

Brauner favours Steiner's use of the phrase 'Jewish condition,' because it denotes either "an irrevocable existential state or a treatable malady" (2001, 2). Following Brauner, one could argue that it is the combination of this identifiable uniqueness and the ambiguity and multivalency of contradictory self-images of Jews in literature that create either an often stereotypical representation of Jewish life or the opportunity to represent Jewish identity as a perpetual construction of changing focalizations.

Geoffrey Hartman is helpful here. He "singles out the domination of the written word (a text-dependency)" that does not "split between letter and spirit, a distinctive humor that assuages the anguish of profanation" (Wirth-Nesher 1994, 4). Giving answers to what Jacobson calls the Finkler Question, Wirth-Nesher suggests that while "the categories themselves may be unstable and problematic, they are an inherent part of the reading process" (1994, 5; see Stähler 2007, 32). Reception shifts the emphasis from definitions of Jewishness to questions that are asked by readers about Jewish identity "with a view to how literary texts can open up the categories that critics too often would close down" (Valman 2012, 218-19). Comedy and Humour are Jacobson's main features to avoid closure and a formal definition of Jewishness: "I don't say comedy is the only means of challenging our routine sympathies and valuations. What, after all, are the interests of the comic novel? If it's written in the spirit of Cervantes then it has no interests, no predetermined direction, nothing to prove" (Jacobson 2010b).

Avoiding content-driven descriptions of Jewishness, Jacobson does not only discuss diverse categories of diasporic Jewishness, but also changes the perspectives on Jewish self-images. This way, Jacobson also mediates between literary conventions shaped by Britishness and those that belong to Jewish traditions. Critics have often acknowledged that Howard Jacobson is one of the few who "has decided to face head on the thorny question of Britishness in his fiction" (Cheyette 2003, 10). Cheyette explains that English national culture is too homogeneous and unchanging in its "idea of the past" to absorb "the Jewish past into a territorial Britishness" (8).

Jacobson claims to be a "Jewish Jane Austen" (Lyall 2010) because he tries to achieve exactly that, to accommodate the Jewish past in a British context in a similar way Austen tried to accommodate a female view in a male society, thus ridiculing femininity with the distance of the narrator's voice and establishing it as a social category. And yet:

> It would be mortifying to the feelings of many ladies, could they be made to understand how little the heart of a man is affected by what is costly or new in their attire. [...] Woman is fine for her own satisfaction alone. No man will admire her the more, no woman will like her the better for it. Neatness and fashion are enough for the former, and a something of shabbiness or impropriety will be most endearing to the latter. – But not one of these grave reflections troubled the tranquility of Catherine. (Austen 1932, 73-74)

Benedict points out that the narrator in Austen's novel *Northanger Abbey* (1818) burlesques "the rationalistic moralism of conventional discourse" (2009, 351) and reveals that fashionable dress is "a part of female cultural competition," "clothes are designed less to make women attractive to men than to triumph over rival women: they are part of a female semiotic system" (352). Austen uses the incongruity between the plural focalization of "women" and the judgment of the narrator to authenticate femininity.[11] In a similar fashion, the character's focalization of Treslove presents self-images of Jews perceived by a Gentile. Stereotypes are ridiculed by the narrator's bemused voice.

Treslove thinks that his heart is breaking with love for Jewish Hephzibah. Finally, he makes up for the disappointment he experienced with Tyler: "Tyler Finkler, not a Finkler! Therefore the deep damp dark mysteriousness of a Finkler woman was still, strictly speaking – and this was a strict concept or it was nothing – unknown to him" (*FQ,* 78). Treslove loves Hephzibah's Jewish humour: "when had poor Tyler ever done what Hephzibah had just done with language?" (*FQ,* 158). Treslove wants to understand Jewish humour, when Hephzibah uses a metaphor to describe Treslove's unadmitted willingness to fall in love with her: "I saw it when I first clapped eyes on you. You were waiting for the roof to fall in.' He went to kiss her. 'And it did,' he said with exaggerated courtliness. She pushed him away. 'I'm the roof now!'" (*FQ,* 158). On the one hand, Treslove is convinced that a "Jewess was a woman who made even punctuation funny" (*FQ,* 158). On the other hand, Treslove cannot work out how Hephzibah uses Jewish humour: "Was it hyperbole or was it understatement? Was it self-mockery or mockery of him? He decided it was tone. Finklers did tone" (*FQ,* 159).

Whether Hephzibah's humour fits conventions of British or Jewish humour is not the question, but how these clichés work with Treslove. Hephzibah changes the meaning of a metaphor to make it macabre belonging to "a literature of the absurd which, by degree if not kind, stands distinctly apart from any European writing" (Ziv and Zajdman 1993, 4). Ziv proposes that black humour may have its true origins in "the *shtetl* tradition of the *schlemiel* and the *schlimazl*" (4). Treslove does not understand that Hephzibah plays with the idea of love being a deadly danger for Treslove. His love for her is as dangerous as a collapsing roof. The ambiguity of this macabre joke is more informed by gender and British humour than Jewish black humour, because "the Jewish joke always has a therapeutic effect: it ridicules suffering and tension" (Hochwald 1996, vii).

What Treslove hopes to discover in Jewish humour appears to be witty in a general sense, rather than being particularly Jewish. The internal does not only tell us about Treslove's inner thoughts but the Jewish narrator's voice ridicules him at the same time. Treslove's expectations are ridiculously blown out of proportion and remind the reader of Jacobson's statement: "Hyperbole is the soul of comedy. Minimalism is its enemy. Freed from the fetters of those who would make us smaller than we are, we glory in the sensation of too-muchness we have regained" (Jacobson 2010b). While this "sensation of too-muchness" is a hope that does not come true for Treslove, it redeems the Jewish protagonists in Jacobson's novel.[12] In contrast, Treslove is funny in his futile attempts to imitate his understanding of what it means to be Jewish: "The Jews were a hyperbolic people. Had he been hyperbolical enough?" (*FQ,* 128).

Jokes based on ambiguities and puns can also be found with Sam Finkler, for example when he uses the sound of /dʒu:/ to confuse Treslove:

> 'Do you know anyone called Juno?' Treslove asked. 'J'you know Juno?' Finkler replied, making inexplicable J noises between his teeth. Treslove didn't get it. 'J'you know Juno? Is that what you're asking me?' Treslove still didn't get it. So Finkler wrote it down. D'Jew know Jewno? Treslove shrugged. 'Is that supposed to be funny?' 'It is to me,'

11 Since the external narrator is always present in Jane Austen's novels, the character is always double.

12 S.B. Cohen explains that the self-critical jokes of Jewish humour are "a major source of their salvation. In laughing at their tragic conditions, Jews have been able to liberate themselves from those conditions" (1987, 108-109).

> Finkler said. 'But please yourself.' 'Is it funny for a Jew to write the word Jew? Is that what's funny?' 'Forget it," Finkler said. 'You wouldn't understand.' 'Why wouldn't I understand? If I wrote *Non-Jew don't know what Jew know* I'd be able to tell you what's funny about it.' 'There's nothing funny about it.' 'Exactly. Non-Jews don't find it hilarious to see the word Non-Jew. We aren't amazed by the written fact of our identity.' 'And d'Jew know why that is?' Finkler asked. 'Go fuck yourself,' Treslove told him. 'And that's Non-Jew humour, is it?' (*FQ* 16-17)

Certainly, this is one of the most prominent scenes in the novel. A Gentile and a Jew negotiate different senses of humour. While Treslove does not get the Jewish part of it, he also fails to get the British one, the pun. Treslove's internal character focalization presents Treslove's view on things most of the time, but the narrator's voice never entirely abandons a Jewish perspective that is closer to Finkler's, who ridicules Treslove for his cluelessness. Treslove cannot step into the diasporic perspective of Sam Finkler.[13] On the basis of this "particular socio-historical condition called 'marginality'" Jewish humour became the "capacity that allows the placement of oneself in the other's position, to look at oneself critically, and to take all serious matters lightly" (Roeckelein 2002, 106). Finkler perceives Jews as existing mainly in the eyes and writings of others. Treslove fails to be accepted by his Jewish friends and this experience keeps repeating itself.

He feels alienated by Finkler's behaviour. Focalization slightly changes between a narrator who comments on Treslove's reaction and Treslove's emotional response as represented by the internal voicing of the fear of not being taken seriously by Jews:

> What Treslove did was exclusion, not jealousy. And though they were related, they were not the same. Jealousy would have made him angry with Hephzibah, it might even have amused him; but all he felt was lonely and rejected. It was like being a child among adults; not unloved but unlistened to. At best humoured. He wasn't the real McCoy, that was what it came to. Not only wasn't he a Jew, he was a jest to Jews. The real McGoy. (*FQ* 260)

Treslove is by no means ignored by Finkler and usually even encouraged, but he is left with a feeling of exclusion nevertheless. The pun on "The real McCoy" uses the American version of the expression (the Scottish one would rather be "the real Mackay")[14] to resonate with the Jewish word for a gentile. While puns belong to British humour, the "Mc," as in "McDonald," might belittle the status of the goy from the diasporic perspective of Jewish humour. Avner Ziv distinguishes Jewish jokes that express "self-deprecation and masochistic self-hatred" from "numerous jokes that on the face of it are Jewish assertions of superiority that deride Gentiles as being stupid (goyischeh kop) and frequently inebriated (shikker is the goy)" (Ziv and Zajdman 1993, 34).

This episode is followed by one Treslove tells about eating tongue with horseradish. His Jewish friends warn him not to burn himself, although it is not hot at all. Treslove sees this as exclusion. He is everybody, "McGoy," to them. Treslove is hurt and wishes his friends would react in a non-discriminatory way to him. However, his thoughts as represented in the focalization make it clear that he is discriminatory himself and feels excluded when it becomes obvious in many places of the novel that he is not:

13 Because of the diasporic character of Jewish humour, the phrase "humor amongst Jews" has been suggested (Roeckelein 2002, 106).

14 Cf. Fergusson: "the real thing; something completely authentic, as in *now that's* the real McCoy! The phrase the real McCoy is the US version of *the real Mackay,* of Scottish origin, which dates from the later 19th century" (1994, 172).

> 'You might not like that, it's tongue, not everybody can cope with tongue.' Not everybody? Did they become everybody the minute they clapped eyes on him? No harm was meant, he knew. Quite the opposite. […] But it wore him down. It wouldn't stop. There was never a time when they opened the door to him and said Julian, how nice to see you, come in, we have nothing in the way of food or other secrets of our culture to test you with today and are no more conscious of your being a Gentile than you are of our being Jews. He was always a curiosity to them. Always a bit of a barbarian who had to be placated with beads and mirrors. He charged himself with ingratitude and humourlessness. Each time he fell into a pet he promised he would learn to do better. But he never did. They wouldn't let him. Wouldn't let him in. (*FQ*, 261)

On the surface, this conveys an exaggerated sense of self-pity and self-righteousness. The focalization makes it quite a complex construction of humorous self-images. Humour is generated by the incongruity between Treslove's hope for recognition by his Jewish friends and his inability not to see the Other in them. The narrator's voice is Jewish. Therefore, the incongruity between Treslove's thoughts, as represented by internal focalization and the narrator's implicitly Jewish focalization describing them, is not only very funny but also presents a Jewish self-image. This self-image represents what the narrator imagines Gentiles see in Jews. The difference could also be described in Füger's terminology as the tension between "autophonic" focalization (focalization using Treslove's voice) and "allophonic" focalization (using the Jewish narrator's voice) (Jahn 1997, 463).

The humour in Treslove's thoughts works both ways. On the story level, this is a humorous narration of a Gentile's self-image and his image of Jews. The narrative form makes it a Jew's self-image and his image of Gentiles. The tension between form and content or between "autophonic" and "allophonic" focalization creates the incongruities of a multi-layered humour that does not match any clichés about either British or Jewish humour, but is certainly quite funny.

The internal or character focalization presents both a Gentile's identification with Jews and a Jewish perspective on Gentiles. This alternating focalization avoids any definition or commitment to Jewish identity. While Treslove suspects his Jewish friends of having an exclusive and well defined understanding of themselves, it becomes obvious that the main character, Sam Finkler, does not live up to this cliché. Finkler keeps turning against his own Jewishness through denial and meets Libor's disappointed comments about Jewish self-hatred:

> The comedic Jewish intonation was meant as a further irritant to Finkler. Libor knew that Finkler hated Jewishisms. *Mauscheln*, he called it, the hated secret language of the Jews, the Yiddishising that drove German Jews mad in the days when they thought the Germans would love them the more for playing down their Jewishness. The lost provincial over-expressiveness of his father.
> 'I don't have friends who are anti-Semites,' Finkler said.
> Libor screwed up his face until he resembled a medieval devil. All he lacked were the horns. 'Yes, you do. The Jewish ones.'
> 'Oh, here we go, here we go. Any Jew who isn't your kind of Jew is an anti-Semite. It's a nonsense, Libor, to talk of Jewish anti-Semites. It's more than a nonsense, it's a wickedness.'
> 'Don't get *kochedik* with me for speaking the truth. How can it be a nonsense when we invented anti-Semitism?'
> 'I know how this goes, Libor. Out of our own self-hatred.'
> 'You think there's no such thing? What do you say to St Paul, itching with a Jewishness he couldn't scratch away until he'd turned half the world against it?' (*FQ*, 45)

The narrator's voice changes from character focalization close to Libor's thoughts to a direct quotation of the dialogue between Sam Finkler and Libor. This way the reader knows where the narrator's sympathies are. The narrator's comment on the futile and dangerous self-denial of German Jews disqualifies Finkler's view. This is supported by the fact that Libor seems to take the part of the more critical and passionate voice speaking out for Jewish self-esteem in the dialogue and warning against Jewish self-hatred. There are several comic effects in this passage although or rather because it is about a serious topic. Libor takes on a "comedic Jewish intonation" staging a stereotypical Jewish self-image of "Yiddishising" that intentionally emphasizes differences and is meant to provoke Finkler.

Jacobson does not present Libor as Yiddish at face value, but speaks of "Yiddishising," indicating that the narrator labels Libor giving him the authenticity of bygone times. Jacobson's humour uses hyperbole and stereotypes when he describes Libor as "a medieval devil." Libor wants to convince Finkler that Jews' self-hatred eventually turns against them and interprets Christianity as a result of Paul's Jewish self-hatred. The narrator shows an angry Libor and sympathizes with his cause to make Finkler believe in himself and to develop Jewish self-esteem.[15]

One of the main purposes of Jacobson's novel is to take on the hideous and self-righteous ways his fellow Englishmen allow themselves in fits of anti-Zionism and anti-Semitism when they talk about Israel. Instead of ridiculing and satirizing the Gentile majority that has increasingly been accepting anti-Zionist and anti-Semitic ideas, Jacobson creates Finkler, who suffers from fits of Jewish self-hatred, and Treslove, who wants to become a Jew but sees no reason to abandon his anti-Israel clichés. The incongruities between these two focalizers show that anti-Zionism is the new form of anti-Semitism (cf. Julius 2010b, 584).

The narrator's voice in the novel is that of Libor who condemns Finkler's Jewish self-hatred and self-denial. In the same way that Libor is the Jewish antagonist to Finkler, Tyler is the Gentile antagonist to Treslove. Neither Tyler nor Libor are the main characters in the novel, but they represent attitudes and ideas Jacobson wants to proliferate. When Finkler declares on Desert Island Discs that although his Jewishness has always been immeasurably important to him, "on the matter of Palestine I am profoundly ashamed," it is not only Tyler who wonders what the connection is. She reveals the hypocritical reasoning behind Finkler's confession: "Profoundly self-important you mean. [...] How could you? [...] A convenient entity your conscience. There when you need it, not when you don't. Well, I'm ashamed of your public display of shame and I'm not even Jewish" (*FQ,* 113). Tyler sees through her husband's shame. She recognizes it to be a ritual he uses to please himself.

Díaz Bild shows how Jacobson manages to explain why some people believe that "nothing good could come out of Israel, whose inhabitants are compared to the Nazis, whereas Gaza is likened to the Warsaw Ghetto" (*FQ*, 91). Díaz Bild explains that Jacobson sees much of the comic anger in *The Finkler Question* resulting

> not so much from the political position of the anti-Zionists [...] but from their attitude of shame: 'What annoys me about it is not the politics, but the idea that what's happening somewhere else is about them. [...] It's the vanity of it; it's the egotism. It's the wear-

15 At the same time, Libor's Jewishness is ridiculed in a British manner reminiscent of Basil Fawlty (John Cleese) in *Fawlty Towers* when he welcomes a customer saying "Oh, German. I'm sorry, I thought there was something wrong with you" ("The Germans." *Fawlty Towers.* Season 1 Ep. 6. 24 October 1975.)

> ing their hearts on their sleeves. It's this carnival of conscience that I make fun of in the book.' (Díaz Bild 2013, 93)

Jacobson could be called a comic genius, but in his novel it is anti-Israeli Sam Finkler who tries to explain how his "comic genius" (*FQ,* 138) results from perpetually renegotiating himself: "Born a Jew on Monday, he had signed up to be an ASHamed Jew by Wednesday and was seen chanting 'We are all Hezbollah' outside the Israeli Embassy on the following Saturday" (*FQ,* 139). The narrator leaves no doubt that he has a different concept of comic genius than Sam Finkler and the journalist who interviews the ASHamed Jew.

Treslove's anti-Zionism quite openly presents itself as anti-Semitism, in Julius's assessment, "most 'anti-Semites' are now 'anti-Zionists'" (2010b, 585). Treslove voices what Jacobson perceives others think of Jews. According to Jacobson, this became obvious with the Six-Day War in 1967: "As long as the world thought that Israel was going to be defeated and destroyed everyone was on the side of 'poor little Israel'. But things changed the moment Israel won: 'Israel winning became a problem. And Israel winning big became a bigger problem.'" (Díaz Bild 95; see also Jacobson 2010c). Jacobson's humour serves a very serious purpose. It tells English Jews what they have known all along, but find more and more difficult to communicate to some of their fellow Jews and many more Gentiles: "All the unsayable things, all the things they know they can't say about Jews in a post-Holocaust liberal society, they can say again now. Israel has desacralized the subject. It's a space in which everything is allowed again" (Judah and Glancy 2015).

Judah and Glancy see the main difficulty all British Jews face in times of growing anti-Zionism in interpreting the potential consequences for them:

> Jacobson had dared to take one massive bet on what the English really thought of the Jews: an impossible mixture of love and hate, repulsion and fascination, envy and deep, if extremely, minutely subtle, racial otherness. They were even more surprised when the non-Jews enjoyed the novel so much they awarded him the Booker Prize. (Judah and Glancy 2015)

When Treslove and Finkler watch a Jewish play together that indulges in anti-Semitism, time has come for Finkler to define himself as a Jew rather than an ashamed Jew. He rejects Treslove's understanding that he could have written this play. Suggesting to Sam Finkler that he is "an ASHamed Jew" and therefore "had to like it," Treslove patronizes not only his friend, but thoroughly misunderstands Sam Finkler: "It was written for you. Could have been written by you. I've heard you speak it" (*FQ,* 252). Finkler is not amused:

> Not those words have you ever heard me speak. I don't do Nazi analogies. The Nazis were the Nazis. Anyway, did you hear me say I didn't like it? I loved it. I only wished there'd been more singing and dancing. It lacked a show-stopper like 'Springtime for Hitler,' that's my only complaint. I couldn't tap my feet. Put it this way, did you see anyone going out humming the Wagner? (*FQ,* 252)

Treslove neither gets the joke nor the message. He does not want to acknowledge this to be a "taste issue […] in the musical sense" (*FQ,* 252), not only revealing once again that he has no sense of humour, neither English nor Jewish, but also takes the issue too seriously to see that it has become a matter of survival for Finkler.

Jacobson does not produce lengthy explanations here, but has Finkler leave the place, not without having wished for "a show-stopper like 'Springtime for Hitler'." Mel Brooks's highly acclaimed film and musical *The Producers* is a perfect example of Jewish humour and what Finkler is commenting on when he speaks out against Treslove. According to Patricia Erens the film's story is "an exercise in Jewish self-deprecation" (1984, 267). Erens quotes John Simon who ironically observed, "not all anti-Semites are Jews" and continues what defines humour in *The Producers*:

> Self-deprecation has long been an element in Jewish humor, perhaps a defense mechanism to soften the blows leveled against the Jews by the Gentile world. In a sense the Jew is saying, 'Your opinions don't count. We have our own insults and certainly these hurt less than those which come from the outside world.' (Erens 1984, 268)

Comparisons between Jewish and Gentile jokes have been made as early as Freud who believed that, by making jokes about themselves, Jews were more in control of themselves and their faults: "When one thinks back to the classic subject in Jewish humor, the Shlemiel, the little man, the outsider, there is always some redeeming aspect which proves engaging" (Erans 1984, 268).

Finkler understands this type of joke when he visits the play with Treslove. The play is not funny, but 'Springtime for Hitler' is because it uses dark Jewish humour to ridicule the unspeakable horrors of Nazi Germany. Finkler is not even "a Shlemiel, or more properly a Shnook (a timid Shlemiel; a passive, ineffectual type), a nobody trying to become a somebody" (268) like Bloom in *The Producers*.[16] In this scene Finkler takes on the part of a critic of Jewish humour because he wants to exclude Treslove and stand in for his Jewishness: "[H]e hadn't escaped what was oppressive about Judaism by joining a Jewish group that gathered to talk feverishly about the oppressiveness of being Jewish. Talking feverishly about being Jewish was being Jewish" (*FQ*, 275).

Jacobson answers the Jewish question with Jewish humour and the form of the "perfect Jewish joke" that never finishes and always responds to the diasporic danger of anti-Semitism and prosecution. Jacobson neither tells specific stories nor does he use any obvious rhetorical features such as hyperbole, but rather relies on a specific form of perceiving oneself as a Jew in the eyes of others and how one perceives others seeing oneself. Consequently, Jacobson achieves humour and comedy mainly by shifting focalization. Avoiding Jewish self-images based on how one sees oneself, Jewishness becomes a detached and humorous representation of what others perceive. *The Finkler Question* does not deny the dangers of diasporic life and therefore its narrator does not deny being Jewish. Nevertheless, Jacobson sees himself in the tradition of Jane Austen, Charles Dickens and many other English writers when he makes a statement about literature that holds true for his Jewish novel, too: "Comedy is a human invention to deal with the sadness of life. It's our greatest achievement. Forget the pyramids. Comedy" (Tracy 2011). Although Jacobson has his characters joking about the never-ending "whole Jewish *gesheft*" (*FQ*, 244) he tries to get away from it and writes an English novel of manners.

---

16 The play Finkler finds without taste matches Nick Cohen's criticism of playwrights who write for the National Theatre whose politics are "a faintly hypocritical and unforgivably shallow version of liberal-leftism" (2010). What Cohen appreciates about Jacobson is that he exposes mediocre art where the positions taken are "fashionable rather than thoughtful, a conscience is no substitute for art" (Cohen 2010).

Works Cited

Austen, Jane. *Northanger Abbey and Persuasion*. Ed. R.W. Chapman, revised by Mary Lascelles. *The Novels of Jane Austen*. Vol. 4. 3rd ed. London: Oxford University Press, 1932.

Bal, Mieke. *Narratology: Introduction to the Theory of Narrative*. Toronto: Toronto University Press, 2009.

Bayer, Gerd. "Alter, Tod, Erinnerung: Lebenswertes und Lesenswertes bei Graham Swift und Howard Jacobson." *Alter(n) in Literatur und Kultur der Gegenwart*. Eds. Rudolf Freiburg and Dirk Kretzschmar. Würzburg: Königshausen & Neumann, 2012. 169-184.

Benedict, Barbara M. "The Trouble with Things: Objects and the Commodification of Sociability." *A Companion to Jane Austen*. Eds. Claudia L. Johnson and Clara Tuite. Malden, MA.: Wiley-Blackwell, 2009. 343-354.

Brauner, David. *Post-War Jewish Fiction: Ambivalence, Self-Explanation and Transatlantic Connections*. New York: Palgrave, 2001.

Cheyette, Bryan. "British-Jewish Literature." *Jewish Writers of the 20th Century*. Ed. Sorrel Kerbel. New York: Dearborn, 2003. 7-10.

Cohen, Nick. "Howard Jacobson Offers a Contrary Voice in the Arts." *The Observer* 17 October 2010. Web. 11 March 2015.

Cohen, Sarah Blacher, ed. *Jewish Wry: Essays on Jewish Humor*. Bloomington, IN: Indiana University Press, 1987.

Díaz Bild, Aída. "*The Finkler Question*: Very Funny Is Very Serious." *Atlantis: Revista de la Asociación Española de Estudios Anglo-Norteamericanos* (AtlantisR) 35.1 (June 2013): 85-101.

Erens, Patricia. *The Jew in American Cinema*. Bloomington, IN: Indiana University Press, 1984.

Fergusson, Rosalind. *Shorter Slang Dictionary*. London: Routledge, 1994.

Gilbert, Ruth. *Writing Jewish: Contemporary British-Jewish Literature*. Basingstoke: Palgrave 2013.

Hochwald, Abraham. *The Harper Collins Book of Jewish Humour*. London: HarperCollins, 1996.

Jacobs, Gerald. "Interview. Howard Jacobson." *The Jewish Chronicle* 9 April 2008. Web. 11 March 2015.

Jacobson, Howard. *Seriously Funny: From the Ridiculous to the Sublime*. London: Viking, 1997.

—. *The Finkler Question*. London: Bloomsbury, 2010a.

—. "On taking comic novels seriously." *The Guardian*. 9 October 2010b. Web. 25 January 2016.

—. "The Plot Against England." *Tablet Magazine*. 11 October 2010c. Web. 11 March 2015.

—. "Dayenu. Enough Already. Perfect Jewish Joke." *Tablet Magazine*. 3 April 2012. Web. 11 March 2015.

Jahn, Manfred. "Frames, Preferences, and the Reading of Third-Person Narratives: Towards a Cognitive Narratology." *Poetics Today* 18.4 (Winter 1997): 441-68.

Judah, Ben and Josh Glancy. "The Jewish Jane Austen, or England's Jeremiah?" *Tablet Magazine* 25 February 2015. Web. 11 March 2015.

Julius, Anthony. "Review: *The Finkler Question*." *The Jewish Chronicle* 28 July 2010a. Web. 11 March 2015.

—. *Trials of Diaspora. A History of Anti-Semitism in England.* Oxford: Oxford University Press, 2010b.

Lezard, Nicholas. "Is Howard Jacobson the Only Person Writing British Jewish Novels?" *The Guardian* 15 October 2010. Web. 11 March 2015.

Lyall, Sarah. "Booker Prize Winner's Jewish Question." *New York Times* 18 October 2010. Web. 11 March 2015.

Maslin, Janet. "Jewish Funhouse Mirror Is Alive and Not So Well." *New York Times* 20 October 2010. Web. 11 March 2015.

Palmer, Jerry. *Taking Humour Seriously.* New York: Routledge, 1994.

Roeckelein, Jon E. *The Psychology of Humor: A Reference Guide and Annotated Bibliography.* Westport, CT: Greenwood Press, 2002.

Roth, Philip. *Operation Shylock. A Confession.* New York, London, Toronto: Simon and Schuster, 1993.

Sacks, Oliver. *The Man Who Mistook His Wife for a Hat and Other Clinical Tales.* London: Gerald Duckworth, 1985.

Steiner, George. *Errata: an Examined Life.* London: Phoenix, 1998.

Stähler, Axel, ed. *Anglophone Jewish Literature: Transcultural and Transnational Studies.* London: Routledge, 2007.

"The Germans." *Fawlty Towers.* Season 1, Ep. 6. Written by John Cleese and Connie Booth. BBC. 24 October 1975.

Tracy, Marc. "Humorous? Yes. Tragic? Definitely. An Evening with Howard Jacobson." *Tablet Magazine* 5 April 2011. Web. 11 March 2015.

Valman, Nadia. "British Literature and Culture: An Introduction." *Whatever Happened to British Jewish Studies?* Eds. Hannah Ewence and Tony Kushner. London: Vallentine Mitchell, 2012. 213-20.

Walton, James. "*The Finkler Question* by Howard Jacobson. Review." *The Daily Telegraph* 30 July 2010. Web. 11 March 2015.

Wirth-Nesher, Hana, ed. *What Is Jewish Literature?* Philadelphia: The Jewish Publication Society, 1994.

Ziv, Avner and Anat Zajdman, eds. *Semites and Stereotypes: Characteristics of Jewish Humor.* Westport, CT: Greenwood Press, 1993.

HEINRICH VERSTEEGEN

When the Professor Loses His Faculties: Uses of the Comic in David Lodge's Novel *Deaf Sentence*

David Lodge's *Deaf Sentence* (2008) received widespread critical acclaim. It was shortlisted for the Commonwealth Writers' Prize 2009 (cf. British Council 2011), and it has been praised for its insightful account and "compassionate understanding" (Cunnen 2009, 34) of aging and mortality. Reviewers' opinions, however, were not quite so unanimous in their assessment of the novel's peculiar combination of funny and gloomy elements. At one end of the spectrum, the novel was called "deeply melancholic" (Conradi 2008), and "a markedly doleful book" (Bray 2008, 59), while, at the opposite end, its major strength was located in "Lodge's comedic talent" (Strout 2010, xciii). Most reviewers, however, were unable to establish any specific aesthetic link between the contradictory styles of the narrative and were content to point out that it "evokes both laughter and tears" (Burkhardt 2008, 120) or that it "cannot be called a comic novel, though it is very funny" (Allen 2008, 21).

As regards the comic element, *Deaf Sentence* is indeed reminiscent of Lodge's earlier campus novels. There is a professor of linguistics in a northern university town,[1] who after taking early retirement still keeps in touch with his old faculty; there is an attractive female American student whose advances flatter the emeritus; and then there is the professor's younger wife, who, as a successful businesswoman, is too busy to keep track of her husband's academic, and other, pursuits. The comic potential of this character constellation is considerable (allowing humorous clashes between old and young, academia and commerce,[2] British and American ways of life[3] and, not to forget, the complications of a love triangle). Likewise, the tone of the narrative is also primarily witty and entertaining. But despite these comic elements, the novel's main subject matter is rather sombre, being about decrepitude, aging and death. Sexagenarian protagonist-narrator Desmond Bates is suffering from progressive hearing loss, which he interprets as an early, if symbolic, harbinger of death, indicated by the title *Deaf Sentence* and numerous other puns on the near-homophony of *deaf* and *death*. Desmond's father Harry Bates, an 89-year-old widower, almost equally deaf, incontinent, and his memory fading, leads an isolated life in his squalid house in southeast London, where he collapses following a stroke and dies a few weeks later, but not until Desmond has arranged for his life-support machines to be cut off. And the gloomy account of the dying father is framed (and punctuated, as it were) by Bates's depressing visit to Auschwitz-Birkenau immediately before the father's stroke and, just after he has decided to let his father die, his equally depressing memories of his first wife Maisie's assisted suicide. The novel ends with the father's funeral

1 Some reviewers seem to think it is the fictitious Rummidge from Lodge's campus trilogy (cf. Schaefer Riley 2008; Cunnen 2009, 34), but the actual town is not named in this novel.
2 Cf. *Nice Work* (1988), which thrives on the comic clash between academia and industry.
3 This is exploited for maximum comic effect in the contrast between Philipp Swallow and Morris Zapp in *Changing Places* (1975) and, to some extent, also in *Small World* (1984) (cf. Ahrens 1992, 281-82).

service, with the mysterious American student faking her own suicide, and with Desmond taking up lip-reading classes.

The exact aesthetic connections between funny and gloomy elements, as well as their relative importance, are obviously somewhat puzzling in this novel. Although it has long been recognized that Lodge's novels, despite "their attractive comic surface, […] are by no means light-hearted entertainment only," but blend "comedy with profounder issues" (Draudt 2000, 241),[4] in none of his previous works did these issues ever reach such a level of darkness and woefulness. I will examine this remarkable clash of moods in *Deaf Sentence* by drawing on theories of the comic, the tragic, and the tragicomic, and I will argue that funny and gloomy parts cannot be regarded as oppositional elements, dividing the novel up into a comical first part and a sombre ending, but that both are ambivalent and fluid modes of storytelling which complement each other. I will also investigate how the ambivalent narrative modes correspond with the novel's thematic focus on the equally ambivalent notions of aging and dying in the 21st century.

The Tragicomic Fallacy

Most reviewers have avoided the word 'tragic' for the more melancholic parts of *Deaf Sentence*, preferring terms like "pathos" (Burkardt 2008, 120) or "darker, more minor scales" (Kakutani 2009, C 29), and very few have used the term tragicomedy to classify the novel as a whole (cf. Allen 2008, 21). This concept, however, has been suggested by one academic critic. Patrick Müller argues that Bates regards his own aging as a tragic affliction (cf. Müller 2012, 157), but then, similar to a character from a comedy of humours, cures himself from his melancholic/phlegmatic state of mind (cf. 158) and learns to accept old age as a meaningful part of the cycle of birth, life and death (cf. 160) – a lesson which Müller calls a catharsis and a piece of universal wisdom, a "*consolatio philosophiae*" (160).[5] This interpretation sounds sleek enough, but it disregards the fact that Desmond Bates himself is anything but sympathetic to the wisdoms of "glib philosopher[s]" (Lodge 2008, 290). In addition, the use of the concept of catharsis is also rather bizarre here, firstly because Müller treats it as an element of comedy, and secondly because the term, at least by common understanding, refers to an experience of the audience, or the reader, but not the protagonist. Müller's interpretation, thus, is neither entirely flawless nor is it helpful since it does not resolve the problem of the ambivalent straddle between comedy and gloom that the novel performs.

Indeed, both 'tragic' and 'tragicomic' are problematic attributes in connection with this novel. One would obviously have to stretch the notion of 'tragic' if one wished to apply it to natural processes of decay like growing old, losing one's hearing, or dying at a biblical age of 89. Not even the assisted deaths of Harry Bates and Maisie, who were both terminally ill, are tragic *per se*, and they are not presented as such in the novel. They are not described as personal crises brought about by a tragic hero's "mis-

4 A similar assessment is given by Walsh, who calls Lodge "[n]ot a comic novelist, exactly" (Walsh 2007, 268).

5 The term was originally coined in Boethius' treatise *De Consolatione Philosophiae* (cf. Boethius, 2002), though Müller does not make any explicit reference to this classical work. Nor can I see any useful link with *Deaf Sentence* – especially since Lodge's fiction is known for its empiricist, anti-philosophical stance (cf. Easthope 1999, 164) and *Deaf Sentence* does not seem to be an exception.

taken choice of an action" (Abrams 1999, 322) or as misfortunes contrived by some impersonal power such as fate (cf. Cuddon 1992, 985). Rather, they are little more than case studies, to be understood as a contribution to the current debate about assisted suicide and the right to die. Nor does the less rigorously defined concept of tragicomedy, in any of its various definitions, quite fit this novel either – neither the old Renaissance definition of tragicomedy as a story which "wants deaths […] yet brings some neere it" (Fletcher, qtd. in Foster 2003, 21), nor in the understanding of modern tragicomedy, as e.g. in the Theatre of the Absurd, in which "the individual is [...] a comic figure in a universe probably tragic or at best uncertain" (Foster 2003, 12). The novel clearly does not "want deaths," as it describes two in detail, and none of the suffering that is entailed in going deaf, growing old etc. in this book is the work of a tragic or uncertain universe. All these afflictions are universally known certainties – though uncomfortable ones.

The problematic application of the concept of tragicomedy may well have been triggered by a – traditionalist – misconception of the terms 'tragedy' and 'comedy' which is encouraged in the novel itself. Where Bates, after many musings about his own aphorism "[d]eafness is comic, as blindness is tragic" (Lodge 2008, 13), finally reaches the supposed insight that "it seems more meaningful to say that deafness is comic and death is tragic, because final, inevitable, and inscrutable" (289), he offers an essentialist definition, suggesting that the concepts of comedy and tragedy are inherent properties of actual situations or even natural conditions – which they are not. Bates is a fallible narrator (and not just in this respect), and the novel itself bears ample evidence that its comic and its quasi-tragic effects do not derive from things as such, but from the perspectives which an outside observer, either a character or the reader, takes on things, or, rather, is made to take on them. This applies particularly well to the many representations of human frailty and inadequacy which form the thematic backbone of the novel. Sometimes they are a source of amusement, sometimes they command sympathy and pity, and sometimes even both at the same time. When Bates thinks his step-grandson Daniel said that "Father Christmas bringed Daniel an icicle," and everybody else in the room laughs because the Christmas present was of course a "tricycle" (177), Bates's defective hearing is amusing, but only from the angle of the immediate bystanders. Even if Bates himself later finds his own mistake funny as well, it is also from the others' point of view. When, on the other hand, during his visit to Birkenau Bates deliberately keeps his "earpieces in because [he wants] to hear the silence, a silence broken only by the crunch of [his] shoes on the frozen snow, the occasional sound of a dog barking in the distance, and the mournful whistle of a train" (255) the mentioning of the hearing impairment enhances the gravity of the situation, not only for Bates himself but also for the reader. Deafness is not comic unless the narrative creates the comic perspective.

Fluid Comedy

Comic perspectives on deafness and other human insufficiencies in *Deaf Sentence* are not only deliberately constructed, but, once constructed, they may just as easily be deconstructed again. They are not fixed, but fluid. Take, for example, Bates's description of his wife's grandchildren, who, he says,

> are beautiful and charming, and at that interesting age when they begin to acquire language with astonishing rapidity, and sometimes make expressive mistakes, if I could only hear them. Today when I complimented Lena on her pretty dress, and she replied that her Mummy had bought it at Marks & Spencer, everybody laughed except me. When I looked puzzled, Fred explained that she had said, 'Mummy bought it at Marks and Spensive.' Then I laughed on my own. (77)

The first reference to deafness in this passage is comic; "if I could only hear them" marks a kind of "descending incongruity" (Spencer qtd in Niederhoff 2014, 38) from Bates's intellectual ability to appreciate children's "expressive mistakes" to his physical inability to hear them.[6] But the next reference to deafness is sad; Bates misses a joke, which excludes him from the family's hilarity. This, then, is again followed by a comic reference to another human insufficiency, little Lena's "expressive" mistake of saying "Marks and Spensive," before the passage is finally concluded on a sad note again – "Then I laughed on my own." It epitomizes the common experience that a joke explained is a joke ruined, for no explanation can ever compensate for the loss of enjoyment experienced in the communal laughter. "Our laughter is always the laughter of a group," says Bergson (1911, 6), and that is why even where Bates finally can laugh, his solitary amusement is another sign of his increasing isolation due to his deafness. Deafness is indeed a source of comedy in these few lines, but it is a fluid, unstable comedy, which shifts between funny and sad, and between light-hearted and heavy-hearted.

Such shifts are of course the manipulative work of the narrative voice. A well-honed technique in this respect, which has already been observed in Lodge's campus trilogy, is the use of "lengthy, complex comparisons" (Draudt 2000, 232) – invented comparisons, to be more precise, between actions or events in the novel and imaginary correspondences which enable the narrator, together with the reader, to take a detached view of the characters' "vagaries in the same way as we look down at a play from our seat in a box" (Bergson 1911, 135). In *Deaf Sentence*, Bates uses this technique to describe misheard conversations as if his own fragmented perceptions were not embarrassing blunders, but carefully crafted artefacts. When the sentence "[w]e were near Carcasonne [*sic*!]. A pretty place, but spoiled by tourism, I'm afraid" (Lodge 2008, 108) in the professor's ears turns into something like "we seared our arses on bits of plate, but soiled my cubism, I'm afraid" (108), Bates the narrator compares this to "a quotation from a Dadaist poem, or one of Chomsky's impossible sentences" (108) – almost as if he were acting in defiant rebellion against his, i.e. Bates the protagonist's, affliction (cf. Eyre 2012, 19).[7] Whereas in Lodge's earlier novels the humorous method aimed at drawing the reader "into an often voyeuristic complicity with the male narrator" (Horlacher 2007, 465), the narrator in *Deaf Sentence* is no such reliable accomplice. The primarily journal-style narrative[8] shifts between de-

6 Bergson also emphasizes the clash between spirituality and physicality as a source of laughter (cf. Bergson 1911, 51).

7 Eyre's interpretation of Bates's hearing-impaired experience of reality as a "carnivalesque inversion of the usual state of cultural affairs"(Eyre, 2012, 20) is not uninspiring, but it omits all the gloomier episodes which suggest that the carnival is over.

8 In some parts, the novel also adopts a third-person narrative with internal focalization (on Bates), though these sections, too, are explicitly identified as stylistic experiments within the journal. Nevertheless, this heterodiegetic narrator offers a somewhat more reliable point of reference – and is therefore especially used in chapters with a slight satirical element. See below.

tachment from and solidarity with the protagonist. The detached perspective is needed for the comic effects, and the solidarity is unavoidable because the narrator and the protagonist are psychologically the same person. One more example of this dual perspective: when Bates discovers a pair of women's underpants in his coat pocket, which Alex Loom, the attractive but manipulative American student, had secretly deposited there during his visit to her flat, he writes in his journal: "I looked at myself in the hall mirror, a gaunt, grey-haired man in a formal dark overcoat holding up a pair of white knickers, like a detective with a piece of incriminating evidence, and wondered what to do with them" (Lodge 2008, 96). In this scene the narrator splits up his protagonist alter ego into two persons, one before the mirror and the other inside the mirror, thus representing Bates as amused and worried, detective and culprit, imagined and real, butt of comedy and object of sympathy, all at the same time. The mirror trick, even more compellingly than the journal method and the invented comparisons, emphasizes the simultaneity of Bates as observer and observed, eliciting simultaneous feelings of detachment and identification.

Comedy of Escape and the Escape of Comedy

In Lodge's classic campus novels most of the comedy served the purpose of satire (cf. Ahrens 1992, 278; Easthope 1999, 28) or even farce (cf. Easthope 1999, 166). In *Deaf Sentence*, by contrast, there is no farce at all, and satirical passages are few and far between. Satirical mockery is used only occasionally, e.g. to lampoon professorial opportunism (in the character of Colin Butterworth), or to deride middle-class decorum or ideologically blinkered Catholicism – most of which is found in chapter 14 (the Christmas celebrations) and chapter 16 (the mini-break in the up-market holiday compound Gladeworld). But on the whole, the unstable comic perspective has a very different function. To understand it, one needs to consider the subversive potential of laughter which is inherent in what I have so far referred to as comic incongruity. Although it has been noted by some critics that incongruity in its simplest meaning, as "discrepancy between the way something is and the way it is supposed to be" (Morreall 2008, 229), is an insufficient concept in a theory of laughter because such discrepancies might also inspire fear or sadness (cf. Morreall 2008, 227; Niederhoff 2014, 31),[9] this concept nevertheless continues to be used in humour studies, as most theorists have specified the relationship between the incongruous elements in various more sophisticated ways.[10] Douglas, in her famous essay "Jokes," argues that comic incongruity is a challenge of "one accepted pattern [...] by the appearance of another [pattern] which in some way was hidden in the first" (Douglas 1975, 96)[11] and that this challenge has a "subversive effect on the dominant structure of ideas" (95). This subversive attack, however, can never completely override the dominant pattern; "a

9 For further objections to the concept of incongruity see Cundall (2007, 203), Morreall (2008, 236), and Veale (2004, 424).

10 All these definitions have integrated a social element, which, for example, can be a "kind of secret freemasonry, or even complicity, with other laughers, real or imaginary" (Bergson 1911, 6), or a correspondence between joke structure and social structure (cf. Douglas 1975, 93), or the existence of a cooperative principle in the humorous process (cf. Raskin and Attardo qtd. in Veale 2004, 424).

11 A similar observation was already made by Bergson: "A situation is invariably comic when it belongs simultaneously to two altogether independent series of events and is capable of being interpreted in two entirely different meanings at the same time" (Bergson 1911, 96). In fact, Douglas's model is an extension of Bergson's and Freud's theories of laughter (cf. Douglas 1975, 95).

successful subversion," according to Douglas, "completes or ends the joke, for it changes the balance of power [...]. The wise sayings of lunatics, talking animals, children and drunkards are funny because they are not in control" (96). All that the joke achieves is that it "affords opportunity for realising that an accepted pattern has no necessity" (96), and the message of jokes is that "the ordained patterns of social life [...] are escapable" (102). As Douglas's analysis is not restricted to standard jokes, but is expressly extended to spontaneous jokes, too, it can be fruitfully applied to the unstable, fluid comedy in *Deaf Sentence* as well. No doubt, Lodge's (or Bates's) hypothetical comparisons mentioned above are a form of spontaneous joking in Douglas's sense. And even the amusement created through the conventions of the comic journal is also the result of an extra-fictional author's deliberate mockery which sets the diarist up as the comic dupe.[12]

A good example where Douglas's joke structure can serve as a useful paradigm is where Bates describes in his journal that, during a clandestine visit to Alex's flat, he turns down the student's request for help with her PhD project (about suicide notes) by arguing that the university would not allow a retired professor to act as supervisor:

> I was glad to have this well-founded reason for declining her request, because otherwise I might have been a little bit tempted by it. The idea of getting involved in some research again, applying my knowledge and expertise to this rather bizarre but undoubtedly interesting topic, and meeting this obviously intelligent and articulate and, let us be honest, very personable young woman on a regular basis to discuss it, was not unattractive. But experience has taught me that postgraduate supervision can be a complex and worrying business: you easily find yourself becoming somehow responsible for the student's achievement, self-esteem, destiny, and it goes on for years. It was a good thing that I didn't even have to weigh up the pros and cons in this case before saying no. (Lodge 2008, 89)

Bates is obviously deluding himself here about Alex's true character as much as about his own motives in allowing himself to be tempted by her request and also in rejecting it.[13] His real interest in the student has already been betrayed in his admiring descriptions of her "naturally shapely figure" (5) and "the shadowy separation of her breasts just visible at the unbuttoned opening of her blouse" (5). Likewise, his assessment of the student as an "intelligent and articulate [...] young woman" is equally misguided, considering that only minutes earlier Alex had put on "a little pouting smile" (88) trying to change the professor's mind, and also considering that Bates feels very ill at ease in her private flat (86). In the same way, Bates's reservations about the alleged complexities of "postgraduate supervisions" are only pretended, too; in truth he has much graver misgivings, especially a sense of distrust in Alex's integrity and a fear of being caught in an illicit relationship with a student, and found out by his wife. In Douglas's terminology, this passage unfolds "one accepted pattern" ('old professor vs. young student') where the old professor's interest is predominantly academic, which is then challenged by a new pattern ('old man vs. young woman') where the old man's interest is chiefly sexual. While Bates describes himself in the 'profes-

12 The fictional personal diary seems to lend itself for comic purposes. Some famous examples would be *The Diary of a Nobody* (Grossmith 1998), *The Secret Diary of Adrian Mole Aged 13¾* (Townsend 1982), or *Bridget Jones's Diary* (Fielding 1996).

13 According to Bergson, a character is comic only if there is "some aspect of his person of which he is unaware, one side of his nature which he overlooks" (Bergson 1911, 146).

sor/student' pattern, the reader sees him in the 'old man/young woman' pattern. The latter pattern is of course hidden in the former (by virtue of the old/young opposition), and, as claimed by Douglas, it subverts the dominant hierarchy in that Bates's professorial stance is obviously fake. Bates is not the academic authority which he tries to act, but a pitiable has-been, who is now afflicted by deafness and boredom, then suddenly flattered by the attentions of a "comely young woman" (5), and (as it seems) only half aware of the "web of deceit" (286) that he is about to weave for himself – egged on by a woman whose surname, ominously, is "Loom."[14] When we laugh about this "old fart" (5), as Bates calls himself elsewhere in self-deprecating irony, this implies, according to Douglas, that the pains and discomforts of old age are "ordained patterns of social life" (Douglas 1975, 102), which have "no necessity" (96) and are, therefore, indeed escapable.[15] The comic perspective diverts the reader's attention away from that uncomfortable social reality by setting up a comic dupe who, however, is not despised (as in satire), but pitied. The insufficiency for which he is pitied is not the biological decay of the human body, but the loss of social participation and his own inability to adapt to the changes brought about by old age and decrepitude.

But this comedy of commiseration, already ambivalent, is even more unstable than it looks at first. At the end of the book Bates admits that he was not completely honest in his journal and that he "turned down opportunities for kinky shenanigans with [Alex] as much out of timidity as principle" (Lodge 2008, 286). At this point, where the subconscious fears turn out to have been conscious ones all the time, the challenging pattern suddenly supersedes the challenged pattern. This changes the "balance of power" (Douglas 1975, 96) and thus ends the comedy. The reader realizes that Bates was not the figure of fun who was ignorant of his own true motives, and the comedy thus escapes from the Alex plotline like air from a balloon. The same development from subversive challenge to complete subversion also occurs in the second comic plotline of the novel, Bates's troublesome dealings with his father Harry. When incontinent Harry Bates is caught short during a motorway journey, but stubbornly refuses to take an emergency stop on the hard shoulder because he might be observed in the act of relieving himself by other motorists (cf. Lodge 2008, 168-69), and when he then wets his trousers inside the car, this is funny because Harry's incontinence challenges his obstinate insistence on decency and decorum. The latter pattern is, of course, not completely invalidated, for the old man is still able to change his wet trousers before continuing his journey in dignity. But the comedy of this plotline, too, dissolves at the very end of the novel. After his fatal stroke, when Harry is confined to a hospital bed and wets himself, not into his trousers, but into a nappy (267), the subversion is complete, the balance of power changes because the old man's incontinence has finally defeated his concern for respectability, and the comedy ends. The same happens to the comic effects arising from Harry's deafness, which is only funny while he is not aware of his impaired hearing, and ceases to amuse the moment when, due to his brain damage, he is no longer fully conscious of anything at all – a situation in

14 Although Bates looks up the word *loom* in the *OED* and gives an extensive list of its many meanings, he makes no explicit mentioning of its foreboding implications (93) – another hint at his unreliability as narrator.

15 Bergson would come to a similar conclusion, though with a slightly different terminology. According to him, we laugh only about what is human, not in the natural sense of physicality, but as a social phenomenon (Bergson 1911, 7)

which laughter would no longer have "a social signification" (Bergson 1911, 8). Thus, the comic framework which Lodge builds around basically pitiable experiences, once it has served its purpose as an escape mechanism, is finally dismantled, leaving only the pity and the sympathy that has been erected together with it.

Deflated Pathos

Lodge's unstable comedy about decrepitude and disability is juxtaposed by more woeful descriptions of misery and grief. Bates's visit to the Birkenau death camp (the only occasion where the narrator denies himself a joke on the *deaf/death* pun), Maisie's death from cancer and her assisted suicide and Harry Bates's last weeks in hospital, as well as his funeral, make up the sombre side of this novel. But if Lodge played hide and seek with the reader's expectations when poking fun at human infirmities, he does nothing less in the more serious sections which centre around social practices of dealing with death and bereavement. He first uses pathos, i.e. he creates "passage[s] designed to evoke the feelings of tenderness, pity or sympathetic sorrow" (Abrams 1999, 205), and, once he has successfully kindled these feelings, he deflates them again by exposing them as conditioned stock responses. Where Bates describes his first wife Maisie's death, the predominantly matter-of-fact tone of the narrative gets tinged with such pathos:

> On the last night of the year I crushed twenty Distalgesic tablets and helped Maisie swallow them in a mixture of warm milk and brandy. She turned up the syringe driver to maximum. I kissed her, lit a night-light candle beside the bed, and lay down beside her, holding her hand, until she fell into a deep sleep. Then I sat in an armchair and watched her breathing until I fell asleep myself. When I woke at 4 a.m., the candle was out, and she was dead, her face quite peaceful, her limbs relaxed. (Lodge 2008, 270)

The ominous mentioning of "the last night of the year," as well as the candle and the fact that it was significantly blown out near the moment of Maisie's death, heighten this description symbolically – as if designed to instil some transcendental light into a dark moment of pain. An even stronger spiritual interpretation of Bates's desolate act is offered by Fred's ethical justification of that act: "'What you did for Maisie was an act of love'" (271). But Bates rejects the romanticizing interpretation with his psychologically more credible confession: "'I'd like to think so,' I said. But the trouble is, I wanted her to die. […] I had to struggle to conceal my relief afterwards, disguising it under grief" (271). The psychological realism in this passage is a functional equivalent to the humour in other passages. By deflating the socially and morally decreed pathos in discourses about assisted suicide, the novel suggests that the proclaimed solemnity is not entirely genuine. Bates's subversive confession of his private experience challenges the accepted pattern of the official rhetoric, showing that the latter also "has no necessity" (Douglas 1975, 96).

Thus, the account of the assisted suicide, although it is anything but funny, does not counteract at all the general drift of the more humorous sections. Both the comic and the serious parts jointly explore the fluid modes with which contemporary culture handles aging and dying. In the society of the Noughties, which is obsessed with the cult of youth,[16] while, paradoxically, its population is growing older and older, attitudes to infirmity and death are in a process of flux and are increasingly losing any fixed points of orientation. And in this novel Desmond Bates is the intellectual epicentre in which the contradictions of contemporary insecurities converge. Numerous debates with his wife, who is a devout Catholic (Lodge 2008, 270), show that he is torn between resentment at and sympathy for religion as ethical guidance (75). His sense of filial duty makes him anxious about his father's well-being, but his monthly visits to him are felt as such a great burden that, when he is stranded in Central London on the day of the 7/7 bombings due to the shut-down of the public transport system, he experiences this day, not as a national tragedy, but as "a kind of unexpected holiday, a reprieve from the tedious duty of visiting Dad" (134). And, finally, he is surprised to find, at his father's sickbed, that other entrenched patterns of meaning are also shaken up: when he spoon-feeds his father, and later when he even has to help the hospital staff to wash him, it becomes clear that neither the familiar division-of-labour routines nor the conventions of the father-son relationship can still be relied on (266-67). The entire Harry Bates plotline can be read as a gradual "reversal of the infant-parent relationship," which is finally taken "through the taboo barrier" (267). Whereas the funny parts of the book show how individuals refuse to accept their experience of aging, thus challenging this experience as basically escapable, the darker parts question some of the more commonly held beliefs about aging and dying.

The line between funny and serious parts, however, is anything but clear-cut. If the funnier sections tend to lapse into more thoughtful moods again and again, the descriptions of the hospital visits and the father's funeral, conversely, are interspersed with dashes of humour. Sometimes the comic note is barely perceptible, as where Bates and his wife are described as chatting cheerfully away to the sick father as if he were a "responsive patient" while the old man is so poorly that he seems to have "regressed even past human infancy on the evolutionary scale" (269). At other times the humour sticks out much more clearly: when Bates visits his dying father in hospital, coming straight from the airport, the effect of his wheeled suitcase in the geriatric ward is described with grim sarcasm: "The old people propped up in their beds in various states of debility and dementia regarded me with alarm [...], as if they feared I was an undertaker come to measure them up" (259). And in the passages about the father's funeral the narrator fully recovers his original, humorous tone of voice once again, exploiting the unintentionally comic potential of solemn officialdom.[17] He presents a detached, "flippant" view of the funeral as "a form of theatre" (274), switches to and fro between a 'normal' and a 'hearing-impaired' perspective, e.g. when praising the superior quality of the "loop system in the chapel" (279), and pokes quiet fun at Father Michael, the minister conducting the service, by dwelling on his Irish accent[18] and his strained efforts to tolerate materialist and downright kitschy elements in an otherwise solemnly religious ceremony (280). Not even in the gloomiest passag-

16 Desmond feels painfully inadequate compared with his only eight years younger, but surgically rejuvenated, wife (cf. Lodge 2008, 65; 72).

17 As I have argued elsewhere, there is strong indication that neither an exclusively serious nor an exclusively jocular way of dealing with death can ever be fully satisfactory and that death rites and jokes are similar in structure and in function (cf. Versteegen 2011).

18 Even the glum Auschwitz passage is touched up with a few comical language mistakes made by the Polish hotel staff: "'*Mrs Bates phoned at 3.15 p.m. Your doghter* [sic] *birthed a baby boy today* [...]'" (257).

es can the reader be quite safe from occasional outbursts of liberating humour, deflating the pathos of established patterns of meaning which are losing their validity in the early 21st century.

Conclusion

It has been claimed that Lodge's novels often centre on a contrast between ideas and experience. Eagleton, for example, has argued that *Nice Work* illustrates "the old English empiricist prejudice that ideas are one thing and life another" (Eagleton 1988, 102), and Easthope reads the characters and plot of *Small World* as representing "an empiricist opposition between the apparent and the real" (Easthope 1999, 168). In *Deaf Sentence*, such an opposition can also be made out, but it is not represented on the level of character and plot (*histoire*), but on the level of discourse. The clash between representations of aging and death as ideas on the one hand and as real experience on the other is contained in the perspectival shifts both in the funny and the serious parts of the novel. In both parts the narrative is structured in such a way that expectations, grounded in "ordained patterns of social life" (Douglas 1975, 102), are built up and then challenged with new experience. The following diagram is a simplified illustration of this pattern:

	ideas		**experience**
funny	old professor's academic authority		sexual desires and fears
	father's stubborn insistence on dignity		infirmity of body and mind
serious	assisted suicide as "act of love"	← challenge	assisted suicide as act of selfishness
	parent/infant relationship, taboo barrier		reversal of parent/infant relationship, breaking through taboo barrier

Unlike Lodge's campus trilogy, where the central academic discipline is literary criticism, the protagonist in this 'off-campus' novel is a professor of linguistics whose field of specialization is discourse analysis. The significance of this particular subject does not lie in its role for the plot, for Bates has no ideological axe to grind with other colleagues, and Alex's PhD could have been in any other subject. But discourse analysis can be read as the analytical template for the novel's central theme. "We live in discourse as fish live in water" (Lodge 2008, 29), as professor Bates used to enlighten his university students, and what Lodge does in this narrative is pitch against each other competing discourses on aging and dying: conventional vs. new, social vs. individual, funny vs. serious.

Eagleton has criticized Lodge for failing, in his early novels, to adopt a distinct position of his own amidst the "caricatured antithesis [of] ideological poles [...] (theory and humanism, [...] modernism and realism [...]), allowing each to put the other into ironic question while the author himself disappears conveniently down the middle" (Eagleton 1988, 97-98). And although the themes of *Deaf Sentence* are not as clearly linked to current ideological debates as those of the earlier novels, no clear-cut authorial stance is visible here either. However, I would not criticize this. Lodge's aesthetic agenda is plainly restricted to raising awareness for the contradictions emerging in a rapidly aging society which idealizes youthfulness. It does not purport to resolve any of the contradictions it exposes. But as regards Lodge's creature Bates, it seems as if he, too, in the end disappears "down the middle." At least his robust sense of humour which set the novel's tone seems to refine itself out of existence. Although in Bates's new post-retirement occupation, the lip-reading classes, there is also "a lot of laughter," this is "laughter of a totally innocent kind" (Lodge 2008, 141). It is a serene kind of laughter, completely oblivious to *double entendre* or innuendo. When, for a class activity, the teacher writes on the board, "'An enormous P –,'" Bates notes that "nobody sniggered or even smiled" (141). It is as if the protagonist had given up his (partly humorous, partly embittered) battle against a world that is unsympathetic to the pains of a professor losing his faculties. For at the close of the novel Bates seems to have taken refuge in the serene company of kindred spirits who when practising words such as "*wet suit* and *wedding suit*, *big kiss* and *biscuits*" (291) respond naïvely and innocently with: "Much laughter" (291). The humorous (self-)mockery so characteristic of most of the novel has been sanitized into a benign and guileless, almost angelic laugh which seems no longer quite of this world. The lip-reading class turns into a kind of pre-mortal Elysium. Or is this only another *Deaf Sentence* pun? The comedy remains ambivalent and fluid till the end.

Works Cited

Abrams, M.H. *A Glossary of Literary Terms.* 7th ed. Fort Worth: Harcourt Brace College Publishers, 1999.

Ahrens, Rüdiger. "Satirical Norm and Narrative Technique in the Modern University Novel: David Lodge's *Changing Places* and *Small World.*" *Literatur im Kontext/ Literature in Context.* Eds. Joachim Schwend, Susanne Hagemann, and Hermann Völkel. Frankfurt: Peter Lang, 1992. 277-95.

Allen, Brooke. "A Tragicomic Meditation on Old Age." *New Leader* 91.5 (2008): 21-22.

Bergson, Henri. *Laughter: An Essay on the Meaning of the Comic.* Trans. Cloudesley Brereton and Fred Rothwell. New York: Macmillan, 1911.

Boethius, Anicius Manlius Severinus. *De Consolatione Philosophiae: Libri Quinque.* Ed. Adrian Fortescue. [1st ed. London, 1925]. Repr. Hildesheim: Olms, 2002.

Bray, Chris. "Seriously Funny." *New Statesman* 137 (2008): 58-59.

British Council. *Writers: Professor David Lodge.* 2011. Web. 24 January 2015.

Burkhardt, Joanna M. "Deaf Sentence." *Library Journal* 133.14 (2008): 119-20.

Conradi, Peter J. "Eeyore Enters the Confessional." *The Independent.* 2 May 2008. Web. 24 November 2014.

Cuddon, J. A. *The Penguin Dictionary of Literary Terms and Literary Theory.* 3rd ed. London: Penguin, 1992.

Cundall, Michael K., Jr. "Humor and the Limits of Incongruity." *Creativity Research Journal* 19.2/3 (2007): 203-11.

Cunnen, Joseph. "Sound of Silence." *America* 200.2 (2009): 33-34.

Douglas, Mary. "Jokes." *Implicit Meanings: Essays in Anthropology.* Ed. Mary Douglas. London: Routledge & Keagan Paul, 1975. 90-114.

Draudt, Manfred. "The Language of David Lodge's Fiction." *Lineages of the Novel.* Eds. Bernhard Reitz and Eckart Voigts-Virchow. Trier: WVT, 2000. 231-42.

Eagleton, Terry. "The Silences of David Lodge." *New Left Review* 172 (1988): 93-102.

Easthope, Antony. *Englishness and National Culture.* London and New York: Routledge, 1999.

Eyre, Pauline. "Deafened by Laughter: Reading David Lodge's *Deaf Sentence* as a Carnivalesque Dismodernist Text." *Journal of Literary & Cultural Disability Studies* 6.1 (2012): 17-34.

Fielding, Helen. *Bridget Jones's Diary: A Novel.* London: Picador, 1996.

Foster, Verna A. *The Name and Nature of Tragicomedy.* Aldershot: Ashgate, 2003.

Grossmith, George, and Weedon Grossmith. *The Diary of a Nobody* [[1]1892]. Oxford: Oxford University Press, 1998.

Horlacher, Stefan. "'Slightly Quixotic': Comic Strategies, Sexual Role Stereotyping and the Functionalization of Femininity in David Lodge's Trilogy of Campus Novels under Special Consideration of *Nice Work* (1988)." *Anglia: Zeitschrift für Englische Philologie* 125.3 (2007): 465-83.

Kakutani, Michiko. "Hearing and Dreams Both Fading." *New York Times.*: C 29. 9 October 2009. Web. 24 January 2015.

Lodge, David. *Changing Places: A Tale of Two Campuses* [[1]1975]. New York: Penguin, 1979.

—. *Small World.* London: Secker & Warburg, 1984.

—. *Nice Work.* London: Secker & Warburg, 1988.

—. *Deaf Sentence.* London: Harvill Secker, 2008.

Morreall, John. "Philosophy and Religion." *The Primer of Humor Research.* Ed. Victor Raskin. Berlin: Mouton de Gruyter, 2008. 211-42.

Müller, Patrick. "'Like walking off a stage': Altern als Tragikomödie in David Lodges *Deaf Sentence* und Ian McEwans *Solar.*" *Alter(n) in Literatur und Kultur der Gegenwart.* Ed. Rudolf Freiburg. Würzburg: Königshausen&Neumann, 2012. 147-68.

Niederhoff, Burkhard. *Die englische Komödie: Eine Einführung.* Berlin: Erich Schmidt, 2014.

Schaefer Riley, Naomi. "His University Career Is over, but not His Academic Studies." *Wall Street Journal - Eastern Edition* 252.85 (2008): D9. Web. 24 January 2015.

Strout, Cushing. "Deafness and the Coming of Death." *Sewanee Review* 118.3 (2010): xcii-xciii.

Townsend, Sue. *The Secret Diary of Adrian Mole Aged 13¾.* London: Methuen, 1982.

Veale, Tony. "Incongruity in Humor: Root Cause or Epiphenomenon?" *Humor: International Journal of Humor Research* 17.4 (2004): 419-28.

Versteegen, Heinrich. "Dying with Laughter: The Inherent Joke Structure of Death and Bereavement." *Journal for the Study of British Cultures* 18.2 (2011): 175-86.

Walsh, Chris. "'Not a Comic Novelist, Exactly': The Academic Fiction of David Lodge." *The Academic Novel: New and Classic Essays.* Ed. Merritt Moseley. Chester: Chester Academic Press, 2007. 268-90.

PETER CHILDS

Sunlight and Dark: Humorous Shades in Ian McEwan's Later Novels

Ian McEwan's debut stories were noted for their mordant tone and Kafkaesque use of violence, fantasy and sexuality. While black comedy marked the early stories and novellas, his writing adopted a more serious register as it developed over the 1980s and 1990s up to the Booker-prize winning *Amsterdam*, his first extended foray into satire. *Amsterdam* was followed by three serious fictions, *Atonement, Saturday* and *On Chesil Beach*, in what has been considered McEwan's mature writing style, noted for its lyrical, cursive sentences. However, in his recent novels, *Solar* and *Sweet Tooth*, McEwan has approached serious subject matter, ecology and espionage, in an archly ironic mode. This essay will characterize the style of McEwan's latest writing while speculating on the historical reasons for his present concatenation of humour and politics in a comic vein.

Ian McEwan's novel *Solar* won the Wodehouse prize for the best comic novel of the year in 2010.[1] Yet McEwan would prefer to say that *Solar* contains humorous sections rather than that it is a comic novel. He concedes that the book has extended stretches aimed in part to amuse, but evidently dislikes the generic categorization: "I hate comic novels; it's like being wrestled to the ground and being tickled, being forced to laugh" (Soal 2008). This suggests if anything that *Solar* is closer to the approach of Waugh than of Wodehouse, with shades of other non-British writers from Kafka to Kundera, Nabokov to Updike, but it raises the question of the capaciousness as well as the category of the comic novel, which might include such diverse anglophone works as *Tom Jones, Tristram Shandy, Catch-22, Ulysses, The Pickwick Papers, The Picture of Dorian Gray, Lucky Jim, Murphy, Cold Comfort Farm, Under the Net, London Fields,* and the novels included in Powell's *A Dance to the Music of Time.* If the designation of comic fiction in part derives from the oeuvre associated with the author then there are comic writers, varying in style from Voltaire or Rabelais to Kingsley Amis or Flann O'Brien, and there are novels with sections that may draw laughter by writers who, like McEwan, are not comic novelists but whose fiction has humorous elements, tragicomic standpoints, sardonic set pieces, or comedic ingredients.

The dominant style of the comic novel of the 20th century appears of a largely different kind from the characteristic mode of the 18th century in Britain, which coincided with a heyday of satire and wit, in writers such as Smollett, Sterne, Johnson, Burney and Swift. Arguably, over the course of the 19th century in-between, and despite the popularity of Dickens, the tone of comedy shifted with more serious but heavily ironical works, such as those of Jane Austen, which have been seen as less theatrical and more novelistic, by which perhaps it is meant more concerned with interiority and the subtleties of human personal and social frailty, as prevalent in 20th-century approaches to humour.[2] As for the 21st century, Jonathan Coe suggests the comic novel is on life-support as the world has turned serious post-9/11 (Coe 2013), but he is also aware that writers like Howard Jacobson, Will Self, Zadie Smith and Coe himself are

1 Its full title is the Bollinger Everyman Wodehouse prize.
2 See the discussion in the Introduction to *The Irresponsible Self* (Wood 2004).

Anglistik: International Journal of English Studies 27.1 (March 2016): 73-83.

keeping the genre alive alongside the varied satirical brio of the likes of Rushdie, Barnes, and Amis. Indeed if one adds the output of Celtic novelists such as Irvine Welsh, or Iain Banks and Niall Griffiths, or the wry, sometimes dour, Spark-inspired humour of writers like A.L. Kennedy, or the gothic Stevensonian satire of Alasdair Gray, or even the English eccentricity of Magnus Mills, it is arguable that comedy, if not the comic novel, has in fact been flourishing, especially away from London.

It seems Ian McEwan has not been interested in the label of the comic novel applied to his fiction, though the Booker-prize winning *Amsterdam* was considered a satire by many, and he has now won a Wodehouse award for a novel set against the 21st-century crisis of climate change. In this essay, I will seek to discuss the ways in which McEwan uses elements of character and plot from the conventions of comedy, and then consider the kind of comic fiction *Solar* might be said to be.

Solar is a novel without commitment. It paints a tragicomic portrait of human nature, depicting the short-term promotion of individual interests and rewards against the collective need for social and ecological care to ensure the well-being in the future of individuals and species. It is not concerned with the rapacious pursuit of greed and power but the rather more quotidian paths of lazy least-resistance and easy quick-wins to achieve creature comfort and selfish benefit. A central theme is irresponsibility, embodied in the central figure of theoretical physicist Michael Beard, head of the National Centre for Renewable Energy near Reading in England. A Nobel-prize winning scientist resting on his laurels, Beard believes "physics was free of human taint, it described a world that would still exist if men and women and all their sorrows did not" (McEwan 2010, 9). In some ways a 21st-century heir to John Self from Martin Amis's 1984 novel *Money*, Beard is similarly a caricature of his times; *Solar* strives to express the concerns of the age but has at its centre a transatlantic representative of callous indifference to the social good. Beard is exploitative while largely lacking in enthusiasm or pleasure. He is described on the first page of the novel as anhedonic (3), and even the motorway out of London along which he travels "demonstrated a passion for existence which he could no longer match" (26). At the turn of the millennium, Beard is middle-aged and dissipated, without insight or vision but at the helm of one of science's attempts to mitigate humanity's exploitation of the earth. At the bidding of politicians, he has invested the efforts of his Centre in micro wind-power machines that ordinary citizens can understand and purchase. However, one of his young postdoctoral researchers, Tom Aldous, proposes a grand scheme that Beard initially thinks is impractical: "Solar arrays on a tiny fraction of the world's deserts would give us all the power we need" (27). The novel's comic thrust derives from the reasons why and the ways in which this idea, positioned in the narrative as a potential partial solution to the threat of climate change, fails spectacularly in practice because of the "human taint," mentioned above.

The book is arranged in three parts, set in 2000, 2005 and 2009 respectively. At the start of the narrative Beard is 53 years old, long past his glory days, and clinging to his fifth marriage to 34-year-old Monroe-lookalike Patrice (7).[3] As the story opens, Patrice has learned of Beard's latest infidelity and decided to begin an affair of her own with their builder Rodney Tarpin. When Beard returns from a climate change expedition to the Arctic he finds that Patrice has also slept with Aldous, whose sudden accidental death when he and Beard are alone in the house leaves Beard with the

3 This may be an allusion to the Terry Johnson play *Insignificance* and its 1985 film adaptation by Nicolas Roeg, in which The Professor, based on Einstein, talks about relativity with The Actress, based on Monroe.

young man's innovative research into artificial photosynthesis. Putting his rationalism to work, Beard calculatedly frames Tarpin for the death. If there is comedy here, it is very much in terms of the Falstaffian irresponsibility striating Beard's behaviour, which rests on a combination of self-delusion and short-sightedness. All is confusion and chance, rationalization rather than reason, opportunity rather than organization, farcical rather than jovial. McEwan explains the appeal of such an approach: "I like the cognitive moment of dissonance when people are so persuaded by something they want to believe that they see or hear differently [...] We're almost defined as a species by our willingness to misunderstand" (Sandall 2008, 6-7).[4] In this spirit the narrative continues, as unplanned courses of action spiral out of control and lead to catastrophic ends that can seem humorous to the reader, in the spirit of Chaplin's view that "Comedy is life viewed from a distance; tragedy, life in a close-up" (qtd. in Levin 1987, 9). Or, in other words, McEwan's chosen mode for the novel matches responses to climate change, which people view from a distance rather than close-up, and so do not take sufficiently seriously in terms of their responsibility.

Part One of the novel is set at the turn of the millennium, in the year when "the earth's fate hung in the balance, and Bush snatched victory from Gore to preside over the tragedy of eight wasted years" (McEwan 2010, 218). Part Two of the novel is set in 2005, the year the Kyoto Protocol came into force following decisions taken at the December 1997 UN Climate Change Conference in Kyoto, Japan, where the delegates agreed to a Protocol that committed industrialized countries to reducing their greenhouse gas emissions. It begins with the phrase "He was running out of time" (107) and this resonant phrase alludes to Beard's and the eco-system's life-threatening condition as well as the more immediate matter at hand, his lateness for a fund-raising speech in London. Beard now has a "mission" (109), which is to put Aldous's research to practical use for his own benefit. He has lost his position at the National Centre in Reading but gained a devoted girlfriend, Melissa Browne, who feels she is herself running out of time to have a child.

Four years later, the third and final Part is contemporaneous with McEwan's time of writing the novel in 2009 and set in the year of the Copenhagen conference that was scheduled to revisit and revise the Kyoto agreement. Part Three finds Beard in El Paso, Texas, having flown in to continue planning his solar project in Lordsburg, New Mexico. Here he aims to produce energy as cheaply as coal through artificial photosynthesis. The novel ends with this plan in ruins and Beard pursued by his business partner, by lawyers investigating his theft of Aldous's research, by the aggrieved Rodney Tarpin, by the spectre of life-threatening ill-health, by his local lover Darlene, and by Melissa, who has brought their daughter Catriona out to the States to see Beard.

The novel abounds with ironic juxtapositions. Central to this is the fact that, while attempting to ameliorate some of the problems of humanity's demand for energy, Beard himself has remarkable "gifts for entropy" (173), as witnessed by his visit to Melissa. "Like many slobs, Beard was appreciative of the order that others created without effort, or any that he noticed" (163). He is someone who brings disorder to the efforts of those around him ("all the books were on the shelves in the right order, at least until he visited" [163]), creating disharmony by his sheer presence at Melissa's: "the sort of place whose ambience Beard could wreck in two minutes by sitting down in it, shrugging off his coat, opening his briefcase and removing his shoes" (163). Beard is also deficient in his care for himself. His health is neglected to the

4 See also Childs (2007).

extent that he sees "his symptoms as crimes. He should see a doctor and make a full confession. But he did not want to be condemned" (185). He makes resolutions such as "no drinks but water, no snacks, a green-leaf salad, a portion of fish, no pudding" but immediately opts for a meal exemplifying opposite nutritional choices (118).

Not surprisingly, one of the novel's central interpretive questions concerns the extent to which Beard can be taken to be representative of humankind and subsequently the degree to which self-interest can be said to drive all the characters in the narrative. Even those portrayed in a kindly light seem to make self-interested choices. Beard's wife Patrice has an affair with Tarpin, then Aldous, to get back at Beard for his affairs. Tom Aldous has an affair with Patrice, taking advantage of a sexual and professional opportunity. Melissa is "truly a good person" (159) yet stops taking the contraceptive pill and becomes pregnant by Beard without telling him. Here is the essence of the book's view of humanity, for which McEwan took inspiration from his trip with the Cape Farewell artists' expedition to the Arctic. The adventure is reworked in the fiction of *Solar* to comic effect but also to illustrate a serious point about human behaviour (49-80). This is most apparent in the "boot room" scene when items go missing. Because the expedition members then indulge in a domino-effect sequence of replacing their own missing gear – such as boots or gloves – by taking items from others, the one scientist (Beard) and nineteen artists visiting the Arctic to study the effects of climate change are presented as emblematic of a wider human inability to work together for the common good when self-interest intervenes. The well-intentioned colleagues end up bringing not camaraderie but chaos to the changing room as each individual ignores a responsibility towards the needs of others. This incident in real life provided the germ for the novel, as McEwan explains in his article "Save the boot room, Save the Earth," where he says: "You might reflect that it is not evil that undoes the world, but small errors prompting tiny weaknesses" (McEwan 2005).

Returning to questions of altruism and collaboration explored from different angles in his earlier novels *Enduring Love* (1997) and *Amsterdam* (1998), for *Solar* McEwan evidently felt his boot-room experience offered a representative and resonant example of how human frailty can sabotage the best of intentions, leading to a collapse of the social contract required for engagement in the pursuit of cooperative solutions to collective problems that in themselves may not appear likely to impinge on the individual. Nonetheless, McEwan's protagonist Beard is a more insidious influence than this, because he is avowedly "not a communally-spirited person" and indeed has "a touch of nihilism:" "The earth could do without Patrice and Michael Beard" (McEwan 2010, 74-75). Beard does not like to be part of a group, but also does not want any group to know this (62). On the trip to the North Pole, he reflects that "the optimism was crushing him. Everyone but Beard was worried about global warming and was merry, and he was uniquely morose. He cared only for darkness and silence" (67). For all his faults, Beard does have a reasonable amount of self-knowledge. With the artists at Spitsbergen, he feels "weary, and too cynical for the company" (67) but at least acknowledges many of his own shortcomings. He does not however believe in inner change but only "slow inner and outer decay" (66).

McEwan's choice of black humour to address such a serious matter as climate change is arguably typical of his approach to fiction. John McLeod observes that since the short stories "incidents are usually described through narrative voices that, in their seeming blankness, their lack of overt moral outrage or compassion, demand precisely that the reader thinks about them in moral, if not political terms" (McLeod 1998, 221). A similar technique is apparent in *Solar*, prompting the reader to think in moral terms about Beard's irresponsible behaviour, and that of the other characters. In political terms, the novel frames its questions for the reader against a mordant recognition of individual self-interest and the tendency of good intentions to be undermined by *Realpolitik*. Several passages in the novel exemplify the slightly cynical and world-weary tone to the narration, which is often focalized through or inflected by Beard's *Weltanschauung*. In Part One, it is noted of the polar expedition that "the guilty discharge of carbon dioxide from twenty return flights and snowmobile rides and sixty hot meals a day served in polar conditions would be offset by planting three thousand trees in Venezuela as soon as a site could be identified and local officials bribed" (McEwan 2010, 46). In Part Two, Beard has espoused the climate-change agenda, largely because he sees the chance for financial gain by exploiting the research of Tom Aldous on a "four-hundred-acre site in the south-western scrub desert of New Mexico" (112). He believes now that "planetary stupidity was his business," posing the question "how could we ever begin to restrain ourselves?" as he surveys from a circling plane humanity's multiplication "like a spreading lichen, a ravaging bloom of algae, a mould enveloping a soft fruit" (111). Beard himself decides that the "disgrace" of the boot room is

> a matter of human nature. And how were we ever going to learn about that? Science of course was fine, and who knew, art was too, but perhaps self-knowledge was beside the point. Boot rooms needed good systems so that flawed creatures could use them properly [...] Only good laws would save the boot room. And citizens who respected the law. (79-80)

With its signature setting of the airplane, as exemplar of personal short-term gain taking precedence over long-term priorities, *Solar* emerges as a book that attempts to view homo sapiens from a distance, and so to paint human nature in the tradition of the bleak comic novel, not as fundamentally noble and essentially public-spirited, but as "somewhat co-operative, somewhat selfish, sometimes cruel, above all, funny" (79). It is clearly the mixed-bag of human nature that interests McEwan, not the characterization that would be underpinned by reference to Rousseau or Hobbes, and this distinguishes the view in *Solar* from McEwan's earlier incursion into environmental concerns in the 1980s, when he wrote more solemnly about how the "growing science of ecology places us firmly within the intricate systems of the natural world and warns us that we may yet destroy what sustains us" (McEwan 1989, 16). The sentiment of McEwan's libretto to Michael Berkeley's *Or Shall we Die?* remains McEwan's humanist message on Climate Change, restated in an article of 2008 entitled "The World's Last Chance:"

> There is a rendezvous next year [2009] in Copenhagen which [...] is the global successor to Kyoto. [...] If it does not result in practical, radical measures, the fight to control our future could well be lost. Every nation on the planet will be represented. The general feeling is that the conference cannot be allowed to fail. (McEwan 2008)

Yet climate change campaigning is unlikely to succeed if the evolutionary reality of human behaviour can be represented by Michael Beard. As Greg Garrard notes, Beard "epitomizes what Mikhail Bakhtin calls 'the grotesque body'" (Garrard 2013, 129). Beard's physical desires constantly undermine any higher thought and his distended stomach not only indicates his overconsumption but his bloated appetite for self-indulgence in general. There is a familiar carnality about Beard and a complacent pomposity that echoes Falstaff. Beard too varies from amusing rogue to imploring child, using the rhetoric of the moment both to promote and disguise his self-interest. While believing the novel's protagonist "personifies human nature" (Garrard 2013, 131), Garrard feels that McEwan, possibly because of his "commitment to Enlightenment values" (McEwan 2010, 130), does not develop Beard's grotesque portrayal into a critique of capitalist consumerism and that the novel has been justifiably met with considerable criticism because as a contribution to the climate change debate it is an insufficiently apocalyptic disappointment. Garrard ascribes some of this failure to McEwan's over-reliance on 'parables,' as he terms the run of allegorical set pieces throughout the novel. This is a frequent characteristic of McEwan's novels, which, from *The Child in Time* (1987) to *Saturday* (2005), and quite explicitly in *Black Dogs* (1992) and arguably *Amsterdam* (1998), often seem to assemble a series of short dramatic scenes, such that as soon as one climax is reached, the reader feels another piece of largely self-contained bravura lurks around the next narrative bend. So, not long after the parable of the locker room comes the similarly illustrative set piece, derived from urban myth, of the indignant traveller helping himself to another person's food he believes to be his own (123-27).

But in *Solar* it is arguably less the fact of this staccato set of narrative allegories that disappoints ecocriticism than their comical emphasis on individual folly. What critics of *Solar* often implicitly find frustrating is the novel's focus, which, despite its title, is not on climate change but on human nature. While set against contemporary concerns over climate change, the impending apocalypse prefigured by the novel's conclusion is that of Michael Beard's world, not of anything planetary. The implication would appear to be that McEwan is more interested in a micro-narrative of the calamity of human self-destruction than in a macro-narrative of ecological disaster *per se*. If human folly leads to planetary devastation, it will be a triumph of self-interested individualism over concern for the survival of the species. The novel's denouement thus has Beard, his solar project and his public life in tatters, contemplating the joint arrival of Darlene and Melissa. But the final word of the novel is "love," used to possibly describe his feeling as his daughter Catriona rushes into his arms (and the "unfamiliar, swelling sensation" in his heart may in fact be a coronary, 279). It is the last piece in McEwan's loose allegorical jigsaw, and indicates faith fragilely placed in emotional attachment to the future, to the child in time. Reminiscent of Larkin's oft-thought-surprising conclusion to his 1956 poem "An Arundel Tomb" that "What will survive of us is love," this attachment can be viewed as sentimental or observational, in terms of kinship or the decision-making influence on the species of selfish genes encoded in DNA. It nonetheless expresses a rationalist approach pressed towards a cooperative rather than competitive response to crisis: "we have to think outside the framework of an individual lifetime and start doing favours for unborn people. The timescales are longer than what human nature is evolved to deal with" (McEwan qtd. in Roberts 2010, 191). It is here that McEwan's literary interest lies, asking the reader to admit the flaws in human nature that are undermining a concerted reaction to climate change: "I think we *do* face a test of our nature, and the more we know about that nature, the better we'll be able to face the test. That's why it's so important to look empirically at what we are, how our cognitive abilities shape our interactions with the world and with each other" (Roberts 2010, 191).

This prompts further consideration of the extent to which Beard is a representative character. Beard is no everyman figure but McEwan insinuates some critical opinions about the drivers of human behaviour through his portrayal of a selfish man. Underlining his inability to share or empathize, Beard is made by his author an only child who "never quite got the hang of brotherly feeling" (McEwan 2010, 193). According to McEwan's narrator, Beard's mother's indulgence of him has left a legacy of "a fat man who restlessly craved the attentions of beautiful women who could cook" (194). At university he "was well known, talked about, useful to people and faintly despised" (197). Like Perowne in *Saturday*, Beard has little affinity with literature, using it only for instrumental ends when he invites out the English Literature undergraduate who will become his first wife. The story of his courtship of Maisie suggests his shallowness, culminating in the sentences: "She also cooked a fine steak and kidney pie. He decided he was in love" (201). Beard finds nothing in literary study "that could remotely be considered as an intellectual challenge" but the reading is a "slog" he is prepared to undertake in his "relentless, highly organised pursuit" of Maisie (201).

Beard is famous for the "Beard-Einstein Conflation" and this phrase is purposeful. McEwan notes in his acknowledgements that he owes a debt above all to Walter Isaacson's biography *Einstein* (285), and Beard's life is a little conflated with Einstein's, but only enough to provoke contrast. Both are figured as early high-achieving geniuses, who lack worldly competency, as illustrated by Beard's sense of victimhood when the signs in his hotel do not indicate where he can find his room, numbered 399. He orbits the building three times before he realizes he has his room card upside down and should be looking for room 663 (217). Yet, the comical point is clear: Beard is not "Einstein," and the two should not be conflated.

McEwan writes a comic novel against the background of, rather than on, a serious subject because his interest is in the foibles of human nature, and particularly *our* ability to mistakenly assume someone else is in the wrong, as Beard does at the Arctic Circle and on the train where he thinks a stranger is eating *his* crisps, while at other times shamelessly and unethically promoting *our* own interests, as Beard does in an extreme example when he steals Tom Aldous's research and frames Rodney Tarpin for Aldous's death. His cognitive ability and his skill for reasoning are tied to rapacious, destructive appetites that mean Beard schemes for his own advantage, from his courtship of Maisie to his get-rich solar arrays in the American desert. Up against these appetites, his own health is not a priority, let alone that of the planet. Beard watches the "livid blotch" that has returned angrily on his hand, but has done little about it for nine months, preferring not to know the results of a biopsy because he wants neither to confront his death nor be admonished by doctors who tell him to change his lifestyle (205). McEwan produces a comic novel because human self-interest, certainly when it stretches to a perverse denial of mortality as in Beard's choice to ignore the signs of cancer, seems incompatible with humanity's interests, and this is a source of ironic humour as much as anger or despair. Beard's venality comes to the fore when he tries to reassure his project partner Toby Hammer, who worries that scientists will decide humans are not the cause of devastating climate change: "'Toby, listen. It's a catastrophe. Relax!'" (217).

However, the humour is dark, reflecting the seriousness of the situation, which McEwan describes in a style that evokes Updike if he were to have written *Catch-22*. The human tolerance of climate change is as absurd as its penchant for war, in which money and adventure are up for grabs, but there is still death, individual (such as Aldous's) and collective: "'Here's the good news. The UN estimates that already a third of a million people a year are dying from climate change" (216). As such, *Solar* is an example of James Wood's category of the "irresponsible self" in comedy, where the humour hangs on the readers' belief that they know more than the character. In distinction from the longer-established comedy of correction that lives on in a satirist like Waugh, the kind of fiction that foregrounds the irresponsible self in comedy, Wood thinks, is a strain entwined with the comedy of forgiveness as the modern novel reveals the complexity of human being in a way that the 18th-century novel did not. Unfortunately for the reader, McEwan provides a variant on the Falstaffian comic grotesque in Michael Beard, and asks if he is not representative of us all collectively "in the boot room;" whether we forgive him ought to depend on whether we forgive ourselves.

Solar uses the approach of comedy for a novel about a shared human disaster. The latter can best be expressed by a concept in economic theory, the tragedy of the commons, according to which individuals consume a common resource, acting independently and rationally according to each one's self-interest but against the long-term best interests of the collective. McEwan illustrates this more directly by showing how Beard's decisions work against him in the long run: his framing of Tarpin for murder, his exploitation of Aldous's research, his unhealthy food and alcohol consumption, his double-dating of Melissa and Darlene, his deferral of the removal of a cancerous lesion. The ways in which these decisions rebound on Beard form the comic plot of the novel, and the mode appears appropriate because self-delusion has long been a staple of humour – but in the modern novel the reader is often drawn in. James Wood describes this in his questioning of Bergson's likening of comedy to watching people dancing through a window without hearing the music (Wood 2004, 15).[5] The absurdity of others' folly, to the mere observer without emotional involvement, is certainly familiar from Shakespearean comedy, for example, but modern humour is less forgiving of the witness, as Wood notes: "What if he felt no advantage over them, but felt, with mingled laughter and pity, that he was watching some awful dance of death, in which he too was obscurely implicated?" (16). This describes *Solar* well, in which the slow dance of death is performed by Beard, whose name arguably indicates he is a cover, someone acting on behalf of another to conceal their identity, which is here perhaps humanity in general and the reader in particular.

This connection to the reader links *Solar* to McEwan's next fiction, *Sweet Tooth*, a very different example of comic writing, deceptive and manipulative. *Sweet Tooth* emerges as a novel that has narratives within narratives, fictions about fictions, stories

---

5 Wood to an extent misrepresents Bergson, who more accurately writes (even if in translation): "Now detach yourself, look upon life as an indifferent observer; many a drama will turn into comedy. It is enough for us to stop up our ears to the sound of music, in a room where people are dancing, for the dancers to appear at once ridiculous. How many human actions would be able to resist a test of this type? And would we not see many of them go from being solemn to funny, if we isolated them from the feeling that accompanies them? Therefore, the comic, in order to produce its complete effect, in the end demands something like a momentary anaesthesia of the heart. It is addressed to pure intelligence" (Bergson 1956, 63).

that tell other stories – and its narrator is a "beard" for another writer. It uses the familiar spy novel structural framework that is akin to a matryoshka doll, and so introduces nested and refracted short stories within an overarching narrative: fictional fragments multiplying the book's examples of confidence tricks, tall tales, and barefaced lies. Consequently, a warning is made to the reader in the first line not to take things at face value: "My name is Serena Frome (rhymes with Plume)" (McEwan 2012a, 1).

A novel of secrets and temptations, *Sweet Tooth* is set in and around 1972 at a time when McEwan was himself a promising but largely unknown writer. The novel is in one sense a shadowy piece of refracted memoir. McEwan's twisted doppelganger is the writer T.H. Haley, who has "published a few short stories and some journalism. He's looking for a publisher" (93). Tom Haley has an undergraduate degree in English from Sussex University, and a Masters Degree in international relations, and now teaches at Sussex while researching a doctorate on Spenser's *The Faerie Queene* (93; 183). The details are in some instances the same as for McEwan's biography (English degree from Sussex University), occasionally altered (McEwan's Masters was in Creative Writing from East Anglia), and sometimes different in time or fact (McEwan did not embark on a PhD or teach at Sussex). In *Sweet Tooth* no one is quite who they seem (none of the principal characters, including Tony, Serena, Tom, and Shirley, is truthful about their activities and identity). To underscore the central act of ventriloquism – that *Sweet Tooth,* a novel by a man in the voice of a woman, appears in fact to be written by Tom, or by Tom and Serena – reference is made to Chet Baker, "a man who sang like a woman" (198). When mention is first made of Tom, Serena Frome is tasked by the secret service department for which she works with reading everything he's published to date, which is also a task the reader might undertake with regard to McEwan in order to appreciate many of the sly in-jokes of *Sweet Tooth,* which incorporates in distorted form several of McEwan's early short stories.

It is perhaps also not coincidental that McEwan has gone on to champion the short story, a form in which he excels and on which *Sweet Tooth* feeds, and to / that he declared in a *New Yorker* blog post that "the novella is the perfect form of prose fiction" (McEwan 2012b). McEwan's choice of the supreme example of the short form is Joyce's "The Dead," which he himself draws on in both *Saturday* and the ending of *The Children Act* (2014), reminding us of Eliot's much misquoted and distorted words:

> Immature poets imitate; mature poets steal; bad poets deface what they take, and good poets make it into something better, or at least something different. The good poet welds his theft into a whole of feeling which is unique, utterly different than that from which it is torn; the bad poet throws it into something which has no cohesion. A good poet will usually borrow from authors remote in time, or alien in language, or diverse in interest. (Eliot 1921, 81)

In McEwan's case, the novelist may self-steal, but it is apparent that in *Sweet Tooth* he has also written something "utterly different than that from which it is torn." There may also be a clue to McEwan's "exquisite scheme" in the example of Edmund Spenser, Tom Haley's thesis subject. For Spenser, the poet "alien in language" from whom he borrowed was Joachim du Bellay, whose sonnet sequence "Antiquités de Rome" Spenser wrought into "Ruines of Rome" in recognition of the "first Garland of free Poesy / That France brought forth," as Spenser notes in an appended verse, addressed to Bellay.[6] This verse is entitled by Spenser "L'Envoi," following in the old French poetry tradition of a detached verse, often used to address the poem to a particular person. It is presumably partly for this reason that "Ruines of Rome" is quoted by Haley (McEwan 2012a, 225), who it seems either composes or collaborates on the many chapters of *Sweet Tooth*, before a final appended letter written in his own voice, addressed to Serena and declaring that he has written a manuscript about her entitled *Sweet Tooth*. In this deceptive novel of surfaces and distorted reflections, we are simply left to calculate the probability of the pattern in the carpet being woven by the writer or simply (mis)perceived there by McEwan's target: us. The author's playfulness in this conniving fiction, for that is the kind of comedy *Sweet Tooth* savours, is exemplified in its emulation of the early McEwan story "Reflections of a Kept Ape" from his 1978 collection *In Between the Sheets*. One of McEwan's "self-reflecting stories" according to its author,[7] "Reflections of a Kept Ape" bears a remarkable similarity to one of Tom Haley's fictions, but it also prefigures the ending of *Sweet Tooth*:

> Only on the last page did I discover that the story I was reading was actually the one the woman was writing. The ape doesn't exist, it's a spectre, the creature of her fretful imagination. *No.* And no again. Not that. Beyond the strained and ludicrous matter of cross-species sex, I instinctively distrusted this kind of fictional trick. I wanted to feel the ground beneath my feet. There was, in my view, an unwritten contract with the reader that the writer must honour. No single element of an imagined world or any of its characters should be allowed to dissolve on authorial whim. The invented had to be as solid and as self-consistent as the actual. This was a contract founded on mutual trust. (193)

Similarly, only on the last pages of *Sweet Tooth* do we find that the story we have been reading is written by, or part-written by, or collaboratively written with, someone else. Though first composed over thirty years ago, like McEwan's short stories, it can only be published in the new century because of the Official Secrets Act. The book in front of us may be that first draft, but if so it is more Tom's fiction than Serena's recollection and has had built into it from the start its anachronous element of hindsight and its approximate year of publication: "almost forty years ago I was sent on a secret mission" (1). Most likely it is the "collaboration" mentioned on the final page (320), but the probability of this is a calculation for the reader, who is placed here in a not entirely dissimilar position to the contestant in the book's central puzzle of the Monty Hall paradox, aware from new information that a first guess at where something lies hidden is now less probable to be correct than it was (203-206). *Sweet Tooth* is an unusual book in that the reader is partially left in a bemused position, trying to work out who has actually written the pages of the novel – unsure by the end whether its putative narrator, Serena Frome, has not disappeared before our eyes, sent up in a plume of smoke in McEwan's hall of mirrors.

Sweet Tooth is simultaneously a novel of undercover agents in between the sheets and a self-reflexive comedy of deceit and intrigue. It is a metafictional entertainment of mistaken identities and of imitations, placed in a cold war setting but light and warm in tone – a novelist's manipulation of a world of espionage and guesswork presented in a kind of breathless memoir that consciously apes a middle-brow prurience about a secret profession and the past of the protagonist. It is not a comedy of irre-

6 "Ruines of Rome" was a piece of juvenilia probably written by Spenser while studying at Cambridge.
7 This is how McEwan describes the story (Hamilton 2009, 15).

sponsibility ultimately or even of forgiveness, as *Solar* might be said to be, but a devious turn to a furtive amusement, a clever confected diversion from the more serious narratives McEwan has undertaken this century in *Atonement, Saturday, On Chesil Beach* and *The Children Act*.

Works Cited

Bergson, Henri. *Laughter: Essays on Comedy*. Ed. and trans. Wylie Sypher. New York: Double Day, 1956.

Childs, Peter. "'Believing is Seeing': The Eye of the Beholder." *Ian McEwan's Enduring Love*. Ed. Peter Childs. London: Routledge, 2007.

Coe, Jonathan. "What's so funny about comic novels?" *The Guardian*. 7 September 2013. Web. 5 November 2013.

Eliot, T.S. "Philip Massinger." *The Sacred Wood*. London: Faber, 1921. 80-93.

Garrard, Greg. "*Solar*: Apocalypse Not." *Ian McEwan. Contemporary Critical Perspectives*. Ed. Sebastian Groes. 2nd ed. London: Bloomsbury, 2013. 123-36.

Hamilton, Ian. "Points of Departure." *Conversations with Ian McEwan*. Ed. Ryan Roberts. Jackson, MI: University of Mississippi Press, 2009. 3-18.

Levin, Harry. *Playboys and Killjoys: An Essay on the Theory and Practice of Comedy*. Oxford: Oxford University Press, 1987.

McEwan, Ian. "Introduction to *Or Shall We Die?*" *A Move Abroad*. London: Picador, 1989. 3-16.

—. "Save the Boot Room, Save the Earth." *The Guardian*. 19 March 2005. Web. 12 February 2014.

—. "The World's Last Chance." *The Guardian*. 19 November 2008. Web. 11 March 2009.

—. *Solar*. London: Jonathan Cape, 2010.

—. *Sweet Tooth*. London: Jonathan Cape, 2012a.

—. "Some Notes on the Novella." *The New Yorker*. 29 October 2012b. Web. 14 November 2014.

McLeod, John. "Men Against Masculinity: The Fiction of Ian McEwan." *Signs of Masculinity: Men in Literature 1700 to the Present*. Eds. Antony Rowland, Emma Liggins, and Eriks Uskalis. Amsterdam: Rodopi, 1998. 218-45.

Roberts, Ryan. "'A Thing One Does': A Conversation with Ian McEwan." *Conversations with Ian McEwan*. Ed. Ryan Roberts. Jackson, MI: University Press of Mississippi, 2010. 188-201.

Sandall, Robert. "*For You*." *The Sunday Times*, Culture Section. 26 October 2008: 6-7.

Soal, Judith. "McEwan sees funny side of climate change in novel reading." 2 June 2008. *The Guardian*. Web. 14 November 2014.

Wood, James. *The Irresponsible Self: On Laughter and the Novel*. London: Jonathan Cape, 2004.

Medienwissenschaft
Anglistik/Amerikanistik

Universitätsverlag
WINTER
Heidelberg

KLECKER, CORNELIA

Spoiler Alert!

Mind-Tricking Narratives in Contemporary Hollywood Film

2015. 172 Seiten, 16 Abbildungen. (Film and Television Studies, Volume 2)
Geb. € 35,–
ISBN 978-3-8253-6473-1

"Mind-tricking narratives almost redefine the concept of spoilers." Films with a surprise ending have become rather frequent in recent years. They are particularly interesting when they offer one plot that contains two storylines, though the second story becomes apparent only in retrospect after this twist ending. The author calls these mind-tricking narratives.

This volume contributes to recent discussions of complex storytelling in film by naming, classifying, and deftly analyzing the "mind-tricking narrative" that is a more precise filmic category than the "twist" or "puzzle" film that other film scholars have identified. The list of films belonging to this category include M. Night Shyamalan's *The Sixth Sense* (1999), David Fincher's *Fight Club* (1999), and Christopher Nolan's *The Prestige* (2006). It also successfully challenges the widespread belief that popular culture equals dumb entertainment and draws upon traditional narratology and cognitive film theory to serve this end.

D-69051 Heidelberg · Postfach 10 61 40 · Tel. (49) 62 21/77 02 60 · Fax (49) 62 21/77 02 69
Mehr Information unter www.winter-verlag.de · E-mail: info@winter-verlag.de

SUSANNE PETERS

A Proletarian Comedy of Menace: Martin Amis's *Lionel Asbo*

1. The Principle of Terrestrial Mediocrity

One of the familiar and often controversially discussed topics of Amis criticism is to point out how, in his novels, everything is going to the dogs.[1] *Lionel Asbo: State of England*,[2] published shortly before Amis's relocation to New York in 2012, takes this bone of contention to new heights in both a literal and a metaphorical sense: dogs play a major role in the novel's configurations of anxiety, but our metaphor of course, and more importantly, also reflects Amis's idiosyncratic diagnosis of a decrepit, violently ignorant English society, as his novel's subtitle aptly flags out: Its eponymous protagonist, a violent and ignorant criminal, assisted by his pair of pitbulls fed on Tabasco sauce and Cobra beer, is an allegory of the state of England. In this essay, I shall discuss whether it is a humorous one.

Martin Amis has found an intriguing phrase for what he thinks is happening in our Western societies today. It is "the principle of terrestrial mediocrity," (129) as the protagonist and writer Richard Tull (whom we can take as the ventriloquist Amis's dummy) assumes in Amis's 1995 novel *The Information* and it is further elaborated as guiding the development of human communities and the history of all art, especially literature: It inevitably leads to moral decay, and finds 20th-century culture in a state of exhaustion. Such downward spiralling history of humankind is aligned with the history of astronomical discoveries, in which man likewise seems to dwindle into insignificance – both processes of persistent humiliation.[3] Perhaps the most characteristic (and often quoted) passage yet in this context can indeed be found in *The Information*, where Richard Tull is questioned by his editor about a new book project:

> 'What's this? *The History of Increasing Humiliation*. Non-fiction, right?' [...] 'It would be a book accounting for the decline in the status and virtue of literary protagonists. First gods, then demi-gods, then kings, then great warriors, great lovers, the burghers

1 In this context, Theo Tait begins his review of *Lionel Asbo* in *The Guardian* (8 June 2012) with the following rather pertinent remark: "It must be hard for Martin Amis, never quite knowing if he's a national treasure or a national embarrassment." The controversy around Amis and his works often rests on the conflicting opinions whether the comic mode is adequate to express serious subjects (e.g. the Holocaust in *Time's Arrow* and in his 2014 novel *The Zone of Interest*). Other accusations are those of sexism, arrogance, and a compassion for America (see Finney 2008, 95-96).

2 Martin Amis's novel *Lionel Asbo* (2012) will henceforth be abbreviated as *LA*. There is an earlier Amis short story entitled "The State of England," published in the collection *Heavy Water and Other Stories* (1998), which also deals in low life. For an analysis of that story with respect to its comic mode see Verrier (2003): "Faithful to the definition of sentimental comedy, the polytonality of Amis's texts, which juxtaposes two rivalling moods, keeps the reader off balance because he/she knows that, at any time, laughter may erupt from social comedy or else horror and desperation may be produced by a random instance of wanton violence" (103).

3 Amis himself has abundantly commented on his views on art in his fiction, in interviews and critical writings, see e.g. "I Am in Blood Stepp'd in So Far," in the collection *The War Against Cliché*, 11-17, esp. 15: "[...] literature [...] has been following exactly the same graph line for two thousand years [...]. If art has an arrow, then that is the way it points: straight downwards, from demigod to demirep." See also Amis's 1984 novel *Money*: "[...] we 're pretty much agreed that the twentieth century is an ironic age – downward looking. Even realism, rockbottom realism, is considered a bit grand for the twentieth century" (248).

> and merchants and vicars and doctors and lawyers. Then social realism: you. Then irony: me. Then maniacs and murderers, tramps, mobs, rabble, flotsam, vermin.' [...] 'And what would account for it?' He sighed. 'The history of astronomy. The history of astronomy is the history of increasing humiliation. First the geocentric universe, then the heliocentric universe. Then the eccentric universe – the one we're living in. Every century we get smaller. Kant figured it all out, sitting in his armchair. What's the phrase? The principle of terrestrial mediocrity.' .' . . Big book.' 'Big book.' And he added, 'Small world. Big universe.' (Amis 1995, 129)

With Lionel Asbo, Martin Amis adds a criminal multimillionaire or, a little more to the point, a multimillionaire criminal to this illustrious collection of literary protagonists referred to in the above quotation. The novel's hero (or rather anti-hero) is a 21-year-old violent and blatant debt collector who changes his surname from a rather innocuous "Pepperdine" to the acronym of Anti-Social-Behaviour-Order, to which he has been frequently exposed from the age of three onwards. While serving yet another term in prison, he wins 134 million Pounds in a lottery, without this undeserved fortune ever affecting his outlook on life, other than making him feel slightly less real.[4] Lionel Asbo has a nephew whom he brings up alone after the death of his sister, and this boy, (at the beginning of the novel) fifteen-year-old soft-footed and gentle Desmond, is to Lionel what Oliver Twist is to Bill Sykes: incorruptible, naïve, submissive to the point of his own detriment, yet desperately striving for education, scholarly knowledge, and love. Conversely, Lionel is premature (he has his first sexual encounter at the tender age of nine), vulgar and addicted to the consumption of pornography, to name but a few of their differences which will be further explored below. While the narrative unfolds its comedy largely upon the utter discrepancy between this odd couple,[5] it depicts the world they live in as humiliating and humbling indeed. In the fictive London borough of Diston, "nothing – and no one – was over sixty years old" (*LA* 9), life expectancy and fertility rates seem to compete with each other for the higher figure, and a cultural ambience pervades that Amis amply captures in Ovid's poetry:

> Each thing hostile
> To every other thing: at every point
> Hot fought cold, moist dry, soft hard, and the weightless
> Resisted weight. (19) [6]

Notwithstanding Ovid's tale envisioning a world *before* the introduction of some kind of order, Amis takes this poetic vision of the state of the world as an adequate description of the contemporary state of England, thus reframing the original by fitting it to his conception of an ending, not – as Ovid does – as a beginning. The hostility and inconsistencies of humankind depicted here can be added onto the deeper, more lasting and universal humiliations as Richard Tull indicated in *The*

---

4 His sense of irreality is described as a feeling of numbness: "See, that's what happens when you win a hundred-odd million quid. You go numb. Not happy. Not sad. *Numb...*" (*LA*, 109).

5 Finney devotes a section to doubling as a major thematic concern of Amis's (2008, 100-105).

6 The lines are taken from Ted Hughes's 1997 translation of Ovid's *Metamorphoses* (the first section is titled "Creation; Four Ages, Lycaon; Flood," n.p.). Interestingly, and perhaps quite revealingly, Amis only quotes the four lines given above. The lines that follow refer to the creation of harmony, a position Amis would clearly reject. They read: "God, or some such artist as resourceful, / Began to sort it out. / Land here, sky there, / And sea there. Up there, the heavenly stratosphere. / Down here, the cloudy, the windy. / He gave to each its place, / Independent, gazing about freshly. / Also resonating – / Each one a harmonic of the others, / Just like the strings / That would resound, one day in the dome of the tortoise."

Information. Amis then seems to indulge in these manifold degradations;[7] and with *Lionel Asbo* it now seems that when the writer has finished writing up his dark profile of humankind's – or at least Britain's – moral decrepitude, his saga of an exhausted culture, his analysis of anxiety and fury about its alleged geo-historical decline, he exits.[8]

On a more cheerful note, and given the novel's concern with sex and crime, power and money, Amis seems to respond to some 'absolute' reader interests. Writing in the first decade of the 21st century, he is not alone in picking the theme of an ordinary man coming to sudden and unearned riches and watching him spend it. Nicholas Shakespeare's *Inheritance* (2010), Allan Hollinghurst's Booker winner *The Line of Beauty* (2004), or Tom McCarthy's *Remainder* (2006) come to mind, which likewise deal with the topic of unforeseen monetary fortunes. In Shakespeare's novel, the protagonist undeservedly inherits 17 million Pounds, Hollinghurst's gains an equally substantial sum and complementary power after his friend puts him in his will and dies, and McCarthy's receives a huge compensation from an insurance company for something falling out of the sky onto his head. Both Shakespeare and Hollinghurst follow conventional reader expectations in having their protagonists act sensibly and responsibly, even charitably, at some point in the story.[9] At the end of these novels, their protagonists appear to be deserving of their wealth, and the storyworld is put back into balance. Not so in Amis's novel. *Lionel Asbo*, like other works in Amis's oeuvre, is typically distinct from these, in a way which McGrath tried to capture succinctly long before *Lionel Asbo* was written: "This recurrent triumph of the primitive and mediocre over the civilized serves to point up the idea that qualities like integrity, breeding, decency, sophistication and confidence are redundant in the face of emergent social barbarism" (McGrath 1998, 6).

Those readers looking for punishment to follow crime, for the villain's fall after his rise, for poetic justice or some kind of closure, are kept waiting in vain until the last page: Asbo is never exposed as a murderer (or at least for complicity in murder), there is no definite answer to the nagging question "who let the dogs in?" Desmond does not call his uncle to account for the ultimate cause of anxiety in the novel, namely the potential mauling of his baby daughter by the pitbulls, and whether Lionel will serve yet another prison term for his many sexual abuses remains an open question. The ending of the novel shows Desmond in a rather psychotic, traumatized condition. At his and Lionel's farewell meeting, he manages to communicate to Lionel how he means to protect himself and his family from his uncle's potential future acts of vengeance, but he also tearfully hugs him before finally taking his leave. The reunification scene between Desmond and his family strikes the reader as very shallow and does not seem proportionate to accommodate the trauma Desmond has experienced and now has to hide from his wife. Thus the story ends without closure, against the grain of what the reader might wish for (Amis experts are of course exempt from

7 On the effects of this paradigmatic view on the downward spiralling history of humankind, as autopoetically reflected in contemporary novels, see Kläger (2009) and, more comprehensively, his major study (2013).

8 An allusion to Amis's relocation to New York in 2012. My argument is in direct contrast to Duggan's interpretation of Amis's position as writer in view of his debased country: "It is at the end of this process of humiliation that the contemporary writer enters the scene" (2013, 104). Although I find this argument convincing in respect to *The Information*, it does not hold, in my view, with regard to *Lionel Asbo*, particularly not after Amis's leaving England after the publication of that novel.

9 McCarthy's protagonist must be excluded here, as he seems to have gone quite mad in the course of the story.

this).[10] However, we do not have to wait until the end to be disappointed in our expectations, the novel's overall make-up is full of such mismatches, oppositions and incongruences. Before I continue to describe these as characteristic features of Amis's peculiar kind of humour, I shall further elaborate on a context that is also referenced by aspects of 'tellability,' namely the novel's response to 'absolute' reader interests. These, I believe, are not nearly as much disappointed as is the reader's generic expectation of, say, a happy ending, or a final release of his tension.

The concept of tellability provides us with some insight into the novel's self-referential quality of refracting its plot in a number of intricate allusions to the yellow press and gratuitous local newspapers. In this context, Amis again plays with the conventions of genre: just as much of the novel's story is tabloid material, the tabloids also become part of its mode of presentation, as the Interview section (*LA* 144-52) serves to demonstrate. *Lionel Asbo* both begins and ends with establishing and upholding its links with the tabloids: Desmond's writing up a letter to an agony aunt on the first page (indeed, the novel's beginning *is* a letter to an agony aunt, the consequences of which are further explored below), while at the end, the bare facts of Desmond's affair with his grandmother and the killing of Rory Nightingale are documented in sealed envelopes and deposited in a safe at the *Mirror* and in the editor's desk at the *Diston Gazette*, to be published in case Lionel dares to attempt another act of vengeance on Desmond and his family. *Lionel Asbo* indeed offers a highly tellable plot, one that we are likely to find in papers like the ones mentioned in the book (*The Morning Lark, The Daily Mirror, The Diston Gazette, The Sun*). There is a fifteen-year-old boy confessing an affair with his own grandmother, an (oedipal?) uncle threatening to kill anybody who dares to sleep with his mother, another boy murdered for sleeping with a woman much older than himself, a common criminal winning millions in the lottery, and finally, the horror story of the (potential) mauling of a baby by two pitbull dogs. The female characters are exclusively cast in supporting roles and not fully developed, as we never read about what goes on in their minds; Granny Grace becomes frail and dies, Dawn is a good daughter (even to her fascist father), loving wife and caring mother, Lionel's playmate "Threnody" acts the part of the glamour girl and celebrity puss, while Cynthia and Gina are portrayed as sex symbols. These bare ingredients of the story make it rather 'tellable,' inherently worth telling, independent of their textualization:

> [...] the dependency of tellability on cultural factors is illustrated by a French recipe for bestsellers that recommends the following ingredients: religion, sex, aristocracy, and mystery. According to this formula – which of course should be taken tongue in cheek –, the ultimate in tellability is achieved in the story: "My God, said the Duchess, I am pregnant. Who done it?" In a list of themes of "absolute interest," the Artificial Intelligence researcher Roger Schank mentions, alongside themes that capture universal hu-

10 Kläger (2009) also discusses the importance of the reader's contribution to the communicative success in Amis's oeuvre: "The author's choice against traditional genres (and its implicit rejection of much of the canon) thus confronts recipients with an assault on their experience and 'reality' on several levels: by rejecting a form that is perceived as 'natural,' both the perception itself and concept of 'nature' are questioned. This endows the anti-generic text with a profound sense of scepticism and doubt, or reinforces it where it is already present in the text" (79).

> man preoccupations (death, danger, sex), narrative topics more typical of Western capitalist societies, such as power or large amounts of money. (Ryan 2008, 590)[11]

Sex, high life, trespasses, crimes – these are themselves not necessarily funny, but their representation through vicious, satiric, ironic, and comic language is. The reader, appreciating these distancing modes of relation, becomes an active participant in the communicative set-up of the novel and in his presumed education that allows him to recognize the set formula of universal topics or human preoccupations from a distance or a somewhat higher point of view. While the 'ingredients' of sex and crime may usually respond to some undeveloped or even voyeuristic public taste, the novel's discourse propels them onto a higher plane, to the pleasant effect that the educated reader seems to get the best of both worlds. Seen in this light, Amis's novel is part crime, part rags-to-riches story of the kind fed daily to the tabloids, albeit presented in the narrator's intellectualized, arrogant, ironic, and satirically – comically – distanced mode. In *Lionel Asbo*, Amis creates a tableau of trespasses on which to present to the reader a comic study in anxiety and humiliation: a proletarian comedy of menace.

2. Anti-Comedy

"The nastier a thing is, the funnier it gets," Amis wrote in his first novel *The Rachel Papers* (1973, 87). We may deduct from this that his idea of comedy, honed over many years, is a kind of anti-comedy: [12]

> What I'm interested in is heavy comedy, rather than light comedy. It's a wincing laughter, or a sort of funky laughter, rather than tee-hee-hee. Sort of a hung-over laughter, where it hurts (qtd. in Finney 2008, 132-33).

Once again extending Richard Tull's views in *The Information* to Amis's own, we may consider his belief that the purity of the genres is no longer to be had. To begin with, Amis adopts Frye's famous theory of the genres, which corresponds to the cycle of the seasons, and adapts this to his own ideas of "something gone wrong" with the genres: "They have all bled into one another. Decorum is no longer observed" (Amis 1995, 53). This "bleeding" into each other ties in with his principle of terrestrial mediocrity, and also, one could perhaps add, seems to reference the second law of thermodynamics, which predicts entropy – a measure of disorder – to take place in all natural processes, such as the cooling off of everything hot. In this context, one also

---

11 The notion of absolute interests has been associated with Labov's concept of tellability. Although originally applied to the oral storyteller, it can also serve in discussing those features of Amis's novel that deal with the kind of keyhole-voyeurism typical of the yellow press. Cf. Ryan (2008).

12 Florian Kläger, who traces the term of such "anti-comedy" back to Giordano Bruno, identifies four characteristics of the genre of anti-comedy and he applies them successfully to *The Information*: "(1) Where 'romantic' relationships may form, they do so between the wrong people or for the wrong reasons [...]. (2) If obstacles are (temporarily) surmounted, it is only to make ultimate failure all the more bitter [...]. (3) It is not society that is renewed by the 'comic' events, but the 'comic' characters are beaten into accepting the prevalent (and deplorable) social *status quo* [...]. (4) Where misconceptions about the identity/personality of any characters are resolved, it is only to their disadvantage [...]" (Kläger 2009, 76-77, see also Kläger and Gill 2013). However, the transgeneric application of these features to *Lionel Asbo* seems not very promising: (1) The romantic relationship in the novel is that between Desmond and Dawn, who make a successful, if shallow, couple; (2) The obstacle in the novel is Lionel himself, e.g. literally taking up most of the space of the flat; he does not, strictly speaking, hinder Desmond in his pursuit of knowledge and education (other than advising him against it). (3) The state of England is indeed deplorable, both at the beginning and at the end of the novel. In this sense, society hasn't changed at all. (4) The characters in the novel cannot be mistaken: they are what they are and remain the same.

recalls Tom Stoppard's play *Arcadia* (1993), in which the stirring of marmalade into yoghurt is theorized emphatically as a process that cannot be reversed. Amis himself reflects the (im)possibility of reversal in his 1991 novel *Time's Arrow*.[13] *Lionel Asbo* is no exception in presenting to the reader a mixed cocktail of anxiety, menace and humiliation together with comic action and occasional slapstick humour (such as Lionel's fight with a lobster); it is a mixture where cruelty and laughter are never far apart, one where cruelty seems to beget irony.[14]

Amis sees himself as a comic writer, and that puts him (among other relations, especially to Henry Fielding) in the tradition of Charles Dickens, whose novels are intricately related to Amis's. Initially, his intertextual indebtedness to Dickens may well be based on his creation of 'bad' characters. Amis seems to appreciate this preference for the 'bad' in the following comment:[15]

> All of Dickens' genius and energy goes into his bad characters, his vamps and fromps and villains and swine, and there's nothing left for his good characters, who are all faceless, and indeed body-less, automatons. (qtd. in Temple 2013)

It is quite obvious how much Amis enjoys creating 'bad' characters as well. Tracing a few of the major similarities between Amis and Dickens, I will use Northrop Frye's essay on Dickens, which is also used by Amis in one of his own reviews of a study of the Victorian author.[16] Two of Frye's ideas serve to supply a trajectory between Dickens and Amis: the idea of the theatrical plot, and the idea of playing off humour types against each other. According to Frye, Dickens used the plot structure of New Comedy for his novels, with its stock devices on both benevolent and sinister sides, and with its cast of humour types serving him to envision a marriage between the realistic and the romantic, or, in Frye's terms, to create "fairy tales in the low mimetic displacement" (2005, 287):

> The structure that Dickens uses for his novels is the New Comedy structure, which has come down to us from Plautus and Terence through Ben Jonson, an author we knew Dickens admired, and Molière. The main action is a collision of two societies which we may call for convenience the obstructing and the congenial society. The congenial society is usually centred on the love of hero and heroine, the obstructing society on the characters, often parental, who try to thwart this love. For most of the action the thwarting characters are in the ascendant, but towards the end a twist in the plot reverses the situation and the congenial society dominates the happy ending. (289)

Stock devices are a natural part of that type of comedy, among which the humours are not meant to be realistic:

---

13 Duggan, on the other hand, writing on *Time's Arrow*, reminds us that there are still purists among us: "The reviewers and critics who see the novel as a[n] obscene 'game,' a 'gimmick' or childish 'play,' are writing from a position that demands the rigorous separation of comic and serious artistic modes and that denies that anything serious or important can emerge from inversions or reversals" (2013, 114).

14 This blending of rather contrastive forces has also led to characterizing Amis's aesthetics as grotesque: "As Stallybrass and White argue, the formal distinction between each element in these oppositions of economy/excess, high/low and beauty/ugliness of necessity paves the way for the grotesque as a mixed form, and a hybrid and corrupt deformation of the privileged term. Amis's grotesque aesthetic, with its mixtures of comedy and pain, its humour and threat, its gleeful wallowing in the present and melancholic nostalgia, is profoundly mixed in this sense" (Duggan 2013, 108).

15 The substantial intertextual relations between Amis and Dickens are also noted by Finney (2008, 93-94).

16 Cf. Frye (2005, 287-308), and Amis (2001, 191-95).

> Most of the people who move across the pages of Dickens are neither realistic portraits, like the characters of Trollope, nor 'caricatures,' so far as that term implies only a slightly different approach to realistic portraiture. They are humours, like the characters in Ben Jonson, who formulated the principle that humours were the appropriate characters for a New Comedy plot. The humour is a character identified with a characteristic, like the miser, the hypochondriac, the braggart, the parasite, or the pedant. He is obsessed by whatever it is that makes him a humour, and the sense of our superiority to an obsessed person, someone bound to an invariable ritual habit, is, according to Bergson, one of the chief sources of laughter. (292)

The theatrical plot structure in a Dickens novel always has its roots in society, with the humours being "'good' if they are on the side of the congenial society, 'bad' or ridiculous if on the side of the obstructing one" (294). The family is the nucleus of society in his novels, and this is where Dickens's famous sentimentality finds a major outlet. Emphasis is not necessarily on the forming of a new society around the marriage of hero and heroine at the end of the novel, but on the maturing or enlightening of the hero. Reading *Lionel Asbo*, one is reminded of these elements that Frye describes in his essay – the theatrical plot structure with the two opposing forces of society, and the clash of humour types – and most clearly, we may now recognize the similarities between Amis's novel and *Oliver Twist*: Desmond, like Oliver, is an orphan, his mother is dead, his father quite unknown. For most of the novel, Desmond is in the hands of a violent criminal, just as soft-minded Oliver is taken on by the gang of criminals led by Fagin and Bill Sykes. And just as we can pair Oliver and Desmond, we can also pair Bill Sykes and Lionel Asbo. Apart from their threatening physiognomy, they share a criminal record, a lack of education, and a disturbed relationship to women (Sykes acting as pimp to Nelly, and Lionel forcing and/or paying Gina and many others to have sex with him). In both novels, these pseudo-parental figures belong to what Frye has termed the "obstructive society," a force that opposes the creation and continuation of a happy family life. The protagonists of both novels are also cut-out humour types: the good characters Desmond and Oliver, who amazingly resist corruption and remain utterly 'good,' even bland and rather faceless, and the 'bad' characters Bill and Lionel, who are mechanically cast outlaws in terms of their criminal trespassing of the rules of society (both being murderers) and therefore excluded from being members of that society. And both novels end, in a sense, happily: *Oliver Twist* celebrates the re-constitution of a nuclear and even extended family, and so does *Lionel Asbo*, if a little on the shallow, prattling side. However, unlike the deathly punishment of the villain Sykes in Dickens, Lionel only falls (terminally?) ill and perhaps will serve another (long?) prison term. Amis uses these ostentatious intertextual references to Dickens in order to constitute his idea of the comic mode: the clashes of the good and the bad are meant to create laughter – however, it is of a kind that sticks in one's throat, because Amis spices it with menace.[17] I do not attempt to limit Amis's sense of the comic to his referencing Dickens; rather, I take their structural implications as a starting point and will now take a closer look at the workings of *Lionel Asbo's* comic mode.

---

17 The theatrical reference is to Harold Pinter's plays that have been described as 'comedies of menace,' a homophonous play on the comedy of manners hinting at a certain climate of anxiety and unexplained, never substantiated fear among the characters on stage.

3. Incongruency

The collision of opposing elements, identified above as structural references to *Oliver Twist*, I will now use as a further stepping stone in my analysis of Amis's technique. Koestler's incongruency theory appears to be rather appropriate to start with in this context. Koestler published a major study of this topic in 1964 (*The Act of Creation*) and also contributed the seminal article on humour in the *Encyclopædia Britannica* where he argues that the source of humour is to be found mainly in extravagantly crafted constructions of incongruency. Applying this conception to narratives, we identify such incongruency at nearly every level, with a juxtaposition of opposing frames of reference found in language, characterization, and plot. According to Koestler, the registering of incongruent elements amounts to an act of bisociation. Pinker succinctly sums up an important passage of Koestler's argument:

> Humour, he [i.e. Koestler] said, begins with a train of thought in one frame of reference that bumps up against an anomaly: an event or statement that makes no sense in the context of what has come before. The anomaly can be resolved by shifting to a different frame of reference, one in which the event does make sense. And within *that* frame, someone's dignity has been downgraded. He calls the shift 'bisociation.' (Pinker 1997, 549) [18]

From the first page onwards, the reader of *Lionel Asbo* is confronted with such scenarios of incongruency, mismatches and twists. Perhaps with the exception of Lionel's pair of dogs, nothing seems to be a fitting match of equals in this novel, an observation that seems to confirm that *Lionel Asbo* is modelled on the familiar Amis topos of the (comic) double. At the outset of the novel, fifteen-year old Desmond is depicted in the conflicting roles of both child and lover; moreover, he is breaking the taboo of incest by admitting to conducting a sexual affair with his own grandmother. His guardian uncle is also introduced in a double role, namely that of protector and predator, prepared to kill anybody who sleeps with his mother. The novel's beginning thus presents to the reader a collection of (partly potential) trespassers that will soon exceed the inner family circle. However, the doubling of parts does not necessarily engender either progression or character development; on the contrary, Asbo remains quite immune to any kind of development to the very last page, his sudden wealth not affecting his behaviour in the least. Lionel's doubling of inherently conflicting roles as *Ersatz* father to his nephew, but also as his potential murderer on the one hand, and Amis's casting of Desmond as both child and incestuous lover on the other seems to lock both protagonists with their opposing roles to an initial, four-folded form of stasis, which generates a lot of tension which is not easily released. Yet it has to be overcome or bypassed in order for its energy to be channelled into a catalyst function to the plot. In Koestler's terms, this presents a pattern that can only be resolved by an act of "bisociation" on the part of the reader: The anomaly of their situation is of course immediately registered by the reader, and it makes sense *because* of its exponentiated unreality (not in spite of it), *because* it is fictional: That is the reason we may laugh *at* these characters who are so tightly locked to each other in their bizarre or grotesque relationship.[19]

18 Pinker's, like a number of other theories of humour and laughter, begins with what happens when we laugh, what facial muscles are affected. I am rather interested in what stimulus is needed to produce these effects.

19 Incidentally, I find Desmond's staying in the flat throughout the story is poorly motivated: why does he not simply move out to a place of his own, at least after his marriage?

Discrepancies and finely calculated mismatches in the novel form the basis of its comic mode, and a closer look at the communicative structure of the first chapter presents to us further instances of incongruency leading to bisociation. It begins with Desmond writing a letter to the agony aunt "Jennaveieve" of the *Morning Lark*, the district's local newspaper. It is the deviant spelling of her name and the numerous errors of a similar kind that ensue, that must first alert the reader to a confession of (the first of many) breaches of the law. Although there doesn't seem to be anything intrinsically funny about this, the reader tends to smirk reading this letter, and this is because we register the discrepancies between referent, phrasing and wrong spelling. The fifteen-year-old's lexicon charts phrases like "a refreshing change from the teen agers I know" insinuating that the boasting boy's sexual experience is not only premature but considerable, and foreign words such as "sophistication"[20] recall another funny discrepancy between phrasing and referent: Desmond reveals himself to be rather unsophisticated (otherwise he would not write this letter in such a style), yet he is prepared to acknowledge it in his lover. As the narrator soon informs us, Desmond's aspiration to higher forms of learning are (at that particular moment) confined to an interest in calligraphy: he only goes for decoration instead of training his mind. A boy from the fictive London borough of Diston aspiring to education may already be a bit of an abnormality, his sexual experience we may grant him, but his preference for his own allegedly sophisticated grandmother rather than for girls of his own age is a gross comic exaggeration (particularly, as there does not seem to be anything really sophisticated about Granny Grace, perhaps apart from her solving *The Daily Telegraph's* heady crossword puzzles). However, Desmond feels that something must be wrong (the reason for writing this letter), and indeed, he is all mixed up: he mistakes his grandmother for a lover, he mistakes sophistication for knowledge and education, calligraphy for good writing skills, he mistakes the *Morning Lark* for a national newspaper and a letter to an agony aunt for a confession (or, without its religious context, a session with a psychiatrist). These examples show that it is the juxtaposition of conflicting frames of reference that are responsible here for the sense of the comic.

As Desmond confides his secret to paper, Amis takes the opportunity to communicate another mismatch to the reader. Secrecy is always levelled against its potential revelation, either intended by publication in the agony aunt column or unintended by Lionel's discovery of it. This threat of revelation/publication is also referred to again at the end of the novel, albeit reversed, where it is ear-marked as a form of protection, and where it is Lionel who has to fear the revelation of "secrets."

With Desmond writing about his affair and unintentionally revealing much more than just the ways and manners of his sexual encounters with his grandmother, accompanied by the supreme voice of the narrator, the reader also registers the allusion to the double structure of epistolary fiction with its twisted grip on time: the time a letter is telling about (here the ongoing affair) plus the present time of the actual writing of the letter both are referenced. Apart from introducing Lionel's part, the allusion to two different time frames is used to slip in Lionel's entry in between these, and Amis thus creates a very impressive first appearance of the violent criminal. Desmond admits to being exceptionally frightened of his guardian uncle whose violence is indeed to be feared, were he to find out about the affair, and the discrepancy between nephew and uncle could not be greater than a comparison of their interests reveals.

20 This can of course also be read as an example of free indirect discourse, with the idiom belonging to the narrator himself and ironically putting it into Desmond's head.

For Desmond, it is the mastering of the apostrophe, for Lionel, it is an act of vengeance:

> *Her son, Lionel, is my uncle, and hes' like a father to me when he's not in prison. See hes an extremely violent criminal and if he finds out I'm giving his Mum one, hell fucking kill me. Literally!*
> It might be argued that this was a grave underestimation of Lionel's views on trespass and reprisal … The immediate goal, for Des, was to master the apostrophe. After that, the arcana of the colon and the semicolon, the hyphen, the dash, the slash.
> *On the plus-side, the age-gap is not that big. See Granny Grace was an early starter, and fell pregnant when she was 12, just like my M*
> He heard the thick clunks of the locks, he looked with horror at his watch, he tried to stand upright on deadened legs – and suddenly Lionel was there. (*LA*, 5)

Desmond's written confessional is thus interrupted by Lionel Asbo, who appears unexpectedly in the door frame. The context for the comic ingredients here, as elsewhere, is the meticulous juxtaposition of incongruent elements – the breaking of rules and the threat of violence – with its ensuing bisociation as exaggerated artificial discrepancy that leads to a relief of the tension in comedy. With this complex framework Amis offers us a slippery comic panorama, as the "relief" section to this dangerous poise on the verge of discovery demonstrates:

> '…What you doing there with that *pen*? What's that you writing? Guiss it.'
> Des thought fast. 'Uh, it's about poetry, Uncle Li.'
> '*Poetry*?' said Lionel and started back.
> 'Yeah. Poem called *The Faerie Queene*.'
> 'The *what*? …I despair of you sometimes. Des. Why aren't you out smashing windows?' (6)

Of course, Lionel hears an allusion to homosexuality in the poem's title ("fairy" as well as "queen" being colloquial terms for homosexuals). Those readers familiar with the colloquial register as well as with Spenser's epic might think his reaction very funny. Of course the same educated reader also registers Lionel's underdeveloped grammar as comic: "Guiss it" is Lionel's shortened expression for "Give us it."

There are many more instances of such comically juxtaposed discrepancies among the two main characters. Apart from those already discussed, one could mention the topic of excessiveness, both in a material and mental sense. The overstepping of limits, either in Lionel's attitude to food and drink or the spilling of money, is mirrored by the narrative's excessive repetitions of depicting Lionel's misbehaviour. However, the notion of excessiveness also meets some limitation, if we apply this opposition to the use of space in the claustrophobic living conditions in the couple's flat: Lionel occupies the substantially bigger one of the two rooms without actually living there, while Desmond, his wife and baby daughter are crammed into the remaining space of the tiny second bedroom. Lionel's excess is perhaps also to be measured against his confinement to prison, which he seems to welcome from time to time ("*Prison's not too bad*, he often said. *You know where you are in prison*" [60]), perhaps as easing the burden of his own excessive self.

As the plot picks up momentum, the differences of the two main characters are extended. On almost every level, they cannot be more apart, to the extent that one is the opposite of the other, and they do not even share the same skin colour. Desmond's love, romanticism and sexual commitment to a single partner is met with Lionel's excessive recourse to pornography and promiscuity which in itself raises (again) two different, perhaps psychologically related, sets of oppositions: his comprehensive denial of his mother's sexuality on the one hand, and his degrading use of the female body (Cynthia, Gina) on the other. Desmond's ideal of education is countered by Lionel's ideal of ignorance, and Desmond's culture is opposed to Lionel's material wealth.[21] Their physiognomy and physical appearance – Desmond is slim, soft, and good-looking and Lionel a square, ugly, mechanical oaf – is also in stark contrast. Desmond is limited where Lionel is unbound and "always one size bigger than expected" (6) until the very end, when this relation is reversed: Lionel is confined to his bed, while Desmond has freed himself from his uncle's revengeful grip on his life.

Another cause of the comic in the novel's discourse is its often hilarious verbal imagery, and, once again, we apply the terms of incongruency and bisociation that result in a brief relief of tension. One example might suffice to shed some light on how it is done, and it seems appropriate to quote the whole section in order to appreciate the build-up to its climax:

> Lionel dressed with slow care. He was going out to dinner. Table for one. Just him and his thoughts. Before he left he popped up to see Scott Ronson: they were going to have a little smoke on his balcony. That feeling again in the elevator. He stepped out and paused. Right floor – but what was the number? Lionel barged around for a bit. Ah, there he was. Scott had just sawn off the top half of the door to his suite, and he was standing there waiting like a horse in a stable. (117)

The two discrepant frames of reference alluded to here are obviously a) the context of an expensive, luxurious five-star hotel and b) the context of a stable yard for animals. They are not simply part of a mixed imagery, they are physically united by the guest having sawn off half of his door, thus making it indeed look like a stable door, an image which is then topped by himself standing there on the lookout for Lionel – exactly, one might think, like a horse looking out for its groom. The reader's act of bisociation then results in a funny realization of this picture puzzle, in which the human and the horse are competingly played off against each other in the mind of the reader.

Apart from these discrepancies and their ensuing bisociations, the aspects of aggression and a subsequent narrative of degradation remain to be explored. As the reader seems to be an essential accomplice to substantiate these comic or semi-comic effects, I will explore these last two points in the remainder of this essay.

4. A Narrative of Degradation

Most theories of humour identify some act of aggression or mock aggression in connection with laughter.[22] In his *Britannica* article Koestler writes:

> There is a bewildering variety of moods involved in different forms of humour, including mixed or contradictory feelings; but whatever the mixture, it must contain a basic ingredient that is indispensable: an impulse, however faint, of aggression or apprehension. It may appear in the guise of malice, contempt, the veiled cruelty of condescension, or merely an absence of sympathy with the victim of the joke [...] (2015).

---

21 Duggan also points this out in his analysis of *Money*: "For Amis, the escape route from money can be seen as culture, as John Self is culturally impoverished because he has not, and cannot, read, and he ends up financially impoverished because he has not read the contracts he has been signing" (2013, 98).

22 Freud's theory of laughter deserves at least to be mentioned. However, he analyzes humour in connection with the human sexual drive and aggression as a release valve, which does not seem to offer much insight here.

The sudden cessation of some imaginary danger can also cause laughter to occur. How can such a connection between danger and fun be accounted for in *Lionel Asbo*? The novel features an intricate pattern of anxiety and threats, from the looming potential revelation of Desmond's secret to the threatening physiognomy and violent behaviour of its anti-hero to its ending with the potential killing of baby Cilla. As we have seen, Amis's sense of the comic is of the rather dark variety, and accordingly, the avoidance of these two imagined catastrophes with their deathly consequences does not on the whole result in a relief of tension. The novel's comic disposition is brought to a rather abrupt end with only partly relieving its tension. We see Desmond still traumatized by fear after his final visit to his uncle: "Des assumed that this feeling would one day subside, this riven feeling, with its equal parts of panic and rapture. Not soon, though" (*LA*, 273).

The tragedy has been avoided and precautions have been taken for it never to happen, and yet a sense of exhaustion and trauma remains. The very last section of the book, which renders the reunification of Desmond's family in the Diston flat ("We're home!" [274]), for the last time opposes ignorance and knowledge: Dawn is unaware of what might have happened 'if.' Desmond's new secret is too frightening to be revealed, and he has to carry the burden of that knowledge alone.

Surprisingly, the notion of anxiety also applies to Martin Amis himself, as he testifies in an interview:

> *Lionel Asbo* took Amis a year to write and a year to revise. "I've never spent that long revising before," he says. "A writer friend asked me, 'What did you put in that wasn't there in the first draft?' My answer was 'anxiety,' there wasn't enough anxiety in it. Books come out of a mixture of ambition and anxiety, and the anxiety has to match the ambition, that's just how it works.' (Lane 2012, 40)

Amis argues for a matching of anxiety and ambition regarding the organisation of his material and anxiety thus even seems to be disguised as ambition. When he mentions it as a factor in composing his novel, it characteristically seems to refer to his idiosyncratic humour, which he mixes, as has been shown in this essay, with anxiety, fear, and threats. In this sense, the writer's anxiety perhaps mirrors that of the reader, who is afraid of having to read a story in which the killing of a baby by two pitbulls is envisaged. This descent in dignity, which the novel shows us, is a trigger for humour, though. As far as this applies to the subtitle of the novel, which references a culture of violence, crime, greed, and lust, and presents it to the reader in funny situations, funny characters and in funny language that mimicks and mocks Lionel's vulgar mispronunciations,[23] it is true. Debased as it is, the fictive world of Diston offers to the reader no comic catharsis. And thus, although one cannot of course speak of a comic *turn* in the works of Martin Amis, as he has always considered himself to be a comic writer, one might well speak of a further – and perhaps even a final – turn of the comic screw in *Lionel Asbo: State of England.*

Works Cited

Amis, Martin. *The Rachel Papers*. New York: Vintage, 1973.

—. *Money: A Suicide Note*. London and New York: Penguin, 1984.

23 The technique of humorous linguistic features is described by Verrier (2003), where he discusses epiphora, stichomythia, mechanical repetition and verbal parrying, deviant spelling, epizeuxis, epanalepsis, cataphoric and anaphoric use, substandard pronunciation, and the use of hyperbole (among others).

—. *Time's Arrow, or, The Nature of the Offence*. New York: Vintage, 1991.
—. *The Information*. New York: Vintage, 1995.
—. *Heavy Water and Other Stories*. New York: Vintage 1998.
—. "The Darker Dickens: A Review of John Carey's *The Violent Effigy: A Study of Dickens' Imagination*." *The War against Cliché*. New York: Vintage, 2001. 191-95.
—. *The War Against Cliché: Essays and Reviews 1971-2000*. New York: First Vintage International Edition, 2002.
—. *Lionel Asbo*. London: Jonathan Cape, 2012.
—. *The Zone of Interest*. London: Jonathan Cape, 2014.
Duggan, Robert. *The Grotesque in Contemporary British Fiction*. Manchester: Manchester University Press, 2013.
Finney, Brian. *Martin Amis*. New York: Routledge, 2008.
Frye, Northrop. "Dickens and the Comedy of Humours." *Northrop Frye's Writings on the Eighteenth and Nineteenth Centuries*. Ed. Imre Salusinszky. Toronto: University of Toronto Press, 2005. 287-308.
Hughes, Ted. *Tales from Ovid*. London: Faber & Faber, 1997.
Kläger, Florian. "Negative Hilarity: Anti-Comedy in *The Information* and *Troilus and Cressida*." *'My age is as a lusty winter:' Essays in Honour of Peter Erlebach and Thomas Michael Stein*. Ed. Bernhard Reitz. Trier: WVT, 2009. 71-84.
—. *Reading into the Stars: Metaphorized Cosmology and the Autopoetics of the Novel*. forthcoming.
— and Patrick Alasdair Gill. "'You didn't set me up. Did you?' Genre, Authorship and Absence in Martin Amis' *London Fields* and *Night Train*." *Trespassing. An Online Journal of Trespassing Art, Science, and Philosophy* 2 (2013): 36-51.
Koestler, Arthur. *The Act of Creation*. New York: Dell, 1964.
—. "Humour." *Encyclopædia Britannica online*. 2015. Web. 3 March 2015.
Lane, Johanna. "Needed: Anxienty." *Publishers Weekly* 259.27 (2012): 40.
McGrath, Patrick. "Her Long Goodbye." The *New York Times*. 1 February 1998. Web. 14 February 2015.
Pinker, Steven. *How the Mind Works*. New York: W.W. Norton, 1997.
Ryan, Marie Laure. "Tellability." *Routledge Encyclopedia of Narrative Theory*. Eds. David Herman, Manfred Jahn, and Marie Laure Ryan. London: Routledge, 2008. 589-91.
Tait, Theo. Review of *Lionel Asbo*. *The Guardian*. 8 June 2012. Web. 4 January 2015.
Temple, Emily. "Martin Amis on Reading, Writing, and What It's Like Inside Nabokov's House." *flavorwire.com*. 24 January 2013. Web. 4 September 2013.
Verrier, Luc. "Sentimental Comedy in Martin Amis's 'State of England' and 'The Coincidence of the Arts.'" *Miescelánea: A Journal of English and American Studies* 28 (2003): 97-108.

BARBARA PUSCHMANN-NALENZ

"Et in Arcadia ille – this one is/was also in Arcadia:" Human Life and Death as Comedy for the Immortals in John Banville's *The Infinities*

Hermes the messenger of the gods quotes this slightly altered Latin motto (Banville 2009, 143). The original phrase, based on a quotation from Virgil, reads "et in Arcadia ego" and became known as the title of a painting by Nicolas Poussin (1637/38) entitled "The Arcadian Shepherds," in which the rustics mentioned in the title stumble across a tomb in a pastoral landscape. The iconography of a baroque *memento mori* had been followed even more graphically in an earlier picture by Giovanni Barbieri, which shows a skull discovered by two astonished shepherds. In its initial wording the quotation from Virgil also appears as a prefix in Goethe's autobiographical *Italienische Reise* (1813-17) as well as in Evelyn Waugh's country-house novel *Brideshead Revisited* (1945). The fictive first-person speaker of the Latin phrase is usually interpreted as Death himself ("even in Arcadia, there am I"), but the paintings' inscription may also refer to the man whose mortal remains in an idyllic countryside remind the spectator of his own inevitable fate ("I also was in Arcadia"). The intermediality and equivocacy of the motto are continued in *The Infinities*.[1]

The reviewer in *The Guardian* ignores the unique characteristics of this book, Banville's first literary novel after his prize-winning *The Sea*, when he maintains that "it serves as a kind of catalogue of his favourite themes and props" (Tayler 2009). Indeed, a manor and park in the heart of Ireland[2] emerge as the setting of this re-narrativization of death, which forces the reader to look in a new way at one of the writer's frequent topics which he believes he was already familiar with (cf. Hand 2002, 176). Here we are confronted with the expected passing away of the famous mathematician and philosopher of science Adam Godley Sr., who boasts of having revolutionized post-Newtonian physics: "[W]e had exposed the relativity hoax and showed up Planck's constant for what it really is. The air was thick with relativists and old-style quantum mechanics plummeting from high places in despair" (Banville 2009, 164). However, the modified Latin phrase from the novel's motto links the text ambiguously to Poussin's and Barbieri's paintings.[3] The grotesque figure, whose appearance in the sophisticated yet neglected setting of Arden House Hermes comments on with "Et in Arcadia ille," is revealed as Pan, the Greek god of pastoral nature, fright and bucolic turmoil. He arrives on the scene of the family gathering at the deathbed of the Godley *pater familias* in the guise of an unexpected and ungainly visitor by the name of Benny Grace, allegedly an old friend of Adam's. The narrative

1 John Kenny focuses on Banville's expertise shown in pictorial descriptions (2009, 147-51). On *ekphrasis* in Banville's work see also Müller (2004) and McMinn (2002). The parodistic function of a pictorial representation is exemplified in Banville (2009, 87).

2 Ireland as the geographical location of Arden is only alluded to (Banville 2009, 100). Critics consider the author a cosmopolitan (post)modernist (cf. Berensmeyer 2000, 247); specifically Irish themes are not characteristic of his work after 1980.

3 "There is, in the world of Banville's fiction, no essential difference between the scientist and the artist. They all arrive at their discoveries by intuition," Imhof states early in the writer's career (1989, 237-38).

Anglistik: International Journal of English Studies 27.1 (March 2016): 99-111.

imitates the paintings: Pan appears in Arcadia, which seems natural, but so does Death. In the end Hermes and Thanatos compete for supremacy (209).

Ostensibly, the narrative obeys the rules of the unity of place and time, whereas the action is duplicated – like two of the characters. The fact that the genius Adam Godley is dying in the "Sky Room," his former study, after he has suffered a stroke which leaves him speechless, paralyzed and presumably unconscious, has drawn the family to Arden House. His second wife Ursula, his son Adam Jr. with daughter-in-law Helen, his daughter Petra and her suitor, two servants, the ominous male friend and Rex the dog assemble around his death-bed; yet another presence and activity contrary in mood and effect to the calamity of the occasion accompanies this day from dawn – delayed for an hour at heavenly bidding – to dusk. Helen, an actress and the beautiful wife of Adam Jr., has attracted the attention of Zeus, the Godfather of Greek mythology and father of Hermes. The latter's presence is required on this occasion, since one of his tasks, according to himself, is to serve as "usher of the freed souls of men to Pluto's netherworld" (15). Adam Sr., when the moment comes for his departure (18), will also be conducted by him. All this the god narrates as a "voice speaking out of the void" (14), even though "cast in the language of humankind, necessarily" (16). Golden-haired Helen, who in outward appearance can compete with her legendary namesake, is designed to play the part of Alcmene in a new production of Heinrich von Kleist's comedy *Amphitryon*.[4] Like Alcmene, Helen Godley becomes for one hour the passionate lover of the godhead himself who, as in the Greek myth, assumes the shape of and marvelously performs the role of her husband, making her pregnant. Hermes colloquially narrates the myth of Zeus and Alcmene who mistook the father of the gods for her husband Amphitryon and became mother of twins, "Iphicles, who was Amphitryon's son and therefore not much heard of again, and Heracles, whom my Dad was pleased to call his own" (211).[5] Though this happened aeons ago, Zeus wants to repeat his experience with the beautiful woman who merely plays Alcmene. At daybreak he leaves Helen Godley in a condition of dreamy euphoria, but during the fateful day he jealously accompanies "his girl" (e.g. 187, 298), not without having arranged for her husband's gift, a ring carved with the initial "A" indicative of further ambiguities (A for Adam, Amphitryon, Alcmene, or is it a Z? [294]). This joyful entanglement is not the only connection tied by divine intrigues: Hermes spends his time appearing as Duffy the cowman to Ivy Blount, offspring of a country squire and housekeeper-confidante to the Godleys, whom he leaves in such a state that she (successfully) proposes marriage to the cowman after inviting him to lunch at the family table (238-39; 266). Later in the afternoon Roddy Wagstaff, who acts as Petra's friend and has punctually presented himself for old Adam's demise, foolishly – or possessed by a god? – molests Helen and has to leave immediately after a thunderbolt announces the jealous godhead's anger at this trespassing (256-58). Petra, the nineteen-year-old, obviously autistic girl who has thus been cheated, she believes, resumes her scarifying, thereby calming herself in a ritualistic and frightening scene (270-78).[6] The saddening and delightful events, mourning and merriment, are thus presented as occurring side by side in one day and one place.

4 This novel repeats Banville the dramatist's engagement with Kleist (1994, 2000 and 2005). In his novel *Eclipse* (2000) he assigns to the actor Alex Vander the role of Amphitryon/Jupiter in the drama which stages a game about identities (cf. Radley 2010, 16).

5 The strategies Banville uses in his tetralogy, especially in *Athena*, to include myths as well as pictorial description are thoroughly discussed in Wilhelmy's study (2004, 338-67).

6 For the character of Petra as representation of a 'posthuman child' see Földvary (2014, esp. 213-14).

The Cast

The company performing the action of this day belongs to two different spheres. The fact that humorous elements spread far into language is exposed not only by the telling names, but equally by meta-narrative epistemological and phenomenological considerations which only a member of the Olympian family can express, because they relativize and dismiss every imaginative concept as anthropomorphous, inferior and as "your constructions," as Hermes condescendingly says. He goes on: "Were I to speak in my own voice, that is, the voice of a divinity, you would be baffled at the sound – in fact you would not be able to hear me at all, so rarefied is our heavenly speech, compared to your barely articulate grunting." Space and time are to the immortals "the infinite here" (16). This divine chronotope will at the moment of death be reflected for the mortals as "fixed for ever in a luminous, unending instant" (300) so that we must conclude that humans can finally somehow participate in the heavenly state of life everlasting.

Regardless of their difference in nature, the gods share feelings with men, assuming an attitude which is a mixture of condescension, benevolence, and envy of mortality. Besides the humorous, the satirical and the bucolic, the grotesque also permeates the plot, variously commented on as "absurdly" or "sadly comical" (e.g. 10) by the divine master narrator. The grotesque becomes evident in the depicted travesty of the great old man's illness (17; 298), moreover in the confusion of lovers and spouses, and even in Ursula's memory of pregnancy, birth and her alcohol abuse. Human suffering, occasionally also experienced by the gods in whom empathy is prevented by this distance from mankind, is scaled down by the messenger of the gods ("Debilitating business, being in love," 299; cf. 73). Despite Hermes' disdainful remarks divine grace eventually makes a conciliatory gift of bliss to everyone from the Olympians (299-300) who hold sway over human life and death 'from A to Z'. Guilt, such as old Adam's neglect of his son and his suicidal first wife Dorothy, is forgiven in the terminal gathering "in the failing evening of the self, solitary and at the same time together somehow here in this place" (300). The cast of this human tragicomedy or farcical tragedy[7] will continue to act in the unceasing drama on the stage set for them by 'fate', playing – if not exactly shepherds, since sheep have here been replaced by cows – but rustic happy farmers, as Hermes' forecast suggests: "Adam will delve and till as his original namesake did, while Helen will wear a bonnet and carry a pail, like Marie Antoinette at the Petit Hameau" (299), presenting a show, just like the unworldly queen. For there is no end to this mystery play of humankind, as Zeus in his last farewell signifies and Helen-Alcmene suggests in her monosyllabic inconclusive "Oh!" (300; cf. 257), which shows her overwhelmed by the god.[8]

The human actors in this play for the main internal focalizer are puppets on a string, with the gods playing a game for their renewed entertainment (15-17) and as evidence

7 The earliest known play dramatizing the myth of Amphitryon, Zeus and Alcmene was a tragedy by Sophocles which is lost; the Roman Plautus first used the term "tragicomedy" in connection with his *Amphitryon* (Radley 2010, 28, n. 5). In early modern theatre, Molière's comedy is the first dramatic adaptation of the material, Jean Giraudoux's not the last one.

8 Similarly, Kleist's Alcmene ends the play with her famously ambiguous "Ach!".

of their benign paternalistic sovereignty.[9] The constellation of characters duplicates the pattern of family relations on the levels of *homo sapiens* and the divinities: above all the triple father-son relationship (the two Adams as opposed to Hermes the son of Zeus, and Pan, son of Hermes [143]) conflates the divine and the human to a degree where – sharpened by Hermes' vernacular – one almost supplies simulacra of the other. Disrespectful comments from the heavenly narrator-son, often combined with truly Homeric laughter (e.g. 12; 50; 61; 79; 186; 258), make the divinities appear equally as funny, quarrelsome, frivolous beings that harbour all the petty faults of ungenerous humans; yet all this imaginary is revealed by Hermes as "only for convenience" (143) to make it somehow expressible "in the common tongue," even though it remains incomprehensible (144). In addition to the hierarchical (vertical) family structures, (horizontal) partner relationships form the main organizational principle. The characters' marriages and criss-crossing ephemeral love relationships enhance the burlesque note. Most of all Hermes' portrayal of the often unlovely outward appearance or unappealing demeanour of humans – above all his description of a Rabelais-inspired monstrous incarnation of the god Pan in a grotesque body (cf. Bachtin 1987, 358-62; 449-50), his bare feet resembling the telltale goatish hoofs – corroborates the distancing view of life and death as a spectacle.

The Stage

Arden House, which one critic refers to as a strange work of art with "a forbidding appearance" (Polvinen 2012, 99-100), including the adjacent estate, evokes Arcadia not without ambivalence: it could be an Edenic place temporarily out of focus, but then graciously restored by the gods to the confused human mindscape.[10] A flashback reveals that Ursula in her youth once had a glimpse of Paradise (Lost) as a signifier of fecundity: "an enclosed garden, with masses of flowers and flowering fruit trees, exotic shrubs, climbing vines, all crowding there together in the sun, profligate and gay" (Banville 2009, 244-45). Tellingly, Adam Sr. and Ursula, who remembers their first home only as "[d]eep winter on Haggard Head" (179), had moved to Arden situated "in the empty middle of the country" (41) from Adam's former home on the hill of Haggard Head which lay next to a deserted golf course high above an ocean that had the bleak look of "an oval sheet of pockmarked steel" (41). At Arden, despite the sad occasion of their present stay, their son "Adam feels like Adam on the first day in the Garden" (89) when he enjoys nature and thinks of his wife's breathtaking beauty – an imp(r)udent feeling of happiness, since it easily provokes the wrath of the gods. The Garden of Eden seems to be briefly restored – like the description of Ursula's paradise it contains strong sexual overtones – in a secluded wilderness on the estate near the holy well, where seduction surprises the rambling Helen accompanied by Ronny. This is revealed as a further touch of irony followed by the latter's expulsion

---

9 Kleist's essay "On the Marionette Theatre" ("Über das Marionettentheater"), in which he sets forth modes of performativity and acting in relation to authenticity and spontaneity, is mentioned by Radley as the subtext of *Shroud* (2010, 24-25). Kenny discusses how consciousness, affectation and natural grace relate according to Kleist and how Banville in his later works (up to 2007) addresses this tension in his characters (2009, 170-72).

10 Imhof refers to Freddie, the male protagonist of *Ghosts*, as eager to build "a negative Arcadia in which the great god Pan is dead" (1989, 235) – this also characterizes Arden at the novel's beginning. Later in *The Infinities*, the narrator Hermes raises the counterclaim: "They told Thamouz [in a story by Plutarch] the great god Pan is dead, but they were wrong" (Banville 2009, 143), because he appears in disguise.

from this spot (254-56).[11] Nature as pastoral landscape expresses life and fertility, of which Pan is the divine patron, and it has a conciliatory effect. The place near the stark roughness of the sea – whose sight is a constant reminder of the dangers harboured in the trespassing of ultimate boundaries –, which Adam Sr. viewed in his youth and imagines in his old age (see Zwierlein 2014, 164), has been left behind. Instead of the grey opaque sea, light and luminosity – as in Banville's 2012 novel *Ancient Light* – now become essential symbols in *The Infinities*. In connection with Helen as with Zeus the epitheton "golden" is repeatedly used to mediate the 'otherworldliness' reminiscent of the Golden Age; descriptions of various shades of light, brightness and the play of colours create an increasing radiance (e.g. Banville 2009, 90). Not only is this unusual in connection with the theme of death in Banville's works, but it also opposes those parts which grotesquely emphasize the corporeal and seem to be degrading. Despite satire and the vicissitudes of human life the country house surprisingly approaches a proverbial "archetype of community," as in the subtitle of Richard Gill's seminal study *The English Country House in Modern Fiction* (1967). Eventually Helen and Adam Jr. will also move to Arden together with 'their' child or children.

Narration, Centre of Consciousness and Thematic Focus

The novel's multiperspectivity with alternating focalizers demonstrates a clear hierarchy. First of all Hermes presents the intrusive, mostly omniscient, alternately hetero- and homodiegetic first-person narrator, by whom the interior and exterior of other characters are revealed; the narrating voice then shifts to Adam Sr., reflecting and remembering and around whom they all have gathered and whose bedside several of them separately visit. Apart from his wife these are his son and daughter, Rex the dog who can see the gods because of his animal nature, and the mysterious unhandsome Benny Grace. The latter's secret observation of the ailing wife Ursula – "a moment out of Watteau, it might be" (264) – and his presumed 'conversation' with old Adam at the end bestow a "Grace" that materializes as a kind of still life where all surround the *pater familias*. He lies gazing into the twilit garden at the French window in the downstairs music room, the servants "like figures in a pantomime" (298) standing apart, his son kneeling before him, his wife at his side, and the whole *tableau* accompanied by pipe tunes, unmistakably, from the old wireless (297-99).[12] This scene is visualized by the family doctor as focalizer: against the backdrop of his sober experienced perception, the aestheticized otherworldliness of Adam's departure stands out and leaves Dr Fortune speechless. The embellishing forms a stark contrast to the preceding artful portrayals of the unpleasantness of Adam's illness, of Benny's physique and gestures, or of the imaginings Petra harbours of men (119-20). As the narratee and with him the reader knows, Adam Sr. will be escorted by the invisible messenger of the gods after being "waited on hand and foot, as he would wish" (299) by his family, whom the physician is able to see.

---

11 In this 'bower-in-the-wilderness' scene memories of Biblical and Catholic beliefs and customs materialize. Related subjects are thematized in the thoughts on guilt and forgiveness as well as the idea of wo/man's release from suffering on earth (120). The neo-paganism paraded in the novel frequently reflects upon the content of Christianity.

12 Kenny underlines the inclusion of musical art in Banville's symbolism (2009, 116-17; 147). Although the visual dominates in this narrative the end of *The Infinities* becomes the epitome of 'harmony,' with a word-play on its literal-musical and its figurative-social meaning intended.

The importance of perception and its narrativization is referred to in the opening scene where young Adam, always in deep thought, is standing at the window at dawn – while his wife is visited by his double – looking out and remembering what his father often told him: "it is [...] a matter merely of perspective. The eye, he tells himself, the eye makes the horizon" (8-9). Similarly, the divine messenger Hermes states: "How all things hang together, when one has the perspective from which to view them" (240-41). Considering this provision the issue of the narrator's and focalizers' reliability is also placed on wobbly ground. Philosophical and scientific issues in *The Infinities* are dealt with in the shape of a mythology revival, with recurrence to the history of European theatre from ancient Greece to modern France and the baroque metaphor of the world as stage.[13] If criticism of Banville (e.g. McMinn 1999, 161) defined the writer's inclination to conceive a sequence of connected narratives as his unique characteristic, *The Infinities*' relationality links it to the poetical variations of one non-mimetic literary work. This novel forms a sequence with the writer's own narrativizations and dramatizations of the "Amphitryon" myth and, moreover, with its mutations by various authors over more than two thousand years. Here Banville favours a hypertextual design of a new, multiple kind.

Berensmeyer in the subtitle of his study defines authority, authorship and authenticity as essential concerns of Banville's earlier novels, which also permeate *The Infinities*. The immortals as the authors both of human fate and its narrativization claim the supreme authority amidst the confusion and struggle of life and death, and while acting-and-disguise emerges as a trope which is explicitly thematized and explored we find authenticity not least assessed by the informal commentaries of Hermes the divine messenger. His role as impertinent son adds a mildly satirical note to the grave events of the plot and to the different forms of comedy surfacing in their representation. In *The Infinities* men and women are poor players and the ancient gods the generous directors who at times meddle with the actors, usually for the better, as with the secret financial support in the case of Adam's career (Banville 2009, 283). Generally they like to consider themselves mere spectators who wish to be entertained in the world theatre: as Hermes initially confirms, "often we will gather at the ramparts of the clouds and gaze down upon them, our little ones" (3). The basic ironical refraction of the novel, which renders it a gentle joke on the reader and the brilliant scientist alike, results from the post-enlightenment prioritization given to the magical and from the post-religious gospel of the unbeliever: instead of revelation and salvation the immortals "offer [...] nothing, in fact, except stories" (91-92) whose authors they are. Representations of stories are ubiquitous in *The Infinities*, inevitably entailing uncertainty and questionable reliability. This ironic twist, part of a metafictional self-reflexivity in combination with the divine characters' playfulness, heightens the narrative's embeddedness in postmodern culture, one of whose hallmarks is the conflation of science and art, which Imhof notices in Banville too.[14] The exceptional narrative

---

13 Berensmeyer investigates intertextuality in Banville's work up to 1997 and emphasizes the wide range of allusions. "This resonance turns his novels into echo-chambers of a literary tradition which is reconstructed into a new text, a hypertext or palimpsest of modernity" (2000, 248). *The Infinities* achieves a peculiar homogeneity.

14 To my knowledge Ian McEwan was the first writer to publish his opinion on the convergence of post-Newtonian physics, which introduced a probabilistic world view and where "[o]bjectivity does not exist" (1983, 13), and the humanities, which explore "the ways we study ourselves and the world" (14). McEwan's oratorio maintains that with the new knowledge about this synthesis, men strive to dissolve determinism and a dualism also expressed in "The Two Cultures" paradigm, including imaginative literature.

situation characterized by dramatic irony, its immediacy established by the supernatural first person, exacerbates the narratee's plight as to whether s/he is being laughed at. The main narrator's position when he addresses the world of the humans to which the narratee – interlocutor of a god – obviously belongs, is analogous, I would argue, to the reader's "paradoxical cooperation of spectacle and engagement" (Polvinen 2012, 109), in which s/he is entangled by the postmodern metafictional discourse.[15] Hermes partakes in the world of his "story" and simultaneously engages in thematizing its discursive quality on the meta-level. Similarly to Adam Sr. he is present yet remote. Even though the human focalizers abstain from addressing the fictionality of what happens several characters occasionally doubt factuality: Helen hesitantly believes in her erotic experience as a dream, Ursula in the haunted house – and the narratee may wonder about the reality status of the narrative offered by Hermes. And yet, mimesis is assessed in the sense that art imitates art through the histrionic re-enactment of the myth in Kleist's play produced with Helen as Alcmene. Fiction substantiates: the *Amphitryon* drama becomes (fictional) reality, and (fictional) life imitates art, with the humans unknowingly performing the tragicomedy.

The narrative displays a macrostructure in three parts. The action of each of the first two focuses on the arrival of a person from outside the family: Roddy Wagstaff and Benny Grace respectively; the third part represents Old Adam's departure as arrival in the family centre. The microstructure of the narration shows Banville's complex style, which, the fiction claims, is accounted for by the divinity of the main first-person narrator whose omnipresence enables him to hurry from room to room and from the space of one consciousness to another. Omniscient as he almost always proves to be – Helen's pregnancy and Petra's interest in Roddy are rare exceptions –, he can pry into the minds of (male) humans, so that the effect of a third-person narration, often as free indirect discourse of various reflector figures with shifting focalization, develops.

In spite of this impression of constantly moving the majority of the novel is told by Hermes, who repeatedly intrudes into the narrative representation and the reading process as he does into the cosmic and the human order on the story level. He occasionally addresses the confusion about the narrator: in the middle of a passage which uses the first person the god interrupts his own speech as in the following example, because he pretends to become suddenly aware again of the difference in perception which distinguishes anthropomorphous concepts from the divine perspective:

> But why do I say *an hour ago*? I have – *he* has, *he* [Adam Sr.], I must stick to the third person – he has lost track of time, he who was once time's master and the keeper of its keys. Now the things that happen merge and flow through each other unresisted, a hopeless mishmash. (Banville 2009, 33)

The poetical scientist Adam Godley may rightly think of himself as having formerly approached supernatural knowledge – shared by the postmodern writer –, which Adam expresses allegorically: "I was the very one who would break time's arrow and discard the slackened bow" (215), namely by doubting and undermining

15 Merja Polvinen's article uses some details of *The Infinities* to illustrate her contribution on the role of mimesis in cognitive literary theory. Like Polvinen (2012, 109), Mark O'Connell (2011, 439) interprets Hermes' voice as that of Old Adam himself, while Tom Payne in *The Telegraph* believes the opposite (2009). I came to the conclusion that the retrospective authorial role of Adam Godley ('godlike') Sr. is eclipsed by the narration of the immortal god Hermes who plays with "the death of the author" trope. Dying Adam's wish to fully enter the community of Arden, which is fulfilled, diminishes his part as 'maker'.

the linear time concept together with the idea of the finite universe.[16] While for whole sections of the novel the focalization is taken over by Old Adam, initially told in the third person (62-71), it later switches to first-person narrative (155-73; 215-36). Adam's memories also explain this enigmatic relation with Benny Grace, his colleague, drinking partner and complementary alter ego, in discovering the infinities. Even in the mind of the dying man, who realizes "I am weakening" (224, 232), the postmodern comic prevails when, as his discoveries suggested, men manage to eliminate that "horizon" in the cosmological concept produced by human eyes: "The world has many worlds, as who should know better than I, each one stranger, more various and for all I know more farcical than the last. Anything is possible" (224). Not one of the world concepts has proved permanent. Thinking about the infinities Adam has to admit "My mind is tired" (233), and finally, in a merging of identities with Hermes, "My mind is going, going" (260).

In the divine narrator omniscience, which only the gods are granted since mortals would find knowing it all insupportable (37-38), unites with unreliability, already expressed in the titles Hermes holds. He, the god of travellers and traffickers, introduces himself as the son of Zeus and Maia, but also enumerates the by-names given to him by the mortals: "trickster, the patron of gamblers and all manner of mountebanks." Immediately he devises and addresses the narratee, a human: "I understand your scepticism" (15). With the familiarizing pronouns "we" and "them" in the opening line (3) a divide has been erected and a riddle proposed, which the reflection about the significance of dawn for humans and Olympians quickly solves: the early morning is merely a funny spectacle the immortals enjoy, while for men it seems a kind of minor resurrection which "we" – the gods – granted them as an efficient comfort for their brief lives (3). Mortality as a fundamental topic has thereby already been raised. That the supernatural narrator, however, alternates between keeping up that divide between the humans and himself, while prying into the minds of his charges and identifying with them, is exemplified when Hermes instructs the narratee about inanimate nature during Helen's romantic expedition into the wilderness: "For nature, my dear, has no purpose, except perhaps that of not being us, I mean you" (254).

Death, subjectivity and the "multiple versions of the self" (McMinn 1999, 162) have been denoted as guiding themes throughout Banville's work, as well as his narrativization of a bi-polar opposition of subject and object or science and art (D'hoker 2004, e.g. 217). *The Infinities* presents the end of compartmentalization and the foresight that "Nothing is separate" (71; cf. 100-101), by which the novel becomes a metanarrative and the god an author in the double sense. The immortal narrator designs fates and imagines the future. His narrative also resumes the tension inherent in duality and otherness, which he is able to mitigate as well as to uphold. Only a god seems capable of such a balancing act (cf. O'Connell 2011, 440), only a god's imagination can author the fictional universe: "And I it is who have contrived these things [...]" (Banville 2009, 29), Hermes claims. He intermittently reminds the narratee of his presence: "I, by the way, in case you have forgotten me, am perched in the middle of the back seat" (99), an invisible eye-witness to all that happens – and its creator. In *The Infinities* the persisting interpersonal and trans-subjective endeavours of Banville's narration,[17] by which a "breakdown between self and other" (O'Connell 2011, 442-43; cf. 440-41) can finally be achieved, paradoxically reaffirm the problem of a

16 On Banville's earlier fictional treatment of time see Val Nolan (2010, 36-38). Above all, his article deals with Banville's fictional representations of astronomy and physics.

17 See, e.g. McMinn (1999, 163); D'hoker (2004, 217-25).

solipsistic self. To have Hermes as first-person narrator tell the events from a perspective other than his own highlights otherness; the narrative almost imperceptibly drifts away from the subject whose view is assumed, as well as from the usurper of this perspective, into an impersonal third-person omniscient narration. Otherness, which old and young Adam constantly and sometimes painfully experience, can be pinnacled by the creation of the male voice expressing a theocentric view that vainly tries to eclipse the anthropomorphic, whose presence is, however, guaranteed through human language. I wish to argue that it over-simplifies the issue at stake to speak of "a closure of the gap of otherness" achieved in *The Infinities* (O'Connell 2011, 441). The narrative mocks a "contraction of the spaces between individual positions" (441), even if it may lead to an occasional confusion of "we" or "I" and "you," thus equally subverting a sense of identity.

Mortality, in *The Sea* a cause of depressing memories, acquires an enviable quality as 'closure' if seen 'from above.' Impiously Hermes comments on the father of the gods, whom he calls foolish, after his adventure with Helen: "Each time he dips his beak into the essence of a girl he takes, so he believes, another enchanting dip of death, pure and precious. For of course he wants to die, as do all of us immortals, that is well known" (Banville 2009, 71). Hermes further explains that *stasis* is the most serious disadvantage the gods have to cope with; and "since nothing may change in our changeless world, either for good or ill" (79) even Zeus "longs for love to kill him" (80).[18] As this never happens Hermes can introduce the baffled narratee to halcyon diversions.

The Comic Turn

The different kinds of the comic in *The Infinities* distinguish the novel from *The Sea* which precedes it, modifying Banville's simultaneously published statement that "at some level [...] all my art is about grief and loss and about the awareness of death" (qtd. from Kenny 2009, 21). Whereas "the awareness of death" is confirmed and symbolically indicated by the connotations of the Latin quotation "et in Arcadia ille," grief and mourning are allayed and eventually muted. This novel disconnects death from loss, melancholia and tragedy and focuses on human nature perceived from a distance, hence admitting the comic.[19] Hermes, who guides the characters with light serenity towards the moment of harmony generated by the gods, specifies "the mortal world [as] a world where nothing is lost" (Banville 2009, 300). Black humour, which in *The Sea* – whose thematic and symbolic reverse *The Infinities* presents – and equally in *Ancient Light* is produced mainly as a result of the protagonist's remembered youthful perspective, contrasts with *The Infinities*' comic turn. Tags such as "comedy of cruelty" (Radley 2010, 13) or "gallows humour" (14) would be insufficient to define the ease and gaiety with which the (self-)ironizing narrator of *The Infinities* steers characters and narratee through the experience of a day. Hedwig Schwall emphasizes that the fantasy genre Banville plays with in *The Infinities* complies with the ludic, thus mischievously subverting conventional novelistic concepts (2010, 102).

Banville's comment on the humour in his work divulges an auto-criticism that writers such as Samuel Beckett or Graham Swift have also expressed: "All my books

---

18 Hermes' remarks play on the ancient poetical meaning of "to die," sporadically still in use, as "[t]o experience a sexual orgasm" (cf. *OED-online* "die, v.1," no. I.7.d).

19 While *The Infinities* seems to be a novel apart, the following novel *Ancient Light* (2012) is classified as the completion of another trilogy together with *Shroud* and *Eclipse* (Haekel 2014).

are funny, if you know how to listen for the jokes. The novel, at a certain basic level, is a comic form" (Banville, Amazon Q&A). One reason for *The Infinities*' new ambience of humour – light not black – lies in the addressing of incongruities in human life, a connection pointed out in the early stages of the English novel (Fielding 1965, 6-7). Informed by the distancing perspective, even the grotesque becomes physical comedy. Elements of the narrative that might be reclaimed for gestures of humiliation from a position of superiority – regularly passages dealing with the humans' bodily functions or situations of heteronomous corporeal precariousness such as illness, birth or death – appear in a benign light and are depicted from the amused divine perspective.[20] The absence – if not of represented unhappiness – of existential fear, isolation or terror, the classical inducements for comic relief, enhances the lightness of tone.[21] If the exceptional example of misfortune is Petra Godley with her disturbed psyche, she also remains the child both her natural father Adam Sr. and the immortals are most emotional and anxious about: "Poor Petra, poor mooncalf, she is the one of all the household who is dearest to us. And because we love her so we shall soon take her to us, but not yet, not yet" (Banville 2009, 120; cf. 299-300). The gods of *The Infinities* appear as condescending, but caring, patronizing figures even though – perfect players on the stage – they also claim the posture of absolute coldness and cruelty (91-92) and reject the image of a Christian god and Saviour. In the represented actions and manifestations of the day they indulge in playing with their "little ones" (3; 61). Under different circumstances these games might seem cruel – cuckolding Adam Jr., for example, or arranging by subterfuge the appearance of Adrian Duffy the cowman at table to fill the empty place of the eminent mathematician Adam Godley dying on the upper floor (202-208) –, yet from the immortal observer's perspective they are comical. At worst they can cause unrest and thus a moment of tellingly "panic fright" (208; cf. 287) instead of anguish. The aim of these protean Olympians lies in the fulfilment of desire and pleasure gain, not in tormenting humans. The distance is reduced again by incongruities, since the gods are themselves vulnerable and possess human weaknesses, so that they equally appear to an observer as actors in a comedy of manners: "gross and lumpy at times," "jealous" (186; 259), sulking and easily bored (72), foolish, envious, and strangers to love. If religion – especially a monotheistic one – usually forbids laughing and makes it very clear "that God does not at all allow to be made fun of," (Schmidt et al. 2014, 3; my translation)[22] Hermes, stimulated to the Homeric laughter which originally also mocked another god, depicts even Jupiter's anger in a way that provokes mirth.[23] If we mostly laugh with this narrator/spectator, we also laugh at him because he changes from the subject of comedy to its object as the reader watches the divinities and, notoriously, "life every where furnishes an accurate observer with the ridiculous" (Fielding 1965, 3). Thus for *The Infinities*, whose mirth diverges from the black humour of other Banville novels, D'hoker's phrase of Banville's "*disturbing* visions of alterity" (2004, 225, my emphasis) has lost its sting.

---

20 Cf. Stierle (1976, 244): "Not the other-directed action itself is comical, but only its perception through another individual's perspective" (my translation).

21 Comic relief and the Shakespearean burlesque, intertextually present in *The Infinities*, are traditionally defined by academic criticism as directed towards the audience of both tragedies and 'dark' comedies. In this novel, serene 'relief' through divine grace is also granted to the characters.

22 "[…] dass Gott gar nicht mit sich spaßen läßt" (Schmidt et al. 2014, 3).

23 The Olympians in the *Odyssey* laugh at the sight of adulterous Aphrodite making love with Ares, caught in a net woven by the betrayed Hephaistos. They laugh at their equals and celebrate the cuckolded husband's inventiveness.

The writer's own explanation of the comic in this book mentions only man's hybrid nature – body and mind – with its creaturely aspects. He maintains that the priority usually given to the mind over man's animal nature – the "simplicity of living" which s/he shares with Rex the dog who is "pure animal" – is continuously undercut by the space granted to physical conditions and needs (Banville qtd. in Radley 2010, 13). The awareness of this unspiritual simplicity also asserts being alive in the world. I have argued that the reader, unreliable in his response,[24] is tempted by the comic, which rests upon numerous incidences of incongruence – between body and mind, the ordinary and the sublime, human and immortal perspectives –, to compassionate and … to laugh. That the reverse of the statement 'the gods are the authors of the mortal (parallel) world' as the bottom line of this novel is also true, namely that the author of the fiction is god, a fatherly (or motherly) figure playing with his little ones in the universe he has contrived, his omnipotence letting him reign supreme, becomes apparent here as in previous novels by Banville (cf. Wondrich 2000, 79; 85). In particular a god-author immersed in the chronotope of the postmodern condition is apt to assume this vain "affectation" – to use Henry Fielding's term for the source of ridicule (1965, 6-7) –, which renders the authorial figure also the object of ridicule.

I wish to address *The Infinities*' position in Banville's recent novelistic production as the contrastive counterpart in a diptych of ambiguity, which divides the epic – like drama – into tragedy and comedy, each selecting from actions and a fable in such a way "that as in the one these are grave and solemn, so in the other they are light and ridiculous; […] lastly, in its sentiments and diction; by preserving the ludicrous instead of the sublime" (2). As regards the "characters of inferior ranks and, consequently, of inferior manners" (2), which Fielding identifies as another source of comedy in the novel, distinctions appear blurred in the 21st-century narrative. Regardless, however, of the 270 years separating him from a contemporary writer, "the misfortunes and calamities of life, or the imperfections of nature, may become the objects of ridicule" (6) when superiority is affected.

With *The Sea*, whose opening sentence, "They departed, the gods, on the day of the strange tide" (Banville 2005, 3), signified an ending or at least its beginning, *The Infinities* forms a complementary pair: "Why in such times as these would the gods come back to be among men? But the fact is we never left" (Banville 2009, 15).[25] Banville regards *The Sea* as the introduction to a shift: "this narrator began to speak – in grief, as usual – and I suspect he's my link. I think this is a transition book" (Banville and Sarvas, 2005). Through its comic turn, including the prophetic glimpse into the future that only a god-narrator can add to the inevitability of death, this novel also implicitly negates loss and once more defends unending openness in the world of the text as well as in infinite parallel worlds. Using the power of textuality the writer evades closure. Besides, with a touch of self-irony, he affirms a poetological proposition: the author/narrator-god has the face of Janus, the god of threshold and transition, who inspects the past and the future, dispensing gloom or brightness, and he is truly "protean"

---

24 For a critical appraisal of very diverse reviews see Radley (2010, 13)

25 Zwierlein's article discusses *The Sea* under the aspect of represented grief (2014, 164-67) and also points out that Adam Sr. is the typical male melancholic, whose imaginings of death are linked to the sea (164). Undeniably Banville has almost exclusively been perceived as the writer of human distress. As Radley remarks humour in his work met with little critical attention. My main objection to Radley's deliberations on *The Infinities* is that he also wants to consider the comic in this novel as equally and uniformly dark (2010, 14).

(Banville 2009, 244).[26] Exceeding the definitions of a Banville novel as "metanarrative which [...] questions its own coherence" (McMinn 1999, 162) or as a literary "hypertext" (Berensmeyer 2000, 248) *The Infinities* presents a fictional meta-discourse on the narrativization of love and death. In Arcadia, the native poetical habitat of love where death is still present, it becomes a comedy. The author's admitted proclivity and relish for the pastoral illuminate this representation of the mortal world: "there is a side of me that is an old-fashioned pastoralist ... an Irish pastoralist. In a way, Irish fiction was always pastoral, even when it was set in the cities. ... It's all pastoral, it's all nature,[27] it's all to do with the countryside" (Banville and Sarvas, 2005).

Works Cited

Bachtin, Michail M. *Rabelais und seine Welt.* Ed. Renate Lachmann. Trans. Gabriele Leupold. Frankfurt/M., Suhrkamp, 1987.

Banville, John. *The Broken Jug: After Heinrich von Kleist.* Loughcrew: The Gallery Press, 1994.

—. *God's Gift: A Version of Amphitryon by Heinrich von Kleist.* [2000]. Loughcrew: The Gallery Press, 2001.

—. *Love in the Wars: Adaptation of Heinrich von Kleist's Penthesilea.* Loughcrew: The Gallery Press, 2005.

—. *The Sea.* London: Picador, 2005.

—. *The Infinities.* London: Picador, 2009.

—. *Ancient Light.* London: Viking, 2012.

—, and Anon. "*The Infinities.* A Q&A with Author John Banville." *Amazon.com.* n.d. Web. 3 January 2015.

— and Mark Sarvas. "The Long Awaited, Long Promised, Just Plain Long John Banville Interview." *The Elegant Variation.* 26 September 2005. Web blog. 4 January 2015.

Berensmeyer, Ingo. *John Banville: Fictions of Order. Authority, Authorship, Authenticity.* Heidelberg: Winter, 2000.

D'hoker, Elke. *Visions of Alterity: Representation in the Works of John Banville.* Amsterdam: Rodopi, 2004.

"die, v.[1]" Def. I.7.d. *OED-Oxford English Dictionary*-online. Oxford University Press. Web. 4 January 2015.

Fielding, Henry. "Preface." 1742. *The Adventures of Joseph Andrews* (with an introduction by L. Rice-Oxley). London: Oxford University Press, 1965. 1-8.

Földvary, Kinga. "In Search of a Lost Future: The Posthuman Child." *European Journal of English Studies* 18.2 (2014): 207-20.

Gill, Richard. *The English Country House in Modern Fiction: Archetype of Community.* Ann Arbor, MI. University Microfilms. 1967.

Haekel, Ralf. "'... no sign at all': Loss in John Banville's *Eclipse*, *Shroud* and *Ancient Light*." *Narrating Loss: Representations of Mourning, Nostalgia and Melancholia in Contemporary Anglophone Fictions.* Eds. Brigitte Johanna Glaser and Barbara Puschmann-Nalenz. Trier: WVT, 2014. 239-54.

26 The artist's protean nature has been famously stated: In a letter to Richard Woodhouse, 27 October 1818, John Keats speaks of "the camelion Poet, [...] he has no Identity, [...] he has no self" (1970, 157), but instead assumes changing identities (157-58). Authenticity is Banville's crucial theme.

27 The relation of inanimate, vegetational, animal and human nature and the divinities in *The Infinities* deserves further critical attention, which would, however, exceed the limits of this article.

Hand, Derek. *John Banville: Exploring Fictions*. Dublin: Liffey Press, 2002.

Imhof, Rüdiger. *John Banville: A Critical Introduction.* Dublin: Wolfhound Press, 1989.

Keats, John. *Letters: A New Selection*. Ed. Robert Gittings. London: Oxford University Press, 1970.

Kenny, John. *John Banville*. Dublin: Irish Academic Press, 2009.

McEwan, Ian. *A Move Abroad: Or Shall We Die?* and *The Ploughman's Lunch*. London: Picador, 1983.

McMinn, Joseph. *The Supreme Fictions of John Banville*. Manchester: Manchester University Press, 1999.

—. "*Ekphrasis* and the Novel: The Presence of Paintings in John Banville's Fiction." *Word and Image: A Journal of Verbal/Visual Inquiry* 18.2 (2002): 137-45.

Müller, Anja. "'You have been framed.' The Function of *Ekphrasis* for the Representation of Women in John Banville's Trilogy (*The Book of Evidence*, *Ghosts*, *Athena*)." *Studies in the Novel* 36.2 (2004): 185-205.

Nolan, Val. "The Aesthetics of Space and Time in the Fiction of John Banville and Neil Jordan." *Nordic Irish Studies* 9 (2010): 33-47.

O'Connell, Mark. "The Empathic Paradox: Third-Person Narration in John Banville's First-Person Narratives." *Orbis Litterarum: International Review of Literary Studies* 66.6 (2011): 427-47.

Payne, Tom. "*The Infinities* by John Banville: Review." 19 September 2009. *The Telegraph*. Web. 8 November 2014.

Polvinen, Merja. "Being Played. Mimesis, Fictionality and Emotional Engagement." Eds. Saija Isomaa et al. *Rethinking Mimesis: Concepts and Practices of Literary Representation.* Newcastle upon Tyne: Cambridge Scholars, 2012. 93-112.

Radley, Bryan. "John Banville's Comedy of Cruelty." *Nordic Irish Studies* 9 (2010): 13-31.

Schmidt, Johann N., Felix C.H. Sprang, and Roland Weidle. "Introduction." *Wer lacht, zeigt Zähne. Spielarten des Komischen.* Eds. Johann N. Schmidt et al. Trier: WVT, 2014, 1-6.

Schwall, Hedwig. "An Iridescent Surplus of Style: Features of the Fantastic in Banville's *The Infinities*." *Nordic Irish Studies* 9 (2010): 89-107.

Stierle, Karlheinz. "Komik der Handlung, Komik der Sprachhandlung, Komik der Komödie." *Das Komische*. Eds. Wolfgang Preisendanz and Rainer Warning. München: Fink, 1976. 237-68.

Tayler, Christopher. "*The Infinities* by John Banville" (Review). 26 September 2009. *The Guardian.* Web. 3 January 2015.

Wilhelmy, Thorsten. *Legitimitätsstrategien der Mythosrezeption: Thomas Mann, Christa Wolf, John Barth, Christoph Ransmayr, John Banville*. Würzburg: Königshausen & Neumann, 2004.

Wondrich, Roberta Gefter. "Postmodern Love, Postmodern Death and God-Like Authors in Irish Fiction: The Case of John Banville." *Barcelona English Language and Literature Studies* 11 (2000): 79-88.

Zwierlein, Anne-Julia. "Lost at Sea: Mourning, Melancholia and Maritime Mindscapes in Early 21st-Century British and Irish Fiction." *Narrating Loss: Representations of Mourning, Nostalgia and Melancholia in Contemporary Anglophone Fictions*. Eds Brigitte Johanna Glaser and Barbara Puschmann-Nalenz. Trier: WVT, 2014. 161-77.

MERLE TÖNNIES

The Use of Comic Effects in Memoirs of British Asian Adolescence: 21st- Century Writers Looking Back at the 1970s and 1980s

This contribution focuses on a particular form of texts which became rather prominent in the British book market at the end of the 2000s and the beginning of the 2010s and is still selling rather well: memoirs of young people of Pakistani origin growing up in Britain (often in the North of England or in other regions with a stereotypically working-class reputation) in the 1970s and 1980s which are told retrospectively and are either directly autobiographical or at least strongly suggest some degree of 'authentic' connection to the author's own life. Some of the most well-known examples are Almas Khan's *Poppadom Preach* (2010), Yasmin Hai's *The Making of Mr Hai's Daughter* (2008) and Imran Ahmad's *Unimagined* (2007). As Esra Mirze Santesso has pointed out (2013, 159; 162), these kinds of "second-generation narratives" can market themselves as "quasi-anthropological studies" which offer 'immediate' access to the experience of how cultures from the Indian subcontinent fared in Britain and at the same time mediate these cultures to the "non-immigrant audience" from the 'safe' perspective of an insider who has (more or less) securely arrived in British society.[1]

Although this form clearly has found a fairly wide readership and is continuing to do so, critical literature has so far addressed it only relatively rarely. Authors who do deal with the memoirs have tended to approach them from two different perspectives: On the one hand, these texts are seen in the general context of postcolonial storytelling or (slightly more specifically) postcolonial autobiography. This means that the analysis focuses on the ways in which the British Pakistani writers take up and/or rework established patterns and techniques of narrative identity construction in postcolonial situations (cf. e.g. R. Ahmed (2012, 57), relating back to the "triumph-over-adversity" model described by Huggan (2001, 161)). On the other hand, critics have situated the memoirs more concretely in the developing genre of 'British Muslim fiction' (cf. e.g. the genre overview by Nash (2012), who, however, does not examine the material analyzed here), as Islam indeed plays an important role in the adolescents' lives and identities. From this point of view, Santesso sees the texts as deliberately moving away from the "disorientation narrative" of first-generation immigrants "frustrated by an inability to negotiate between the Islamic faith and the Western, secular state" (2013, 163). In contrast to their parents' generation, the characters define themselves as British and quickly learn to manage their lives in between different cultures (cf. 163-64), though characteristics of 'disorientation' do manifest themselves in their mothers' lives (cf. 169-74). Claire Chambers even goes a step further and affiliates the stories and their marketing with what she names "'Muslim Kool'" (drawing together 'Cool Britannia' with 'Asian Kool'). In that understanding, the memoirs "plac[e] discussion of music, fashion, night life, and university study alongside analysis of identity politics, Thatcherism, and Islamophobia" and deliberately oppose the awareness of diverse Muslim identities to existing "'misery memoirs'" about a monolithic, oppressive Islam (2013, 88; 91).

1 On the more general demand for 'exotic' autobiography see also Huggan (2001, 155-76) and Hawthorne (1989).

Anglistik: International Journal of English Studies 27.1 (March 2016): 113-124.

While all of these contextualizations can help to study the texts, they often pay relatively little attention to one important characteristic that the memoirs share, namely the use of comic characters and scenes.[2] In some cases, these elements evoke open laughter; in others, there may be darker implications which only allow the reader to smile – but attention to the comic potential of growing up as a British Pakistani in the 1970s and 1980s is one of the features which (apart from those already given above) allows us to understand the books as a fairly consistent corpus of material. This is why the present article chooses the 'Black British Bildungsroman' as a comparative framework for the texts – a prominent genre of the 1990s and early 2000s in which protagonists from a non-white ethnic background try to find their way into British society, with varying degrees of success.[3] One could argue that the memoirs treat the same issues of divided loyalties, conflict and racism as the novels but use various techniques to highlight their comic potential. Maybe the fact that the authors recall their own lives rather than creating fictional ones and moreover do so from a distinct distance in time, i.e. at a point where they have probably come to terms with the problems of their youth, gives them the necessary freedom to see this potential in constellations which generally come across as much more serious and oppressive in the Black British Bildungsroman. Moreover, this might also liberate the audience to actually laugh at these experiences (even if it is not always unproblematic laughter), which may also have contributed to the memoirs' success in the book market. In this way, the development from the Black British Bildungsroman to the 21st-century memoirs can indeed be understood as a certain 'comic turn' within Black British literature, i.e. a turn towards attempting to represent and use the comic potential of intercultural contradictions and conflicts.

In order to capture the specific qualities of the selected texts, the term 'memoir' (rather than autobiography) is chosen here – as well as in most of the sparse secondary literature on them.[4] The designation 'memoir' has been said to highlight the interrelations between the individual life at its centre and the cultural context of the time, primarily asking "what is the place of this writer in the culture represented?" (Buss 2001, 595; see also Smith/Watson 2001, 198). In this vein, G. Thomas Couser situates memoirs "on a continuum from [texts] focused on the author to those focused on an other" (2012, 21). He also highlights that 'memoirs' tend to concentrate "only on a discreet part of the life" (23) – with the texts under consideration here, childhood and especially adolescence and young adulthood. Last but not least, 'memoir' also captures the predominant quality of the narrative voice in the works, as it stresses the reliance on 'memory' ("a notoriously unreliable and highly selective faculty" [19]) already etymologically. This fits in well

---

2 Santesso touches upon some of these elements in *Poppadom Preach*, albeit from a rather derogatory perspective which does not take the comic effects seriously as a topic for analysis: "Both Abdullah [in *Life, Love and Assimilation* of 2006] and Khan lean heavily on a traditional compilation of types: abusive father, repressed mother, rebellious adolescent. They shy away from topics that lie outside the purview of the formula; [...] they never engage with them [controversial issues like abuse and racism] deeply enough to threaten the familiar stereotypes or the expected plotline" (2013, 162).

3 For a seminal study of this genre see Stein (2004), who stresses its transformative potential for British society already in the title of his book. For the different forms of the Black British Bildungsroman with a special focus on gender distinctions see Tönnies (2013). Chambers touches upon this connection by briefly mentioning "auto/biographical *bildungsroman* style" with regard to *The Making of Mr Hai's Daughter* and also naming the representative authors Hanif Kureishi and Meera Syal, but she does not examine the context of the Black British Bildungsroman any further (2013, 78; 84).

4 See especially R. Ahmed (2012) and S. Ahmed (2010, 154). Santesso, on the other hand, uses the designations 'novel' and 'narrative' for *Poppadom Preach*, thereby to some extent begging the issue of authenticity.

with the informal, often episodic and chatty tone of the books which helps the comic effects to arise. As both Buss (2001, 595) and Couser (2012, 18) point out, this characteristic has often led to a rather derogatory treatment of memoirs by established critics (see also Rak 2004, 486-88). Although Couser (2012) considers this to be more a thing of the past now, exactly such a stance can indeed sometimes be found with regard to the texts under consideration here (see fn. 2 above).

Apart from *Poppadom Preach*, *The Making of Mr Hai's Daughter* and *Unimagined*, which were already mentioned above, the present analysis includes Zaiba Malik's *We Are a Muslim, Please* (2010) and *Greetings from Bury Park* by Sarfraz Manzoor (2007). The overall corpus thus contains three female and two male perspectives on British Asian adolescence. The authors all have Pakistani ethnic origins and were born in the 1960s or early 1970s. Manzoor and Imran Ahmad (*Unimagined*) stick out a little bit as they were born in Pakistan (with Ahmad – born in 1962 – also being a few years older than the others), but they both moved to Britain at a very young age (two in the case of Manzoor and three in Ahmad's, who significantly starts using the present tense at this stage of the narrative [cf. 2011, 27]). So all five memoirs show childhood and adolescence as firmly rooted in Britain and have a temporal focus on the 1970s and 1980s (with wider temporal perspectives included in an epilogue in *Unimagined* and in a prologue in Malik's *We Are a Muslim, Please*). As already briefly suggested above, the British spaces in which the narratives are set are held together by an almost stereotypical sense of disadvantage and marginalization. Bradford is the main focus in both *Poppadom Preach* and *We Are a Muslim, Please*, while Ahmad's adolescence takes place in South London and Hai's in Wembley. Manzoor – when describing how his mother finally moved to Britain with the children to join their father, settling down in Luton – explicitly points out the city's "dire reputation," which he and his family, however, "did not know" (17). At the same time, the texts differ to some extent in the parents' outlook and the ways in which they try to shape their children's lives – ranging from the extreme conservatism of Dilly's home in *Poppadom Preach* to the radically liberal attitude of Hai's father, who – while opposing 'Westernisation' through television and popular culture – consistently insists on her and the whole family being as 'modern' as possible and not 'held back' by the rules of Islam (77-79).

The memoirs usually stop at the point where the author has found some sense of a social identity for him/herself. This is often also connected with a spatial relocation, but the main focus of the overall narrative remains on the time and locations of adolescence. Manzoor deliberately moves to Manchester to study in order to get away from his father. At the end of the book he has become a journalist in London, but still continues to recall events from his earlier life. The extremely neat chronology of *Unimagined* (with chapter headings giving the protagonist's age throughout) leads up to the end of Ahmad's student years at Stirling and then through to his first job at Unilever in London. Yasmin Hai is a TV producer in London at the end of her memoir and has seemingly grown into the role of 'Mr Hai's daughter' (which is also the title of the final chapter), while Zaiba Malik studies at Nottingham University and then becomes a journalist in London. She mentions typing the final chapters of her memoir in the British Library (2011, 226) – an explicit parallel to Manzoor (2008, 70), which really seems to intertwine these very similar life stories. *Poppadom Preach* leaves its protagonist Dilly in 1986 when she is about to fly to Pakistan to her sister's wedding and is making plans to find a husband there to finally allow her to get away from her parents, finish her education and find a job. Although the final paragraphs hint that these plans may not work out so easily (Khan 2011, 374), there is at least a sense in which Dilly is finally moving away from her childhood home mentally as well spatially (flying to Pakistan, which has always been denied to her so far). Thus, one can definitely discover the basic pattern of the Black British Bildungsroman here by which the protagonist starts out in a marginal position and finally manages to get closer to the social (and also spatial) centres of British society – although this is never an unproblematic integration process.[5]

In the memoirs, this is often stressed by concluding references to 7/7 and the traumatic effect of the event and its aftermath on the situation of British Muslims. Hai is breastfeeding her little son in front of the current television footage (2009, 327), Manzoor returns home to Luton "on the first weekend after the bombing" (2008, 263), and Malik intersperses messages to one of the bombers, who lived quite near her old home in Bradford as a child (2011, 246), throughout the book in a different typeface, before addressing "A Letter" to him in the epilogue (to some extent echoing the prologue about being interrogated in a Bangladeshi prison and being denied a Muslim identity there; 4; 245). Especially in this case, but also with Hai and Manzoor, one can argue that the bombings played an important role in the motivation to write the memoir – not wanting to allow extremists the only voice on the British Muslim community but taking part themselves in the discussion about the Britishness of 'Asian Muslims:' "After all, this is our country too" (Hai 2009, 334). This urge to contribute one's own experience to an ongoing debate may to some extent explain the fact that all of the selected memoirs were published within a relatively short time period, and there is also a connection here to their pervasive insistence on authenticity. Malik reproduces photographs from her life throughout the text and includes a dedication to her mother, who also features prominently within the book; Manzoor explicitly names friends and family from the narrative in the acknowledgements, and Ahmad stresses before the actual memoir that "[t]his entire account is completely true" (2011, 16). Similarly, Hai (apart from a photograph of herself as a child, waving a little Union Jack, on the cover of the paperback edition) inserts an "Author's Note" where she stresses that despite some changes to disguise identities, "every story I tell is based on first-hand experience or rooted in testimonies related to me by witnesses. Every event I write about happened" (2009, xiii). And even with *Poppadom Preach*, where the protagonist Dilly is first of all a fictional character, the reader can hardly notice that the author, too, is a Pakistani who was born and raised in Yorkshire and claims Bradford as her hometown (cf. Khan n.d.), without being tempted to establish links between her and her character. Thus, there is a sense that the authors are all at least in some ways trying to convey the 'real' experience of second-generation British Pakistanis to a wider (and also white British) readership, wanting to alter the status quo many of them observe in media representations: Although there are more Asian characters on TV in the 2000s than in the 1980s (when – as Manzoor notes – they "were almost invisible" and, if present at all, were used only for offensive comic relief [2008, 245]), Hai still notes: "[U]p to now the only time British Asians made it onto the telly was in BBC2 documentaries about the British Empire or Enoch Powell's 'rivers of blood' speech" (2009, 226). What is missing in the media is "everyday [British Asian experience], the one we live [...], but never [see] on television" (226).

5 On spatial and social movement and the problems involved in this for both male and female characters in the Black British Bildungsroman see e.g. Stein (2004, 39), Sommer (2001, 113; 126) and Tönnies (2013, 52-53).

This programmatic focus on the authentic 'everyday' runs through all of the memoirs and plays a prominent role in the comic effects they produce. A dominant technique is the representation of contradictions here – between the rules of Islam and/or Pakistani culture on the one hand and those of British society surrounding the home and at school on the other. Moreover, disparities are shown to obtain almost as prominently *within* the home and its culture. Such contradictions are sometimes pointed out openly in the memoirs, and the retrospective perspective of telling the narrative from a considerable time distance is, of course, helpful here: Manzoor describes with a deliberate parallelism in the sentence construction that "while [he] spent [his] afternoons poring over discarded porn magazines or browsing the videos on the top shelf of the video store in the Purley Centre, [he] spent [his] evenings reading the Koran" (2008, 184). Similarly, with regard to discrepancies within the home, Malik mock-naïvely wonders why the Asian dramas watched by the family "were always about girl and boy falling in love," while real-life marriage had to be arranged (2011, 148).[6] More often, the reader him/herself is allowed a more active role in the recognition of contradictions than the narrator-protagonist, and as the combination of disparate elements is pushed to the point of absurdity, laughter is evoked despite the serious background of these scenes. This laughter usually contains a degree of superiority over characters who seem to be caught in contradictions they cannot fully understand, let alone change. Thus, a leitmotif of television bringing unfiltered British values into the home runs through the memoirs; "[w]atching television with [the] family [is] a minefield" (Manzoor, 2008, 184), as kissing and nudity must not appear. The narrator-protagonists often wonder which programmes might be 'safe,' and if offensive images appear out of the blue, everyone has to rush to the TV set as fast as possible to change channels: "These [bra advertisements] were always tricky at a time when we had no remote control for the TV" (Malik 2011, 60). Noticeably the narrator-protagonist to some extent distances him/herself from the family circle here, which makes it easier for the reader to laugh, but still remains part of the group. The absurdity of the situation is pointed out explicitly with regard to other families: When describing how the Khan family make their three-year-old son stand in front of the TV set whenever an inacceptable scene comes up, Hai comments: "Why no one ever thought of just changing channels, I don't know" (2009, 42). The contradictions between British popular culture and British Pakistani lives can also directly affect the narrator-protagonists themselves. Ahmad, for instance, repeatedly recounts his difficulty in achieving identification with TV heroes like James Bond, as he feels he would not be allowed to kiss women, and the television characters of course do not have arranged marriages (cf. 2011, 40; 123; 125). As Ahmad seems very distant from his young self throughout the memoir, often creating dramatic irony for his audience by stressing his own former lack of insight,[7] the reader is encouraged to laugh directly at the young protagonist here and make light of his 'problems.'

---

6 The term 'contradiction' is also explicitly used by Ahmad (incidentally on the same topic as in Malik's above statement (131)) and Hai (2009, 160). R. Ahmed (2012, 61-65) foregrounds it as a special characteristic with regard to Hai's memoir.

7 This attitude is already visible in the cover photograph of the paperback edition, which apparently reproduces Ahmad's appearance in the "Karachi 'Bonnie Baby' contest" at the age of one: "I looked like James Bond [...]. I was also somewhat unsteady on my feet" (2011, 23). Correspondingly, the "Afterword by the Author" ends with a friend concluding about the narrated I: "At the end of *Unimagined*, you are still pretty narrow-minded and quite unpleasant in many of your views" (299). Indeed, the reader is frequently invited by the narrating I to see through limitations of his younger self's knowledge and/or unthinking belief in ideological tenets like the moral goodness and supportive community of all Muslims (cf. e.g. 61; 67-68; 71; 92; 98-99; 128).

Apart from British culture entering the home through the media, all the characters at least sometimes have to interact with the world in the English language. The contradictions between society's expectations and the actual situation particularly concern the mothers of the families here. In *Poppadom Preach*, Dilly uses this discrepancy to get her own back at least temporarily against her oppressive and even abusive parents, prompting the readers to share her momentary triumph in laughter. She for instance sells a note from the Electricity Board to her mother as a sick note from the doctor forbidding her to do any housework: "She had to take my word for it; she'd been stuck in Early Reader books for years" (2011, 151; cf. also 119). The effect on both Dilly and the audience is intensified when her mother then proceeds to show the electricity card to the truant officer from school to account for her daughter's absence (152). Even Malik and Hai, who have a much better relationship with their parents, repeatedly comment on their mother's inability to speak English correctly in such a way that she is held up for ridicule. The title of Malik's book refers back to "an announcement Umejee [her mother] used to make, say, once every couple of months when we were in our teens, or whenever she felt the need. [...] It was a phrase she would also use in the outside world. In front of strangers who, quite frankly, didn't give a shit" (2011, 11). Malik also details how her mother used to "pronounce [...] England 'Ingerland' and Channel 4 'China 4'" (21), while Hai quotes her mother trying to show off her command of English idioms in "You were apple of eye" (2009, 31). Interestingly, Hai then later on invites the reader to laugh *with* her mother, who manages to reinvent herself after her husband's death and is shown to use the role of the linguistically incompetent 'Asian woman' deliberately to get a better deal from the builder (209). This incident is, however, conspicuously singular in all the memoirs; far more usually, the narrators blame their mothers rather than the British environment for the ridiculous contradictions.

In all the texts, contradictions are moreover a staple of the children's and adolescents' lives as far as their experiences at school and with their white British friends are concerned. It becomes abundantly clear that even with a liberal home like Hai's, a young British Pakistani could not but live in two worlds simultaneously in the 1970s and 1980s, constantly forced to juggle the different rules and conventions. Explicit references to this situation recur frequently (cf. e.g. Khan 2011, 73; 261; Ahmad 2011, 37; Malik 2011, 76; 100; 140; 188; Manzoor 2008, 245; Hai 2009, 68; 89), irrespective of the protagonist's sex or his/her family's social status. Typically, the memoirs crystallize these contradictions in concrete conundrums pinpointed almost epigrammatically to produce a comic effect. Thus, Manzoor realizes that his father's reluctance to go on holiday ("typical of an entire generation of Asian fathers") regularly causes problems at school because after the holidays the pupils are "expected to write essays on what we had been up to" (2008, 124). Ahmad is laughed at by his classmates because he truthfully writes in an assignment that the only thing he got for Christmas was a tin of biscuits from the neighbour – "the usual January problem" (2011, 60). Similarly, Hai feels embarrassed when her uncle's visit from Pakistan means that cultural traditions are resurrected in her home and her schoolmates might see her with "this Asian Father Christmas lookalike:" "My carefully cultivated English image would surely fall apart" (100). Moreover, she gets into a fight with an Asian friend at school who draws the attention of their classmates to the fact that Hai unthinkingly put a lot of pepper on her school-lunch. Being accused of liking spicy food seems to be a serious insult and leads to an absurd competition between the two girls about whose mother cooks the most British meals (84-85).

At the same time, there are also repeated scenes in the texts where it does seem possible to live in both worlds at once. Many of the protagonists and their families seem to be fascinated with the Royal family and events like the wedding of Prince Charles and Diana in 1981 (cf. Manzoor 2008, 123; Kahn 2011, 273; Ahmad 2011, 157; Malik 2011, 105), and Malik's mother even esteems the Queen so much that her daughter has to write letters to her in the mother's name offering direct support: "You are like a Pakistani family. I will work for you for free" (20). In a number of situations such intercultural combinations seem to work out completely naturally. Hai's mother "in her best sari" watches proudly as her daughter participates in the Brent Primary Schools Country Dancing Championships and receives the teacher's congratulations (2009, 69), while Hai herself solves the problem of teachers not being able to pronounce her first name by adopting Jasmin as her "Christian name" – "your other name, which meant nothing to you or your family but which everyone in England could pronounce. [...] Calling it your 'Christian name' gave it more legitimacy" (71). Similarly, Ahmad (2011, 61-62) and Malik (2011, 116) love singing Christian hymns at Assembly,[8] and Khan's Dilly is very keen to take part in the nativity play at school (45; cf. also Ahmad 2011, 59-60). In these cases, the reader is mostly left to notice the potential culture clash on his/her own, without prompting by the narrator-protagonist or other characters. S/he is thereby encouraged to question in how far real incompatibility exists or whether his/her realization of a discrepancy and the laughter that expresses it might be grounded in stereotypes.

Apart from intercultural contradictions, the memoirs also show the Asian community itself as a site of disparities. Very concretely, the parents regularly have style concepts for the home that seem strange to their children – and to the reader (cf. Hai on installing a fish tank in the bathroom [2009, 163] and her perception of "true Wembley style" with "hideous shades of lilac and pistachio green" [218]). Obscure but apparently well-established rituals of home furnishing seem to concentrate on sofas in the memoirs, with Manzoor's parents keeping a "magnolia shroud" on the "three-piece suite" which then has to be whisked off quickly when guests arrive (2008, 157), and Hai's mother leaving the plastic wrapping on the sofa backs – "another 'fancy' touch" (2009, 219). On a more fundamental level, a veritable leitmotif develops in the texts concerning contradictions between words and deeds, specifically relating to the families' fathers. Especially the strict fathers are characterized by conspicuous hypocrisy, preaching diligence and obedience but themselves avoiding chores in the house as well as religious obligations or at least carrying them out in a very makeshift form (cf. e.g. Manzoor 2008, 28-30; 33; 221; 225; Khan 2011, 10; 97). Hai's father (the most liberal male parent in the memoir corpus) does help with the housework but here, too, there is a certain discrepancy between appearances and reality, as he proves to be exceedingly incompetent in this realm. As Hai's mother details, "'[o]ne time, he wash dishes with baby bib on. And next time, he feed your sister, he put my apron on her'" (45). In such scenes of contradictions within the British Pakistani homes the reader is typically invited to take the narrator-protagonist's side and share his/her down-to-earth approach to furniture as well as his/her ability to look below the surface. This is often supported by his/her use of irony, so that Dilly for

8 Malik's memoir also contains a list of items from both cultures that she mixes as a teenager (125). This can to some extent be seen as a counterpoint to Hai's food contradictions, as typical dishes play a prominent role here. However, this example also shows the serious background behind the play with discrepancies, as the meticulous listing of the different points she combines is followed immediately by a reference to her falling silent for a year because the two sides of her life have become too incompatible (125-27).

instance comments in mock wonder: "It was strange that an educated man like my father couldn't seem to work out how to use a washing machine" (109).

Interestingly, the memoirs mostly adopt the same approach with regard to Islamic beliefs and practices, so that the narrator-protagonist becomes the reader's point of identification who looks at his/her family and wider community from the outside and even invites deflating laughter at them. The basis of this approach is the British Pakistani children's and adolescents' frequent experience of Islam as a set of totally incomprehensible rules which nevertheless need to be followed meticulously. Manzoor states his regret about not being allowed "to feel sorry for Jesus" when watching a TV programme on his life at the age of six, only being told that the reason for this prohibition is his religion: "That made no sense to me" (2008, 214). Similarly, he describes replying to his white British friends that toys are against his religion without getting the connection (215), while Ahmad even only learns from a brief comment made by a schoolmate's mother that he does not eat pork (a "commandment" issued by his parents [34]) "*because of* [his] *religion*" (46). Malik describes that she "developed Islamic Obsessive Compulsive Disorder" (2011, 56), desperately obeying all the rules to the letter "[t]hough a lot of times I didn't understand why" (57), which obviously did not make the observance of the rules any easier. The emptiness of the incomprehensible rules becomes very obvious when Manzoor, on having completed one reading of the Koran, is told that now he simply has "to read the whole thing again." His reaction to this pointedly conveys deadpan irony in its brevity: "Great" (2008, 220).

Observations of Muslim religious practice are also repeatedly shown to trigger amused incomprehension on the narrator-protagonists' part, which the reader is invited to share: Malik describes her father's ablutions in the kitchen-sink in uncomprehending detail, pointing out that he was "all the time flooding the adjoining gas cooker, Umejee's spice jars and the lino" (2011, 38). Her father's frequent attendance at the mosque remains a total mystery to her; "I never really knew what Dad did" there (41) – paralleling Khan's Dilly who seems to consider the main purpose of the mosque to be calming down her father after family quarrels (cf. 2011, 221; 224). When Malik goes to the mosque herself, the imam appears to her as "a Pakistani Norman Collier, the northern comedian whose routine was based around a faulty microphone" (2011, 43). Similarly, Ahmad describes feeling totally out of place at the mosque because he does not understand the rituals at all and can only get through them by copying the others (2011, 47-48). Some of the memoirs point out explicitly why the children feel so lost with regard to their religion: The teachers at the Koran school speak no English (cf. Malik 2011, 43), so that the whole institution becomes a rather absurd affair which can also be painful, because the teachers regularly hit their pupils (cf. Khan 2011, 155; 157). Ahmad does describe learning "the basics" about Islam at the Islamic school (2011, 76; cf. also 67-68) – though his first insights into Islam apparently came from a programme on British television rather than from any members of the Muslim community (37). By portraying Islam from an ironic distance (at least as far as their own youth is concerned) and encouraging the audience to respond to its apparent absurdities with laughter,[9] the narrators often create stereotypical representations which are close to the potentially hostile hetero-images of the Muslim community and

9 The distancing from Islam is so dominant that even in *Unimagined* (where Ahmad mostly holds up his younger self for ridicule) the reader is clearly invited to be on the narrator-protagonist's side in these instances, against the seemingly incomprehensible and limiting religion. Malik uses direct addresses to the reader as an additional strategy to bring him/her closer to the narrating I (cf. e.g. 2011, 116; 170; 182). This 'you' seems to waver to some extent between a British Pakistani person who for instance shares the experience of being excluded at school (116) and a more broadly constructed readership.

its rituals current in the dominant white British society of the time (and perhaps even at the time of writing the memoirs). This problematic aspect is not really addressed in the texts; it seems that the authors' fundamental experience of the limitations imposed by Islam still influences them so strongly that they cannot (or do not want to) address the ideological implications of their portrayal of religion.[10] Manzoor most succinctly sums up that even as a teenager "[t]o be a Muslim [... still primarily] seemed to involve not being able to do things" (2008, 228).[11]

Indeed, there is a sense in the memoirs that the narrator-protagonists often not simply fail to understand how Islam works but that they actively dig up contradictions and hold the Islamic community up for ridicule. Repeatedly, Islamic practices are shown as disorganized and inefficient, so that the congregation at the mosque sometimes ends up praying in the wrong direction (Malik 2011, 250; cf. also Hai 2009, 118 on technical difficulties involved in private prayer) and shoes are stolen there (Malik 2011, 67). The difficulty of ascertaining the new moon for the celebration of Eid gives rise to "pandemonium" at the mosque (73), and "frantic calls to Pakistan [are] made" to obtain more information (Hai 2009, 112). Malik even deflates the community spirit at her father's wake with the "stench" of the "dozens of pairs of shoes [...] piling up" near the door, mixing with the smell of curry further into the house and making her "want to retch" (Malik 2011, 159). In addition to such strategies of narrative protest, already the young protagonists show their disagreement with the limitations imposed on their lives by finding covert ways of subverting them and/or turning them to their own advantage. Dilly is especially creative in this respect, engaging in a shoe-stealing game at the mosque (called "Hop Home, Mister," as they only take left shoes) together with her siblings and friends (Khan 2011, 182-83) and escaping from having to fetch vegetables from the garden by "tak[ing] ages" to find the scarf she is meant to wear outside (82). When all the girls of the family are made to practice wearing a burkha before a trip to Pakistan, Dilly's sister Egg quickly sees the advantages of this piece of clothing despite its confining effects: "[...] No one knows who we are. It's like being invisible. [...] [W]e could go shoplifting" (369). The sense of being confined by rules is definitely strongest in this memoir, but so is the protagonist's resilience and resourcefulness, which make the reader laugh with her despite his/her recognition of the serious background behind the episodes.

It fits in with this approach on Khan's part (and potentially also with the fact that this is the memoir with the most obvious use of fictional elements in the whole corpus) that *Poppadom Preach* even evokes laughter at very obvious suffering inflicted by the rules of the community – embodied by British Pakistani wives literally shut in in their homes. Repeatedly, young Dilly describes how she and her siblings annoy either their own mother or another woman, knowing full well that their opponent will not be able to do anything about it, because she cannot go out through the front door (cf. e.g. 2011, 20; 83; 91; 99). When one of these women is allowed to leave her house for once, Dilly observes in an apt analogy that she has "been given a day pass

10 This is all the more conspicuous as in a number of other cases the same texts show an awareness of stereotypes. Khan for instance has Dilly quote with playful irony the image of an Asian family piling on top of each other in an already overloaded car, adding that her mother told them "to stop fussing, and didn't we know that they can get six people on a motorbike in Pakistan" (2011, 286), while Hai describes the "very Asian chaos" of her home (38) and the "Asian Mothers' Mafia" living up to their reputation of attempting total community control together with the "aunts" (81; 157).

11 See also Ahmad, who (with characteristic self-mockery) has his eleven-year-old self conclude that "Christianity appears so much easier. You don't seem to have to do anything much except sing hymns" (2011, 80).

by her husband" (285) – inviting laughter with her wit at the shut-in neighbour's expense.[12] As Dilly herself is progressively confined to the house in the course of these scenes, her cruel treatment and representation of the other women may appear as a desperate attempt to distance herself at least emotionally from a fate she knows she cannot avoid.

In surveying the use of comic elements in the memoirs so far we can sum up that they very often position the reader more or less obviously on the narrator-protagonist's side, usually very clearly set apart from his/her family and community. There are, however, some instances where this set-up changes and the audience finds itself at a noticeable distance from the narrative voice. This happens especially when – in direct opposition to the already analyzed tendency to show the Muslim community as 'strange' – the narrator-protagonist presents events as 'normal' that definitely seem extraordinary to the reader. This may lead to disconcerted laughter by which the audience distance themselves from the perceived attack on established standards of behaviour. *Poppadom Preach* goes furthest in this respect. Dilly is regularly confronted with direct verbal and physical violence in all surroundings, especially in her own family, and stresses throughout that this is 'normal' for her (cf. e.g. Khan, 263; 274; 305; 345) – "a family tradition, part of the fabric of our universe" (319).[13] Thus, ironically, being beaten at the Koran school makes her "feel right at home" (157), and in describing family quarrels Khan often introduces a slapstick tone that induces the reader to laugh despite the brutality (e.g. 317-18), especially as Dilly seems to be enjoying herself thoroughly when for once she is not actively involved. Thus, she says about the prospect of her sister getting hit, "[i]f there was any slapping going on, I wanted to watch" (269), and comments on an escalating altercation between her father and her sister-in-law, "it was a lot more interesting than the video" (316). One might argue that the normalization of violence is a strategy for emotional survival on Dilly's part; as an adolescent, she does not see any opportunity to escape from her family, so she simply accepts the given conditions as 'normal' instead of wasting her energies in futile protest. At the same time, the narrating I clearly knows that her youth was far from 'normal' and uses this knowledge to play with the reader's emotions, sending him/her back and forth between laughter and outrage.

There is a further category of comic elements which occasionally features towards the end of the memoirs and introduces a potential distance between the narrator-protagonist and the reading audience. These effects are based on dramatic irony – the reader's (apparently) superior knowledge which makes him/her laugh fairly automatically at the characters' lack of insight, because it is rather pleasant to feel more knowledgeable. Some of the narrator-protagonists foreground their impression that Muslims become increasingly integrated in Britain in the 1990s and that this goes together with a reduced importance of religion in the British Muslim community. Tellingly, such views are always recorded for the period before 9/11 and 7/7, so that the reader is led to realize the immense difference that the early 2000s made in this respect. When Hai states confidently that British Pakistanis of her age will "never have to live under the shadow of those dark [religious] rules" (2009, 109) and that "no one of [her] generation [will] ever sympathise with" the fatwa against Salman Rush-

12 In an earlier scene where Dilly and her sister visit this woman at home she is already exoticized as a "strange creature" instead of being perceived as a human being (131).

13 Manzoor is not beaten by his father but his childhood includes routines like massaging his father's feet in the evenings and being humiliated in front of his father's friends, which he presents as 'normal' in a similar way (cf. 2008, 34-35; 63; 92).

die (212), the reader smiles somewhat sadly at her ingenuousness, just as when Ahmad calls the *Satanic Verses* "bound to be somewhat obscure: I don't think it's going to be of any consequence" (2011, 282). Characteristically, Ahmad leaves the reader's distance from the character intact, whereas Hai in both instances has the narrating I add the same qualification which draws in the audience again: "Or so I thought" (2009, 109; 212). Manzoor intensifies the reservations compared with Hai and thereby foregrounds the narrating I even further, so that no real superiority can establish itself on the reader's part: "The search for an identity I could feel comfortable with had, *I believed*, reached its destination. *I was wrong*" (2008, 261; my emphasis). The overall approach is the same, however: Through the demonstration that positive statements about integration and an open-minded third generation of British Pakistanis can only seem hopelessly naïve after 2005, the reader is made to feel exactly how much has been lost through the growing fundamentalism as well as the white hostility towards British Muslims. This of course fits in very well with the authors' motivation for writing the texts in the aftermath of 7/7 (cf. above).

All in all, the memoirs thus use a range of different comic elements to influence the readers' relationship with the narrator-protagonists and the course of their lives. In this way, the audience is made to experience directly the contradictions between British Pakistani and white British culture, often being encouraged to laugh at the same time as realizing the much bleaker subtext which the scenes have for the young characters. When the focus is on contradictions and absurdities within the British Pakistani community itself, the narrator-protagonist usually places him/herself at a conspicuous distance from the other characters, including his/her family, and close to the reader. This positioning is not simply a mediator role, however, but can lead to the reproduction of stereotypical hetero-images, especially when Islam and its practices are portrayed. This may make the audience aware of their own potential stereotypes, but primarily comes across as the narrator-protagonists' way of fighting back against the limitations that Islam and the Muslim community imposed on their young selves. The memoirs combine this approach with a normalization strategy which shows their characters trying to cope with violence and abuse, often making the audience's laughter at the 'strange' plot events stick in their throats. Compared with the Black British Bildungsroman, the memoirs thus manage to involve the readership more directly through the creation of comic effects which generate fairly automatic responses. The devices thereby far transcend simple comic relief and also help to weave the British Pakistanis' experiences in their youth together with ways in which they cope with their past and with their present lives as adults. This comprehensive perspective also means that the readers immediately share the impact of the post-2000 development of the Muslim community in Britain on the individuals they have come to identify with despite all factual differences. In this way, the memoirs manage to realize their repeatedly declared aim of giving a voice to the 'normal,' non-fundamentalist British Pakistani population. At the same time, the emotional connections created by the comic elements can be taken to play a central role in the texts' successful appeal to a fairly broad readership.

Works Cited

Ahmad, Imran. *Unimagined: Muhammed, Jesus and James Bond*. 2007. London: Paper Books, 2011.

Ahmed, Rehana. "Reason to Believe? Two 'British Muslim' Memoirs." *Culture, Diaspora, and Modernity in Muslim Writing*. Eds. Rehana Ahmed, Peter Morey and Amina Yaqin. New York/London: Routledge, 2012. 52-67.

Ahmed, Sara. *The Promise of Happiness*. Durham/London: Duke University Press, 2010.

Buss, Helen M. "Memoirs." *Encyclopedia of Life Writing: Autobiographical and Biographical Forms*. Ed. Margaretta Jolly. Vol. 2. London: Fitzroy Dearborn Publishers, 2001. 595-96.

Chambers, Claire. "Countering the 'Oppressed, Kidnapped Genre' of Muslim Life Writing: Yasmin Hai's *The Making of Mr Hai's Daughter* and Shelina Zahra Janmohammed's *Love in a Headscarf*." *Life Writing* 10 (2013): 77-96.

Couser, G. Thomas. *Memoir: An Introduction*. Oxford: Oxford University Press, 2012.

Hai, Yasmin. *The Making of Mr Hai's Daughter: Becoming British*. 2008. London: Virago Press, 2009.

Hawthorne, Susan. "The Politics of the Exotic: The Paradox of Cultural Voyeurism." *NWSA Journal* 1 (1989): 617-29.

Huggan, Graham. *The Postcolonial Exotic. Marketing the Margins*. London/New York: Routledge, 2001.

Khan, Almas. *Poppadom Preach*. 2010. London: Simon & Schuster, 2011.

—. "Almas Khan." Amazon. Author's Page. *Amazon.co.uk*. n.d. Web. 22 February 2015.

Malik, Zaiba. *We Are a Muslim, Please*. 2010. London: Windmill Books, 2011.

Manzoor, Sarfraz. *Greetings from Bury Park: Race, Religion and Rock 'n' Roll*. 2007. London: Bloomsbury, 2008.

Nash, Geoffrey. *Writing Muslim Identity*. London: Bloomsbury, 2012.

Rak, Julie. "Are Memoirs Autobiography? A Consideration of Genre and Public Identity." *Genre* 37 (2004): 483-504.

Santesso, Esra Mirze. *Disorientation: Muslim Identity in Contemporary Anglophone Literature*. Basingstoke: Palgrave Macmillan, 2013.

Smith, Sidonie and Julia Watson. *Reading Autobiography: A Guide for Interpreting Life Narratives*. London and Minneapolis, MN: University of Minnesota Press, 2001.

Sommer, Roy. *Fictions of Migration: Ein Beitrag zur Theorie und Gattungstypologie des zeitgenössischen interkulturellen Romans in Großbritannien*. Trier: WVT, 2001.

Stein, Mark, *Black British Literature: Novels of Transformation*. Columbus, OH: Ohio State University Press, 2004.

Tönnies, Merle. "Feminizing a Classical Male Plot Model? Black British Women Writers and the 'Bildungsroman.'" *Anglistik: International Journal of English Studies* 24.1 (2013): 51-61.

STEPHAN KARSCHAY AND JOANNA ROSTEK

"Man haf fe do wha man haf fe do:" Humour and Identity (Re)Formation in Bernardine Evaristo's *Mr Loverman*

On reading the blurb of *Mr Loverman* (2013), one is led to assume that Bernadine Evaristo's seventh novel has a particular literary staple in its sights: the eternal conflict between the needs and desires of an individual on the one hand and the normative behaviour expected and often prescribed by society on the other. *Mr Loverman* examines why individuals end up opting for imperfect compromises and the price they pay for the choices they make. The novel demonstrates how we fashion ourselves and are perceived by others through a range of markers that dissect identity into separate categories, such as class, race, age, gender, sexual orientation, or family status and how each of these categories triggers distinct social expectations. Problems arise when one's individual needs begin to jar with cultural norms, and when the expectations resulting from one particular marker of identity (for instance race) cannot be reconciled with those stemming from another (for instance sex).

Mr Loverman's flamboyant protagonist, Barrington Jedediah Walker, is the bearer of a whole set of culturally charged identity markers: he is an affluent, married septuagenarian black man of Caribbean descent who is also a closeted homosexual. Up to his present age of 74, he could not allow himself to be all of these things openly and simultaneously. Instead, Barry had to give priority to one part of his personality to the detriment of another: in order to do justice to a particular concept of masculinity – one that in turn was shaped by his Caribbean provenance – Barry has until now concealed his homosexuality and his decades-spanning love relationship with fellow Antiguan Morris De la Roux. In what Kate Colquhoun has termed a "tale of the complicated untruths that can fester at the core of a tight community, the bluster that masks fear and, ironically, the importance of restraint" (2013), *Mr Loverman* shows the reasons for and the consequences of Barry's dissimulation, depicting the scars it has left on him, his lover Morris, his two daughters, and – above all – his wife Carmel. It traces the protagonist's gradual acceptance of an alternative but more truthful identity that is grounded in his open homosexuality and that supersedes his more conventional position as the patriarchal head of an extended family of immigrants. Barry can only overcome his late-life crisis and envision a golden old age once he manages to acknowledge the complexities of his own identity and to harmonize what at the beginning of the novel seem to him to be mutually exclusive and therefore 'unliveable' dimensions of his character:

> They think they know me.
> Husband of Carmel.
> Father of Donna and Maxine.
> Grandfather to Daniel.
> Retired engine-fitter.
> Man of property.
> Man of style.
> *Buggerer of men…* How I go live with that? (Evaristo 2013, 134)

While the difficulty of balancing individual and social needs may be a universal concern of literature, what makes Evaristo's novel special for our reading is that Barry unwittingly holds the answer to his above question – and thus the key to his self-made closet – in the method of his trademark sense of humour: "I am the Great Mood Levitator. I am the Human Valium" (Evaristo 2013, 4), is one of Barry's earliest self-characterizations. Through his sprightly first-person narration that dominates the novel (a more despondent foil is provided by the less frequent interior monologues of Barry's wife), Evaristo often turns a comic eye on the painful issues of deception, self-denial, and regret, without ridiculing the serious topics at the heart of her text. Even though *Mr Loverman* is a novel about lies, repression, and aging, critics have characterized it as "funny" (Thomson 2013), "sometimes hilarious" (Colquhoun 2013), and in parts "comical" (Canning 2013). It is the aim of our article to analyze the function of Barry's humour on his troubled journey to self-knowledge. More specifically, we will investigate to what extent *Mr Loverman*'s protagonist uses the comic as a strategy to cope with the discursive categories of race, gender, sexuality, and age in the process of his identity (re)formation.

Before embarking on a close reading of the novel, it is worth asking why humour might be a particularly useful tool for exploring the serious vicissitudes of age, gender, sex, and race as well as the overarching issue of identity formation. As a starting point, it is helpful to quote Gaby Pailer's observation that there is "a remarkable intersection between gender theories and theories of laughter, the comic, and comedy: in both areas the question of physicality for shaping or expressing identity is a major issue, and in both fields critics claim the subversive potential of bodily acts towards a cultural norm" (Pailer 2009, 7).

Manfred Pfister, commenting on the connection between laughter and sexuality, likewise stresses that "[t]hey are both closely linked to our corporeal nature" (2002, vi) and also notes:

> In both cases, an instinctual drive or corporeal reaction forms the anthropological basis that is given widely divergent socially acceptable expression [*sic*] and functions in the various cultures; and in both cases, the anthropological drive – sexual desire or the *vis comica* – constantly threatens to subvert the social bounds set up to contain it. In the case of both sex and laughter, what emerges is that both their histories are mainly histories of attempts to limit, control and civilise them, be it through negative injunctions and taboos or through setting up particular forms of gender relations [...] or particular forms of laughter [...] as positive models to be aspired to. (v-vi)

Pursuing this line of thought further, one may note that besides gender and sexuality, race (by way of skin colour) and age (by way of changes in the body's cellular structure) similarly involve a manifestly corporeal element, which, however, is culturally overdetermined. What humour thus shares with categories such as age, gender, sex, and race, is a dual nature, i.e. a material, bodily dimension on the one hand that evolves in and interacts with a non-material, cultural realm on the other. The tensions adherent to this dualism lie at the core of *Mr Loverman*, which portrays how cultural norms have shaped the protagonist's aging, black, male body, and his "full-blooded, hot-blooded, pumping-rumping, throbbing organ of an uncontainable, unrestrainable, undetainable man-loving *heart*" (Evaristo 2013, 17). For Barry, humour is a strategy that imitates, masks, and helps to bridge the tensions between 'nature' and 'culture' that act upon him.

Laughter can be variously untamed, uncontrollable, and subversive, or regimented, disciplinary, and order-affirming. Pfister notes, moreover, that it "is always caught up in the distinctions between centre and margins every society employs to establish and stabilise its identity" (2002, vi). While in some cases, laughter emerges as a defiant strategy of excluded outsiders, in other contexts, as Andreas Böhn points out, the comic "does not necessarily tend to overcome traditional oppositions and ideological boundaries" (2009, 62). Andy Medhurst points to yet another possible effect of humour in the process of identity formation: "It is exactly because identities are so disputed, so slippery, so rocky and so anxious that the celebration of belonging offered by comedy is all the more welcome" (2007, 19). Humour is thus, like identity itself, a complex, multi-layered phenomenon and invariably serves different, at times conflicting, ends. It is therefore fitting that Evaristo's protagonist uses his comic versatility to defend *and* to attack; to exclude *and* to include; to ward off *and* to accept; to alleviate *and* to circumvent painful introspection.

From Barrysexual to Homosexual: Humour and the Investigation of Race, Gender, and Sexuality

Barry is a uniquely garrulous narrator with an opinion on almost everything ("Sociology, Psychology, Archaeology, Oloyology – you name it. English Literature, French Language, *naturellement*." [Evaristo 2013, 8]), and thus much of the comedy in *Mr Loverman* is of a rhetorical, rather than a theatrical, nature. Stupendously versed in Shakespeare's *oeuvre*, Barry fashions himself as an armchair poet worthy of the highest accolades: "Derek Walcott? You listening over there in St Lucia? Mi no care if you did get the Nobel Prize for poetry, you better watch out, because Barrington Walker's goin' steal the linguistic march on you, fella" (11). A part of Barry's humour, then, is notable for its sheer irreverence and its creative amalgamation of apparently incompatible rhetorical compounds. It can be related to the incongruity theory of humour (cf. Morreall 1983, 15) whose essence is captured in a comment by the 17th-century writer and natural philosopher Blaise Pascal: "Nothing produces laughter more than a surprising disproportion between that which one expects and that which one sees" (Pascal qtd. in Morreall 1983, 130). Barry's ability to create amusing linguistic inconsistencies is directly linked to his Caribbean heritage. An autodidact of many parts, he can "speak the Queen's as well as any Big Englander" (Evaristo 2013, 6), but will, on occasion, "mash up the *h-english linguish* whenever we feel like it, drop our prepositions with our panties, piss in the pot of correct syntax and spelling, and mangle our grammar *at random*" (6-7). Inventively mingling standard speech with Jamaican patois, *Mr Loverman* easefully moves between registers whose combination creates humour out of incongruence. Pondering the troubled relationship with his daughters, for instance, Barry invents mock-Shakespearean words, which he then arranges in a *figura etymologica* to enhance the hyperbole that is so characteristic of his speech in general: "Donna, in particular, stored up all her beshittery for her father – who was beshat upon from a great height" (134).

Just like Shakespeare's own examples of the genre, *Mr Loverman* is a comedy which ends with the reconciliation of two lovers (Barry and Morris), the symbolic expurgation of a blocking figure (Barry's wife Carmel) and the restoration of a certain order out of chaos. Yet Barry's story at times veers dangerously close to a tragic outcome, since his particular quest for happiness involves the difficult examination of race, gender, and sexuality as ambiguous and often contradictory fields of identity formation. In a reading of contemporary Caribbean fiction by Michele Cliff and H. Nigel Thomas, Timothy Chin has emphasized the importance of such an examination for a progressive development within and between individuals of different cultures:

"These sites of ambiguity and contradiction – which often reflect how 'differences' are actually lived and negotiated – are, paradoxically perhaps, the ones that can potentially enable new forms of social and cultural relations" (1997, 139). Barry himself has been witness to such newly formed social and cultural relations in his immigrant experience of a more tolerant and less racist British society. On remembering how the managing director of Ford Motors ("Mr Lardy Comb-Over") patronized him at his retirement party by explaining the word *raconteur*, in the assumption his former employee might not understand "words of five syllables or ones that was a bit Frenchified" (Evaristo 2013, 7), Barry's temper briefly flares up again, yet he happily admits that racist taunts are a thing from the past: "Never no mind. Those days long gone. I've not been called no names by nobody except the wife for at least twenty years" (6).

Of humble origins in Antigua, Barry has managed to rise in the ranks of British post-war society to a position of upper-middle-class affluence. The driving force behind this story of a successful acculturation is, however, a deep-seated fear of cultural ostracism as Barry's confessional statement, "I don't like being an outsider" (159), makes clear. Yet while this anxiety has proved to be conducive to Barry's economic success and the confident assertion of his Black Britishness, it also prevents him from aligning his gender identity with his homosexuality. More specifically, Barry finds himself in a critical conundrum (in both senses of the word 'critical') that Dwight McBride has identified as a major stumbling block in the study of culture:

> When we give "race," with its retinue of historical and discursive investments, primacy over other signifiers of difference, the result is a network of critical blindnesses that prevents us from perceiving the ways in which the conventions of race discourse get naturalized and normativized. These conventions often include [...] the denigration of homosexuality and the accompanying peripheralization of women. Underlying much of race discourse, then, is always the implication that all "real" black subjects are male and heterosexual. (1999, 263)

In a similar way, by having predominantly defined himself in terms of race – as a London-based black Briton of Caribbean descent – Barry impedes a self-investigation of his troubled gender identity. Despite his assertion that "I am an anti-discriminatory person" (Evaristo 2013, 137), he conforms to the normative standards of a patriarchal gender ideology that is both openly misogynistic and homophobic. Furthermore, it is telling that Barry's liberal claim is only part of his interior monologue and does by no means tally with his explicitly voiced statements, thus making again visible the lie he lives.

In light of the unresolved conflict between his 'racial' and his gender identities, Barry's witty statements can be partly explained by the relief theory of laughter. Originating in the works of the third Earl of Shaftesbury in the 18th century, the relief theory was prominently elaborated by Herbert Spencer in the 19th century and transposed to the field of psychoanalysis by Sigmund Freud in the early 20th. Its basic idea is that humour serves the physiological function of releasing a surplus of nervous energy, in an analogous way to a steam cooker, which will release extra pressure through a relief valve (cf. Morreal 2009, 16). Arguably, Barry's humour can be read as such a coping strategy which allows him to externalize his inner tension. This explains why many of his humorous remarks have a derisory and discriminatory edge. Through his biting comments, Barry can vocalize but also mask (from others and from himself) his hidden rage and despair.

The third chapter of Evaristo's novel is teasingly titled "The Art of Being Normal" (31) and elaborates on the gender scripts black men feel obliged to follow, regardless of their actual sexual orientation. Barry explains the motivating reason why his lover Morris married his since-divorced wife Odette: "[H]e couldn't be a West Indian and not start a family – *man haf fe do wha man haf fe do*. Truth is, both of us was desperate to be anything other than what we was" (32). In Barry's and Morris's lives, race trumps sex in the performance of gender – and that is their potential tragedy. Having internalized orthodox gender stereotypes, Barry seems to hold the essentialist belief that gender is an innate part of human nature, rather than an ideological and discursive position. According to Barry, "The Art of Being a Man" (the title of the novel's ninth chapter) thus consists in complementing women's strengths and compensating for supposedly inborn female weaknesses: "Women are wired differently to men. Oh, yes, they can put on an emotional performance when it suits them, but they're not so hot when it comes to technical things" (168). At several points in the novel, this gender orthodoxy tips over into misogynistic vitriol barely tempered by Barry's amusing metaphors. In an evening introductory course on feminism at the adult education centre in Hackney, Barry lectures his fellow students about the Aristotelian view that "the female is a female by virtue of a certain lack of qualities," in other words by "a natural defectiveness" (127). Incongruously, Barry rejects the notion of patriarchal oppression by fusing the two alternative default positions women are allotted in patriarchal discourses of race and gender: "[A]nyone thinking women are oppressed should meet some of the bush women from my part of the world. Trust me, if they could get away with it, they'd cut off a fella's balls, pluck them, chop them, marinate them, stew them, serve them up on a plate with rice and peas and present the fella with the bill" (127). Barry here employs humour as "an instrument of discrimination, [...] ridicule and humiliation" (Pailer 2009, 8), and the comedy evoked by his grotesque recipe hardly glosses over its more sinister undertones. Apparently, Evaristo's protagonist can only imagine two types of women: submissive guardians of the hearth and dangerous *femmes fatales*. He fuses these patriarchal stereotypes of orthodox femininity into the image of the 'Devil in the House' threatening the male sex with a symbolic castration. That this is a fear evidently entertained by Barry himself is made clear by his unflattering hyperbolic description of Carmel as "the Sphinx guarding the city of Thebes:" "Head of a woman, body of a lioness, wings of an eagle, memory of an elephant, bite of a saltwater crocodile with 2,000 pounds per square inch of pressure, ready to snap my head off" (Evaristo 2013, 14). Although Carmel is meant to function as the comical object of this ludicrous characterization, the acrid humour ultimately mirrors Barry's own frustration that his lived identity is just as grotesque and disjointed as the incongruent body parts out of which he imaginatively assembles his wife. His making fun of Carmel is but projected self-loathing.

This hidden self-contempt is related to the fact that Barry's cultural background has fostered a tacit homophobia within himself. When day-dreaming about a life as an out-gay couple, Barry's ideal vision of the future smacks of the very stereotypes about gay life which make his coming-out such an arduous process. "How about Miami?" he suggests to Morris, adding: "I hear that place is full of pooftahs. Maybe we can live in a luxurious bungalow in Florida with sprinklers on the lawn and half-naked butlers serving up our evening aperitif" (45). This sexualized image of decadent wealth and the designation of other gay men as 'pooftahs' show to what extent Barry has internalized the prejudices of his own culture. At a later conversation with Morris about the highly controversial gay writer, actor, and style guru Quentin Crisp – whom Barry ridicules as an "eccentric pooftah with blue-rinse hair," Barry's anti-gay statements do not fail to incense his more self-conscious lover: "This is your problem, Barry. He was the same as me and you. So that makes you a pooftah too" (137). Yet Crisp's camp performances jar with Barry's understanding of virile masculinity.

At this point, Barry's humour bespeaks a sense of superiority towards the supposed emasculation of a certain gay life-style: "Morris, when did you ever see me flapping about with limp wrists and squealing like a constipated castrato?" (138). Thomas Hobbes – one of the most prominent proponents of the superiority theory of humour – characterized such moments as a "[s]udden glory," which can be caused "by the apprehension of some deformed thing in another, by comparison whereof they [i.e. the persons laughing] suddenly applaud themselves" (qtd. in Morreall 2009, 6). Hobbes further noted that this kind of humour was most prevalent in those jokers "that are conscious of the fewest abilities in themselves; who are forced to keep themselves in their own favour by observing the imperfections of other men" (6). Thus Barry's show of superiority can be understood as a vainglorious attempt to mask his own sense of insecurity about his homosexuality. He is not yet ready to fully embrace his identity as a gay man and refuses to be pigeonholed by society: "I am an individual, specific, not generic. I am no more a pooftah than I am a homo, buller or anti-man" (Evaristo 2013, 138). That Barry is already struggling with the push-and-pull of his contradictory ideological positions becomes clear when he starts humming Gloria Gaynor's famous gay anthem "I Am What I Am," without any sense of self-irony. Ultimately, however, he refuses to accept a label that is not of his own making and stumblingly asserts: "I ain't no homosexual, I am a … Barrysexual!" (138). On the one hand, this creation of a neologism to characterize his individual identity could be read as typical of Barry's trademark rhetoric of humour and as an attempt to transcend limiting and ready-made identity markers. On the other hand, the evident effort it takes the otherwise quick-tongued protagonist to disgorge a rather uninspired pun suggests that at this stage, Barry's bravado is only skin-deep. His secretly lived homosexuality gives the lie to his show of masculinity and it appears even more difficult to detach his sexual and his gendered selves.

To claim that Evaristo's protagonist has made a deliberate decision to dissociate the performance of his gender from his sexual identity as a gay man would be to ignore the powerful shackles of racial and gender ideologies. In an important article on Queer Criticism, Judith Butler revisited her seminal study *Gender Trouble* (1990) to clarify the possible misapprehension that the performance of gender is best understood as a series of conscious acts, "as one puts on clothes in the morning" (Butler 1993, 21). Butler rejects such a "voluntarist account of gender" (21) as it assumes a fully evolved subjectivity antecedent to its own gendering:

> Gender is performative insofar as it is the *effect* of a regulatory regime of gender differences in which genders are divided and hierarchized *under constraint*. Social constraints, taboos, prohibitions, threats of punishment operate in the ritualized repetition of norms […]. To the extent that this repetition creates an effect of gender uniformity, a stable effect of masculinity or femininity, it produces and destabilizes the notion of the subject as well, for the subject only comes into intelligibility through the matrix of gender. (21-22)

In this understanding of gender performance, misogyny and homophobia are the markers of a heteronormativity that Barry is constrained to perform under ideological duress. His dilemma suggests that homosexual love is cast as an unspeakable transgression, under constant threat from a disciplinary regime of power.

Evaristo gives this oppressive regime and its material effects a prominent place in her novel. In the seventh chapter, Barry recalls the killing of Delroy Simmons, a local electrician of Jamaican descent, who was rumoured to have been cheating on his wife with another man (Evaristo 2013, 113-14). The memory of finding the murder victim right outside his house makes Barry emphasize: "*No wonder I couldn't leave Carmel back then*" (114). That homophobic violence is by no means a thing of the past is made clear by Evaristo's reference to the gruesome assault on Ian Baynham in Trafalgar Square in 2009, when a teenage girl and her friends trampled the 62-year-old civil servant to death in front of a group of tourists. In Barry's case, these reflections are not only a reminder of the hypothetical dangers he might be facing as an out-gay man, but they are mementos of how narrowly he escaped a similar attack in 1977, when he was badly mangled by a group of thugs reviling him as "Batty man! Bum bandit! Poofter! Anti-Man!" (122). In the light of this experience, Barry's comic denigration of camp homosexuals like Quentin Crisp can also be read as a psychological mechanism that helps him work through trauma. In one version of the relief theory of humour, Sigmund Freud saw in humour the narcissistic victory of the pleasure principle over trauma. According to Freud, humour was thus best understood as having both a liberating and a sublimating effect:

> The grandeur [of humour] clearly lies in the triumph of narcissism, in the triumphantly asserted invulnerability of the ego. The ego refuses to be hurt by causes in reality, to be obliged to suffer, it insists that the traumas of the outside world cannot get near it, indeed it shows that it sees them only as occasions for the gain in pleasure. (Freud 2006, 562)

Read in this way, Barry's humorous bravado acts as a shield against both the dangers of a homophobic world and the painful realities of an identity in denial of itself.

At the same time, it can be argued that Barry's humour also serves as the novel's central tool of empowerment to reach an 'authentic' identity that harmonizes the apparently incongruous categories of race, gender, and sexuality. This process involves first and foremost the dismantling of Barry's own patriarchal stereotyping of women and gay men. Expecting to find "attention-seekers" like Quentin Crisp in a modern gay bar, he is surprised to realize that these men are remarkably 'normal:' "They're just regular guys […]. Just goes to show how even my assumptions might, upon occasion, be misconceptions" (Evaristo 2013, 248). Similarly, Barry must recognize that the denial of his own identity has almost ruined his wife. Formerly the voracious virago of his misogynistic stereotypes and the butt of his unkind jokes, Carmel, by the end of the novel, appears to him as the victim of a terrible injustice – an injustice that requires serious, vocal redemption: "And I sorry. Carmel, I sorry" (305). The naming of things for what they are finally also leads Barry to contemplate that he "might be okay with [being] a Barrysexual, correction, *homosexual* (la-di-dah) grandfather" (299). That the conciliatory hint of irony in this statement is directed at Barry himself registers that the functions of his humour have changed with the strenuous process of self-recognition. Maggie Gee argues in her review of *Mr Loverman* that Evaristo gives "her readers time to move from laughter to sympathy" (Gee 2013). Such a development is likewise traced by the novel's protagonist: while his urge to make fun remains intact, it undergoes a turn by the end of the narrative in losing some of its previous acerbity and malignance which was but an expression of Barry's inner pain. After his coming-out and the realignment of his racial, gendered and sexual identities, much of Barry's earlier laughter emerges as a grinning yet grim mask which, while it allowed him to cope with his troubled life, paradoxically prevented him from smiling.

"Your Daddy Still Got His *Joie De Vivre*:" Humour as a Means of Valorizing Old Age

Having scrutinized the functions of humour with regard to the categories of race, gender, and sex, it is instructive to consider *Mr Loverman*'s engagement with an additional marker of identity, namely age. Richard Canning asserts that "the most radical reversal of expectations in *Mr Loverman* relates to the paucity of novels in which older gay experiences and perceptions play any role" (2013). Yet what makes Evaristo's novel stand out is not only the prominent place it assigns to an elderly gay character, but also the positive stance it adopts on the issue of (male) aging in general. Old age in Western culture is frequently perceived as a problem-ridden and negatively connoted stage of life. It is seen as marked by nostalgia, anxiety, and depression; determined by the deteriorating and ailing body; bereft of future, except the certain prospect of death; devoid of sexual desire and pleasure. In order to challenge this negative view of old age, Evaristo resorts to a 'comic turn.' Importantly, the kind of humour she employs in this context is not predominantly grim and cynical, but optimistic and life-affirming. In this, *Mr Loverman* departs from texts about the process of aging which use gallows humour as a strategy to brave what is nevertheless perceived as a painful ordeal. In Evaristo's novel, humour is not aimed at the allegedly pathetic and ridiculous 'side effects' of aging, but functions as a means of injecting old age with energy and life.

With respect to race, gender, and sex, the many ways of theorizing them in the course of the past few decades add up to a joint effort to move these categories away from the realm of 'nature' and situate them closer to the domain of 'culture.' Concomitant with these attempts has been the positing of such categories as constructed and performative – and thus open to change and reinterpretation – instead of considering them as fixed and universal phenomena. The challenge in addressing aging in similar terms is that old age is associated with a 'natural,' certain, and fearsome fact of life: death. Kathleen Woodward notes that "[i]n physiological and anatomical terms (this is biological or functional aging), aging is undeniably associated with a loss of function, one whose upper limit is death" (2006, 171). For this reason, the boundary line between 'natural' and 'cultural' processes gets easily blurred: the gradual changes to our bodies over time and the growing physical limitations are undeniable, which makes it easy to overlook what is cultural about growing old. Yet age is similar to other discursive categories of identity. In an important essay on "The Double Standard of Aging," Susan Sontag claimed as early as 1972 that growing old "is much more a social judgment than a biological eventuality. […] The calendar is subject to variations from country to country. […] Aging also varies according to social class" (1997, 21). Brett Mills has more recently concurred that "'[b]eing old' is […] an outcome of an individual's interaction with society rather than an intrinsic fact of a physical body, and so exploring representations of age and ageing can tell us something about how the category of 'the elderly' is constructed in this society at this time" (2015, 273). In the light of this remark, it is noteworthy that *Mr Loverman* represents growing old in a positive way and entertainingly challenges a series of ageist prejudices. In the process, it relies on humour as a marker of intellectual vigour.

Barry's self-characterization in the novel's first chapter in this regard is typical of his attitude toward aging, which fuses self-irony with optimistic defiance:

> I am still a Saga Boy. Still here, thanks be to God. Still spruced up and sharp-suited with a rather manly swagger. Still six foot something with no sign of shrinkage yet. Still working a certain *je ne sais* whatsit. I might have lost the hair on my head, but I

> still got a finely clipped moustache in the style of old Hollywood romancers. Folk used to tell me I looked like a young Sidney Poitier. Now they say I resemble a (slightly) older Denzel Washington. Who am I to argue? [...] I can still bedazzle with my indestructible ivories. Must be the only 74-year-old in the land with his own full set, not a single one extracted, capped, veneered or crowned. (Evaristo 2013, 8; 10)

As becomes obvious from Barry's anything but modest self-description, he is not a depressed aging man whose remaining energy is spent on nostalgic reminiscences and past regrets. Nor does he see his body as a site of decay; quite the contrary, he is attentive to and proud of it, even verging on the vain. This attitude does not mean that he fails to register the challenges and limitations that come with age. His narrative is interspersed with sometimes self-mocking, sometimes more serious reflections on his stage of life:

> [T]he inescapable truth is that it's not easy approaching your ninth decade. You look back with nostalgia on the time when the force of your piss could dislodge bricks in a wall, from two whole yards away. You remember the time when your body moved as fast as your mind, and it didn't feel like your legs was filled with concrete when you tried to run. You remember the time when you had hair on your head. These days you have a little heartburn, you think you having a heart attack. The finishing line got that much closer. (44)

Despite approaching the "finishing line," Barry continues to engage in activities that he enjoyed as a younger man, such as going out with Morris, having passionate sex with him, eyeing potential sexual partners, or simply being cheeky and irresponsible. This 'youthful' behaviour is here appropriated by the older generation, and one of the novel's greatest merits lies in the representation of Barry's self-diagnosed "*joie de vivre*" (91) without making him appear absurd or pathetic.

Barry is not a pitiable age-denier fighting a vain and embarrassing fight against the inevitable. Instead, what he does refuse is to succumb to social expectations regarding 'age-appropriate' behaviour. These are prominently voiced by his younger daughter Maxine, who suggests that instead of having the occasional night out, her father should consider "going to bed at a reasonable hour with a mug of Horlicks... or... something stronger, *whatevs*" (91). Barry is patronized by his middle-aged daughter like a naughty child that needs to be reprimanded and taught to conform to social rules. The irony is that at forty, without a partner, a child, or a steady income, obsessed with fashion and diets, and desperately trying to conceal her age ("I've been twenty-nine for eleven years already" [96]), Maxine herself is a victim of standards of 'age-appropriate' behaviour. She is ahead of her father in terms of the realization that race, gender, and sex are largely socially constructed categories: in fact, she is the one to introduce Barry and Morris to Soho's multicultural gay scene. But her conventional notion of age is at odds with her otherwise progressive stance. The resulting irony resurfaces when she tells Barry after he comes out to her: "You've been trapped inside yourself, which can lead to a very distorted view of things. My advice to you is to join a gay pensioners' club for support, where you can share experiences with fellow old-timers over a gentle game of table tennis or croquet" (220). While urging her father to step out of one trap (that of heteronormativity), Maxine inadvertently pushes him into another (that of old age). But Barry humorously reminds her that despite its corporeal dimension, aging is (like gender) very much a matter of performance: "Maxine [...], you love the fact that I don't *act* like some old codger with one foot in the grave, so don't give me any of that Horlicks crap" (91, my emphasis). The interaction between

Maxine and Barry suggests that in the process of identity (re)formation, the younger generation can learn from the older and vice versa.

The novel's ending, which envisages a hopeful future for Barry, Morris, and Carmel, moreover works against the perception of age as a stage of life dominated by the prospect of death. It is true that the characters are to a large extent preoccupied with the burdens of their past lives. After all, Barry notes, "[t]his is what happens when 75 per cent of your life is in the past. Each step forwards triggers a step backwards" (134). *Mr Loverman* demonstrates, however, that there are steps forwards still to be taken at a later stage of one's life – Barry's coming-out being the most illustrative instance. But also Carmel, having discovered that her husband had used her as a cover-up for his secret life as a homosexual, decides that despite her pain, frustration, and anger, she will "look to the future now and not waste any more time regretting the Big Bad Decision that changed the course of your life" (289). The novel ends with Morris reminding Barry that now they finally have "a future to look forward to together" (307). Some critics have understandably expressed reservations about Evaristo's unconditionally cheerful ending which miraculously grants happy prospects to all its aging protagonists. Yet what on the one hand seems unrealistic might on the other be read as a programmatic decision on the author's part not to reduce aging to "plans for funeral plots, metaphorically speaking" (298), but to imbue it with humour, optimism, and a future.

Mr Loverman thus challenges what Kathleen Woodward has termed "[t]he youthful structure of the look – that is, the culturally induced tendency to degrade and reduce an older person to the prejudicial category of old age" (2006, 164), and Barry's *joie de vivre* plays a significant role in this process. Regarding the categories of race, sex, and gender, Barry's humour frequently serves as a coping strategy masking and, at the same time, helping him to externalize his inner conflict. With respect to age, Barry's humour assumes a different function and is, as it were, more authentic: it is not 'faked' laughter variously hiding and giving expression to sorrow, but the manifestation of contented acceptance regarding the fact of growing old. If, as readers, we are struck by Barry's behaviour as too farfetched for a man of his age, we may of course accuse Evaristo of an aesthetic failure in devising an implausibly youthful and cheerful old character. At the same time, however, it is instructive to keep in mind Nela Bureu Ramos's observation that "[d]esire or love knows no age, nor does imagination or creativity. Culture tells you when to start or end phases of existence, and how to live these phases" (2010, 17). A sceptical reaction to Barry's vitality might thus reflect discursively constructed expectations about age that Evaristo's protagonist gleefully sets out to revise.

Conclusion

While Andreas Böhn is right in claiming that "[t]he comic is not the ultimate locus from which one can embark on revolutionizing the world" (2009, 62), Bernardine Evaristo's *Mr Loverman* suggests that humour may nevertheless facilitate such a revolution in the context of identity formation. Yet the novel makes it clear that comedy alone will not suffice: establishing an 'authentic' identity – at whatever age – requires the dismantling of ideology's simplistic binarisms that cast people in preconceived uniform moulds. Furthermore, the authenticity of one's identity must become manifest in language: "Yes, sah. Yes, Morris. Yes, Lola and fellow *attention-seekers*, I feel myself coming out, no *so-called* about it" (274). That Barry's comic rhetoric points the way to a satisfactory resolution of his identity crisis is one of the great strengths of

Mr Loverman: Barry must learn to harmonize those elements of his identity that seem to him at first incompatible – in the same way his humour harmonizes apparently incongruous compounds. With regard to the power of puns, Jonathan Culler has noted how "boundaries [...] count for less than one might imagine and [are sites] where supposedly discrete meanings threaten to sink into fluid subterranean signifieds too undefinable to call concepts" (1988, 3). Barry finally accepts that the fluid categories of identity formation such as race, sex, gender, and age need not be mutually exclusive, that they need not cancel each other out. It is as possible to be an energetic septuagenarian out-of-the-closet black man as it is rhetorically possible to mix high and low cultural references or Jamaican patois with the Queen's English.

Mr Loverman thus demonstrates that the perceived 'naturalness' and inescapability of identity markers may effectively imprison and damage those who are unable to meet the culturally prescribed standards of 'normality.' In keeping with his own experience, Barry demands at one point: "If someone asks for their freedom, you got to give it to them; otherwise you become their jailer" (Evaristo 2013, 79). The problem about this request, however, is that the walls of society's prison are frequently invisible to its inhabitants. *Mr Loverman* aims at making us aware of the structures that confine us and it encourages us to realize that they are not impregnable. In this respect, it is highly symbolic that the novel ends with the gay lovers' road trip in a convertible and with the three protagonists – Barry, Morris, and Carmel – refurbishing their old homes, knocking down walls, and assigning new functions to old rooms (290; 295). The message is clear: while it is impossible to live without the framework of a 'home,' its outline and furnishings are not immovable. The process of recreation and of turning one's life around may be an arduous one, yet it may prove just as liberating and energizing as the humour with which it is laced.

Works Cited

Böhn, Andreas. "Subversion of Gender Identities through Laughter and the Comic?" *Gender and Laughter: Comic Affirmation and Subversion in Traditional and Modern Media*. Eds. Gaby Pailer and Susanne Bach. Amsterdam: Rodopi, 2009. 49-64.

Bureu Ramos, Nela. "Introduction: The Aching of Desire." *Flaming Embers: Literary Testimonies on Aging and Desire*. Ed. Nela Bureu Ramos. Bern: Lang, 2010. 7-22.

Butler, Judith. "Critically Queer." *GLQ: A Journal of Lesbian and Gay Studies* 1.1 (1993): 17-32.

Canning, Richard. "Book Review: *Mr Loverman*, by Bernadine Evaristo." *The Independent*. 13 September 2013. Web. 5 January 2015.

Chin, Timothy S. "'Bullers' and 'Battymen': Contesting Homophobia in Black Popular Culture and Contemporary Caribbean Literature." *Callaloo* 20.1 (1997): 127-141.

Colquhoun, Kate. "Book Review: *Mr Loverman*." *Sunday Express*. 1 September 2013. Web. 5 January 2015.

Connell, R. W. *Masculinities*. [1995]. Cambridge: Polity Press, 2005.

Culler, Jonathan. "The Call of the Phoneme: Introduction." *On Puns: The Foundation of Letters*. Ed. Jonathan Culler. Oxford: Basil Blackwell, 1988. 1-16.

Evaristo, Bernardine. *Mr Loverman*. London: Penguin, 2013.

Freud, Sigmund. "Humour." [1928]. *The Penguin Freud Reader*. Ed. Adam Phillips. London: Penguin, 2006. 561-66.

Gee, Maggie. "*Mr Loverman* by Bernardine Evaristo – Review." *The Guardian*. 31 August 2013. Web. 5 January 2015.

McBride, Dwight A. "Can the Queen Speak? Racial Essentialism, Sexuality, and the Problem of Authority." *Black Men on Race, Gender, and Sexuality: A Critical Reader*. Ed. Devon W. Carbado. New York: New York University Press, 1999. 253-75.

Medhurst, Andy. *A National Joke: Popular Comedy and English Cultural Identities*. London: Routledge, 2007.

Mills, Brett. "Old Jokes: *One Foot in the Grave*, Comedy, and the Elderly." *British TV Comedy: Cultural Concepts, Contexts and Controversies*. Eds. Jürgen Kamm and Birgit Neumann. Basingstoke: Palgrave Macmillan, 2015. 265-277.

Morreall, John. *Taking Laughter Seriously*. Albany, NY: State University of New York Press, 1983.

—. "A New Theory of Laughter." *The Philosophy of Laughter and Humor*. Ed. John Moreall. Albany, NY: State University of New York Press, 1987. 128-38.

—. *Comic Relief: A Comprehensive Philosophy of Humor*. Malden, MA: Wiley-Blackwell, 2009.

Pailer, Gaby. "Introduction." *Gender and Laughter: Comic Affirmation and Subversion in Traditional and Modern Media*. Eds. Gaby Pailer and Susanne Bach. Amsterdam: Rodopi, 2009. 7-14.

Pfister, Manfred. "Introduction: A History of English Laughter?" *A History of English Laughter: Laughter from Beowolf to Beckett and Beyond.* Ed. Manfred Pfister. Amsterdam: Rodopi, 2002. v-x.

Sontag, Susan. "The Double Standard of Aging." [1972]. *The Other Within Us: Feminist Explorations of Women and Aging*. Ed. Marilyn Pearsall. Boulder, CO: Westview, 1997. 19-24.

Thomson, Ian. "*Mr Loverman*, by Bernardine Evaristo – Review." *The Spectator*. 14 September 2013. Web. 5 January 2015.

Woodward, Kathleen. "Performing Age, Performing Gender." *NWSA Journal: National Women's Studies Association Journal* 18.1 (2006): 162-89.

MARION GYMNICH

Elements of Satire and Romantic Comedy in a Portrayal of British Society at the Beginning of the Millennium: Sebastian Faulks's *A Week in December*

1. Themes and Structure of *A Week in December*

Sebastian Faulks's *A Week in December* (2009) has been hailed as "an attempt to write a new kind of condition of England novel" (Dix 2012). This categorization of Faulks's novel seems justified given the fact that *A Week in December* addresses a remarkable range of problems British society has to face at the beginning of the new millennium, including for instance the fear of terrorism, challenges in the field of health care as well as the increasing lack of trust in the international financial and banking system. *A Week in December* seeks to provide a panoramic picture of life in London in the 21st century by introducing a considerable number of characters who differ in terms of their age, education, ethnicity or income. To a certain extent, these characters may be read as representatives of particular social groups. Upon closer examination, however, one realizes that many of the characters actually face what appear to be variations on the same problem. There are for example several individuals whose lives have been significantly shaped by some kind of alternative/virtual reality, be it "Parallax, the newest and most advanced of alternative-reality games" (Faulks 2010, 3) available on the internet, the temporary escape from reality that is promised by drugs, hallucinations caused by a psychological disorder or the increasingly virtual world of global finance, which is even referred to as "Fantasy Finance" by one of the characters (129).

Despite conveying an impression of life in the 21st century that is without doubt quite dismal in many respects, *A Week in December* is also highly entertaining and thus can be seen in the context of a comic turn in British literature. Many Condition-of-England novels written in the 19th century, when the genre had its heyday, adopted a predominantly serious, at times almost didactic tone in their assessment of contemporary society, seeking to respond to problems of their time by advocating social reforms. Elizabeth Gaskell's industrial novels *North and South* (1854-55) and *Mary Barton: A Tale of Manchester Life* (1848) are cases in point. Though being quite clearly didactic, Charles Dickens's *Hard Times* (1854) combines a sentimental depiction of the plight of workers in a fictitious industrial city called 'Coketown' with a good deal of humour and satire on human flaws and social institutions (e.g. the Victorian education system). One could argue that Faulks follows in Dickens's footsteps by adopting a satirical and humorous approach in his assessment of the shortcomings of society.[1] In his examination of social problems Faulks in fact draws upon different comic traditions, ranging from satire to romantic comedy – a mixture which has interesting implications for the evaluation of society undertaken in this specific literary text.

In one of the few articles that have discussed *A Week in December* so far, Hywel Dix argues that "Faulks's main theme is how people in contemporary London have

1 The recurring references to the tradition of the Victorian novel scattered throughout the text additionally draw the readers' attention to similarities between Faulks's *A Week in December* and the 19th-century novel.

become atomised, disconnected from each other in their daily lives and therefore lacking in emotional contact or any sense of mutual co-existence" (Dix 2012).

While the isolation experienced by individuals is undeniably highlighted throughout *A Week in December*, at least some of the characters turn out to be able to overcome their emotional disconnection in the course of the novel. This development even culminates in a striking rediscovery of the experience of old-fashioned romance for these characters, as will be shown below. In terms of its structural features, Faulks's novel at first sight seems to support the conclusion reached by Dix, since *A Week in December* juxtaposes several plot strands revolving around different characters, which results in a largely episodic structure. Nevertheless there are several narrative strategies which ensure a certain amount of coherence and even serve to evoke the impression that the lives of people living in the modern metropolis are connected after all. This notion of connectedness is partially evoked on the plot level. In the first chapter of the novel the readers are told about plans for a dinner party, and the list of guests provided in the text (Faulks 2010, 5-7) causes the reader to expect that this party will eventually bring together many of the novel's characters.

There are also further, arguably more subtle hints which remind the readers time and again of the fact that the lives of the different characters are linked in manifold ways, even if the individuals are not aware of these connections. The readers for instance gradually realize that several characters are likely to visit the hospital that has been singled out as the target of a terrorist attack. In this way a certain amount of suspense is created, and the readers are reminded of the sinister truth that the threat of terrorism is one of the factors that connect the people living in a modern metropolis like London. The photograph of one of the characters that is featured on an internet website providing pornographic material is seen by several other characters, including the members of a terrorist cell who use exactly this photograph to exchange secret messages. Moreover, contemporary consumer culture is shown to link the characters' experience in more mundane ways: Some of them have dinner at a (fictitious) restaurant chain called Pizza Palace, while another character buys marijuana in one of the chain's restaurants, and yet another hopes to win a literature award sponsored by the same chain. As these examples demonstrate, the meticulous references to what characters eat, where they happen to be at a particular moment, what they read about and what they are exposed to in the media, are characteristic of the narrative style employed in *A Week in December* and constitute a means of showing that the characters are already connected simply due to the fact that they move within the same framework of references within contemporary consumer culture.

In particular from the bird's eye perspective frequently adopted by the heterodiegetic narrator of *A Week in December*, who makes ample use of the psychological and spatial privileges conventionally associated with this type of narrator, the overall impression of life in London at the beginning of the 21st century appears to be significantly less informed by isolation than one might perhaps expect. Instead, the novel even seems to suggest that one may at any moment run into someone who will end up having an important impact on one's life in one way or another: This person may be a terrorist, but he or she may just as well be someone one falls in love with – an idea that has been reiterated countless times in the genre of romantic comedy. On the second page of the novel, the heterodiegetic narrator draws upon the spatial privilege to establish a link between two characters:

> Some yards below where Gabriel sat reading was an Underground train; and in the driver's cab a young woman called Jenni Fortune switched off the interior light because she was distracted by her own reflection in the windscreen. (2)

In retrospect, what looks like a purely spatial 'link' between the two characters turns out to have been an instance of foreshadowing since Gabriel and Jenni soon begin to forge a romantic relationship. The references to the genre of romantic comedy one encounters throughout *A Week in December* are a feature of the novel which time and again serves to undermine the impression of isolation prevailing in many portrayals of contemporary society.

2. The Parallels to the Romantic Comedy *Love Actually*

In terms of its overall structure and even with respect to some of the themes that are addressed, *A Week in December* bears some striking similarities with one of the most successful recent British romantic comedies: Richard Curtis's film *Love Actually*, which was released in 2003.[2] A structural feature *A Week in December* and *Love Actually* share (besides featuring London as their primary setting) is the juxtaposition of a number of separate, yet occasionally intertwining plot strands and the resulting episodic structure of the overall narrative. Moreover, both the novel and the film present characters from very different layers of society, ranging from the working class to a fictitious Prime Minister in Curtis's comedy and the Prince of Wales in *A Week in December*. (The latter appears briefly when one of the characters is awarded an OBE, cf. Faulks 2010, 284-87). As far as the topics that are addressed in the course of the narrative are concerned, there are also a number of parallels between the film comedy and Faulks's novel. Both include references to pornography, mental care facilities and the impact of 9/11 on contemporary society.

A structural feature that additionally reinforces the similarities between the film and the novel is the fact that they are both set shortly before Christmas. The 'week in December' the title of Faulks's novel refers to is the week from the 16th to the 22nd of December 2007, whereas the plot of *Love Actually* covers several weeks before Christmas. Yet the references to Christmas which are already suggested by the temporal structure also serve to highlight crucial differences between the two portrayals of life in the British capital at the beginning of the new millennium. While *Love Actually* can certainly be classified as a fairly traditional 'feel-good' Christmas movie, there are hardly any traces of what might be called 'Christmas spirit' in *A Week in December*. One of the comparatively few references to Christmas occurs relatively early, in a passage that summarizes the musings of London Underground driver Jenni Fortune as follows:

> The week before Christmas was the worst time of year for people throwing themselves on the track. Nobody knew why. Perhaps the approaching festivity brought back memories of family or friends who'd died, without whom the turkey and the streamers seemed a gloomy echo of a world that had once been full. Or maybe the advertisements for digital cameras, aftershave and computer games reminded people how much they were in debt, how few of 'this year's must-have' presents they could afford. Guilt, thought Jenni:

2 Curtis, who wrote and produced *Love Actually*, also created several other well-known romantic comedies, including *Four Weddings and a Funeral* (1994) and *Notting Hill* (1999). *Love Actually* is thus part of what Neale refers to as the "new cycle of romantic comedies" (Neale 1992, 287) – some of which are among the most successful British films since the 1990s (cf. Helbig 1999, 300).

> a sense of having failed in the competition for resources – for DVDs and body lotions – could drive them to the rails. (3)

The fact that Jenni sees a link between the approaching holidays and the increasing frequency of suicides certainly serves to present Christmas in a very bleak light. On the whole, there does not seem to be any room for Christmas in the lives of the characters who are presented in Faulks's novel. Even the blatant consumerism typically associated with Christmas, which is briefly alluded to in the passage above, does not play a significant role in the novel. What the characters are shown to purchase in *A Week in December* (i.e. drugs or the ingredients for a bomb) contributes to revealing the cynical egoism governing the rules of consumption in the society depicted by Faulks – an entirely secular society which by and large seems to have shed even the vestiges of altruism one might hope to find in the act of buying Christmas presents. It is telling that it is Jenni Fortune, one of the (few) likeable characters in Faulks's novel, who thinks about Christmas presents at all.

Despite the cynical attitude prevailing in *A Week in December* there is a surprisingly large number of characters in the novel who end up finding romance: Tube driver Jenni Fortune and barrister Gabriel Northwood; professional football player Tadeusz 'Spike' Borowski and his Russian girlfriend Olya, a model for internet pornography; and even would-be terrorist Hassan al-Rashid and the liberal-minded Iranian PhD student Shahla. In this way the novel conforms to the convention of the happy ending viewers expect to see in romantic comedies. In particular the romance developing between Jenni and Gabriel is strikingly devoid of erotic overtones, thus echoing the tradition of the romantic comedy in which

> the question at stake […] is not just sexual (or not just a matter of fucking), however stated. It is rather one of coupledom, compatibility and, precisely, romance; and hence of the (changing and often contradictory) social conditions, institutions, discourses and practices that define and underpin them. (Neale 1992, 286)

The romance plot focusing on Jenni and Gabriel is perhaps the most conventional one in terms of its "persistent evocation and endorsement of the signs and values of 'old-fashioned' romance" (Neale 1992, 295), including a slightly awkward first date and Jenni daydreaming about future domestic bliss with Gabriel. The genre of romantic comedy is also explicitly referred to on the story level when Shahla invites Hassan to watch "some sort of romcom" (Faulks 2010, 265), which he likes despite his initial aversion to what he considers a product of shallow western culture: "Hassan had not intended to like the film, but after fifteen minutes he could no longer stifle his laughter" (266). All in all, the pattern of the romantic comedy constitutes one of the central reference points in Faulks's novel, as the examples provided above indicate.

3. The Main Targets of Satire

Notwithstanding the recurring allusions to the genre of romantic comedy in *A Week in December*, at least the most prominent plot strands seem to be indebted first and foremost to the tradition of satire. These plot strands differ quite clearly in terms of how daring the satirical approach appears to be. The plot revolving around Ralph Tranter provides a relatively uncontroversial satire on the literary scene and the current state of the education system. Oxford-educated misanthropist Ralph Tranter, a failed novelist and author of spiteful reviews, is a type of character whose literary predecessors seem to include (minor) characters in Dickens's and Jane Austen's novels and perhaps even the comic stereotypes familiar from Ben Jonson's comedy of humours. What Tranter truly enjoys is writing and reading unfavourable reviews of literary works written by others:

> Crash was what he wanted: crash and burn – failure, slump, embarrassment. He liked it when ascerbic youngsters teased established writers and he relished it when old pipe-suckers slapped down a lively newcomer. [...] Literary setbacks came in many shapes, and Tranter relished all of them: he was a connoisseur of disappointment, a voluptuary of disgrace. [...] But reading praise for the work of a British contemporary gave him a stomach pain as fierce as the cramps of gastroenteritis. (21)

Given his single-minded interest in finding fault with the achievements of others one is almost tempted to argue that Tranter embodies the vice of jealousy; his disposition is taken to its comical extreme in a scene where he is shown to feel envy when confronted with the clichéd predictions provided by an internet horoscope for a fictional character he at some point in the past created himself:

> Tranter logged on to the e-mail at his white PC. There was the usual Sunday horoscope from Stargazer. "Hi, Bruno Banks! A good week awaits you! Venus is in the ascendant, which means you are going to get lucky in love! Professional openings are abundant. [...]" Tranter envied Bruno his auspicious life. Unfortunately, Bruno was a fictional character Tranter had invented for a novel he'd abandoned two years earlier. As inspiration waned, he had looked to the Internet for help and hoped that signing up to a horoscope as Bruno Banks would give him ideas. It hadn't. (18-19)

The entertaining presentation of grumpy, cynical misanthropist Tranter is combined with a satire on both the current literary scene in Britain and the contemporary education system. After all, the literary world in which Tranter fails to achieve fame is one in which success is largely measured by means of awards sponsored by pizza and coffee chains, whereas the shortcomings of the British education system allow Tranter to earn a substantial amount of money by correcting the spelling and grammatical errors in official reports written by the teaching staff of a prestigious private school.

Reality TV constitutes a further target of satire in *A Week in December*. The various types of entertainment subsumed under the label 'reality TV' (docusoaps, makeover shows, etc.), which have become increasingly popular since their emergence in the 1990s, have often been criticized for their banality as well as for the exploitative structures inherent in this particular TV format.[3] Nevertheless reality TV continues to enjoy enormous popularity; in an article published in 2009, i.e. in the same year as *A Week in December*, Beverley Skeggs points out that "the 'reality' television format now occupies up to 78% of national free-to-view television and 47% of non-terrestrial television, with up to 92 screened programmes a week" (Skeggs 2009, 627). The fictitious reality TV show featured in Faulks's novel, which is called *It's Madness*, "is imagined as a televised competition in which psychiatric patients compete for the right to hospital treatment" (Dix 2012). Thus, the way the show is presented lends itself to combining media satire with a satirical criticism of the state of health care in contemporary Britain. Psychological disorders are anything but a marginal problem in British society at the beginning of the new millennium. The report commissioned by

---

3 Cf. Piper: "By May 2003, the experience of shows such as *Wife Swap* (Channel 4, 2003–) and *I'm A Celebrity Get Me Out of Here* (ITV1, 2002–), along with the prospect of a summer of 'sick TV', prompted various commentators, psychologists and Tessa Jowell, the Minister for Culture, to call for a viewer 'revolt'. Jowell's argument, in particular, was that 'quality' drama, comedy and current affairs were all under threat as broadcasters fell over themselves to cater for what, by implication, were increasingly debased pleasures" (2004, 273).

the King's Fund and published by Paul McCrone et al. in 2008 in fact states that "[m]ental health problems affect more than 8 million people in England, and account for more NHS expenditure than any other health programme" (McCrone et al. 2008, 5). Thus, providing appropriate mental health care without a doubt constitutes one of the major challenges British society currently has to face. The somewhat dystopian idea that people suffering from psychological disorders might have to compete for proper treatment in a TV show raises the question of whether politics will be up to coping with this task.

The description of the fictitious TV show suggests that its overall concept is indebted to *Big Brother*, which may very well be regarded as the prototype of a particular type of reality TV which involves a competitive element and adopts the disguise of "a social experiment that aims to explore the patterns of interaction between people under various kinds of 'natural' and 'artificial' pressures" (Bignell 2008, 208). *It's Madness* even features a kind of '*Big Brother* house', i.e. "a remote but well-appointed one-storey house (the so-called Barking Bungalow)" (Faulks 2010, 44) where the contestants' actions are recorded by "[h]idden cameras [...], watching them sleep and eat and clothe themselves, scrutinising their attempts to communicate with one another" (44). As a rule, reality TV in the tradition of *Big Brother* has been designed to provide viewers with "the over-arching pleasure of voyeurism, of watching what is normally private and 'forbidden'" (Crisell 2006, 92). The show that is imagined in Faulks's novel is more ruthless in its voyeurism than what has come to be expected with regard to reality TV, given the fact that *It's Madness* features contestants who suffer from various psychological disorders and thus are particularly vulnerable. The cast of *It's Madness* includes patients afflicted by bipolar disorder, schizophrenia and chronic depression, who are routinely exposed to merciless ridicule by the 'celebrity judges' on the show. Whenever a contestant is asked to comment on the symptoms of his/her disorder, he/she is interrupted by one of the 'judges', who seize every opportunity to make cheap jokes at the expense of the patients.[4] Serious psychological problems are thus trivialized, and the 'judges' continuously seek to make the audience feel superior to the participants in order to generate comic effects. The type of comedy staged in *It's Madness* – and indeed in reality TV in general – thus can be accounted for by "[s]uperiority theories [which] ally humor principally with ridicule and the enjoyment of one's own superiority in pinpointing the foibles or weaknesses of another" (Dadlez 2011, 2). The so-called 'therapeutic challenges' the contestants are exposed to include the attempt "to go for two days without medication" (Faulks 2010, 272), talking about their sexual fantasies (273) as well as obligatory karaoke performances, which constitute "one of the most popular elements of the entire show, the so-called 'Loony Tunes' evening" (154) and are clearly yet another strategy for exposing the participants to ridicule. The patterns which emerge by means of the description of *It's Madness* thus allude to "the now paradigmatic

4 Cf. the following descriptions of what is happening in the show: "The first patient on *It's Madness* was suffering from 'bipolar disorder'. 'Sounds like something you get in the Arctic,' said Lisa, one of the celebrity judges. 'Is it anything like frostbite?' The audience began a long helpless chuckle as the patient – a red-faced, bedraggled woman in her twenties – explained her symptoms." (Faulks 2010, 41); "The bipolar woman, who'd now been given the nickname Captain Scott, was explaining how at other times she was caught in a downswing that could last for months. 'Then it's like I'm in a world which is only black and white before colour had been invented and I'm like so tired I can't move, I just want to stay in bed for days and days.' 'Yes, Scotty, we've all had days like that,' said Terry O'Malley, the boss of the panel. 'It's called a hangover.' He waited for the laughter to subside [...]" (42).

dilemma of fascination/contempt for a form at once 'compulsive' and 'repugnant'" (Piper 2004, 274-75).

As Dix points out, the concept behind *It's Madness* seems to take the exploitative format of reality TV to "a logical extreme" (Dix 2012): While ordinary shows of this kind typically invite their viewers to derive voyeuristic pleasure from "see[ing] the participants in states of undress and dishevelment" (Crisell 2006, 93) as well as from witnessing "intimate encounters: squabbles or sexual activities" (93), *It's Madness* breaks a taboo by turning people who are ill into a public spectacle. What is presumably even more disturbing than reflections on the possible (dystopian) future of reality TV is the fact that the show featured in Faulks's novel seems to have been inspired by real-life precedents. Dix notices a striking parallel to a contestant who appeared in a British talent show in the year Faulks's novel was published:

> This [i.e. the concept of *It's Madness*] appears to be a caricature of Susan Boyle, who competed in another televised talent competition, *Britain's Got Talent*, in 2009 and became a media and marketing phenomenon, known as much for overcoming serious learning difficulties as for her own performances. In his fictional version of the contest and its entrants, Faulks takes to a logical extreme what is already implicit in the structure of such cultural products. Susan Boyle became successful – the media were quick to point out – despite the disadvantage of having learning difficulties, so that those very difficulties became part of the narrative of her success. Contestants in Faulks's world cannot succeed in spite of their psychiatric problems; on the contrary, they must enact those very problems if they are to succeed in the competition that they have entered. (Dix 2012)

Beyond the parallel observed by Dix there is an even more striking precedent in the history of *Big Brother*:

> In 2006 *Big Brother*'s housemates included Pete Bennett, who has Tourette's syndrome. His inclusion could be seen as a move towards greater visibility on television for disabled people. [...] After two weeks of the seventh series of *Big Brother* in 2006, charities and mental health groups, including the Samaritans, Sane, Rethink and the Mental Health Foundation, made public criticisms of the programme over its casting of participants with mental health problems. (Bignell 2008, 231)

The possibility of addressing psychological disorders in the format of reality TV in order to achieve "greater visibility on television for disabled people," which is mentioned by Jonathan Bignell in the quotation above, is clearly undermined by the way the patients are treated in the fictitious show *It's Madness*. Instead of rendering people who are often socially marginalized more visible, the show systematically exposes their problems to ridicule.

As Minna Aslama and Mervi Pantti point out, "[s]hows such as *Big Brother* basically consist of talk in a closed laboratory setting in which there is not much else to do, and in which the management of one's emotions is the key to the participants' success" (Aslama/Pantti 2006, 171). *It's Madness* features contestants who appear to be singularly ill-equipped for meeting the emotional challenges inherent in this particular TV format; they are thus exposed to a lot of pressure, which finally even culminates in one of the participants committing suicide. The emotional strain experienced by the contestants in the fictitious show appears to be characteristic of reality TV as a form of entertainment "where the outbreaks of raw emotion figure prominently in the attraction and popularity of the genre" (168) as such.[5] Yet, while one may assume that contestants in reality TV shows generally are aware of the potentially humiliating exposure typical of the format and may in fact be anything but authentic in their own performance,[6] the participants of *It's Madness* are portrayed as helpless victims of both television entertainment and a flawed health care system which denies them proper treatment, thus forcing them to accept public humiliation for the sake of winning "free private treatment for their condition for a whole year in Park View, England's top hospital" (Faulks 2010, 271).[7]

The satire on reality TV provided in Faulks's novel is rounded off by the portrayal of a viewer who enjoys this type of entertainment. Most of what the readers learn about *It's Madness* is filtered through the perspective of sixteen-year-old Finbar Veals, who regularly watches the show while eating his pizza and smoking joints. Although Finbar may not be the most trustworthy critic of what is happening on the show, even he cannot help but wonder why it is so popular (cf. 273). He classifies *It's Madness* as "modern comedy" (41), and this indeed seems to be the most appropriate label for a type of entertainment that has been more and more designed to encourage viewers to mock the show's participants since its emergence in the 1990s. Being familiar with contemporary media culture, Finbar sees through the unreliability characteristic of reality TV and thus, for instance, doubts the qualifications of the alleged 'experts' appearing on the show: "Two psychiatrists (though he doubted they were really qualified) gave an assessment of what treatment the patient needed, how much it would cost and whether she should be admitted to a hospital" (42).[8]

Although Finbar is convinced that "[t]elevision was all a con – everyone knew that" (42), at least the contestants assembled in the 'barking bungalow' seem to be actually suffering from psychological disorders, as has been pointed out above. It is part of the black humour that is at times apparent in *A Week in December* – and perhaps it also borders on poetic justice – that Finbar, who gets a kick out of watching people afflicted by psychological disorders exposed to public humiliation on TV, finally ends up in a ward for mentally ill people. Whether the symptoms of psychosis he suddenly displays are merely a temporary side-effect of drug abuse or will prove to be permanent is left open at the end of the novel, but at least the readers can rest assured that Finbar – unlike the contestants on *It's Madness* – will have access to proper medical treatment thanks to his rich parents.

A further, even more controversial topic that is dealt with in a satirical manner in *A Week in December* is the threat of Islamist terrorism. Many British novels written in the wake of 9/11 and the disaster on 7 July 2005, in which "52 Londoners were killed

---

5 According to Aslama and Pantti, reality TV in this regard seems to respond to more general preferences in contemporary culture: "Interest in the emotions of other people seems to be very much a part of contemporary culture, as is a pressure to reveal emotions and talk about them in both private and public forums […]" (2006, 167).

6 Cf. Bignell: "Just as in docusoap, the realism of 'reality TV' is partly performance, and it is telling that several *Big Brother* contestants have subsequently become television presenters" (2008, 209).

7 Worries about the future of the health care system in Britain are certainly among the challenges British society has to face at the beginning of the new millennium. Already in 2001, Ken Judge, Jo-Ann Mulligan and Bill New (2001, 321) observed that "[t]he public seems to be increasingly worried about the government's ability to fund and run the NHS. While GPs and other health professionals continue to enjoy public confidence, there are signs that specific aspects of both the hospital service and the primary care sector are under increasingly visible strain."

8 The appearance of experts, including psychologists, constitutes a recurring feature of reality TV inherited from factual television (cf. Aslama and Pantti 2006, 172). In fact, "realism was emphasised in the first British version [of *Big Brother*] by the prominence of inserted sequences featuring the programme's two resident psychologists analysing and discussing the behaviour of the participants" (Bignell 2008, 208).

and at least 770 injured by 4 suicide bombers in central London who [...] attacked the Underground railway and bus network" (McLeod 2011, 241), have addressed the topic of terrorism by focusing primarily on people's fear of another attack. Ian McEwan's novel *Saturday* (2005) is a case in point.[9] Sebastian Faulks, in contrast, approaches the topic of terrorism from a more daring angle, by offering a quite detailed depiction of the preparations for a terrorist attack on the (fictitious) Glendale Hospital in London. The assessment of the suitability of this particular target that is at one point provided by a member of the terrorist cell may shock the reader; yet it undeniably sounds like the kind of reasoning one may assume to be behind terrorist attacks: "It's an ideal target. It ticks all three boxes. News impact. Density of population. And third, though this is less important, scarcity of Muslim victims" (Faulks, 291). Nevertheless the meticulous description of the preparations for the attack, which involve for instance using internet pornography for communicating secret messages, at times also evokes comic effects by departing from what the readers are likely to expect – a strategy which corresponds to the assumptions of "[i]ncongruity theories [which] link humor to the defeat of expectations, to a clash or dissonance that is enjoyable rather than distressing or confusing" (Dadlez 2011, 2). The fact that Faulks does not shy away from tackling a highly sensitive topic like Islamist terrorism in a satirical manner confirms the impression that *A Week in December* could be situated in a tradition of English satires that can be traced back to Daniel Defoe's *The Shortest Way with the Dissenters* (1702) and Jonathan Swift's *A Modest Proposal* (1729), which likewise seek to foreground social criticism by breaking taboos and whose "outrageousness [...] is arresting, immediate, and easy to spot" (Boyle 2007, 199).

The plot strand addressing Islamist terrorism revolves around the student Hassan al-Rashid, son of "chutney magnate" (Faulks 2010, 5) Farooq al-Rashid, who is awarded an OBE on the very same day his son, who has joined a terrorist cell, is preparing a terrorist attack in the British capital. The passage in the first chapter which introduces Hassan starts out as a description of an average, perhaps even somewhat goofy young man and ends in a twist that may come as a shock for the reader:

> In the rear carriage of Jenni Fortune's Circle Line train Hassan al-Rashid sat staring straight ahead. Normally, without a book to read, he would move his head up and down so that the reflection of his face in the convex window opposite would develop panda eyes, elongate like an image in a fairground mirror and then pop. But this was not the day for such frivolity: he was on his way to buy the constituents of a bomb. (14)

In the course of the novel the readers learn quite a lot about Hassan's background as well as about his reasons for joining a terrorist cell due to the fact that he is often used as character focalizer. Thus the readers are invited to develop a certain amount of empathy with Hassan and "to imagine what it is like to live the life of another person who might, given changes in circumstance, be oneself," as Martha Nussbaum (1995, 5) puts it. Hassan's choices seem to derive from his personal experience of injustice, but even more from his wish to find "a superior way of life" (Faulks 2010, 107) for himself. Hassan thus could be categorized as a misguided idealist, frustrated by the lack of values he is faced with in a secular British society at the beginning of the 21st century.

---

9 Cf. the following description of *Saturday*: "An atmosphere of terror pervades the novel throughout, and is linked explicitly to the aftermath of 9/11 in the opening pages as Perowne [i.e. the protagonist of the novel], waking at dawn, watches a burning aircraft pass over his house attempting to approach Heathrow Airport" (McLeod 2011, 256).

Ultimately, the plot strand focusing on the activities of the terrorists ends on a surprisingly optimistic note. The plans for the terrorist attack fail due to a combination of Hassan's dismal sense of direction, his low blood-sugar level, which makes him dizzy, and, last but not least, "a bicycle with no lights on" (380) which almost knocks him down. One may certainly interpret the cyclist as some kind of *deus ex machina*, who somehow manages to trigger a radical change in Hassan's way of seeing the world and who thus brings about a happy ending, which has not seemed at all likely up to this point. All of a sudden, Hassan appears to consider his previous convictions to have been ridiculous, which gives rise to a cathartic laughing fit. Once he finally manages to stop laughing he deliberately throws his rucksack, which contains the fuses for the explosives he is supposed to take to Glendale Hospital, into the Thames, thus effectively putting an end to the planned terrorist attack (at least for the time being) as well as to his own involvement with the terrorist group: "[…] something had happened on that bridge. Something more than the shock of almost being knocked down by a speeding cyclist… Something profound and real at that moment had changed in him, had shifted on its axis; and it was never going back" (384-85).

The unexpectedly optimistic ending of this plot strand, which is made possible by Hassan's cathartic experience, once more recalls the happy ending typical of romantic comedies: Hassan confesses his love to Shahla, and the couple kisses. At this point the reader may again be reminded of the film by Richard Curtis. At the beginning of *Love Actually* the introductory voice-over explicitly refers to 9/11 in the following way: "When the planes hit the Twin Towers, as far as I know none of the phone calls from people on board were messages of hate or revenge, they were all messages of love" (Curtis 2003, 00:01:36-00:01:50). Here the reference to the terrorist attacks is integrated into the general optimism that is typical of the genre of romantic comedy. In *A Week in December* terrorism on the whole is shown in a much more sinister and threatening light, but the outcome discussed above suggests a twist which echoes the optimism that sets romantic comedy apart from satire.

On the last pages of the novel, some of the major and minor plot strands are shown to unravel in quite an optimistic manner, and this hopefulness is stressed by numerous references to laughter and smiles (cf. Faulks, 382; 383; 385) – something one may also expect at the end of a romantic comedy. Yet when laughter is referred to in the very last sentence of the novel the implications are strikingly different: "As he stood with his hands in his pockets, staring out over the sleeping city, over its darkened wheels and spires and domes, Veals laughed" (390). That hedge-fund manager John Veals is shown to be laughing at the very end of Faulks's portrayal of British society appears to be particularly significant since he is a character who so far has been presented as lacking any sense of humour. At one point in the novel, his wife Vanessa even complains: "I could forget the lack of fun […] or his dread of parties or holidays or romance, I could forget everything if I could just once see him laugh" (101). While Hassan's laughter is cathartic and redeeming, reconnecting him with a desire to live, Veals's laughter is triggered by the fact that he has just started a global banking crisis, which will ruin many people around the world, but will in the end leave him even wealthier than before:

> When, or rather if, the financial crisis ever stabilised, there would be a recession in what journalists charmingly termed the 'real' economy. Millions around the globe would lose their jobs; other millions would go without food, or at least see their modest lives stripped of comfort. But I have mastered this world, thought John Veals, passing his hand over his newly shaved chin. (390)

This time there is no *deus ex machina* who comes to the rescue. The hedge-fund manager apparently cannot be stopped anymore, and his evil machinations will ruin people around the globe. Hassan's sudden change of mind in fact seems to leave Veals in the role of the real villain in the novel. While Hassan's actions have at least always been motivated by a struggle to define who he is and by a search for what is right, Veals's decisions are entirely devoid of any ethical considerations: "The distinction between 'legal' and 'ethical' was of no concern to him – or to anyone he'd ever met" (69).

The hedge-fund manager is presented as a kind of self-made man, whose knack for financial matters was supposedly inspired by "his first experience of markets, at the age of fourteen" (10), when his uncle, a bookmaker, let him in on the secrets of his profession. Unlike many of the other characters in the novel, Veals is isolated indeed and does not even care about his wife or his children; he has no real friends or hobbies: "The only activity, the only aspect of human life, that interested John Veals was money" (269). Paradoxically, he is not even very much interested in spending money; his sole aim in life seems to be making money for money's sake. With its portrayal of a hedge-fund manager who could not care less whether his actions have terrible consequences for other people the novel leaves no doubt that Veals is the embodiment of 'the evil banker,' who arguably has become one of the new 'bogeymen' of 21st-century society in the wake of the financial crisis. Faulks's *A Week in December* is set at the end of 2007, shortly before the global financial crisis reached its peak in 2008. Thus the novel can also be read as a response to this crisis, seeking "to engage with, and make sense of, the financial turbulence of the 21st century," as Katy Shaw (2014, 44) puts it.

4. Conclusion

Sebastian Faulks's novel *A Week in December* may certainly be seen first and foremost as a satire on British society at the beginning of the new millennium (cf. Dix 2012), featuring contemporary television, the health care system and the financial system as some of the main targets of criticism.[10] In particular the manner in which Faulks approaches the topic of Islamist terrorism and the exploitative structure inherent in reality TV, which may escalate further in the future, certainly borders on the kind of violation of taboos which is not uncommon in satires. Yet Faulks also draws heavily upon the more light-hearted tradition of romantic comedy, as has been illustrated above. This mixture of satire and romantic comedy as two very different ways of creating comic effects gives rise to fundamentally different assumptions about the outcome of social developments. As Valentine Cunningham points out, "[s]atire does not do happy endings. Its wastings and trashings go on irreversibly. *Dei ex machinae* steer clear of satirical fictions" (2007, 419). Yet happy endings are one of the staple features of the genre of romantic comedy, which is also drawn upon in Faulks's novel.

10 Dix emphasizes that the readers are also invited to read some of the characters as satires on actual celebrities: "There is a strong sense of irony in Farooq al-Rashid's receiving an OBE from the royal family when the businessman on whom he might have been modelled, Mohamed Al-Fayed was in reality snubbed by the Queen, Duke of Edinburgh, Queen Mother and Prince of Wales, who withdrew their royal warrants from Harrods, the fashionable department store owned by Fayed. There is also a strong identification between Lisa, the presenter of television game show *It's Madness* who had 'been lead singer with a successful but short-lived band called Girls From Behind' and Cheryl Cole, sometime singer with the pop group *Girls Aloud* and presenter of televised talent competition *X Factor*" (Dix 2012).

As a consequence, the overall impression of British society is not quite as bleak and dismal as it might be; there is a lot of hope and even a *deus ex machina*. The author juxtaposes different comic traditions in his panoramic picture of life in London at the beginning of the 21st century, stressing that comic modes of storytelling are compatible with the aim of providing topical social criticism in a modern Condition-of-England novel.

Works Cited

Aslama, Minna and Mervi Pantti. "Talking Alone: Reality TV, Emotions and Authenticity." *European Journal of Cultural Studies* 9.2 (2006): 167-84.

Bignell, Jonathan. *An Introduction to Television Studies*. 2nd ed. Oxford and New York: Routledge, 2008.

Boyle, Frank. "Jonathan Swift." *A Companion to Satire*. Ed. Ruben Quintero. Malden, MA, and Oxford: Blackwell, 2007. 196-211.

Crisell, Andrew. *A Study of Modern Television: Thinking Inside the Box*. Houndmills, Basingstoke: Palgrave Macmillan, 2006.

Cunningham, Valentine. "Twentieth-century Fictional Satire." *A Companion to Satire*. Ed. Ruben Quintero. Malden, MA, and Oxford: Blackwell, 2007. 400-33.

Curtis, Richard (dir.). *Love Actually*. Working Title Films/United Pictures, 2003.

Dadlez, E.M. "Truly Funny: Humor, Irony, and Satire as Moral Criticism." *The Journal of Aesthetic Education* 45.1 (2011): 1-17.

Dix, Hywel. "From Markets to Metafiction: Satires of the Literary Marketplace at the Dawn of Two New Centuries." *Revue Interdisciplinaire 'Textes & Contextes'* 7 (2012). Web. 10 February 2015.

Faulks, Sebastian. *A Week in December*. [2009]. London: Vintage, 2010.

Helbig, Jörg. *Geschichte des britischen Films*. Stuttgart and Weimar: J.B. Metzler, 1999.

Judge, Ken, Jo-Ann Mulligan and Bill New. "Public Attitudes and the NHS." *The Contemporary British Society Reader*. Eds. Nicholas Abercrombie and Alan Warde. Cambridge: Polity, 2001. 321-28.

McCrone, Paul et al. *Paying the Price: The Cost of Mental Health Care in England to 2026*. London: King's Fund, 2008.

McLeod, John. "Writing London in the Twenty-First Century." *Literature of London*. Ed. Lawrence Manley. Cambridge: Cambridge University Press, 2011. 241-60.

Neale, Steve. "The Big Romance or Something Wild?: Romantic Comedy Today." *Screen* 33.3 (1992): 284-99.

Nussbaum, Martha C. *Poetic Justice. The Literary Imagination and Public Life*. Boston, MA: Beacon Press, 1995.

Piper, Helen. "Reality TV, *Wife Swap* and the Drama of Banality." *Screen* 45.4 (2004): 273-86.

Shaw, Katy. "'Capital' City: London, Contemporary British Fiction and the Credit Crunch." *The Literary London Journal* 11.1 (2014): 44-53.

Skeggs, Beverley. "The Moral Economy of Person Production: The Class Relations of Self-Performance on 'Reality' Television." *The Sociological Review* 57.4 (2009): 626-44.

ULRIKE ZIMMERMANN

More Than Just an Effect: The Comic in British Women's Contemporary Short Stories

1. The Comic and the Short Story – Highlighting Change

Comic writing in recent years seems to have changed its appearance and part of its functions, branching out into genres and topics which do not inherently lend themselves to comic treatment and representation. "Comedy" proper, across a multitude of cultural products, is still valid as a term; one can unthinkingly refer to a novel, a film, or a play as comedy. But there is more. The comic seems to appear more frequently in unexpected contexts; arguably it infests culturally serious locations and topics which in and of themselves do not necessarily give rise to comic treatment.[1] To find the comic in a short story which sets out to be humorous from the start is no surprise. To find the comic in all sorts of contexts and all sorts of themes, and increasingly so after the turn of the millennium, says something about the cultural framework we are living in. Currently the comic is making a strong move towards the centre of attention. A cultural product need not explicitly be labelled as "comedy" to be unabashedly and insistently comic, and it may take the liberty to approach deadly serious issues. This is particularly interesting since, generally, comic productions are still underrated, in the sense that they only slowly come to be trusted with serious topics.

The comic has been the subject of countless analyses over time. Classifying the comic is notoriously difficult, and no approach seems fully satisfactory. In this article, the focus will be on only a few of the many phenomena: first, incongruity, and, related to this, free play with scale and measure. The result of these two often is a conceptual dissonance for the readers, which is pleasurable rather than irritating. The conception of the comic as the result of incongruity ultimately goes back to Immanuel Kant, who, in his *Critique of the Power of Judgment,* notes that the unexpected, or the jolting of expectations, has a gratifying effect on beholders – like the punch-line of a joke, for example. Incongruity is often achieved via a juxtaposition of unlikely or unsuitable elements.[2] Laughter, according to Kant, is an expression of the realization of incongruity and the concomitant pleasure. One of the advantages of the incongruity approach since Kant is the fact that there is no built-in agenda in the assessment of an incongruity phenomenon. It is hardly possible to explain comic phenomena without their social and political implications, but incongruity approaches usually do not commit themselves as to whether the comic in a particular case is affirmative or subversive. This can be done by a critic using the incongruity explanation but the decision can also be kept open. Several 20th-century critics have broadened Kant's basic definition and also expanded on his terminology, but the incongruity principle itself has remained relatively intact.

A second approach to the comic worth noting for literary interpretation is Henri Bergson's definition of the comic as "something mechanical encrusted on the living"

1 The writer of this paper believes that the comic has always had the tendency to be transgressive and to "bleed" into all conceivable cultural products, habits, and rituals. The increase in this tendency, and the contexts in which it happens, would merit research far beyond the scope of this paper.
2 For a brief overview on incongruity theories of the comic, see Zimmermann (2013, 33-35).

(1980, 84). Bergson's basic idea is that life is a fluid state, and that any society accordingly has to rely on its members to be flexible at all times. This works on a literal level (the human body has to be flexible) and on a metaphorical one (life requires humankind to be flexible). Comic effects are created when a living being behaves like a machine – by repetitive behaviour, or by being unable to accommodate an unexpected occurrence.

Addressing serious matter in a comic way may also bring up thoughts of Sigmund Freud and his theory of the comic as taboo-breaking activity. In his *Jokes and their Relation to the Unconscious* (1905), he conceives of joke-work as he did of dream-work, which would turn jokes into another kind of social safety valve: the release of pressure brought to the individual through strains and regulations around them by making jokes. This relief theory of the comic can be an angle of approach, but is hardly sufficient on its own. However, Freud's theory certainly provides a convincing explanation for the frequent proximity of the comic to the very serious: conceivably, it can be argued that the more sensitive a subject is, the greater the tendency will be to address it in comic ways.

No matter from which angle one approaches the topic, it is important to note that the comic is not just a decoration or an aesthetic effect – although it can be used for these purposes. The use of the comic most frequently is much more; it has reverberations on the meanings a text can carry, and on its agendas. My interest is with texts which are not necessarily comic at first glance, but have the comic as part of their innermost structure. The short stories which comprise this case study employ the potential of the comic to open up fresh perspectives on difficult and serious topics. Muriel Spark's "The Young Man Who Discovered the Secret of Life" (first published in 2000) and Fay Weldon's "The Site" (2002) are examples by well-established authors with a diverse body of work, with the stories sharing surprising similarities in their sardonic look at life. Both include supernatural elements. Marina Lewycka's "The Importance of Having Warm Feet" (2009) and Jackie Kay's "Not the Queen" (2006) both have women narrators,[3] and they ask questions about identity, social positioning, and life in the United Kingdom in the 21st century.

An analysis of comic productions by women can end up in an awkward double bind. Comic literature, while it may be appreciated for its entertainment value, has had to cover a long distance to become a critical subject in its own right. The same can be said about women's writing,[4] which has a long and partly torturous history towards full critical acknowledgement. In addition to that, women and the comic still seem to be a volatile combination. In many societies and contexts there are social restrictions on how women receive and produce comic effects, many of them still firmly in place. Arguably, comic writing by women is hence marginalized twice over. Nevertheless, the idea that comic literary products by women are *per se* subversive because of the conditions in which they were written may be attractive but is also essentialist as well as unsupported by evidence.[5]

3 So does Weldon's story – Spark is the exception here; her narrator is identified as an author who hears about the protagonist's experiences through letters to her publisher ("her," if we posit a woman narrator, or Spark herself).

4 The notion here is that writing by women is by no means a definable entity or in any way summarily different from men's writing. But women's writing is taken to be bound up in and subject to different social, moral, and political conditions and hence can be located in different areas of experience.

5 Second-wave feminism in particular subscribed to the idea of an inherent subversiveness of women's humour but also did invaluable work in re-assessing the comic in texts by women authors. Criticism on

The current state of the British short story is too diverse to be tied up nicely in definitions.[6] Liggins, Maunder and Robbins address the irony of the project of trying to define the *British* short story, as any criticism will have to include Edgar Allan Poe and the American tradition (cf. Liggins 2011, 2).[7] As length, although relative, remains a defining factor, they note that the short story tends to come across as less weighty and important than epic forms (2). In that sense, the short story shares the dimension of being underestimated with women's writing and with comic writing.[8] Moreover, it has frequently been noted that particularly in the second half of the 20th century, the short story became a space for debating current issues, "particularly popular with women writers and with others who feel in some ways marginalized or not fully secure within their communities" (16). Brosch states that the short story by tradition is concerned with liminality, crises, and transgression processes (Brosch 2007, 23), which is true for all of my examples.

Liggins et al. conclude that, despite its somewhat erratic critical history in the UK, the short story is a form which is alive and kicking, open to experimentation but also used by writers in traditional ways of narration.

> The British short story is thus a complex, multiform creature. It is made up of relationships between the material world of the demands of publishing and the marketplace, specific aesthetic schemas and programmes, the conventions of genre and the influence of the writers of other nations. It is a mongrel or, perhaps more kindly, a hybrid, and its names and forms are legion. (Liggins et al. 2011, 5)

2. Mapping Out Comic Territory: Muriel Spark and Fay Weldon

Both Muriel Spark (1918-2006) and Fay Weldon (born in 1931) are British writers of note. Texts working with the comic have been an essential part of their repertoire; they are shapers of traditions in their own distinct ways. For present purposes, two recent examples will come under consideration. Muriel Spark was a critic before she became an acclaimed writer; she has always been firmly identified as Scottish.[9] Spark is probably best known for her novel *The Prime of Miss Jean Brodie* (1961), but was also a prolific writer of short stories. Her humour is dark, and her short stories thematically varied throughout her career.[10]

Spark's late short story "The Young Man Who Discovered the Secret of Life" is a very short, roughly three-page vignette from the daily life of a workman, "a plasterer's

---

comic literature by women is rapidly expanding. The introduction by Stetz to her monograph (2001) may provide a good starting point. See also Zimmermann (2013, 39-47) on gendering the comic.

6 As Brosch puts it, "Die short story ist sympathisch resistent gegenüber Definitionen" (Brosch 2007, 9).

7 On the concept of the British short story see Korte (2003, 9-19). Korte analyzes the interplay and interdependence of the various cultural and geographical identities in the UK with regard to the short story.

8 For a linguistic analysis of the comic in short stories see Ermida (2008).

9 Her Scottishness seems to rest largely on her Scottish father and her spending her formative years in Scotland; for a differentiated, personal view on her identity see her interview with Martin McQuillan (2002, 226-27); for the connections with religion – and Spark's conversion to Catholicism – see, for example, Carruthers (2010). For brief biographies see also "Writing Scotland" (2015), and McMillan (2015). Peter Kemp's monograph (1974) still belongs to the most relevant studies on the earlier Spark; see Randisi (1991) on the satirical tradition – however, Spark's comic work to my mind goes far beyond the domain of satire.

10 Spark's "The Black Madonna" (1958) is an early take on migration to the UK, with ethnicity, class, and religious hypocrisy at its centre. Spark is also strong on stories with a supernatural element to them, as in "The Portobello Road" (1958) or "Miss Pinkerton's Apocalypse" (1955); all in *The Complete Short Stories* (2002).

apprentice" (Spark 2002, 254) who keeps encountering a ghost, emanating from a chest of drawers. The short story derives its comic effect largely from incongruity, made visible from the very beginning. "The main fact was, he was haunted by a ghost [...]. But I have been told on good authority that this is absolutely absurd. There is no such thing: plasterers do not have apprentices" (254). The reader is expecting to be told that ghosts do not exist, but instead is confronted with the mundane and potentially irrelevant assertion that plasterers' apprentices do not exist. The narrative has its fun here with the epistemological status of human beings and ghosts. The ghost in Spark's story is a rather snobbish one, as he[11] comes from "the top drawer" (255), and hence feels entitled to pass sarcastic comments on the young man's life. He is also jealous of the apprentice's girlfriend. The young man is irritated with the ghost, but soon finds out that the latter is able to predict which horse will win at the races and profits from his advice. When the protagonist gives up his attitude of superiority towards his girlfriend and proposes marriage, the ghost reluctantly vanishes for good. "This quenching of the ghost [the young man reports] is to me the secret of life" (Spark 2002, 256) as he is sure the ghost was after his soul (257). In fact, the ghost seems far too trivial and nagging to be capable of such a project. The story blends the fantastic and the comic; it approximates magical realism in the status it accords to the supernatural.[12] The story imbues an unspectacular, precarious existence and a budding relationship with secrecy and glamour. It is telling that the ghost vanishes with the marriage and ensuing prosperity. The young man goes on to have a good life, successfully "specializing in crazy-paving" (257).[13]

Fay Weldon is still writing and very productive; she is a feminist with a controversial agenda of her own.[14] "The Site"[15] is a story playing with history, the last things, and the individual's role in both. It is a longish piece, allowing itself time to develop the setting and the unnamed narrator, accelerating towards the end towards a surprising dénouement, which comes with the force of a punch line, thus revealing – despite the relative length – the genre's relation with the anecdote. The narrator is a typical Weldonian middle-aged, disillusioned, intelligent woman who is a sculptor. When an ancient Roman grave is discovered on the building site for a shopping mall, the works come to a halt. The archaeologists that are called in turn out to be at the side of the developers, wanting to get the bones off the site so that the construction can continue. The narrator is outraged and calls in the church, "but the bishopric was unmoved" (Weldon 2003, 40) – the skeletons are presumed to be "pagan and [have] nothing to do with the Church" (39). The narrator comes up with an outrageous idea. She tells the "hippie silversmith" Carter Wainwright (42), "'My point is, Carter,' I said, 'if they

11 The ghost is addressed as male throughout the story.

12 Arguably, the way in which the story plays down the very impact of the supernatural, trifling with the ghost, sets it apart from the Latin American type of magical realism.

13 The top drawer and the crazy paving are good examples of Barreca's (1988) observation of reliteralizations of metaphors in women's comic writing, see below in the analysis of "Not the Queen."

14 See, for example, her interview with Saner (2009) and her homepage, both of which display Weldon's sense of humour, and her pleasure in working against the grain. Weldon's homepage speculates about the year of her death and addresses academics who are in the process of writing studies on her. For a brief biography, see also Patten and Smith (2013). It is an interesting coincidence that Weldon, too, received her university education in Scotland at the University of St. Andrews. Weldon has been frequently criticised for being too economically-minded, as it were (allowing herself to be sponsored by Bulgari for her 2001 novel *The Bulgari Connection*). A case in point is, for example, O'Kelly's introduction to her review of *Nothing to Wear and Nowhere to Hide* in *The Guardian* (2002).

15 The collection *Nothing to Wear and Nowhere to Hide*, in which "The Site" appeared, received mixed reviews. See for example O'Kelly, Moore, and the review in *The Scotsman*, all 2002.

found an early Christian cross in this grave tomorrow, they'd have to believe'" (43). She takes a small piece of wood from the gravesite, and the two proceed to forge a cross and place it at the site. The press is called in and the British Museum declares the cross to be genuine (44-45). "Priceless, or at any rate in the region of several million pounds" (46). The forgers, after an initial episode of panic, are relieved. The site development goes on but "a service of reconciliation" (47) is held by priests over the graves before the remains are removed. The story ends on a conciliatory note. "I think we will be forgiven for our deceit: we were meant to do what we did" (48). The narrator has never revealed herself as particularly religious, but she does have a pragmatic set of beliefs she lives by.[16]

A fake, the story seems to suggest, is quite as good as the real thing if it causes people to behave with dignity. The story delivers sharp digs against venerated institutions and their hypocrisy; the church does not move on behalf of the unknown dead, and the academics put their faith where the money is, with the developers. The question of religion and the basic human right to a burial is at the centre of the text, addressed in a tongue-in-cheek way. Interestingly, Britain's past is presented as multicultural and multi-faith (there is no knowing which religion, if any, the buried people followed), while its presence is largely class-ridden, governed by ruthless economic interests. The story's concerns are implicitly gendered by the fact that it is a woman who brings about change by working quietly and subversively behind the scenes. Additionally, the comic action – a desperate, hasty forgery setting the wheels of the world of high culture in motion – also takes place behind the scenes.

3. Fighting the Cold: Marina Lewycka, "The Importance of Having Warm Feet"

Marina Lewycka, born in 1946, is a British writer of Ukrainian origin. Her literary work – she is mainly known as a novelist – is informed by a double perspective on life in contemporary Britain and the lives of immigrant communities from Eastern Europe.[17] She has a keen sense of the comic and sees herself firmly rooted in the tradition of comic literature, which to her constitutes the "mainstream," as she stated in an interview with Doris Lechner, talking about her second novel.

> DL: You place *Two Caravans* within the tradition of English literature with an epigraph from Chaucer's Canterbury Tales.
> ML: ...especially in English comic literature really. Which is, I suppose, the mainstream of English literature. Shakespeare was also a very great comic writer. (Lechner 2010b, 457)

The importance she places on the comic in literary history, and accordingly in her own work, is striking.[18]

Lewycka's short story "The Importance of Having Warm Feet" was a donation to a four-volume collection of original stories for Oxfam, which was published in 2009. The story has a striking *in medias res* beginning, a stark image of Napoleon Bonaparte's defeated troupes retreating from Russia in 1812. Marching through the Ukraine

16 Arguably, the story's concern not just with death but with the material consequences of death – decomposition – could open up the text to a Freudian reading of the comic: breaking the taboo of death, providing relief for the readers in the face of their own mortality. The creative construction of historical facts by the narrator could be read as a release of the pressures of a limited human existence.

17 For Marina Lewycka's biography see, for example, Tranter (2008), "Writers. Marina Lewycka."

18 Natalia Feduschak's article in the *Kyiv Post* (2011) also picks up on this pervasive strain in Lewycka's texts. Lewycka herself as quoted above speaks about English literature but it is suggested here that her work is part of the larger context of contemporary British literature.

in the dead of winter, "[t]hey would knock on the doors, and plead, 'For the love of God, give me refuge, mon ami.' The villagers called them 'monamishchiki'" (Lewycka 2009, 107). The dry statement of the French-Ukrainian neologism, coined by the civilian inhabitants for the desperate remains of a great army sets the tone for the story as a whole. The great narratives of the history books are juxtaposed with the everyday life of the common people, who are either never touched by history or at best passed by its straggling remains. The immense loss of life in the French invasion of Russia is stated equally laconically, only to be followed by a private assessment: "Of some 500,000 who had set off to conquer Russia, barely 10,000 made it back to France. And it was all because of unsuitable footwear, my great great-great-grandmother told my great-grandmother, who told my mother, who told me" (107). Effortlessly and briefly, true to its genre, the story sweeps from the wastes of frozen Russia and Ukraine in 1812 to the narrator of the story, presumably located in the present time of the early 21st century.[19] The importance of the right kind of warm shoes and socks, and of keeping one's feet warm in all conceivable situations is a leitmotif in the text.

In flashbacks, the narrator reminisces about her childhood as a Ukrainian girl in Bradford. "The other kids laughed at my sensible shoes and woollen socks. They sniggered at my long plaits, and my funny name, and my brand-new school satchel" (108). The narrator is chosen for the role of the Virgin Mary in the primary school's nativity play and has a hard time as her main bullies play Joseph and the innkeeper. Her mother, however, has different worries. "[... I]t's December, and the school hall will be cold. What will you wear on your feet?" (111). As the shoes seem too heavy and unsuitable for the Virgin, mother and daughter decide just on the socks. The teacher takes issue with them, and obediently the narrator takes them off. Some time later, the performance is unexpectedly interrupted: "[...] before the innkeeper could answer, someone burst onto the stage and rushed up to me. In her hands was a pair of grey woolly socks. 'Put them on at once!' my mother exclaimed. 'You'll catch your death of cold!'" (113). Predictably, the innkeeper greets Mary and Joseph with "'My, what a lovely pair of socks'" (114), and the nativity play comes to a halt. "The shepherds laughed. The choir of angels laughed, the three wise men laughed. Even the ox and the ass and the piglet laughed" (114). The text transforms from slapstick to something larger with these sentences. The parallelism enforces the effect of the whole biblical world bursting out laughing: men, spiritual beings, animals. This nativity, staged by young children, is informed by and comes to life with laughter; at the same time, the narrator's mother unwittingly points to the bigger picture: what did Mary and Joseph seek if not shelter and – warmth? Here the socks, lowly everyday objects, are incongruous in the setting of a re-enactment of scenes from the New Testament. The actors and the audience laugh in their appreciation of this incongruity.

"I never forgave my mother for that until her dying day, but on her dying day I forgave her" (115). The story ends with the narrator, who turns out to be in her fifties at the time of narration, at her mother's deathbed. Dying of cancer, her mother complains of cold feet, for her a sign of her impending death. When the daughter puts bed socks on her feet, she remembers the episode and reminds her mother of it. With

19 In her analysis of Lewycka's novels, Lechner makes use of Marianne Hirsch's concept of postmemory to describe the passing on of (traumatic) memories through the generations in Lewycka (cf. Lechner 2010a, 438-39). The short story touches briefly on trauma in family history. Puschmann-Nalenz, in her study of representations of the East in recent short fiction, points out the insistent "[p]resence of the [p]ast" in some of her material (Puschmann-Nalenz 2010, 389-95).

hindsight, her mother finds her own action "terrible" (116). "'You did everything right,' [the narrator tells her], and kissed her cheek. 'It mattered then, but is doesn't matter now.'" (116). The relationship between the generations is a loving and close one, epitomized by the image of the socks. The narrator stays close to her mother until the end, and the story closes with her beginning her mourning process. "But I was glad, too, that when she stepped out on her last long march into the cold unknown, at least her feet were warm" (116). If you have to die, at least you should be comfortable in the process – unlike the masses of defeated Napoleonic soldiers with whom the short story opened, who are invoked once more with the image of the mother stepping out on a march into afterlife.

In Lewycka's text, the year 1812 is linked to the present time by a (seemingly) insignificant commodity of daily life: footwear. But there is another strand woven into the story linking the past and the present: images of death and dying, and, together with this, the insistence on the human desire for protection for oneself and loved ones. The basics, the story seems to say, are not basic at all. "The Importance of Having Warm Feet" is a condensed narrative imaginatively spanning two centuries and a genealogical line which has proved strong enough to survive into the present time.[20] Its humour lies in the juxtaposition of the little and the great, the insignificant and the historic, the spiritual and the corporeal. Laughter itself becomes a focus only briefly but in that brief moment it encompasses the globe. It should be noted that the protagonists of the story are women. Maleness only has fleeting appearances in the image of a retreating army, and in the attribution of the soldiers as Napoleon's. The bullies at the narrator's primary school are also boys. Women are positive characters: the narrator's mother and her teachers. The obsession of the female family members with warm feet and hence appropriate socks (the Bergsonian element in the story) could arguably be read as clichéd: femininity and knitwear go together, with the additional element of caring and nurturing. The humorous tone of the story is a redeeming factor here, as is the conclusion that the women possess an enormous strength: the little Ukrainian girl has grown into a woman who can tell a story and has a very strong bond with her mother. The teachers are the ones who restore order, in the chaotic music lesson as well as in the near wreckage of the nativity play. The text plays with measurements, notions of greatness and smallness, according the same (probably even higher) importance to socks, the comfort associated with them and warm feet as to world history. Lewycka's story effortlessly includes death – the death of masses in an army and the individual death of a loved one – childhood memories and family traditions in a story which insists that the great and the small are both part of the complexities of human life.

4. Who to be in the 21st Century? Jackie Kay, "Not the Queen"

Jackie Kay, a black Scottish writer born in 1961, has been concerned with questions of belonging and identity for most of her writing career, which began with the poem series *The Adoption Papers* in 1991. The greater part of Kay's oeuvre consists of poetry and short stories.[21] It is interesting that Liggins et al. in their chapter on the contemporary British short story "focus on Scottishness, as the genre has proved particularly malleable in the hands of a new generation of Scottish writers who have been prepared

20 If one likes, the time span is even wider to include the beginning of the Christian era with the staging of the nativity play.

21 See also Tranter (2008), "Writers: Jackie Kay."

to take risks with the parameters and conventions of the form" (Liggins et al. 2011, 247). Kay is one of the most noted practitioners of this generation.[22]

Kay's short story "Not the Queen," which came out in her 2006 collection *Wish I Was Here*, is a deceptively light piece on identity and biography.[23] The story outlines the life of a Scottish woman of Drumchapel, Glasgow, who happens to look like Queen Elizabeth II. It is also a doppelganger story that touches upon the fantastic and upon Freud's uncanny. The focus, however, does not lie on the potentially dark implications of this state of things (enhanced by the fact that the woman is of the same age as Queen Elizabeth). The basic situation is the material of a pure comedy of mistaken identity,[24] but like the cliché of a true comedian, Maggie Lockhart is a serious, secretly unhappy person who has spent her life failing to come to terms with her dubious fate.[25] Most of all she wants to be taken seriously, which is hard in her position as a striking double of the Queen. Her mindset does not help her to cope. "Maggie didn't have a temperament for teasing; never had been good at being teased, even as a child [...]" (Kay 2006, 109). In this, she is similar to the protagonist of Lewycka's short story, sharing with the latter an insecure childhood. The uncanny intrudes upon the story several times, but is always kept in check by the protagonist's no-nonsense approach. The idea of not seeing yourself but somebody else when you look in the mirror is deeply unsettling but makes Maggie rather irritated and irritable:

> Nobody could see her face without thinking of the other one's: not the man or the woman in the street, not the total stranger at the bus stop, not even her own family. And even she had the odd feeling when she glanced in the mirror that she wasn't seeing herself, but the bloody Queen. No, no seriously. (109)

Maggie fails to see what the point of all this might be. She struggles through life as the object of countless stares and the butt of countless jokes, and she is permanently unhappy about her looks. "Maggie couldn't joke about her face; it was no laughing matter. It had ruined her life" (111), and to make it even worse, "Maggie was shy and didn't like talking to strangers particularly [...]" (112). Both are not the best characteristics to accompany her outward appearance. She can lead a quiet life now that she has retired, and she still thinks with horror of her professional life as a wages clerk, when she continuously had to listen to the same kind of tired jokes (114). She is in a good marriage with Charlie, who has always enjoyed being married to the spitting image of the Queen, with the result that over the decades he has committed a series of dreadful blunders towards his wife. Charlie seems to be a balanced and content man, undisturbed by the social pitfalls Maggie has to face on a day-to-day basis throughout their married life. On their wedding night, he tries to joke with her about sleeping with his "very own wee Queen" (115), which makes Maggie jump out of the bed and force the promise out of him to avoid this kind of joke for the rest of their time together. From then on, Charlie has his fun in silence, of which Maggie nonetheless is very well aware. "No many men got to see the Queen naked so they didn't no they

---

22 It would go beyond the scope of this essay to include the role migration experiences play in Kay's work. A case in point would be "Trout Friday," which uses subtle humour for its unspectacular, friendly depiction of a young woman in search of her place in society in contemporary Britain, see for example Zimmermann (2008, 131-34).

23 On (women's) identity in Jackie Kay's short stories, including darker examples, see Zimmermann (2008).

24 This kind of comedy is part of a very long tradition, going back to Plautus's *Menaechmi* and then Shakespeare's *Comedy of Errors*.

25 Arguably, she has a telling last name, having locked her heart against positive strategies to cope with her looks, and against her fellow beings who like to make fun of her, but are generally harmless.

didn't" (Kay 2006, 115). Years later, he dares to bring back a mug[26] with the Queen on it as a souvenir from London, which also upsets Maggie, who "[...] yanked it off him and put it in the box for the jumble" (114).

Maggie remembers a small, but decisive event when her car broke down twenty years before the time of narration, and the arrival of the AA mechanic brings quite unexpected consolation.

> He lifted her bonnet and peered into her engine. "Has anybody ever told you, you're the double of –" "The Queen," Maggie said, cutting him dead. "Aye!" he said. "I'm no kidding but it's a wee bit freaky so it is. Go and look away, will you, while I fix your motor cause you're putting me aff. Jesus, whit a predicament fir ye. An' I suppose this is jist gonna oan and oan. Whit a burden fir ye, hen." It seemed to Maggie that the AA man was the very first person to ever truly understand. (110)

The sentence "Whit a burden fir ye" will stay with her for the following decades. The mechanic's initial reaction to Maggie's looks is not unusual. But then, the complete stranger seems to sense that she does not live comfortably with these looks, but is harassed by them, that they are indeed a "burden," blighting her whole life. The implicit understanding and the consolation the mechanic offers are extremely important to her. The narrative here has a quiet joke on Maggie at the beginning of the passage quoted above. When the mechanic "lifted her bonnet and peered into her engine," the subject matter is Maggie's car which metonymically (by way of *pars pro toto*) turns into Maggie herself. The AA man in fact sees into her inner workings, her mind and soul.[27]

With hindsight, Maggie believes that in the grand scheme of things her car broke down so that she would not get into a fatal accident, and so that she would meet the mechanic (cf. 111). For her, his blunt statement – a rather meagre consolation, if truth be told – represents an acceptance of her lot she has always longed for but never been given by anybody. "What a burden" is what she from then on often says to herself in front of a mirror (112). Apart from this, Charlie's love and understanding are the only bright lights in a world Maggie has come to see as stupid and rude. Charlie likes to play along when people stare at Maggie. "The big limping swine loved to see her awkward and embarrassed and to take her arm and rush off as if the pair of them were famous" (113). He always walks a bit behind her to defend her against stares and comments if necessary, and once he playfully suggests hiring a bodyguard for her – which Maggie cannot find funny at all (114). Looking the way she does forces Maggie to think about the implications of identity with an intensity she might not otherwise have had. "Everybody knew the Queen. Everybody knew what the Queen looked like. Nobody would ever say to the Queen, 'You are the double of Maggie Lockhart' [...]" (113). Presumably, this is what makes her feel so insecure about herself. She can never be truly herself because there is always someone who is well-known, overshadowing her appearance but also her achievements. No one, Maggie's very life seems to suggest, can compete with the monarch of the United Kingdom and the Head of the Commonwealth.

Maggie has always pretended not to be interested in the Queen in the only gesture of defiance open to her, for instance when a colleague of hers, unfortunately obsessed

26 The text puns on the meanings of "mug" – large cup – and "mug" as a colloquial reference to a face here. The individual person's face, her relationship to her own looks, and the impact one's face can have on one's life are, after all, the central motif of the text.

27 One could possibly read sexual undertones into this particular line – after all, the AA mechanic is the only man who seems to understand Maggie's feelings.

with royalty, keeps talking to her about the Queen: the fact that she never seems to smile, her relationships with her children, and her corgis (cf. 115). But over the years, Maggie finds herself thinking about the Queen rather often. "She couldn't help herself, especially when they were both getting on. Not many people had a double to compare themselves to unless they were identical twins" (115-16). Maggie starts comparisons on how well the two of them age: posture, skin, health. Interestingly, she does not come out of this totally defeated although the Queen seems to win on quite a few points. But then, she has always had advantages over Maggie: "(Mind you, think of all the expensive moisturizers.)" (116). Although Maggie has spent her life nagging about her fate and developing a defensive attitude towards humankind, she is revealed as a likeable and down-to-earth character.

Finally, she reaches the decision to do something about her situation and have cosmetic surgery on her nose to have its appearance changed. She saves her money, going about all the preparations secretly, and takes herself off to London under false pretences. Going through the city in a taxi, however, she starts asking herself questions: "Had she not just been a bit touchy all her life? Couldn't somebody who liked a good laugh have enjoyed herself with the Queen's face?" (119). Now that the decision has been made, she wonders about the meaningfulness of it, and she knows instinctively that liking to laugh is a quality which might be covetable as it can make life easier. The phrase echoes the most famous witty woman character of British literature, Elizabeth Bennet, who "dearly love[s] a laugh" (Austen 1966, 39). The recognition of her true situation comprises the last page of the story Maggie Lockhart has to tell. "[…] had she really suffered?" (Kay 2006, 119). With her decision on surgery made, she is suddenly free to think about her life in a detached manner, and as a consequence can find the comic side of her situation, which so far has eluded her completely. This is what would have helped her beleaguered psyche, her stressful social interactions, had she thought of it earlier in her life. Instead of being a permanent butt of jokes, she could have laughed with people and possibly even turned the tables on them. She realizes she could have found relief in laughter, but as it was, she merely provided comic relief for others. The final decisive factor is the absent Charlie, who is waiting in Glasgow for Maggie's return from the purported visit to her sister: "[…] he'd treated her like his Queen" (119). Here, the word "queen," denoting a factual monarch, is turned into a metaphor. This is a movement between the literal and the metaphorical which Regina Barreca has identified as a technique frequently used in women's humorous writing.[28] Maggie comes to realize that she would frighten and hurt her husband if she suddenly came back with a different nose. "He would hit the roof. […] And then he would probably cry" (119). She remembers the only two occasions in their marriage when Charlie cried: the death of his father, and the World Cup of 1974, when Scotland was knocked out of the tournament by goal difference. To all intents and purposes, she is not willing to be the cause of the third time: "To hell with it. Have the Queen's face and put up with it. Maggie looked out of the black-cab window as it passed Picadilly Circus only to see some people excitedly looking in. She gave them the smallest of waves" (120).

28 Barreca (1988) focuses on the strategy of re-literalizing metaphors and incorporating them into humorous narratives, but as Kay's text plays with the literal and the metaphorical meaning of "queen," going back and forth between the two, Barreca's point seems to be noteworthy here. However, the question of whether this is a strategy preferred by women writers remains open. It certainly strikes the eye in a number of comic texts by women.

These are the last sentences of the short story. At a very mature age, Maggie Lockhart finally comes into her own, accepting her appearance and making the best of it. She can recognize the comic potential of her situation, and hence, the positive side of the bane of her existence can finally be acknowledged and possibly even exploited. Ironically, with her shy, tentative wave, which is a first huge step towards acceptance of her appearance and a willingness to play along with what life has thrown at her, she comes very close to her double without realizing it. The Queen, after all, will always wave in a very restrained, lady-like fashion, which is exactly what Maggie is doing now, at the end of the text, in her taxi.

Jackie Kay's short story relies structurally on diverse variations of the comic, which, however, cannot and should not be divided. Maggie is a Bergsonian protagonist in her insistence on her negative attitude. To the treatment at the hands of others, even friendly and well-meaning people who could be her friends, she reacts stubbornly and always according to the same reaction pattern. The reader feels the need to cringe, torn between pity and exasperation for this protagonist who always has to listen to the same kind of joke and never manages to break out of her offended sulking. To cope with the vicissitudes of life, however, one has to be as pliant and fluid as life itself.[29] Probably even more important is the fact that the story is brimming with incongruous moments. Maggie Lockhart is a simple woman in a circumscribed life. Drumchapel, with its housing estates of the 1950s and '60s, is one of the districts of Glasgow, which was often under political debate and became the site of various municipal improvement schemes.

Maggie never mentions living in a difficult part of her native city, but the choice of location makes it clear that Drumchapel and Buckingham Palace could not possibly be further apart. Throughout the text and Maggie Lockhart's life, Queen Elizabeth II is a faraway but pervasive and stable presence. The people around Maggie are interested in the Queen and always read press reports about her. All who get in a word, including Maggie herself, concede that the Queen does not seem to have much fun in life either. Her royalty-obsessed colleague notes her lack of smiles; Maggie assumes that "[i]f you could look into the Queen's eyes for a long time, you'd find that she was shy just like Maggie" (116). The Queen holds Maggie's life and the story together, and presumably she does so with the UK, creating a sense of unity and continuity just by *existing* and performing a set of functions (of which presence is probably the most important). The remote monarch of the Commonwealth is pulled into a Glaswegian suburb and into the daily life of one of its humble inhabitants.

Part of the comic effect comes from the recognition of this insurmountable distance, which nonetheless is constantly bridged by a totally arbitrary twist of fate: Maggie's looks. This leads to deeper questions about social identity: how is it that two women with near-identical faces lead such fundamentally different lives? Implicitly, the text addresses discourses of class and power. The very arbitrariness of Maggie's fate raises the question of whether the distribution of power and social standing is not equally arbitrary. The accident of birth placed Maggie in her specific life; but the same could be said for Queen Elizabeth II, who is a monarch by the same token. The story cannot be called anti-monarchist, but it does ask rather tongue-in-cheek questions about the meaning and consequences of class, and about the state of the nation.

29 In Bergsonian terms, the people who make jokes about Maggie are also comic by themselves because they keep repeating the same kind of observation. However, it can be assumed that quite a few of these people meet Maggie for the first and only time, so they are not necessarily part of a mechanistic repetition. But for Maggie of course it would have to appear this way.

Kay's text also brings up the issue of Scottish identity in relation to a British national identity. The person of the Queen seems to be the only element which brings Maggie's Scottish world and the rest of the UK together, and it comes as a surprise to the reader that Maggie goes to London for her planned surgery. For her, this is as far as she could possibly go: from a Glaswegian perspective, London is a remote place. The Scottish vernacular figures largely when the characters have direct speech, something Kay likes to do, giving many of her texts a distinctive Scottish quality beyond locations and place names.

The third element of the comic structure topicalizes the comic itself. The crucial turning point of the story is Maggie's moment of realization that laughter and a sense of the ludicrous would have made her life so much easier. The short story ends on a hopeful note and the idea that Maggie now will set out to catch up on all the fun and laughter she has missed. Nevertheless, the text is also tinged with sadness since she had to reach her seventies to come to that conclusion.

5. Conclusion

The short stories of this case study rely heavily on incongruity and juxtaposition for their comic effects. The small rests next to the great, and the two together mirror the reality of daily life. The last things and the big questions on personal identity, love, religion, and death, are equally important to a person's outer appearance or choice of footwear. Ghosts get their say as well as flesh-and-blood human beings, and the dead receive a dignified treatment only with the help of some creative action, which fools the authorities and makes fun of them, revealing them as inadequate, if not inhumane. The movement between the historic and the trivial in the stories is an almost telescopic zooming in and out, back and forth, and the ultimate effect is the realization that the trivial is of course not insignificant but loaded with cultural and emotional meaning. By incorporating the comic, the texts can address emotions without being sentimental in any way. The stories' implications and the statements they make would be totally different without the comic perspective on relationships, history, gender, and class. On an additional level, it is also suggested that a sense of the comic may help to cope with the vicissitudes of life. This may be particularly true for women protagonists, but the question remains open of whether the comic releases subversive potential or has a conciliatory effect, enabling the protagonists simply to go on as before. Weldon's protagonist certainly takes subversive action, and Kay's Maggie is about to find new options of behaviour by beginning to appreciate the comic. The texts do not use slapstick, and they are not for laughing out loud, avoiding too explicit appeals to the readers' emotions. It is important to note that – as the work by Muriel Spark and Fay Weldon shows – the use of the comic as depicted here is not a short-lived trend, and has not come out of nowhere. There are traditions at work which seem to converge and become more and more pronounced around the turn of the millennium.

The comic in these texts works as a strategy of representation and narrative structuring of experience. The comic must be allowed to speak about all manner of things, not just about light ones, and not just about itself. It must be allowed to speak about all facets of human experience, and to conceive of the comic just as a means of entertainment and relief (albeit good things in themselves) is a blatant underestimation. The comic is not exclusively a mode or a decorative effect. In many texts, it is constitutive, no matter the topic. Comic texts cannot be taken any more lightly than serious ones. They approach their topics and their agendas with the same kind of intellectual *gravitas* and must be accorded the same kind of cultural importance. Indeed, comic texts might have an advantage over other kinds by their capacity to sneak in their agenda under the cover of smiles and laughter – which makes them potentially dangerous, speaking for the subversive potential of the comic.

Works Cited

Austen, Jane. *Pride and Prejudice.* [1813]. Ed. Donald J. Gray. New York: Norton, 1966.

Barreca, Regina. "Metaphor-Into-Narrative: Being Very Careful with Words." *Last Laughs: Perspectives on Women and Comedy.* Ed. Regina Barreca. New York: Gordon & Breach, 1988. 243-56.

BBC Two. "Writing Scotland. Muriel Spark." *bbc.co.uk*. Web. 15 February 2015.

Bergson, Henri. *Laughter.* Ed. Wylie Sypher. Baltimore, MD: Johns Hopkins University Press, 1980.

Brosch, Renate. *Short Story. Textsorte und Leseerfahrung*. Trier: WVT, 2007.

Carruthers, Gerard. "'Fully to Savour Her Position': Muriel Spark and Scottish Identity." *Muriel Spark. Twenty-First Century Perspectives*. Ed. David Herman. Baltimore, MD: Johns Hopkins University Press, 2010. 21-38.

Ermida, Isabel. *The Language of Comic Narratives. Humor Construction in Short Stories*. Berlin: Mouton de Gruyter, 2008.

Feduschak, Natalia A. "Marina Lewycka, Writer of Ukrainian Descent, Puts Comic Spin on Immigration." *Kyiv Post*. 11 February 2011. Web. 23 January 2015.

Freud, Sigmund. *Jokes and their Relation to the Unconscious*. Ed. and trans. James Strachey. London: Hogarth Press, 1975.

Kant, Immanuel. *Critique of the Power of Judgment*. Ed. and trans. Paul Guyer. Cambridge: Cambridge University Press, 2003.

Kay, Jackie. "Not the Queen." *Wish I Was Here*. London: Picador, 2006. 107-20.

Kemp, Peter. *Muriel Spark*. London: Paul Elek, 1974.

Korte, Barbara. *The Short Story in Britain. A Historical Sketch and Anthology*. Tübingen: Francke, 2003.

Lechner, Doris. "Eastern European Memories? The Novels of Marina Lewycka." *Facing the East in the West. Images of Eastern Europe in British Literature, Film and Culture*. Eds. Barbara Korte et al. Amsterdam: Rodopi, 2010a. 436-50.

—. "Interview with Marina Lewycka." *Facing the East in the West. Images of Eastern Europe in British Literature, Film and Culture.* Eds. Barbara Korte et al. Amsterdam: Rodopi, 2010b. 451-59.

Lewycka, Marina. "The Importance of Having Warm Feet." *Ox-Tales: Earth*. Eds. Mark Ellingham and Peter Florence. London: Profile Books, 2009. 105-16.

Liggins, Emma, Andres Maunder and Ruth Robbins. *The British Short Story*. Basingstoke: Palgrave Macmillan, 2011.

McMillan, Dorothy. "Muriel Spark 1918-2006." *Scottish Poetry Library*. 2015. Web. 15 February 2015.

McQuillan, Martin. "'The same informed air:' An Interview with Muriel Spark." Martin McQuillan, ed. *Theorizing Muriel Spark. Gender, Race, Deconstruction*. Basingstoke: Palgrave, 2002. 210-229.

Moore, Charlotte. "Tales of the Expected Unexpected." *The Spectator*. 5 October 2002. Web. 15 February 2015.

O'Kelly, Lisa. "Hotel du Slack." *The Guardian*. 22 September 2002. Web. 15 February 2015.

Patten, Eve and Jules Smith. "Writers. Fay Weldon." *British Council Literature*. 2013. Web. 15 February, 2015.

Puschmann-Nalenz, Barbara. "West Faces East: Images of Eastern Europe in Recent Short Fiction." *Facing the East in the West. Images of Eastern Europe in British Literature, Film and Culture*. Eds. Barbara Korte et al. Amsterdam: Rodopi, 2010. 381-95.

Randisi, Jennifer Lynn. *On Her Way Rejoicing. The Fiction of Muriel Spark*. Washington, D.C.: The Catholic University of America Press, 1991.

Saner, Emine. "I'm the only feminist there is – the others are all out of step" [Interview with Fay Weldon] . *The Guardian*. 22 August 2009. Web. 15 February 2015.

Spark, Muriel. "The Young Man Who Discovered the Secret of Life." *The Complete Short Stories*. London: Penguin, 2002. 254-57.

—. *The Complete Short Stories*. London: Penguin, 2002.

Stetz, Margaret D. *British Women's Comic Fiction, 1890-1990. Not Drowning, But Laughing*. Aldershot: Ashgate, 2001.

Tranter, Susan. "Writers. Jackie Kay." *British Council Literature*. 2008. Web. 23 January 2015.

—. "Writers. Marina Lewycka." *British Council Literature*. 2008. Web. 23 January 2015.

Weldon, Fay. "The Site." *Nothing to Wear and Nowhere to Hide*. [2002]. London: Flamingo, 2003. 33-48.

—. "Nothing to Wear & Nowhere to Hide." Book Review. *The Scotsman*. 14 September 2002. Web. 15 February 2015.

—. "Fay Weldon. Novelist – Writer." *fayweldon.co.uk*. 2015. Web. 15 February 2015.

Zimmermann, Ulrike. "Out of the Ordinary – and Back? Jackie Kay's Recent Short Fiction. *Multi-Ethnic Britain 2000+*. Eds. Lars Eckstein, Barbara Korte, Ulrike Pirker and Christoph Reinfandt. Amsterdam: Rodopi, 2008. 123-37.

—. *Comic Elements in Women's Novels of Development from the 1960s to the 1980s*. Würzburg: Königshausen & Neumann, 2013.

ARTICLES

ELIN KÄCK

Revisiting Europe: American Constructions of Europe in Poetry of the 20th and 21st Centuries

The intricate question of how America relates to Europe has been the subject of numerous debates throughout history. Europe has been a steady site for struggle also in American poetry, offering various positions and stances. To indicate the range of these, we might pit T.S. Eliot's *The Waste Land* (1922), which depends on Europe for many of its learned references, against William Carlos Williams's *Spring and All* (1923), which invokes Europe in an antagonistic framing, working to undo its hegemonic hold on American writing. While their handling of Europe may differ, these texts reveal the prevalence of Europe in American writing at the time. In fact, in the 1923 *Studies in Classic American Literature*, D.H. Lawrence suggests that the Euro-American relationship is central to American writing: "Somewhere deep in every American heart lies a rebellion against the old parenthood of Europe. Yet no American feels he has completely escaped its mastery" (Lawrence 1971, 10). In relation to poetry, Stephen Fredman has similarly argued that "the [American] poet finds him or herself in the awkward position of a latecomer to a European tradition that is both constitutive of and alien to the conditions out of which the poet writes" (Fredman 1993, 17). Aside from the Europe of tradition, the Europe of Modernism and the avant-garde has historically been viewed as equally problematic in relation to America. A 1921 article in the first number of the magazine *Broom* has it that "in Europe these things represent the extreme tip of growths, the roots and trunks and heavier branches of which are in its own soil. In America such tips produce the effect of hanging in the air" (Sanders 1921, 92). Given the significant American participation in the transatlantic Modernist movement, however, one might ask how the sense of belatedness has evolved in the years after Modernism and whether the relationship with Europe in poetry has taken on new forms in the course of the 20th and 21st centuries.

If, to simplify somewhat, the task of American poetry in the early 20th century was to prove its independence from Europe and thus to serve a highly symbolic purpose of establishing a national high-cultural identity, in the early 21st century, that task has changed significantly. Checking in on the issue as it stood at mid-century, in his historical overview Robert von Hallberg argues that "[t]he question in the 1950s was no longer whether American culture was fecund enough to produce a world-class literature" but rather whether "Americans [could] assume the custodianship of European cultural traditions as adroitly as military and economic responsibility was being shouldered?" (von Hallberg 1985, 71). How did American poetry get from Eliot's learned references, Pound's bardic voice in a largely Eurocentric cultural landscape, or even Williams's counter-hegemonic rendering of the "swarming European consciousness" (Williams 1923a, 174), to the self-assured mid-century stance described by von Hallberg? And where has it gone since? With globalism continually restructuring and negotiating this mid-century American cultural, economic and military hegemony, and with the recent economic upheaval in Europe and a widening of the scholarly field away from Eurocentric paradigms and towards new perspectives, the time has come to sketch some ways in which the Euro-American relation has operated on or been processed in American poetry in the past century.

The following, then, will trace the question of how some American poets relate to or use Europe, beginning with William Carlos Williams, going through Charles Olson and Kenneth Koch, and ending with the contemporary American poets John Ashbery, Charles Bernstein, Laura Mullen, Bernadette Mayer, and Fanny Howe. These represent some of the most vocal American poetry movements or groupings of the past century, such as Modernism, the Black Mountain Poets, the New York School and Language Poetry, thereby suggesting the scope and width of the preoccupation with the Euro-American relationship in writing. Yet, the poems included in this discussion have been selected for their engagement with this problematic rather than as representatives of different groupings. Rather than suggest that what we might call the Europe trope is central to these poets, I argue that these poems reveal the persistence of the Europe trope in American writing and, more importantly, demonstrate the transformations it has undergone in the course of nearly a century. By no means exhaustive, and in most cases limited to single poems, this should be seen as an initial, loosely chronological, mapping of some of the strategies employed by poets that in different ways take up, reformulate or turn away from the Euro-American concerns of the 1920s.

In order to understand the transformations of the Europe trope in almost a century of American poetry, it is crucial to comprehend its particular stakes and difficulties. In the 1920s, many of Williams's works deal with America's relationship to Europe, but rather than simply reject Europe in favor of a Nativist stance or, conversely, embrace Europe as a viable route to authority for American writing, he displays the ways in which either option is untenable. Thus, a work that includes an inaugural act of killing Europe still sees European tropes and myths organizing much of what follows. Ultimately, because America is bound to Europe, particularly England, through language, and because many of the myths, symbols and allusions used in writing link to a European past, Europe is unavoidable. The death of Europe as well as its persistence in language and allusions will be operative also in the work of later poets, but they will, as will be shown in the following, seek other ways to deal with Europe, ways informed by both political changes to America's position on a global stage and by new ways of conceptualizing belatedness in the wake of unoriginality.

At the beginning of *Spring and All*, in one of its many polemical prose sections, the speaker fantasizes about a recreation of the world brought about by the imagination, a force as real as reality itself. First, however, the world has to be destroyed: "Kill! kill! the English, the Irish, the French, the Germans, the Italians and the rest: friends or enemies, it makes no difference, kill them all" (Williams 1923b, 90). However, the destruction of Europe does not accomplish a clean slate for American writing. Further on in *Spring and All*, in poem VIII, we see a host of European references in conjunction with an American landscape both pastoral and commercial: "Persephone's cow pasture" and John Pierpont Morgan ("J. P. M.") "cutting / the Gordian knot / with a Veronese or / perhaps a Rubens–" (109-110). This poem demonstrates how historically European concepts saturate the American present, from the notion of the pastoral as such to the formulating of problems: a Gordian knot to be solved by the American businessman by means of either a Rubens or a Veronese, which seem interchangeable and reduced to their market value as cultural capital, means that not only is the way of phrasing and understanding a problem completely guided by European precedent, the route to solving it lies in accumulating markedly European cultural capital. Whether or not the poem is in fact critiquing this European viewpoint, this "consent" given to the leading party, to use Antonio Gramsci's definition of hegemony (Gramsci 2001, 1142), the poem itself will also be complicit in perpetuating or validating this Eurocentric paradigm by way of invoking these terms.

When the Gordian knot occurs in *The Great American Novel* the same year, the implications are similar: "Where in God's name is our Alexander to cut, cut, cut, through this knot" (Williams 1923a, 174). Here, the knot is not named, but instead the story of Alexander the Great cutting the Gordian knot is invoked. The knot to be cut in *The Great American Novel* is the relationship with Europe, the "swarming European consciousness. But there it is much simpler – No good to us" (174). There seems to be no other way of conceiving of a solution to the American problem than to produce or imagine an Alexander so that European history gets inscribed as a layer above the American text in process. If, with Mikhail Bakhtin, we view the word as "half someone else's" and therefore as carrying with it traces of former use, then we also recognize the impossibility of writing outside the power structures of that former use (Bakhtin 2008, 293). Williams makes explicit the power structures that inform European hegemony and reveals the limitations put on the American poet's project. Writing in a borrowed language, already used in canonical works in the English tradition, means that every word written may end up being an instance of citing.

The Designification of "Europe"

While many poets of Williams's generation dealt explicitly with European cultural lore, the work of some contemporary poets indicates that there has been a shift in the dealing with Europe in American poetry, one that is indicative of a larger shift in the view of America as a cultural producer. Charles Olson and John Ashbery both have poems with "Europe" in the titles, but they feature not the expected reckoning with Europe in terms of monuments or cultural encounters. Rather, they rewrite this preoccupation in a way so as to make the term "Europe" a mere signpost signifying nothing more than a semiotic marker and emptied of its former significance as a symbol of the entire cultural history of the Western world. Olson's 1950s poem "The Death of Europe," for example, performatively declares Europe effete and thus no longer a problem to solve. It is a funeral poem for Rainer M. Gerhardt, a German champion of Pound's work and a poet who looked to America for new developments in poetry. The death of Gerhardt gets to symbolically equate the death of Europe, but the phrase makes a larger claim. Gerhardt is figured as the "last poet / of a civilization" and "the first of Europe / I could have words with" (Olson 1987, 312; 309). These two statements mark the end of what is construed as an already short and uncertain Euro-American dialogue, since Gerhardt is then both the first and the last poet with which the American poet has been able successfully to communicate. If, in a Bakhtinian sense, the word has to be expropriated by the new poet for use, Olson's having "words with" implies rather a fraternal sharing.

In an earlier Olson poem, "To Gerhardt, There, Among Europe's Things of Which He Has Written Us in His 'Brief an Creeley und Olson'," the speaker claims that "place / as a force is a lie" (Olson 1987, 214). Insisting that his poem will not contain "proper names" of European places or poets (213), Olson's speaker discounts the currency of European cultural monuments as well as the power of appropriation that previous poets might have attempted to tap in their use of European proper names or names of canonical writers: "naming them as though, / like your litany of Europe's places, you could take up / their power [...]" (214). No such appropriation can be achieved. Europe invoked so as to be subsumed always presumes Europe as arbiter of cultural, canonical and symbolic power. Olson's poem indicates a change in attitude towards the Europe question, so that it no longer becomes a matter of effectively procuring power through poetic appropriation of European symbols and names, what Foucault has described as "the usurpation of power, the appropriation of a vocabulary turned against those who had once used it" (Foucault 1977, 154). Olson's procedure also departs from what Paul Giles takes to be Emerson's method, i.e. "taking icons and ideas from classical European culture and spinning them round in a new way" (Giles 2011, 7). Rather, it becomes a matter of neglecting Europe as a site for battle and turning elsewhere for historical origins and cultural models. At the same time, this does not seem to me to be effectively performed, since the poem clearly engages with Europe and takes as its antagonist (and in the later poem as its object of praise) the German poet doing Poundian historical investigations while also acknowledging American poetic advances.

What the speaker in the poem offers Gerhardt is "a present" (Olson 1987, 216). This present, American, comes with precursors that "though they are not our nouns, the verbs are like!" (219). There are two ways of approaching this nounless state of predecessors: either they are American poet precursors who, by virtue of being American, are not yet the kind of invokable noun that stands for a totality of cultural capital, canonical status and tradition, or they are European precursors that can never be *our* nouns, and thus cannot be invoked as the kind of scaffolding Olson suggests with the reference to accumulating their power earlier in the poem. Being a "noun," is to be emblematic, while having "verbs" that are "like" implies that the work that poetry performs, the actual writing, is on a par with that of noun-precursors. In this way, Olson shifts the focus from status to poetry as work, as action, as accomplishing something of importance, a shift which, lastly, works to the advantage of American writing, which is then equal to that of any canonical previous writing.

Olson remains preoccupied with Europe and repeatedly enacts his stance toward the burden of predecessors. We may only recall the compelling authoritative voice in "Maximus to Gloucester, Letter 27, [withheld]" declaring the battle with European antecedents ended, the poem itself enacting the break: "[...] this, / Greeks, is the stopping / of the battle" (Olson 1983, 184). The battle is stopped, furthermore, through words, but words historically and bodily situated: "It is the imposing / of all those antecedent predecessions, the precessions / of me, the generation of those facts / which are my words [...]" (184). The lecturing, authoritative voice of the American poet-speaker is intervening, through poetry, in the ongoing chain of reiterated battle, performatively stopping it. He does so by imposing not only his voice upon it, but also his body, which is a body made up of "occasions," interestingly enough not marked as a product of linear history, but rather of space and relations: "No Greek will be able / to discriminate my body. / An American / is a complex of occasions, / themselves a geometry / of spatial nature" (184-185). Emphasizing space, geometry and the relation between occasions, Olson foregrounds another value system than that which endorses Eurocentric hegemony: America as spatial as opposed to temporal makes for a different power-relation altogether. "To have any chance of being noticed and accepted, American writers needed to contest the temporal law instituted by Europe," Pascale Casanova has argued (Casanova 2004, 243). Yet, as in the previously discussed Olson poems, there is a sense in which even a dismissal of Europe becomes an affirmation of its importance. As Alan Sinfield has argued, dissidence "has to invoke those [dominant] structures to oppose them, and therefore can always, ipso facto, be discovered reinscribing that which it proposes to critique" (Sinfield 2001, 47). After all, what use is there to challenge an opponent or even declare a struggle ended which is not of importance?

John Ashbery's poem "Europe" from *The Tennis Court Oath* (1962) performs a different operation on the concept of Europe. While, like Olson's poem, it refuses to engage with monuments, it is a poem concerned with the war, which in itself is invested in both the erecting and destruction of monuments. Starting in England and moving on to Paris, the poem draws on a semantic war register with words such as "bombs," "Zeppelins," "aviators," "Morse code," "gas jet." Thus, it is no longer preoccupied with images of the intellectual, the avant-garde or the bulk of culturally significant artifacts normally used in Europe poems by American writers, but instead usurped by the war. The image of Europe is altered, and the scene is its destruction, not its cultural durability. Despite the fact that several European place names occur in the poem, the word "Europe" occurs only once, in a brief couplet that figures space and geography as receding: "But the map of Europe / shrinks around naked couples" (Ashbery 2008, 102). Not only is the space narrowing, the very map, in itself a version of the cartography of monumental place names at work in many previous Europe poems, is shrinking too, as though the store of available meaningful place names is equally eroding. As the title is "Europe," Europe becomes equated with war and destruction and stands for the end rather than the beginning, origins, of something. In an interview, Ashbery explains that the poem was named after the Paris Metro station, Europe, and also states that although the poem comprises European things, "of course they can also be found anywhere else" ("John Ashbery in Conversation" 1988, n.p.). The lack of specificity in relation to Europe, the insistence that whatever is there can also be found "anywhere else," is, I argue, emblematic of a shift in attention from the concern with Europe as the central site of struggle and of coming-into-being for American poetry to a much more guarded stance, even surpassing that of the mid-century poets who von Hallberg claims faced European monuments with "equanimity" (von Hallberg 1985, 72). In Ashbery's poem, and indeed in Bernstein's as we will see further on, statues and monuments are not even recorded. It is as if those measures of culture are no longer applicable: even if a poem is called "Europe," there is no claim to specificity or uniqueness. This absence of specificity, the space left by the monument removed, produces, opens up, a field for other possible writings.

Battling Europe Vicariously through Modernism

Europe as a particular locus, comprising different sites and places, is one way of figuring Europe, but what I call the Europe trope holds more than just geographical space. As has already become clear in the poems discussed thus far, it is a construct that includes poets, artists, monuments and art works that belong to the "imaginary cultural unity" that has gone under the name of Western or European culture (Guillory 1994, 42). In other words, it is deeply connected to the idea of precursors and tradition. In Kenneth Koch's poem "Fresh Air" (1955), we see first anxiety toward and then excessive violence against predecessors. This poem is, indeed, a reckoning with Europe, but it comes mainly in the guise of a reckoning with the Modernists and other more recent poets. The speaker asks, for example: "Who are the great poets of our time?" and "(Is Eliot a great poet? no one knows), Hardy, Stevens, Williams / (is Hardy of our time?)" (Koch 1999, 231). Tracing an uncertain genealogy of poetic lineage, and rejecting academic notions of poetry in a violent, highly performative way, reminiscent of *Spring and All*, Koch goes in for the kill, just like the "Kill! kill!" of Williams: "Agh! Biff! A body falls to the moving floor" (232). The discourse in Koch's violent passages is saturated with popular culture and the exclamations native to the comic strip, an allusion one would not find traces of in Williams's work, but the indictment of the arbiters of poetic tradition, who get the brunt of the attack, can be traced back to Williams's collection.

The preoccupation with poetic lineage and with establishing an operative tradition is one shared by critics, poets and theorists in the late 20th century, sometimes referred to as the possible "Age of the Anthology" (von Hallberg 1985, 26). The polemical piece takes into its sphere not only tradition as in European tradition, but also American tradition, which implies, firstly, that there now is, securely, such a thing, and secondly that the European preoccupations are less acute than previously. But Koch does not escape them entirely. The drawing in of "Helen of Troy," "Zeus," and "Ulysses" as characters (234), contributes to the perpetuation of the importance of Europe. Bourdieu has shown that even a dismissal of something might be, in effect, only contributing to its importance, since "the struggle tends constantly to produce and reproduce the game and its stakes by reproducing […] the practical commitment to the value of the game […]" (Bourdieu 1991, 58). Ridicule, parody and pastiche are known ways of counteracting power, but I would argue that Bourdieu's assessment is applicable also here.

Robert von Hallberg has claimed that as the American hold on the global economy and market grew after World War II, so American poetry changed vis-à-vis Europe: "By fountain, statue, palazzo and piazza, the poets were demonstrating their ability to write intelligently, tastefully about the outward signs of the cultural heritage America was taking over after the war […]" (von Hallberg 1985, 72). Rather than acknowledge any shortcomings, these poets met monuments with composure, von Hallberg argues, "as though the contemplation of a monument were a test of strength and a flinch could cost the game. American writers (and some tourists, too) are painfully aware of the need to prove themselves culturally" (72). But in Charles Bernstein's 1980 piece "The Italian Border of the Alps," what does the geographic marker signify? No vista is offered, no monument, no description. The sentences and phrases that make out the piece seem disconnected from any Italian context, as though the geographical indexing is gratuitous or meaningless. There is no Byronic hero brooding on these Alps, nor is there a reworking of that old motif. What does the European location do here, then? Italian Alps are of course still emblematic of something – some remnant of the romantic lyric still lingers in the very phrase, as does, perhaps, some echo of a *Bildungsroman* or the Grand Tour, but none of these are supported by the text. The words "summits," "panorama" and "ravine" are really the only links to the title in the text.

The expected sublimity appears, although not as first-hand account, but as something cited from elsewhere, i.e. distinctly not found in the presence of these Alps, but at a remove from it, and as such arguably not sublime in the sense we expect, since such a presence of the sublime would be overpowering, unquotable. Instead, it is intellectually approached as a cited phrase of the expected: "Obsequiousness turned into alteration, illusion ushering in 'these sublime distances'" (Bernstein 2010, 50). A broken-up structure of correspondence, letters, phone calls and conversations serves to loosely link the cut-off or decontextualized sentences of the piece, but the type of correspondence one would expect from a solitary poet speaker in the Italian Alps is intertwined with the correspondence between parent and child during summer camp, dinner-party commentaries, and work-ethic talk of the magazine interview or job interview kind, so that the Italian exile situation that might lie inherent in the poem because of its title never takes precedence over those other potential contexts.

If explicit signs of the Italian Alps, or even Italy, are non-present in the work, what I would suggest is highly present is the male high-Modernist trio of Pound, Williams and Eliot, the last of whom is mentioned by name. Pound is echoed in the phrase "& then went down to the ship" (51); Williams in the more domestic "Please, place the plums" (49), a request which is suggestive of both Williams's poem "This Is Just to Say," where the plums have been placed in the ice box by the poet's wife, and of the attention to form and line breaks – the placing of the word – in Williams' poetry in general; and Eliot appears in a more essayistic comment on poetics: "If Eliot is read with attention, he raises questions which those who differ from him politically must answer" (52-53). As we can see, these three allusions cover the domestic, the mythic/traditional and the metapoetic or scholarly discourses that work on the text.

Whereas Pound's generation had dealt with Europe directly, as a force to be reckoned with and as a route to American poetry, like Koch Bernstein deals more with the legacy of the Modernists here than with Europe as such. The conflation of Modernism and Europe deserves some attention here. The critique against the Eurocentrism of Modernism, voiced for example by Susan Stanford Friedman, who declares it "the dominant centrism to confront" when it comes to Modernist studies, has meant a reshaping of our understanding of the period (Friedman 2010, 476). Thus, when Bernstein substitutes the American Modernist trio of Pound, Eliot and Williams for the expected European scenery, the poem works to problematize this very point. In their works, however different and with whatever stance taken toward Europe, Europe plays a major role. Situating their poems in a European landscape highlights their embeddedness and complicity in that Eurocentric narrative of Modernism.

Reframing through Unoriginality

If Bernstein's hint at Europe is either vague, arbitrary or misleading, then Laura Mullen's rewriting of Wordsworth in "I Wandered Networks Like a Cloud" (2011) does something very different vis-à-vis the European tradition as represented by iconic male writers of classics in the English language: "I Wandered Lonely as a Cloud." Claiming the right to use traditional forms has historically been a route to authority for poets. This kind of appropriation of old forms in itself performatively declares the right to use them and is therefore connected to the question of poetic authority. "To decontextualize and recontextualize a text is [...] an act of control," Richard Bauman and Charles L. Briggs argue in "Poetics and Performance as Critical Perspectives on Language and Social Life" (Bauman and Briggs 1990, 76). Furthermore, it concerns "legitimacy" in that one has to be "accorded the authority to appropriate a text" so that the "recentering" is seen as "legitimate" (76-77). Who has the authority to use cultural lore in this way? Or could in fact the act of recontextualizing cultural lore in itself confer authority onto the new poet?

What is at stake here is not so much originality as it is exploration by way of investigation and critique. Indeed, the turn to unoriginality, for which Marjorie Perloff marks *The Waste Land* "a foundational text" (Perloff 2010, 12), acts transformatively on the issue of Europe in American writing. If being original is no longer the objective, and if authorship is no longer conceived of as individual genius, then the battle with tradition is significantly less dramatic. The American writer can then rewrite old writings, or recite them, doing something to them which can be at least as counter-hegemonic as a Williams piece of the 1920s. Even conceptual writing and the use of constraint can be translated in these terms, for the constraint chosen by the conceptual poet functions much like a traditional genre by imposing upon the text certain formal limitations within which writing must take place, but these limitations are not necessarily European, not necessarily part of a literary tradition like the English, but chosen by the poet. It can be seen as effectively taking the battle elsewhere, and thus actually performing the move Olson envisioned in his counter-European poems.

The rewriting of Wordsworth by Mullen is playful in its application of that poem to our contemporary lives and concerns. She takes the loafing poet figure, lying restive on his sofa conjuring up poems from the sights of the day, and transforms it into what is ultimately an indictment of that poet figure: in this contemporary version, what is considered on the sofa is the news and the pleasure the I feels here is that of being distant – that very distance from the object of the poem that Wordsworth's poet needs in order to turn it into poetry – a distance of contemplation. That distance, however, is instantly compromising when the object is war rather than daffodils. It becomes cynical, detached and a symbol of bourgeois contentment:

> A poet could not but be gay,
> Far from such desperate company:
> I gazed – and gazed – but little thought
> What wealth the show to me had brought: (Mullen 2011, 9)

The Wordsworthian poet figure goes where others do not, sees what others do not, detects and discerns. Anyone can watch the news.

The ironic close of the poem, where our speaker revels in her distance from these horrors, however, ends up making this a poem more about our response to catastrophe and our responsibilities than the horrors themselves: "And then my heart with pleasure fills, / To channel surf the world's ills" (9). There is an information fatigue, too, at work here. Whereas Wordsworth sees daffodils doing something astonishing and records it, our speaker sees yet another generic war report and it is just like all other war reports, only with different people dying. The remove at which Mullen's poet encounters war is echoed by the remove at which Wordsworth's daffodils appear. In other words, the motif of daffodils cannot be treated as an original experience, as a first sighting, or mediated without an account of Wordsworth's rendition. For the Western poet safely ensconced in a sofa in the 21st century, war is similarly presented at a remove, mediated by the screen, and thus runs the risk of being met with the same generic staleness as the flower motif in poetry.

Archival Investigations at the Intersection of Europe and America

While most of the poems we have dealt with here suggest that contemporary poetry turns from a preoccupation with the classical and symbolic high-cultural artifacts and myths of Europe, Bernadette Mayer's *The Helens of Troy, N.Y.* (2013) serves as a qualification of such a conjecture. Researching Troy, NY, Mayer does the work of the anthropologist and historian in capturing life in a town with one of America's many highly charged place names, carrying with them their European double. We might recall Olson's rejection of such place names and conclude that Mayer's project makes it clear that American geography resists such categorical rejections; the American "Rome," "Troy," "Paris," and "Ithaca," to name just a few such names, will demand to be citable as poetic material. The problematic lies in the matter of distinction, for is the American "Ithaca" really citable without the NY qualification attached to it? Considering the plethora of American towns named Troy, furthermore, this tag of identification serves to distinguish Troy, NY from both the ancient Troy and the other American towns named Troy. In Mayer's poems, Troy appears both with and without specification, enhancing the doubleness and investigating that problem of citationality.

The Helens of Troy, N.Y. entails research going to the very beginnings of the Euro-American power structure. Mayer's portraits and interviews with the various Helens of Troy, furthermore, act as both a direct link between the US now and antiquity and as a means for probing the question of their interrelation. It is as much a critical portrait of the decay of small-towns in post-industrial times, with towns that no longer have markets (Mayer 2013, 27), as it is an investigation into the expectations of the American dawn and early settlement: "there's a lot of greek revival architecture in troy / named troy like ithaca & the other troys to honor the people / in greek democracies," we read in "Helen Rezey Sestina" (27). The contrast between the concept of Greek democracy and a complete lack of markets is of course stunning, but even more significant is the distortion of the history of the name. Troy does not connote the people in Greek democracies so much as power, glory, and a history that is recited and deemed recordable.

Writing about her project in a piece named "The Faces that Launched a Thousand Ships," a title which twists the notion of historical time, precedent and hierarchy, Mayer explains that encountering "these Helens is seeing a part of history that wouldn't exist, wouldn't have to exist either, if I weren't doing this; there are lots of people & things, including books, that are already there, but being alive is different maybe" (Mayer 2012, 81). The distinction between "being alive" and being "already there" is one of being alive and of being taken up into literature, being recorded, being there as print, as traceable and part of documented history. Mayer is transferring these Helens, as well as Troy, NY, into the literary, so as to offer textual (and photographic, documentary) existence to them. The distinction between the original Troy and Troy, NY, is always present, perhaps even more so in its textual absence, i.e. in the cases where no "ancient" (29) or "n.y." (53) modifies Troy. Mayer's project is, in effect, a challenge to this hierarchy in that it places Troy, NY on a literary map, making it a site for poetry precisely within these multiple tensions of Europe-America, old-new, democratic-capitalist, and settler-colonialist. The stance toward Europe or history is less oppositional in Mayer's work than in Olson's or Koch's, but her topic is itself precisely the site of struggle: the relationship between Europe and America, the imposing of one culture (from the Greek revival architecture to the ousting of the Native Americans) on another, and, crucially, the power of language and naming.

Returning to the Site: 21st-Century Travelogue Poetics

If Robert von Hallberg emphasizes the composure with which poets met European monuments mid-century, Fanny Howe's 2009 poem "Oxford" offers a different way of handling epitomized European sites in the 21st century. Inserted into the catalogue of historically significant place names, like "Christ Church," and author names, such as "Larkin" and "Eliot," is a name of global modernity, "Pret Manger," presumably the fast food chain "Pret A Manger" (Howe 2009, 140). Such juxtaposition reveals how the function of historically significant place names and monumental sites as signposts in the European space is blurred by the global capitalist signs imposed on such spaces. No only that, whereas Oxford's "Christ Church" is singular, "Pret Manger" is ubiquitous and thus an uncertain sign-post for orientation, as there are commonly multiple such restaurants in one place. Much like the unspecified European things in Ashbery's poem, a place such as "Pret A Manger" can be found anywhere, and one in Oxford does not differ from one in London, Paris or Boston. While placing these side by side might seem to reveal the power of the one type and the weightlessness of the other, in fact it rather serves to deflate the meaning of those old, symbolic names, whose topography is now overwritten with the global palimpsest of consumer capitalism. If Williams had pitted American capitalism against European culture in his allusions to John Pierpont Morgan and masters of European painting, Howe's poem reveals the invalidity of that formula post globalization. They are no longer easily distinguishable.

In the final stanza, the situation of discovery of Europe is summarized: "Everything you see is finished. / Even the ground underfoot and ahead" (141). This might indicate the end of Europe, much like Franco Moretti has argued in *Distant Reading* (2013), "the conditions which have granted European literature its greatness have run their course, and only a miracle could reverse the trend" (Moretti 2013, 42). It is also, because of the references to other previous poets, a statement of belatedness, of coming into that European space only after it is "finished" so that whatever Eliot came there to find is no longer there. Mullen's account of Wordsworth rests on the fact that "daffodils" are poetically finished, no longer available as motifs for poetry apart from through citing, just like Bernstein's sublime is present only through quotation. A first encounter, a first experience, in Europe seems impossible. Aptly then, the line "There is no present" highlights the historicity of Europe and its museum-like space (Howe 2009, 140). Unlike the Modernists or even the post-war poets assuming cultural hegemony, however, the contemporary poet realizes that capturing the items of this museum in form, which von Hallberg has claimed is one way of exerting power in the face of European culture (von Hallberg 1985, 74), is now an obsolete move. These items have already been enmeshed in an entire history of poetic excavation.

Europe and America in Poetry: New Forms of Negotiation

This paper set out to sketch the American poetic interaction with Europe as motif, theme, subject, or source by means of allusion or comprising a selection of culturally significant and citable works of art. Our brief investigation has yielded at least five different ways of dealing with Europe in the past century: the polemical yet citational mode of Williams, with its conflation of American capitalism and European cultural capital; the refusal of Europe as a site for battle and the performative ending of the battle of Olson and to some extent of Bernstein and Ashbery; the editing or rewriting of canonical texts in the English-language canon by Mullen; the revisiting of emblematic European sites that no longer offer first-hand experience or have become non-descript through the spread of the emblems of consumer capitalism as in Howe's poem; the archival work of Bernadette Mayer, which works through a range of poet-anthropologist-historian methods to uncover and explore the link between an American present and a European past.

Doubtless, these are only some possible methods for engaging in a question dating back to the beginnings of America, and these methods are not to be taken as a definitive diachronic trajectory through the terrain this question offers. Yet, placing Olson side by side with Williams, for example, reveals a new stance in relation to the European past as citable, as material for text. The addition of Bernstein, furthermore, deepens this rift between early 20th-century accounts of the Euro-American relationship in poetry and later ones, since it completely displaces or drowns out the European locus advertised in favor of a Modernist presence that is taken up also by Koch in his battle with antecedent. Mullen's and Mayer's work, the most recent of the poems discussed in this paper, suggests a contemporary reworking of the question in the wake of the turn to unoriginality and conceptualism. Once what is at stake is no longer originality, and once writing as citing is no longer seen as a specifically American predicament linked to the previously used English language, but as a fundamental property of texts, poetic authority may be rephrased to accommodate a non-European vantage-point, may even finally contest such a hegemonic paradigm. We might of course add that the texts or problems addressed by these recent works are still firmly European, alluding to canonical works as well as emblematic place names, and that such a preoccupation in itself signals an ongoing interest in the question of the Euro-American power relation historically, politically, culturally, and poetically. However, the methods of editing, rewriting and researching point to a more definitive and authoritarian stance vis-à-vis these materials, so that it moves beyond subversion and into a realm of investigation and research. Therein a space opens up also for wholly different questions: that of the detached poet, that of being as text and being as flesh, and of the post-industrial topography of America itself.

Works Cited

Ashbery, John. "Europe." *Collected Poems 1956-1987*. Ed. Mark Ford. New York: Library of America, 2008. 91-113.

Bakhtin, Mikhail. "Discourse in the Novel." *The Dialogic Imagination: Four Essays*. 1981. Ed. Michael Holquist. Trans. Caryl Emerson and Holquist. Austin, TX: University of Texas Press, 2008. 259-422.

Bauman, Richard and Charles L. Briggs. "Poetics and Performance as Critical Perspectives on Language and Social Life." *Annual Review of Anthropology* 19 (1990): 59-88.

Bernstein, Charles. "The Italian Border of the Alps." 1980. *All the Whiskey in Heaven: Selected Poems*. New York: Farrar, Straus and Giroux, 2010. 49-54.

Bourdieu, Pierre. "The Production and Reproduction of Legitimate Language." *Language and Symbolic Power*. Ed. John B. Thompson. Cambridge: Polity Press, 1991. 43-65.

Casanova, Pascale. *The World Republic of Letters*. Trans. M. B. DeBevoise. Cambridge, MA: Harvard University Press, 2004.

Foucault, Michel. "Nietzsche, Genealogy, History." *Language, Counter-Memory, Practice. Selected Essays and Interviews*. Ed. Donald F. Bouchard. Trans. Bouchard and Sherry Simon. Oxford: Basil Blackwell, 1977. 139-164.

Fredman, Stephen. *The Grounding of American Poetry: Charles Olson and the Emersonian Tradition*. Cambridge: Cambridge University Press, 1993.

Friedman, Susan Stanford. "Planetarity: Musing Modernist Studies." *Modernism/Modernity* 17.3 (September 2010): 471-499.

Giles, Paul. *The Global Remapping of American Literature*. Princeton, NJ: Princeton University Press, 2011.

Gramsci, Antonio. "The Formation of the Intellectuals." *The Norton Anthology of Theory and Criticism*. Ed. Vincent B. Leitch et al. New York: Norton, 2001. 1138-1143.

Guillory, John. *Cultural Capital: The Problem of Literary Canon Formation*, 1993. Chicago, IL: Chicago University Press, 1994.

Hallberg, Robert von. *American Poetry and Culture, 1945-1980*. Cambridge, MA: Harvard University Press, 1985.

Howe, Fanny. "Oxford." *Poetry* (November, 2009): 140-41.

"John Ashbery in Conversation With John Tranter, New York City, May 1988." jacketmagazine.com. *Jacket Magazine*. Web. 5 December 2014.

Koch, Kenneth. "Fresh Air." *The New American Poetry 1945-1960*. Ed. Donald Allen. Berkeley, CA: University of California Press, 1999. 229-236.

Lawrence, D.H. 1923. *Studies in Classic American Literature*. Harmondsworth: Penguin, 1971.

Mayer, Bernadette. "The Faces that Launched a Thousand Ships." *I'll Drown My Book: Conceptual Writing by Women*. Eds. Caroline Bergvall, Laynie Browne, Teresa Carmody and Vanessa Place. Los Angeles, CA: Les Figues Press, 2012. 81-82.

—. "Helen Rezey Sestina." *The Helens of Troy, N.Y.* New Directions Poetry Pamphlet 3. New York: New Directions, 2013. 27-29.

—. "A History of Troy, NY" *The Helens of Troy, N.Y.* New Directions Poetry Pamphlet 3. New York: New Directions, 2013. 49-55.

Moretti, Franco. *Distant Reading*. London: Verso, 2013.

Mullen, Laura. "I Wandered Networks Like a Cloud." *Dark Archive*. Berkeley, CA: University of California Press, 2011. 9.

Olson, Charles. "Maximus to Gloucester, Letter 27 [withheld]." *The Maximus Poems*. Ed. George F. Butterick. Berkeley, CA: University of California Press, 1983. 184-185.

—. "The Death of Europe." *The Collected Poems of Charles Olson*. Ed. George F. Butterick. Berkeley, CA: University of California Press, 1987. 308-316.

—. "To Gerhardt, There, Among Europe's Things of Which He Has Written Us in His 'Brief an Creeley und Olson'." *The Collected Poems of Charles Olson*. Ed. George F. Butterick. Berkeley, CA: University of California Press, 1987. 212-222.

Perloff, Marjorie. *Unoriginal Genius: Poetry by Other Means in the New Century*. Chicago, IL: The University of Chicago Press, 2010.

Sanders, Emmy Veronica. "America Invades Europe." *Broom* 1.1 (1921): 89-93.

Sinfield, Alan. 1992. *Faultlines: Cultural Materialism and the Politics of Dissident Reading*. Oxford: Oxford University Press, 2001.

Williams, William Carlos. "The Great American Novel." 1923a. *Imaginations*. Ed. Webster Schott. New York: New Directions, 1971. 158-227.

—. "Spring and All." 1923b. *Imaginations*. Ed. Webster Schott. New York: New Directions, 1971. 88-151.

ROBERTO DI SCALA

At the Crossroads of the Global and the Local: Suggested Future Directions for 21st-Century ELT

When we speak about *English*, *which* English do we refer to? If the issue may seem either unproblematic or irrelevant to some (maybe, many) people, it is not to language professionals, such as teachers, who use English as the object of their job.

This contribution tackles the pluralistic nature which is increasingly being attributed to English in terms of varieties and variants, and its subsequent impact on English Language Teaching (ELT). After some introductory remarks on the most recent attempts at defining the plurality of English, the focus will be on the need for teachers (and students) to become informed about it. Suggestions will be made in order to abandon the supposed global primacy of a single national variety (e.g. British English) in favour of the awareness that the language is locally realized according to specific contexts of learning and use. The need for global teaching aims to be adapted to meet the local needs of each learning context will thus be brought to the foreground. A final note will remark on the resistance to this tendency which is still present in the educational sector, and the conclusion will be reached that, in order to be really effective for today's students, 21st-century ELT directions should lead towards the acceptance of what yesterday seemed deviant.

English at the Global Level

It is by now an established reality in the field of linguistics that there is nothing which can be unequivocally termed 'English' as a precise, clear-cut and defined linguistic entity. It is more of a "protean entity" whose fabric and uses in the world "are being constantly re-shaped and transformed in multiple ways" (Leung and Street 2014, xxi). As a consequence, the question arises which meaning should be attached to the word *English* when it stands alone. Blommaert (2010, 100) proposes a distinction between two senses of the term: English_1, which is an idealised, homogeneous, ideological construct or object, and English_2, which refers to a "locally organised pragmatics of using 'English' in ways rather distant from English_1" (Ferguson 2012, 177). English_1 may therefore be interpreted as a vast, virtual repository of linguistic resources which are pragmatically realized in different ways by different speech communities (see also Seidlhofer 2011). Each realization gives rise to a specific variety with its own set of codified norms.

In the light of the developments in English studies during the last thirty years, the best way to deal with the issue is to adopt the term *Englishes*, which suggests that in today's world "the language needs to be viewed not as a single, monolithic entity, but as something that has multiple varieties and forms" (Seargeant 2012, 1). These forms are not only linguistically "interesting" (Seargeant 2012, 2) but also "equal" (Kirkpatrick 2014, 33. See also Kirkpatrick 2007; Kachru 1985; 1992; Kachru and Smith 1985; Wolf and Polzenhagen 2009; Motschenbacher 2013).

The movement towards the 'pluralisation' of English started around the mid-1980s when Kachru defined his theory of the 'three circles' model (Kachru 1985). The Kachruvian model leads to a distinction between English as a first, second, and foreign language. Before turning to the question of English as a first language, let us see how English in its role of second language can be defined. Seargeant (2012) defines English as a Second Language (ESL) as

> a term used to refer either to the use of English in countries where it has some official status (mostly due to the legacy of colonialism), or in which it is the predominant means of communication and is being learnt by people (often immigrants) from non-English speaking backgrounds. (Seargeant 2012, 192)

English as a Foreign Language (EFL) is defined as

> the use or variety of English in contexts where it neither has an official status nor is widely used as a means of intranational communication. Instead, the language is taught as being explicitly associated with countries traditionally perceived as English-speaking (e.g. the UK, the USA). (Seargeant 2012, 191)

As far as English as a first language is concerned, in the countries belonging to Kachru's Inner circle the language is realized in different ways. These differences may concern grammar, lexicon, phonetics, and any other level of language, and they are usually restricted to the single speech communities and nations where they are used. These varieties are usually defined as English as a Native Language (ENL). A somehow richer and wider definition has recently been introduced by Kirkpatrick (2007), namely that of English as a Nativised Language. He defines a nativised variety as one "that has been influenced by the local cultures and languages of the people who have developed the particular variety" (7). On the grounds of this suggestion, then, "all varieties of English that are spoken by an identifiable speech community are nativised" (7), while the traditional distinction between English as a Native Language and English as a Second Language would only be important "in contexts where a so-called native variety, such as British English, is set against a so-called nativised variety, such as Malaysian English" (Kirkpatrick 2007, 7) which, in Kachru's terms, would be a distinction between Inner Circle and Outer Circle English.[1]

As too many definitions are likely to create too much confusion, the terms chosen for this contribution are: English as a Nativised Language for Kachru's Inner and Outer Circle Englishes; English as a Foreign Language for Kachru's Expanding Circle Englishes; World Englishes to refer to the field of study which has nativised varieties as its main object of research. At the same time, equal status is recognised for all varieties of English as a Nativised Language, and the plural noun *Englishes* is considered to be as representative as possible of said plurality.

---

1 Other terms have been proposed in order to account for all the Englishes spoken worldwide, among which World Englishes, English Language Complex, and English as an International Language. World Englishes (WE) refers to both "all local English varieties regardless of which of Kachru's three circles they come from" (Jenkins 2009, 371) and the field of study of which Englishes around the world are the main object of research (see also Kirkpatrick 2007; 2014; Kachru 1985; 1992; Kachru and Smith 1985; Wolf and Polzenhagen 2009; Motschenbacher 2013; Seargeant 2012). English Language Complex (ELC), instead, refers exclusively to all varieties of the language which are "distinguishable according to some combination of their history, status, form and functions" (Mesthrie and Bhatt 2008, 3; also McArthur 1998; 2003; Seargeant 2012). Finally, English as an International Language (EIL) recognizes World Englishes as having all equal status of legitimacy while being used for international, and consequently intercultural, communication (Sharifian 2009). Therefore, the ability to negotiate diverse varieties in order to facilitate communication is of crucial importance (Canagarajah 2006; Sharifian 2009) and, therefore, instructors should focus on teaching communicative strategies aimed at negotiation which leads to the avoidance of misunderstandings among the interlocutors (Lee McKay 2009).

English at the Local Level: Countable, Plural. The Case of English as a Lingua Franca (ELF)

The approach to the teaching and learning of English which has been chosen for this contribution goes against the single variety bias which seems to characterize the main trends of research in Second Language Acquisition (Kachru 1994; Sridhar 1994; May 2011; 2014). In the light of the role English plays in today's communicative scenario, traditional approaches to teaching the language seem anachronistic if they alone are granted legitimate status and validity. As a matter of fact, the motto at the heart of contemporary ELT should be 'teaching Englishes.' Consequently, the issue of the plurality of English should be included in school curricula and syllabi. Besides being acquainted with the different realizations of the language, teachers should therefore also be aware of the importance of inserting topics such as language awareness,[2] World Englishes, and the pragmatics of intercultural communication in their daily classroom practice.

From this perspective, one aspect of traditional approaches to ELT which should be progressively overcome is the so-called primacy of the native speaker. The validity of this model has been unquestioned for many decades by too many ELT professionals: crucial importance has been attached to acquiring native-like competence in language performance, and in most cases this has always meant that learners were expected to reproduce as closely as possible the way British English was spoken by natives. In spite of all this, many scholars have recently criticized the primacy of the native speaker model as they consider it to be no longer fit for ELT (see Derivry-Plard 2013; Hall 2011; Holliday 2005; 2006; 2013; Motha 2014). If native speakerism[3] were definitely no longer considered the benchmark for ELT, many teachers who are not native speakers of any ENL variety would be given a chance to overcome their feeling of inadequacy, "unease and insecurity" (Jenkins 2012, 492), a feeling they experience whenever they compare their language mastery to that of the idealized native speaker which is still so pervasive in the available teaching material (see also Buckledee 2010).

If 21st-century ELT is to be really effective for contemporary learners, though, acknowledging that native speakerism is out of place and that all ENL varieties have equal status and a right to be part of school curricula and syllabi is not enough. Another issue is to be taken into consideration, namely English as a Lingua Franca (ELF). ELF is a variant of English which is intended as a function of the language. It is used to communicate by people who do not share a common language when engaged in a communicative exchange and is considered a means for reaching mutual understanding through a number of pragmatic strategies which allow interactants to co-construct meaning (Jenkins 2000; 2007; Seidlhofer 2011; Mauranen and Ranta 2009; Björkman 2011; Mauranen 2012; Hülmbauer 2013; McKenzie 2013; Vettorel 2013; 2014; 2015; Bayyurt and Akcan 2015).

2 Language awareness, defined by the Association for Language Awareness (ALA) as "knowledge about language, and conscious perception and sensitivity in language learning, language teaching and language use" (ALA n.d.), helps learners to develop their observation as well as critical skills so that they may acquire a more profound understanding of the mechanisms of the language. At the same time, language awareness allows learners to become autonomous and independent by giving them the tools to learn how to learn (Lazzari and Panichi 2005).

3 Native speakerism is "a pervasive ideology within ELT, characterized by the belief that 'native-speaker' teachers represent a 'Western culture' from which spring the ideals both of the English language and of English language teaching methodology" (Holliday 2005, 385).

What should be highlighted at this point is that ENL and ELF are not mutually exclusive. The two can coexist within the English classroom as the distinction between English for Specific Purposes and English for General Purposes proposed by Seidlhofer 2011 suggests:

> we might start thinking of learning speaking and writing ENL as ESP – English for Specific Purposes, and where such purposes can be specified in advance, adherence to [native speaker] norms is obviously an entirely appropriate objective. But most learners have other and far less specific and predictable purposes, and it does not seem reasonable to impose such ESP objectives on them, especially since they are unlikely to attain them anyway. What they need is what is usually referred to as EGP – English for General Purposes – English that can be adapted to any purpose and made appropriate to any context. This is still generally assumed to be standard ENL, but as far as international uses of English are concerned, it is clearly not this English but ELF that serves these general purposes: it is ELF that is EGP. The pedagogic implication of this is that if the language subject is to prepare learners to use English for general purposes, it needs to develop not a *specific competence* but a *general capability* for use. (Seidlhofer 2011, 200)

The main focus is thus on the use of the language. This implies that students should be considered *users* of the language more than mere learners: an active role in the educational process of acquiring English will help them to become competent communicators – provided that they are able to choose which English to use according to the different contexts. As users, students may sometimes need to adhere to the formal structures of a specific ENL variety while, on other occasions, they may be required to use the flexible, informal structures of ELF. It is therefore important to teach the prescriptive, codified norms of a specific ENL variety and to present typical ELF features (Ferguson 2012; McKenzie 2013). This is possible only if language awareness is explicitly and adequately raised in the students. To do so, standard school curricula should contain both issues concerning the plurality of Englishes and basic notions of the pragmatics of intercultural communication. Though the learning of a specific ENL variety will still play a major role, it will no longer be the sole objective of language education. Once students are informed about the existence of different realizations of English (both ENL varieties and ELF), they will be able to make an informed choice on what linguistic resources to activate (if those related to ENL or those typical of ELF) according to the communicative context of use (Grazzi 2013). Theoretically, towards the end of their school years students should be autonomous users of Englishes: they should be acquainted with at least one ENL variety while also being ELF-informed. On the one hand, mastering one ENL variety will ensure they are able to use it appropriately on all occasions when they are requested to conform to formal communication. On the other hand, being ELF-informed will allow students to manage situations where informal communication is needed.[4] In this way, "issues of appropriateness as and when the particular interaction requires" (Illés 2013, 91) would be solved. Also, ELF features will have been awarded a legitimate role along with ENL forms because a "proficient speaker of English in the postmodern world needs an awareness of both of them" (Canagarajah 2013, 7).

---

4 'Formal communication' comprises, among others, international standard tests for language assessment (e.g. Cambridge or Trinity exams), business letters, and official reports for international institutions. 'Informal communication,' instead, refers to any exchange where interactants are free to use the language without being compelled to comply with the standard rules of a single ENL variety (e.g. when non-native speakers exchange information about their likes and dislikes).

English at the Local Level: The Role of Teachers

What does all this entail for teachers? Any innovative educational practice needs to be supported and performed by informed as well as motivated instructors. In the case of ELT, teachers must be informed about the plurality of English as well as about the existence of ELF. Above all, though, teachers must consider this approach to ELT a valid one and adopt it in their daily teaching practices. Also, they must start to consider students as users of the language rather than mere learners. In the light of all this, instructors must thus turn into educational facilitators. Teachers must be able to equip students with effective tools to make autonomous, informed choices on the appropriateness of the English they are to use. In the particular case of ELF, teachers should have clear in mind the transition of students from the role of speakers of English as a Foreign Language (EFL) to ELF users. For teachers, "acceptance and recognition of such a transition will be proof that they themselves have become advocators of awareness raising and that they are in a position to transmit it to their students" (Mansfield and Poppi 2012, 164). Jenkins (2012) expresses the same recommendation when she maintains that teachers must decide if and to what extent ELF is relevant to their classes on the grounds of the different contexts of use. Dewey (2012) suggests that teachers should become aware of these issues (plurality of English and ELF) during their initial training (see also Björkman 2010; Pedrazzini and Nava 2010; Bayyurt and Sifakis 2015; Bozzo 2015). Up to now, though, it seems that little has been discussed about how to translate the said theoretical pedagogical issues into practice (see also Dewey 2012). The issue calls for a reconsideration of the whole teaching scheme which many instructors are familiar with, especially in classes where students of different nationalities and lingua-cultural backgrounds sit side by side. A revision of the traditional objectives for language learning is therefore needed: its focus must shift from achieving the competence of a native speaker to the communicative process and the ways "to adapt what one wishes to say to the needs of the interlocutors" (Ferguson 2012, 178). In this way the process of negotiation which leads to online meaning making is brought to the foreground and awarded a central role within the teaching practice (Illés 2011; Canagarajah 2013; Illés 2013; Madhav 2013). A number of strategies should be adopted in the language class: paraphrase, repetition, redundancy, and the exploitation of shared plurilingual resources are keys to an awareness-raising language education. This, in turn, will help students to develop their intercultural awareness as well as their Intercultural Communicative Competence (ICC) and to become competent intercultural communicators (Vettorel 2010; Mansfield and Poppi 2012; Canagarajah 2013).

Teachers have to keep in mind "why [they] teach English, who [they] teach English to and what [they] teach English for" (Weber 2013, 12). They are requested to change their attitude to language proficiency: they have to consider language not only as a system but as a social practice as well (Canagarajah 2013, 7). Also, teachers have to acknowledge the important of negotiation strategies and the primacy of pragmatics[5] within ELF, and be able (and willing) to teach discourse strategies (House 1996; 2010) as well as language awareness (Seidlhofer, Breiteneder, and Pitzl 2006; Mansfield and Poppi 2012).

Teachers' willingness to change their mindset, though, is not so easy an objective to achieve. Making a breach in the wall of long-standing teaching practices may be extremely difficult (Buckledee 2010; Seidlhofer 2011). A large number of language

5 House (2002) expects major emphasis to be put on what she terms 'pragmatic fluency.'

class curricula and syllabi include traditional methodological and conceptual standards which, though perceived as slightly outdated in current research, provide ready-made solutions teachers can easily manage with little effort. As far as Englishes are concerned, much resistance is to be found at the institutional level as to awarding legitimacy and equal status to the different ENL varieties as the object of teaching (and thus to considering British English as *one* of the many varieties and not *the one* variety to be taught). At the European level, for instance, the sublimation of British English as the major ENL variety worth teaching and learning is institutionalized through the Common European Framework of Referece (CEFR). It "persists in its orientation towards native-speaker norms" (Seidlhofer 2011, 185) while making "clear reference to the [native speaker] as benchmark for language proficiency" (Weber 2013, 8). The idea is supported by the member states of the European Union: the design of the curricula for teaching and learning foreign languages at school set forth by the different ministries of education mirrors this basic approach (Weber 2013). There are cases of ministerial guidelines for teaching English which are not updated in terms of contents and methodological issues.[6] Furthermore, most textbooks and course materials devote little space to Englishes and language awareness so that students are presented with an essentially monolithic approach to a single ENL variety (which, in most cases, is British English). Given this institutional and editorial landscape, many teachers continue to teach their students notions in the traditional way. These 'singularist' instructors are convinced (either consciously or unconsciously) of the primacy of one ENL variety; they ignore or even thwart the plurality of English, sometimes because they know nothing about it, sometimes because of professional laziness: relying on one's well-established working method is easier and less demanding than questioning one's old beliefs.

Conversely, 'pluralist' teachers are experts in one ENL variety, know about the others, and support the idea that English, in one of its forms (i.e. ELF), can work as a function of the language. These instructors will equip students with the instruments to choose the right kind of English for the right context, and will (try to) turn them into skilled communicators.

Conclusion

The position endorsed in this contribution stands somewhere between the urge for change and the need for reassuring habits and entails a tension between the global and the local dimensions of teaching English. It is at school that most people should learn how to become competent users of the language. In this light, then, innovation can be seen as the local realization of a new, global approach to ELT. At the theoretical level, the said approach is globally valid for any situation: at the practical level, though, it must be adapted to meet the local needs of each class. If 21st-century teachers want to bridge the gap between the classroom and the outer world, then ELT professionals must not be afraid of stepping forward: globalization requires multicultural and multilingual competent communicators to be educated in places where the plurality of English is duly realized in effective ways at the local level. In this view, "the criterion for selecting the language to be taught is not whether it is proper English as measured

6 A case in point is Italy. The latest guidelines issued by the Italian Ministry of Education for upper secondary education contain only hints at the need to instruct students about the existence of ENL varieties other than British English (which, by the way, still remains the standard reference variety of teaching). No explicit mention is made of language awareness, World Englishes, and ELF.

against standard norms or the conventions of [native speaker] usage but whether it is appropriate English – locally appropriate to the purpose of developing a capability in the language" (Seidlhofer 2011, 199), where 'locally' refers to the local, pragmatic realizations of the potentialities of English$_l$. Therefore, here is where we are: at the crossroads of the global and the local.

Works Cited

ALA – Association for Language Awareness. "About." n.d. Web. 11 May 2015.

Bayyurt, Yasemin, and Sumru Akcan, eds. *Current Perspectives on Pedagogy for English as a Lingua Franca*. Berlin: De Gruyter, 2015.

Bayyurt, Yasemin, and Nicos C. Sifakis. "Developing an ELF-Aware Pedagogy: Insights from a Self-Education Programme." *New Frontiers in Teaching and Learning English*. Ed. Paola Vettorel. Newcastle-upon-Tyne: Cambridge Scholars Publishing, 2015. 55-76.

Björkman, Beyza. "*So you think you can ELF*: English as a Lingua Franca as the medium of instruction." *Hermes – Journal of Language and Communication Studies*, 45 (2010): 77-96.

—. "The pragmatics of English as a lingua franca in the international university: Introduction." *Journal of Pragmatics*, 43 (2011): 923-925.

—. *English as an Academic Lingua Franca. An Investigation of Form and Communicative Effectiveness*. Berlin: De Gruyter, 2013.

Blommaert, Jan. *The Sociolinguistics of Globalization*. Cambridge: Cambridge University Press, 2010.

Bozzo, Luisa. "Which English(es) to Teach? Empowering EFL Trainee Teachers to Make their Choices." *New Frontiers in Teaching and Learning English*. Ed. Paola Vettorel. Newcastle-upon-Tyne: Cambridge Scholars Publishing, 2015. 103-128.

Buckledee, Steve. "Global English and ELT coursebooks." *EIL, ELF, Global English: Teaching and Learning Issues*. Ed. C. Gagliardi, A. Maley. Bern: Peter Lang, 2010. 141-151.

Canagarajah, A. Suresh. "Changing communicative needs, revised assessment objectives: Testing English as an International Language." *Language Assessment Quarterly* 3.3 (2006): 229-242.

—."Redefining proficiency in Global English." *Contextualizing the Pedagogy of English as an International Language: Issues and Tensions*. Ed. N. T. Zacharias and C. Manara. Newcastle-upon-Tyne: Cambridge Scholars Publishing, 2013. 2-10.

Cogo, Alessia. "Strategic use and perceptions of English as a Lingua Franca." *Poznań Studies in Contemporary Linguistics*, 46.3 (2010): 295-312.

Derivry-Plard, Martine. "The Native Speaker Language Teacher: Through Time and Space." *Native-Speakerism in Japan. Intergroup Dynamics in Foreign Language Education*. Eds. Stephanie A. Houghton and Damian J. Rivers. Bristol: Multilingual Matters, 2013. 249-261.

Dewey, Martin. "Towards a *post-normative* approach: learning the pedagogy of ELF." *Journal of English as a Lingua Franca*, 1.1 (2012): 141-170.

Ferguson, Gibson. "The Practice of ELF." *Journal of English as a Lingua Franca* 1.1 (2012): 177-180.

Grazzi, Enrico. *The Sociocultural Dimension of ELF in the English Classroom*. Roma: Anicia, 2013.

Guido, Maria Grazia, and Barbara Seidlhofer, eds. *Perspectives on English as a Lingua Franca. Textus* XXVII, 1 (2014).

Hall, Graham. *Exploring English Language Teaching. Language in Action.* Abingdon / New York: Routledge, 2011.

Holliday, Adrian. *The Struggle to Teach English as an International Language.* Oxford: Oxford University Press, 2005.

—. "Key Concepts in ELT. Native-speakerism." *ELT Journal* 60.4 (2006): 385-387.

—. "'Native Speaker' Teachers and Cultural Belief." *Native-Speakerism in Japan. Intergroup Dynamics in Foreign Language Education.* Ed. Stephanie A. Houghton and Damian J. Rivers. Bristol: Multilingual Matters, 2013. 17-26.

House, Juliane. "Developing pragmatic fluency in English as a Foreign Language: routines and metapragmatic awareness." *Studies in Second Language Acquisition*, 8.2 (1996): 225-252.

—. "Developing pragmatic competence in English as a Lingua Franca." *Lingua Franca Communication.* Ed. Karlfried Knapp, and Christiane Meierkord. Frankfurt am Main: Peter Lang, 2002. 245-267.

—. "The pragmatics of English as a lingua franca." *Handbook of Pragmatics. Volume 7: Pragmatics across Languages and Cultures.* Ed. A. Trosborg. Berlin: Mouton de Gruyter, 2010. 363-387.

Hülmbauer, Carolina. "From within and without: the virtual and the plurilingual in ELF." *Journal of English as a Lingua Franca* 2.1 (2013): 47-73.

Illés, Éva. "Communicative language teaching and English as a lingua franca." *VIEWS*, 21, 1 (2011): 3-16.

—. "Something old, something new. Coursebooks for teaching ELF." *ELF 5. Proceedings of the Fifth International Conference of English as a Lingua Franca. May 24-26 2012.* Ed. Yasemin Bayyurt and Sumru Akcan. Boğaziçi: Boğaziçi University Press, 2013. 91-96.

Jenkins, Jennifer. *The phonology of English as an international language: new models, new norms, new goals.* Oxford: Oxford University Press, 2000.

—. *English as a Lingua Franca: attitude and identity.* Oxford: Oxford University Press, 2007.

—. "English as a Lingua Franca: Interpretations and Attitudes." Section 2 of M. Berns, J. Jenkins, M. Modiano, B. Seidlhofer, Y. Yano, "Perspectives on English as a Lingua Franca." *World Englishes. Problems, Properties and Prospects.* Ed. T. Hoffmann, L. Siebers. Amsterdam / Philadelphia: John Benjamins Publishing., 2009. 369-384.

—. "English as a Lingua Franca from the Classroom to the Classroom." *ELT Journal*, 66.4 (2012): 486-494.

—. *English as a Lingua Franca in the international university: the politics of academic English language policy.* Abingdon / New York: Routledge, 2014.

Kachru, Braj B. "Standards, codification and sociolinguistic realism: The English language in the outer circle." *English in the World: Teaching and Learning the Language and Literatures.* Ed. Randolph Quirk and Henry G. Widdowson. Cambridge: Cambridge University Press, 1985. 11-30.

—. "World Englishes: Approaches, Issues And Resources." *Language Teaching* 25 (1992): 1-14.

—, and Smith, Larry E. "Editorial." *World Englishes* 4 (1985): 209-212.

Kachru, Yamuna "Monolingual Bias in SLA Research." *TESOL Quarterly* 28, 4 (1994): 795-800.

Kalocsai, Katerina. *Communities of Practice and English as a Lingua Franca. A Study of Students in a Central European Context.* Berlin: De Gruyter, 2014.

Kirkpatrick, Andy. *World Englishes. Implications for International Communication and English Language Teaching*. Cambridge: Cambridge University Press, 2007.

—. "World Englishes." *The Routledge Companion to English Studies*. Ed. C. Leung, B. V. Street Brian. Abingdon / New York: Routledge, 2014. 33-45.

Lazzari Anna and Luisa Panichi. "Presentazione." Eds. Anna Lazzari and Luisa Panichi. *English in Economics and Business. Guida all'inglese del mondo dell'economia e del commercio*. Milano: Hoepli, 2005. i-vii.

Lee McKay, Sandra. "Pragmatics and EIL Pedagogy." *English as an International Language. Perspectives and Pedagogical Issues*. Ed. Farzad Sharifian. Bristol: Multilingual Matters, 2009. 227-241.

Leung, Constant, and Brian V. Street. "Introduction." *The Routledge Companion to English Studies*. Ed. Constant Leung and Brian V. Street. Abingdon / New York: Routledge, 2014. xxi-xxx.

McArthur, Tom. *The English Language*. Cambridge: Cambridge University Press, 1998.

—. "World English, Euro English, Nordic English?" *English Today* 19.1 (2003): 54-58.

McKenzie, Ian. *English as a Lingua Franca. Theorizing and Teaching English*. Abingdon / New York: Routledge, 2013.

Madhav, Kafle. "Reconceptualizing EIL pedagogy: from mastery to successful negotiation." *Contextualinzing the Pedagogy of English as an International Language: Issues and Tensions*. Ed. N. T. Zacharias and C. Manara. Newcastle-upon-Tyne: Cambridge Scholars Publishing, 2013. 58-74.

Mansfield Gillian and Franca Poppi. "The English as a Foreign Language / Lingua Franca Debate: Sensitising Teachers of English as a Foreign Language Towards Teaching English as a Lingua Franca." *Profile* 14.1 (2012): 159-172.

Mauranen, Anna. *Exploring ELF. Academic English Shaped by Non-Native Speakers*. Cambridge, Cambridge University Press, 2012.

—, and Elina Ranta, eds. *English as a Lingua Franca: Studies and Findings*. Newcastle-upon-Tyne: Cambridge Scholars Publishing, 2009.

May, Stephen. "The Disciplinary Constraints of SLA and TESOL: Additive Bilingualism and Second Language Acquisition." *Linguistics and Education* 22.3 (2011): 233-247.

—. "Disciplinary Divides, Knowledge Construction, and the Multilingual Turn." *The Multilingual Turn. Implications for SLA, TESOL and Bilingual Education*. Ed. S. May. Abingdon / New York: Routledge, 2014. 7-31.

Mesthrie Rajend and Rakesh M. Bhatt. *World Englishes: The Study of New Linguistic Varieties*. Camrbdige: Cambridge University Press, 2008.

Motha, Suhanthie. *Race, Empire, and English Language Teaching. Creating Responsible and Ethical Anti-Racist Practice*. New York: Teachers College Press, 2014.

Motschenbacher, Heiko. *New Perspectives on English as a European Lingua Franca*. Amsterdam / Philadelphia: John Benjamins, 2013.

Pedrazzini, Luisa, and Andrea Nava. "The ELF of English language teachers." *EIL, ELF, Global English: Teaching and Learning English*. Ed. Cesare Gagliardi and Alan Maley. Bern: Peter Lang, 2010. 283-299.

Seargeant, Philip. *Exploring World Englishes. Language in a Global Context*. Abingdon / New York: Routledge, 2012.

Seidlhofer, Barbara. *Understanding English as a Lingua Franca*. Oxford: Oxford University Press, 2011.

—. "Key concepts in ELT. English as a lingua franca." *ELT Journal*, 59.4 (2005):339-341.

—, Angelika Breiteneder and Marie Louise Pitzl. "English as a Lingua Franca in Europe: challenges for applied linguistics" *Annual Review of Applied Linguistics*, 26 (2006): 3-34.

Sharifian, Farzad. "English as an International Language: An Overview." *English as an International Language. Perspectives and Pedagogical Issues*. Ed. Farzad Sharifian. Bristol: Multilingual Matters, 2009. 1-18.

Smit, Ute. *English as a Lingua Franca in Higher Education. A Longitudinal Study of Classroom Discourse*. Berlin / New York: De Gruyter, 2010.

Sridhar, S. N. "A Reality Check for SLA Theories." *TESOL Quarterly* 28, 4 (1994): 800-805.

Vettorel, Paola. "English(es), ELF, Xmas and trees: Intercultural Communicative Competence and English as a Lingua Franca in the primary classroom." *Perspectives. A Journal of TESOL Italy*, 37, 1 (2010): 25-52.

—. "ELF in international school exchanges: stepping into the role of ELF users." *Journal of English as a Lingua Franca*, 2, 1 (2013): 147-173.

—. *English as a Lingua Franca in Wider Networking. Blogging Practices*. Berlin: De Gruyter, 2014.

—, ed. *New Frontiers in Teaching and Learning English*. Newcastle-upon-Tyne: Cambridge Scholars Publishing, 2015.

Weber, Elisabeth. "English as a Lingua Franca and appropriate teacher competence." *ELF 5. Proceedings of the Fifth International Conference of English as a Lingua Franca. May 24-26 2012*. Eds. Yasemin Bayyurt and Sumru Akcan. Boğaziçi: Boğaziçi Unversity Press, 2013. 7-13.

Wolf Hans-Georg and Frank Polzenhagen. *World Englishes. A Cognitive Sociolinguistic Approach*. Berlin: De Gruyter, 2009.

REVIEWS

Oliver Scheiding and Martin Seidl, eds. *Worlding America: A Transnational Anthology of Short Narratives before 1800.* Stanford: Stanford University Press, 2015. 264 pp.

Many literary anthologies on the market today force the diversity of American writing into more or less neatly organized categories based on specific (and often rather exclusive) notions of nation, genre, period, gender, or race. *Worlding America: A Transnational Anthology of Short Narratives before 1800*, meticulously edited by Oliver Scheiding and Martin Seidl, ventures beyond such conventional paths of anthology-making, urging its readers to think outside of established parameters and rethink common trajectories of American literary history.

The anthology embraces what may seem at first to be a relatively narrow generic and temporal scope – short narratives before 1800 – but which turns out to be a courageously broad corpus that includes writings by Native American, African American, French, English, German, and Spanish authors. The "America" of the title thus includes North America and the Americas as well as the Circum-Atlantic world, avoiding what Scheiding and Seidl call "a national fallacy" by moving from a "U.S.-centric bias" to a transnational, and indeed global perspective rooted in the concept of *worlding* (9; 10). They derive this concept from Martin Heidegger's *Sein und Zeit* (1927) via Susan Gillman and Kirsten S. Gruesz[1], who develop a "text-network model" of *worlding* that "is based on iteration rather than origination and examines the pluridirectional flow of texts across different languages, cultures, and nations" (10). *Worlding* provides a productive framework for the anthologized short narratives, turning the focus away from "specific genres [...], national origins, and periods" (11), according to which the collected narratives would merely constitute an aesthetically inferior prehistory of the American short story. As such, it shifts our attention to "a new understanding of the literary text not so much as a work that can be ascribed to a particular author, place, and time of publication, but rather as a network of multiple intentions, writing practices, and print traditions that stretch across time and space" (10-11).

Reflecting this reorientation from literary work to literary networks, the volume is divided into five sections (Life Writing, Female Agency, The Circum-Atlantic World, Cultures of Print, Ghost Stories). Each of these sections is subdivided "into units of interrelated narratives of different times and backgrounds" (14), as the editors explain in their excellent introduction (for example, Orientalism, Migrant Fictions, and Sensationalism in the Cultures of Print section). These sections and clusters follow no rigid pattern of organization, moving from the literary mode of life writing and a focus on the agency of female writers/writing to the geographical lens of the Circum-Atlantic world and the framework of print culture, concluding with a theme-oriented

---

1 See Susan Gillman and Kirsten S. Gruesz. "Worlding America: The Hemispheric Text-Network." *A Companion to American Literary Studies*. Eds. Caroline F. Levander and Robert S. Levine. Chichester: Wiley-Blackwell, 2011. 228-247.

section on ghost stories. Avoiding common patterns of organization (chronology, region, nation, etc.) reinforces the editors' attempt to "encourage […] readers to explore stories in ways that re-create modes of world-making grounded in cross-cultural and cross-temporal texts in motion" (14). Each of the sections begins with a headnote that introduces the featured texts and outlines the print practices and cultural circumstances that shaped their production, publication, and circulation as well as the broader field from which these narratives are drawn. The headnotes offer preliminary analyses that equip the reader with a sophisticated understanding of why these texts matter and how they may be studied. The editors also provide information about the frequently convoluted publication history of each text (placed in a footnote after the title of each narrative), explanatory endnotes for each text, and suggestions for further reading at the end of each section.

The ultimate value of *Worlding America* lies in the textual materials it collects, in annotated and contextualized form, as a corrective to existing canons of American literature. Only if these texts can challenge received notions of American literary history will the anthology achieve its self-declared objectives. In my estimation, the anthology admirably meets its ambitious aims. My reading experience was one of continuing fascination, stimulating surprise, and a satisfying sense of discovering new historical dimensions and literary connections among writers as diverse as the French Jesuit missionary Paul Le Jeune's report of negotiations with the Natives in New France, the English Edward Taylor's remarkably un-Puritan account of his voyage across the Atlantic, the German printer Christoph Sauer's promotional missive extolling the benefits of life in Pennsylvania, the Spanish Carlos de Sigüenza y Góngora's transcription of Alonso Ramírez's travel experiences in Mexico, the African American Thomas Powers's confession written before his execution, the violent captivity narrative of Marie Le Roy and Barbara Leininger, the French military officer Jean-François de Saint-Lambert's sentimental story about a Jamaican slave rebellion, Philip Freneau's depiction of the hardships faced by ship captains in the Circum-Atlantic trade, post-revolutionary narratives by anonymous writers that had been popular in Europe before publication in the U.S. and appealed to the literary tastes of magazine readers, and ghost stories by anonymous European American writers as well as Native Americans such as Chiricahua and K'iche' Maya.

Scheiding and Seidl have assembled a well-balanced anthology of lesser known short narratives from canonical writers (Freneau, Cotton Mather, Benjamin Franklin, as well as Washington Irving and Nathaniel Hawthorne, the latter two illustrating the transition from pre-1800 narratives to the post-1800 genre of the short story) and texts that most Americanists and students of the colonial era will not have previously encountered. *Worlding America* is an impressive anthology that will undoubtedly prove to be highly useful as a scholarly resource and teaching tool.

DANIEL STEIN

Reingard M. Nischik, ed. *The Palgrave Handbook of Comparative North American Literature*. Houndmills, Basingstoke: Palgrave Macmillan, 2014. 512 pp.

This *Handbook* comes as a timely volume, monitoring as it does a significant re-orientation in American and Canadian studies, from the study of literature and culture within national paradigms to a transnational perspective. Divided into five sections, its seventeen chapters – all except two being original contributions by Canadian, US-American and German scholars – deal with central areas of North American Literature Studies, showing how comparative investigations can be fruitfully applied to these areas in order to arrive at a deeper understanding of cultural factors and processes in a (globalized) North American context.

In her introductory chapter, the editor defines the aims and scope of comparative North American literature studies within a network of intersecting disciplines (Canadian studies, American studies, global and hemispheric studies, inter-American studies and border studies), providing valuable clarifications in face of a proliferation of terms and concepts. Taking account of globalizing tendencies in the western hemisphere, comparative North American (literature) studies may redress deficits of national approaches, such as for instance the fact that 'Canadian studies' have become virtually synonymous with the study of English Canada, to the exclusion of Québécois literature and culture (cf. 7 f.). As Nischik rightly remarks, North American Studies "does not refer to clear-cut geographies and agendas, but is subject to political, institutional, and, last but not least, personal practices, which are geared to traditions and cultural hierarchies, yet may change over time" (5). She therefore emphasizes the need for a comparative approach, and a "combined view of US and Canadian (and Québécois) literatures" (16). Indeed, as she claims, "Comparative North American Studies [...] decenters the view of individual countries and cultures and does not privilege one over the other" (17). It allows for analysing cultural and socio-political developments in a wider perspective, without entirely displacing "national, identity-based approaches" (18). Chapter 2 by Rachel Adams ("Imagining North America") concludes the book's first section, whose aim is that of "Charting the Territory," by circumscribing the range of conceptualizations of 'North America,' from the utopian visions of explorers and early settlers to a concept of the North American continent "that is informed by, but cannot be reduced to, economic and political relations" (42).

Including chapters on the black and Native populations in Canada and the US, section II ("Perspectives on Multiculturalism") is dedicated to multiculturalism as a defining aspect of North American societies, analysing its social, cultural and political manifestations, and the frequent divergence between theory, ideology and practice. In chapter 4 ("Comparative Race Studies: Black and White in Canada and the United States"), Eva Gruber shows how 'race' is frequently elided from Canadian public discourse, due to different historical backgrounds and a much greater heterogeneity of Canada's black population as compared to that of the US, with those African Canadians who have lived in the country for generations now being greatly outnumbered by recent immigrants especially from the Caribbean. Katja Sarkowsky's chapter on Indigenous literatures focuses on renderings of the US-Canadian border in Indigenous writing, this border being irrelevant to the collective identities of Native

North Americans, and the self-positioning of Indigenous writers like, for instance, Thomas King (cf. 90), while being strongly effective in other respects (cf. 86). In her chapter on "Naturalization and Citizenship in North America," Mita Banerjee surveys the troubled history of Asian immigration to Canada and the US, which illustrates the preference/exclusion of immigrant groups according to "cultural compatibility," (103) discussing Denise Chong's novel *The Concubine's Children* (1996) as a prominent literary rendering of the way in which 'racial prerequisite cases' or the 'queer domesticity' among the Chinese communities in the wake of immigration restrictions concerning wives and families were used for denying citizenship.

Section III ("French-Language and English-Language Cultures in North America") deals with Francophone literature and culture within and beyond Quebec. Marie Vautier, in a historical survey of "Comparative Canadian/Québécois Literature Studies," corrects the wide-spread view that Canadian literatures in English and French have largely been studied separately, stressing the primary importance of comparative criticism in the field within the Canadian context. Chapters on Québec and US-American literary relations, especially on the various phases of the reception of American literature in Québec (Jean Morency), and on French language and culture regions other than Québec (Monika Giacoppe, "North America's Francophone Borderlands") complete the differentiated assessment of North American *Francophonie* in this section.

The chapters in section IV ("Regions and Symbolic Spaces") deal with national borders (Canada-US, US-Mexico) as multiply inscribed sites of division and contact, and their reflection in 'border fiction' (Claudia Sadowski-Smith), and with the importance of regionalism in US and Canadian literature (Florian Freitag). Reviewing concepts of region and regionalism, Freitag emphasizes that Comparative North American Studies "offers an opportunity to consider regions, regional writing, and regionalism in contexts that transcend the national" (201), thus enabling the profiling of parallels and differences. Christa Kannenberg's chapter on "The North in English Canada and Quebec" elaborates on the importance of 'North' as an element in Canada's understanding of herself as a nation, as expressed in the title of Sherrill Grace's seminal study *Canada and the Idea of North*, or in Louis-Edmond Hamelin's influential concept of 'nordicity.' The chapter also shows how conceptions of 'North' differ in Anglophone Canada, where 'North' denotes the distant arctic regions, and Québec, where the province itself is already seen in terms of 'North.' The section concludes with a chapter by Caroline Rosenthal on "North American Urban Fiction," which offers a penetrating account of Canadian and US 'literary landscapes' since the early 20th century. The comparative perspective here brings to focus the cultural-historical significance of differences, like the lack of modernist urban fiction in Canada *versus* renderings of the big city as the epitome of modernity in the US, the ensuing questioning of modern myths by postmodern US writers such as Paul Auster on the one hand, and an emphasis on exploring the metropolis as a multiple ethno-cultural space in contemporary Canadian writing on the other.

Section V ("National, Transnational, Global Perspectives") places cultural-historical developments in Canada and the US within larger frames. Demonstrating the benefits of comparative literary history, two authoritative and elegantly written chapters on modernism (Jutta Ernst) and postmodernism (Julia Breitbach) in the USA and Canada cast new light on well-established tenets, such as for example the lack of 'high modernist' writing in Canadian literature, and the complex connection between postcolonialism and Canadian postmodernism. These chapters are followed by an investigation of literary celebrity as a socio-cultural phenomenon in a globalized literary market (Lorraine York), and a concluding chapter by Georgiana Banita on "North American Literature and Global Studies: Transnationalism at War," which illustrates the transnational re-orientation in North American Literary Studies through the example of writing about war from Canada and the US.

Reingard M. Nischik has assembled a rich, informative, and critically astute collection of essays, which will be an indispensable reference work for Canadianists, Americanists and students of world literature alike. Meticulously researched and carefully edited, the chapters in this *Handbook* offer innovative approaches to their subjects, while at the same time providing a reliable compendium of information on cultural-historical backgrounds and developments. Together with perceptive readings of representative literary texts in many of the chapters, the volume combines comprehensiveness and detailed analysis in a remarkably balanced manner. The concentration on Canada and the US, with only the occasional glimpse at Mexico, may be regretted by some, but has greatly contributed to a focussed and homogeneous volume, an impression that is further enhanced by consistent cross-references between the individual chapters, an extensive listing of reference works and a detailed index.

MARTIN LÖSCHNIGG

Kate Macdonald and Christoph Singer, eds. *Transitions in Middlebrow Writing, 1880-1930*. Basingstoke: Palgrave Macmillan, 2015. 240 pp.

'Middlebrow,' 'highbrow' and 'lowbrow' were relatively short-lived critical terms that entered the literary field in the 1920s. 'Middlebrow' writings were taken to be less intellectually distinguished, aimed at a middle-class audience, and set off against the intellectualism of literary modernism on the one hand and lower-class mass print on the other. In use until the 1940s, the term was of dubious origins, deriving from the 19th-century phrenological idea that intellectual capacity was inferable from the height of people's foreheads. Rather surprisingly, it has since been excavated by scholars from the 1990s onwards in order to designate middle-of-the-market publishing phenomena of the inter-war era that addressed a readership "normally categorized by its recent acquisition of literacy, and its new economic power" (3). While much definitory work has been done,[1] the term has almost become naturalized (again), in the publication under review and elsewhere, which tends to obliterate its denigrating connotations. Indeed, most chapters of the present collection comment on the anachronism of using the term 'middlebrow' for texts written between 1880 and 1930. Notwithstanding, the collection succeeds in pointing out the "provisional" nature of

1 See Ann Ardis. *Modernism and Cultural Conflict, 1888-1922*. Cambridge: Cambridge University Press, 2002; R.M. Bracco. *Betwixt and Between: Middlebrow Fiction and English Society in the Twenties and Thirties*. Parkville: Melbourne University Press, 1990; R.M. Bracco. *Merchants of Hope: British Middlebrow Writers and the First World War*. Oxford: Berg, 1993; and Ina Habermann. *Myth, Memory and the Middlebrow: Priestly, du Maurier, and the Symbolic Form of Englishness*. Houndmills: Palgrave Macmillan, 2010.

literary taxonomies (2); as Macdonald and Singer argue, "[o]ne person's establishment norm is another person's avant garde" (1). They propose to read the 'middlebrow' as an "alternative cultural formation" that was more inclusive and less policing of its boundaries than high culture: "Middlebrow culture was denigrated by critics, whereas criticisms of the avant garde came from consumers" (6). But although the introduction surmises that the 'middlebrow' was bolstered by a "particularly British taste for the ordinary and recognizable" (5), it is precisely because they choose to see the 'middlebrow,' implicitly or explicitly, as a democratic force that editors and contributors occasionally downplay the conservatism, patriarchalism, and collusion with the market evinced by some of these mainstream literary products.

Above all, however, the collection manages admirably to readjust our conceptions of 'literary history.' Thus MacLeod, in the fascinating first chapter, details "What People Really Read in 1922," the year of modernist masterpieces (*Ulysses*; *The Waste Land; Jacob's Room*). Judging by numbers, it appears they read A.S.M. Hutchinson's novel *If Winter Comes*, a bestseller whose commercial success was matched by its critical acclaim, and which ramified into literary spin-offs, music, theatre, cinema, and home-furnishings. Similarly, Frost who introduces Part I: "The Market," demonstrates that before critical evaluation separated them out, Joseph Conrad, Rudyard Kipling, and the now forgotten Francis Marion Crawford were grouped together "as common competitors within the same literary market" (41); he retraces their similarities in terms of style, plot, and gender norms. Part II on "Middlebrow Reactions" offers insights into self-reflexive moments in Scottish Kailyard fiction (Walton) or novels by John Galsworthy (Hurlburt) and H.G. Wells (Miller). Walton shows how Kailyard escapism, with its backlash against modernist formal experiments and shifting gender norms, was rewritten not only by anti-Kailyard satires but also by Kailyard novels themselves, as they "often obliquely acknowledg[ed] […] a sense of historical transition and call[ed] attention to their own literary artifice as a nostalgic and impossible fiction" (154). Galsworthy's anti-modernism and investment in materiality is seen by Hurlburt as "a strategic response" to economic and social change (104), a reading which all but erases the backwardness of this 18th-century Country Whig position. It remains debatable whether novels "about the dangers of change" simply produced "a sense of stability in a time of transition" (117; 118), or whether their biologizing descriptions of "emancipated people" as no more than "an excrescence, small, and noisy" (quoted from Galsworthy, 117) were dangerous in themselves. And we cannot but observe that despite the "potentially revolutionary" (137) and non-realistic elements of Wells's *The Sea Lady* (1901) as analysed by Miller, gender norms are firmly in place here, with the *femme fatale* figure and the sexual double standard: "the [male protagonist's] desire for a greater spiritual and sexual freedom" (121), just like the dissatisfaction with conventional domestic arrangements voiced in Hugh MacDiarmid's androcentric *A Drunk Man Looks at the Thistle* (1926) (see Walton 153), reveal an underlying conservatism that could have been addressed more fully.

Several contributors underline how classifications of literary texts as 'middlebrow' were liable to change either during the print-run of a magazine such as *To-day*, with its various readjustments to changing readerships (Kane), or in a transnational perspective, as Part III emphasizes: Here we gain fascinating insights into Flaubert's English 'middlebrow' translations and appropriations (Atkinson). Van Puymbroeck shows how French critic Henry David Davray's penchant for realism made him focus on the British 'middlebrow' from across the channel; Rymenants explores the cross-traffic between British and Dutch conceptions of the 'middlebrow' in literary critics Arnold Bennett and Herman Robbers; and Sanders and Rutten analyse the case of Edgar Wallace, who as a result of Dutch translations, marketing and criticism was "[i]n 1930 […] by far the most popular author on the Dutch book market" (223). With the exception of Sitch's chapter on artist Charles Marriott, the volume remains in the fields of the literary, textual and bibliographical – sometimes resulting in lengthy close readings. Some deeper engagement with how the term 'middlebrow' relates to the notion of the 'popular' would have been desirable, perhaps with reference to John Storey's[1] work. Both high literary modernism and mass culture are only sketchily defined throughout, although we are offered fascinating glimpses into differential readings of the 'middlebrow' through suggestions that *If Winter Comes* was indeed taken by its readers to be 'high art' (McLeod), or that the marketing strategies adopted by May French Sheldon for her translation of Flaubert's *Salammbô* imitated those of the mass market (Atkinson). By means of meticulous case studies such as these, this eminently useful and enjoyable collection points the way towards further explorations of shifting and transitional cultural formations.

ANNE-JULIA ZWIERLEIN

Brigita Jeraj. ***Tendenzen der*** **Female Gothic Fiction** ***im 20. Jahrhundert.*** **Würzburg: Königshausen & Neumann, 2015. 352 pp.**

This informative study of female Gothic fiction - a term the author has adopted from Elaine Showalter - offers a useful introduction to a subject that has received widespread interest in recent literary and cultural criticism, even though it is primarily descriptive rather than explanatory. The immense popularity of Gothic romance since the publication of Horace Walpole's *The Castle of Otranto* and the manifold variations in literature as well as in other media of what was regarded as Gothic in the late 18th and 19th centuries deserve our attention - especially in the context of 20th-century literary criticism. Jeraj is courageous (especially because this is her PhD thesis) because she pays attention to texts that have been considered trivial or merely paperback romances and hence not worthy of academic scholarship in spite of their popularity with readers. Her study also deserves recognition as she works in an exemplary interdisciplinary way: by linking British Gothic fiction to texts written by Irish, US-American and Canadian writers (both female and male), the book is also of interest to readers whose academic focus is not necessarily English literature. Moreover, Jeraj also discusses the manifold adaptations - especially of du Maurier's *Rebecca* – in film and the recent musical adaptations with the same title by the German artists Kunze and Levay.

Jeraj begins her study with an ambitious discussion of Gothic fiction from its beginnings to the present in order to define her concept of the Gothic and the

1 See John Storey. *Cultural Studies and the Study of Popular Culture*. Edinburgh: Edinburgh University Press, 2010.

immense interest in the genre for both women writers and readers since the late 18th century. Even though this short discussion (about 10 pages) is necessarily somewhat cryptic it reminds the reader of the necessity to interpret these texts written by women, for women, and about women (ch. 1.3) from a historical perspective. Unfortunately, the author offers very few explanations for the new tendencies in female Gothic fiction since the late 1920s. To argue, for example, that the new quality of these texts is the exploration of extreme states of women`s psychological disturbances and emotional fears is certainly a correct observation. Yet, she merely finds the reason for this phenomenon in the fact that women are sensitive and more emotional than men (30). Such an explanation – and there are many of this kind – is at best trivial and in terms of gender politics hardly acceptable.

The author pays particular attention to du Maurier's novels and short stories, which she convincingly discusses in terms of a very close reading. Even though the reader gets literally buried under an avalanche of well-known encyclopaedic details Jeraj shows how du Maurier's seemingly trivial texts need to be read in a very sensitive way in relation to the long tradition of Gothic fiction, in particular to all the texts produced by women writers in the 20th century. The reader particularly appreciates that Jeraj includes a discussion of du Maurier's contemporary Michael Avallone, who published a lot of his Gothic romances under a female penname. On the basis of texts published in the 1960s and 70s, she demonstrates how he imitated a female writing strategy in order to attract women readers as well as to achieve commercial success. As many of his roughly 1,000 publications are only available as manuscripts in the Howard Gotlieb Archival Research Center in Boston, MA, and hence not easily accessible, this part of the book deserves praise, especially because Avallone's work is – unfortunately – still neglected in recent studies of Gothic fiction.

Moreover, this – albeit somewhat long – chapter of about 150 pages (half of the book) helps her to demonstrate in later chapters how various Gothic romances adopt and rewrite du Maurier, and how film adaptations work, such as Hitchcock's *Rebecca* or the recent musical of the same title. Her project is also of major interest because she interprets du Maurier's texts interculturally in relation to Margaret Atwood, Angela Carter, Emma Tennant, Shirley Jackson, Elizabeth Bowen and many others. She succeeds in demonstrating how these writers have not merely continued the long tradition of women's Gothic fiction but also redefines both the male and female Gothic from a late 20th-century perspective. Her interpretation of Angela Carter's texts is very suggestive because, on the one hand Jeraj works out how Carter's fiction should be read in terms of the long tradition of women writers who have adopted the Gothic to make their readers aware of the frustrations of women in a patriarchal society. On the other hand, however, she also convincingly illustrates how Carter probes into the construction of female and male sexuality from a 20th-century feminist perspective and how she – for example in her canonical *The Bloody Chamber and Other Stories* – reshapes the tradition of the female Gothic by way of deconstructing its genre conventions. Moreover, she also shows why it is legitimate to see Carter as a major representative of so-called modern female Gothic fiction because of her way of exposing stereotypical gender myths in terms of the politics of capitalist power relations.

Unfortunately, the author remains essentially descriptive and leaves the reader alone to find her or his own explanations. Yet, she has succeeded in reminding the reader of the importance of studying these texts and explore their – albeit controversial – cultural and political potential. In spite of all critical remarks made here the book is a very suggestive introduction to Gothic fiction written by women in the 20th century. Moreover, the book is also helpful for students who wish to pursue this subject further in their BA and MA theses.

STEPHAN LIESKE

Wieland Schwanebeck, ed. *Über Hochstapelei: Perspektiven auf eine kulturelle Praxis*. Berlin: Neofelis, 2014. 226 pp.

This volume collects the papers of an interdisciplinary conference of young academics held in 2013 and dealing with a topic that has generated a number of publications in recent years.[1] The interest in impostors can be explained on the one hand by the continued medial presence of many spectacular cases of identity fraud and deception, which are often taken to herald a cultural malaise, and on the other hand by their scholarly evaluation as symptoms of a postmodern culture in which they subversively expose how any claim to an authentic identity is inevitably undermined by the ubiquity of performance. The book, however, does not see itself as a mere reflection of current trends, but rather argues for imposture as a "timeless cultural practice," perhaps even an "anthropological constant" (14, my translation). In fact, the critical epilogue by Stephan Porombka suggests that the heyday of the impostor has been passé since the beginning of the 20th century. The lessons that the impostor can teach us about society and culture have long been internalized, which is why a historicized examination of the phenomenon is appropriate (217-221). Accordingly, the book sets out to pursue an appreciation and analysis of imposture's various manifestations and contextual conditions of formation (16).

In order to draw attention to the multiplicity of how imposture pervades cultural and social discourses, the book sports an appropriately interdisciplinary approach, featuring contributions from the fields of literary studies, media studies, cultural studies, psychology, and sociology. The danger of such an approach is of course that the multifarious perspectives on and understandings of the subject matter are so varied that their consolidation in one volume appears strained or even incongruent. While the collection can certainly be called eclectic, this is not to the detriment of the book, however. Occasionally, the way in which the concept of imposture is imposed upon some of the material does feel a bit labored and is not always entirely convincing, and one can come away with the feeling that if you handle the concept loosely enough, you can find imposture wherever you choose to look. But what the productive arrangement of the articles in thematic clusters rather than disciplinary fields accomplishes is that the individually fruitful analyses enrich each other by mutually highlighting shades of significance and ways to grasp the manifold implications of the concept.

---

1 See Caroline Rosenthal and Stefanie Schäfer, eds. *Fake Identity?: The Impostor Narrative in North American Culture*. Frankfurt: Campus, 2014; and Wieland Schwanebeck. *Der flexible Mr. Ripley: Männlichkeit und Hochstapelei in Literatur und Film*. Wien, Köln, Weimar: Böhlau, 2014.

The first thematic cluster examines the relationship between imposture and lying. Markus Wierschem argues that 20th-century American literature (exemplified by Eugene O'Neill's *The Iceman Cometh* and Kurt Vonnegut's *Cat's Cradle*) celebrates the lie as a meta-literary argument for the need for fiction by showing how destructive the positivist excesses of truth can be. Sophie Spieler reads the ubiquity of lies and various forms of imposture among virtually all the characters in Tom Wolfe's *The Bonfire of the Vanities* regardless of their social status as weakening the novel's criticism of the elite, yet at the same time fueling its social satire by emphasizing how the shrewd maneuvering in a "landscape of lies" becomes a value in itself. While both articles have their flaws in the way they build their argumentation, they are a stimulating read and complement each other by teasing out the ethical dimensions of lying in differing literary contexts. They are enriched by a contribution from the field of psychology that highlights the scientific limits of lie detection and by a (tongue-in-cheek?) street art/photography project by Lukas Stopczynski.

The second thematic cluster focuses on the pretense of expertise as a particularly topical manifestation of imposture. Especially thought-provoking are the contributions by Sonja Veelen and Wieland Schwanebeck, who, respectively, take a critical look at how the socio-cultural discourses of job interviews and the university, particularly the humanities, foster a climate in which the effective staging of expertise more often than not counts for more than its substantiation. Schwanebeck reads the case of Karl Theodor zu Guttenberg's plagiarized dissertation refreshingly against the grain as a reflection of the flaws of a university system in which imposture is facilitated by the pressure to shore up knowledge capital in a fairly self-contained environment. He delineates the spectrum of academic fraudulence from "bullshit bingo" (150) papers to full-blown plagiarism, and while the tone changes between ominous and jocular, the insights undeniably invite a much-needed critical self-reflection. Anne Herrmann makes similar points about the endemic nature of imposture in expert interviews on television, but her example of the 9/11 broadcast on RTL does not yield the most felicitous illustration of her arguments. Felix Lempp and Jannis Funk, finally, read making-ofs of current blockbuster films as marketing tools that generate curiosity by claiming authentic insights into the production process. The making-of parody "Rain of Madness," documenting the production of Ben Stiller's war film parody *Tropic Thunder*, exemplifies their arguments convincingly if unsurprisingly.

The final thematic cluster looks at the impostor as a cultural type. Sebastian Thede's contribution about the significance of imposture in Werner Serner's novella *Die Tigerin* seems to hide its own meaning behind a barrage of stilted lingo so difficult to decipher that I have wondered whether the article is a hoax serving to illustrate Schwanebeck's arguments about the inherent fraudulence of academic institutions (including its meaning-averse jargon). In contrast, the subsequent article by Bernhard Stricker about the Hollywood classic *All About Eve* delivers a fine reading of that film's condemnation of its protagonist's imposture and in the process, following the philosophy of Stanley Cavell, suggests the ethical relevance of opposing authenticity and theatricality. The final article is another tongue-in-cheek art piece by Stopczynski that consists entirely of Latinate dummy text, which effectively pretends erudition but is in effect nonsensical filler.

The closing epilogue usefully qualifies and reclassifies the introduction's claim to the ubiquity of imposture and rounds off an altogether recommended volume on a topic whose continued relevance for interdisciplinary analysis is undoubtedly demonstrated.

MARTIN HOLTZ

Sonja Fielitz, ed. *"...that I wished myself a horse." The Horse as Representative of Cultural Change in Systems of Thought.* Heidelberg: Winter, 2015. 226 pp.

Among the numerous recent developments in literary and cultural theory, one of the most fruitful and burgeoning enterprises is the study of literary and other texts from an ecological or environmental perspective. Amongst other things, it conceives of literary texts as the main realm of a processural, emergent form of ethics that works by means of fictionalised accounts of possible worlds and imagined consciousness of others, thus maintaining the value of literature in the negotiation of what it means for humans – and the humanities – to be part of a more-than-human world. In this ecocritical context, exciting and challenging work is being done in what has come to be known as, variably, animal, or human-animal studies, zooanthropology, or animality studies: research that aims at understanding the cultural representation of, and epistemological engagement with 'nonhuman animals' in all its various, discourse-forming articulations and the implications of these praxes for the conceptualisation of the human.

Sonja Fielitz's collection of essays positions itself in the context of this 'animal turn' by discussing, from a variety of historical and disciplinary perspectives, the horse as "Representative of Cultural Change in Systems of Thought." The book presents a number of essays divided into three main conceptual parts, 'Authors and Texts,' 'Aesthetics,' and 'Linguistics,' thus seeking to offer a most welcome interdisciplinary engagement with its subject matters beyond mere *Motivgeschichte*. As Fielitz points out in the introduction, the volume rather seeks to interrogate "the dichotomy between horses and humans, and with this a particular focus on the dichotomy of 'body' and 'mind'" (8). This is a large claim indeed, and one certainly difficult to achieve. The first thing that struck me as valuable is the collection's broad historical focus, beginning with, and putting special emphasis on, early modern texts from the 16th and 17th centuries. Thus, the first section, dealing with authors and texts, discusses Shakespeare and Marlowe (Stanley Wells & Paul Edmondson), the Irish 'Ulster Cycle' and 'Finn Cycle' (Erich Poppe), Marvell and verse satire (Roy Eriksen and Kirsten Juhas, respectively), and the works of Jonathan Swift (Hermann Josef Real), thus offering a helpful and enlightening historical depth that much contemporary work on literary engagements with animality seem to be lacking. From there, it moves on to Victorian texts (*Black Beauty* unsurprisingly features twice) with essays by Francesca Orestano and Susanne Peters, and contemporary works such as *War Horse* (Peters, too, and Anja Müller) and *The Studhorse Man* (Martin Kuester).

It is never easy to summarise a wholly diverse collection of essays in the space allotted to a brief review. Much more could be said about the individual essays and their take on the editor's claim that the horse be thought of as 'a representative of cultural change,' and much more could be written about the insightful and studious engagements with an author's life, times, writings, and companion species relationships, such as portrayed in Hermann Real's impressive discussion of Swift's passion for horseback riding (in relation to his works, especially of course *Gulliver's Travels*, his illness, and his stance towards marriage against which he suggests one "could have afforded a Horse for less Money" (62) in one of his letters). I found Susanne Peters's essay "Writing/Riding on Non-anthropocentric Horses," discussing Sewell's *Black Beauty* and Morpurgo's *War Horse*, to be particularly insightful with regard to the questions posed by the introduction, namely, in how far "the psychology of human-animal stories is […] revealing in terms of […] [the] place we ascribe them in our culture" (114). In the course of her essay, Peters sets out to discuss the narrative discourse of said stories, arguing that it is there that literature succeeds in rendering graspable to its readers glimpses of a more-than-human world. Animals, she points out, "appear to possess a sophisticated consciousness which we might then imaginatively access via literature" (115) because via the narrative situation employed, "[d]irect speech [can be] turned into perceiving and interpreting […] The horses feel and think, but they do not speak in human voices" (115). This is not to say that the insights of literature can necessarily be privileged over other engagements with non-human animals; as Peters convincingly shows, while literary texts function as a "testing ground for communicative possibilities without the restrictions of reality and under no obligation to depict something as true," this potential comes as "a mixed blessing: the stories as stories can never be anything but anthropomorphic" – but they do succeed, after all, in rendering animals, or, in this case, horses, "as agents" (117). It should be added that Anja Müller's subsequent piece nicely adds to these findings through a sustained discussion of the implications of having a horse as a reflector, especially concerning narrative voice and the question of realism in novels such as *War Horse* and its stage version.

The following section of 'Aesthetics' explores forms and codes of horsemanship as a sensuous and emotional experience, discussing Equestrian Ballet between 1500 and 1700 (Barbara Ravelhofer) as well as contemporary forms of Freestyle Dressage (Sonja Fielitz) and contextualising these discussions with an essay on neoclassical poetics and the art of horsemanship, by Rolf Lessenich. Fielitz's endorsement of the notion of presentism and presence effects, on the one hand, and the reference to bodily sensations and respective cultural studies, which in the case of the chosen topic have to be redefined in terms of bodily interplays of two agents, seems promising indeed. All in all, one would have wished for more engagements with theoretical tools that would have to be shown to be capable of performing the task of thinking anew about human-animal relations, as promised in the introduction. That is to say, the great historical breadth of the articles and the diversity of horse-related phenomena under scrutiny unfortunately tend to come with a lack of serious engagement with human-animal studies from a theoretical perspective. (The seeming lack of a thorough proofreading is another, if more formal, problem of the volume.) In how far, then, can one say the book is more than *Motivgeschichte*?

One reason is its inclusion of linguistic research. Despite the institutional closeness of literary studies and linguistics, it is somewhat rare to find a collection of essays dedicated to what at first sight seems to be literature-and-culture based inquiry completed by findings from the field of linguistics, which is why I much enjoyed reading the piece by Rolf Kreyer, who presents a discussion of the lexeme 'horse' and its close lexical neighbours 'steed,' 'mare' and so forth from the vantage point of two linguistic corpora covering no less than 30 million words from different literary texts.

Christoph Schubert, drawing on Conceptual Metaphor Theory, discusses metaphors, idiomatic phrases and proverbs and shows how in the cultural memory of English, 'the horse' has functioned and still functions as a vehicle conveying ideas of strength, value, and, more generally, positive connotations as well as a lively storehouse of conceptual means of (re)thinking animality.

Now, in conclusion, back to what the book does and what it does not. Although it sets out to be more than a 'mere' history of motifs and representation and aims at providing a functional history of texts with regard to the idea of cultural change and the interrogation of, for instance, Cartesian mind/body dualisms, I find some of the essays strangely lacking in references to and engagements with the critical literature that has become more and more prominent over the last ten or so years. Susan McHugh's work on animal narratives, Donna Haraway's idea of companion species, Philip Armstrong's discussion of animal imaginaries in the fiction of modernity or Matthew Calarco's philosophical debates on the role of animality in the more recent history of philosophy all would have provided helpful analytical frames and terminological and conceptual means of moving beyond the very restriction on the motif refuted in the book's introduction. On the other hand, it is to the book's definite merit to have assembled a historically thorough and exhaustive collection of texts may stand as a useful introduction to this exciting field of research: Taken as a literary history of the horse in English literature and language, it will, without doubt, benefit students and scholars alike for whom the present findings will be even more helpful if read along more theoretically oriented works by Cary Wolfe, Jacques Derrida, or Erica Fudge.

ROMAN BARTOSCH

Claudia Lamb. ***Die*** **Authorized Version of the Bible (1611)** ***und ihre Sprache.*** **Heidelberg: Winter, 2013. 393 pp.**

There are numerous incentives for a historical linguist to dedicate their time and expertise to the *Authorized Version*, also known as the King James Bible (henceforth KJB; Lamb uses both names and their abbreviations interchangeably throughout her work). Printed for the first time in 1611, it is after all one of the most expressive and revealing representatives of a potentially quasi-standard linguistic status quo in England, emerging right in the transitional period between Middle and Early Modern English. As her own two overarching goals, the author of this monograph set out to "describe the text's genesis in detail" and to provide "a comprehensive and systematic analysis" of what she refers to as "the most significant linguistic aspects that distinguish [the KJB's] language from today's English" (21).

In Chapter 1.4, Lamb formulates five claims she seeks to argue and substantiate in her extensive study, including (1.) the identification and classification of archaic linguistic features from a modern perspective, (2.) as well as within the text's own synchronic frame. Claim (3.) postulates that the language of the KJB in fact was not the actual role model for Modern English inflection, morphology and lexis, while (4.) seems to modify the former, arguing that modern phraseology does indeed reflect major influences and continuations of the KJB's idiomatic repertoire. The author's final point (5.) seems to have been formulated as a mere add-on to the latter, shifting the focus to a cross-linguistic juxtaposition of the idioms identified in the KJB and their equivalents in Modern German.

Before this review moves on to discuss the actual contents of Lamb's work, it has to be pointed out that one of the first impressions this monograph creates is that it is the outcome of what has been both systematically and meticulously conducted analytical research work. In fact, within the ten chapters this book is made up of, the author focuses on dissecting the individual historio-linguistic layers in the primary text so distinctly that she sees the need to provide her readers with two versions of her table of contents: a concise one displaying the chapters in their condensed form, and the actual, detailed one that stretches over six full pages (9-14) and displays the subchapters counted up to six digits (e.g. 5.7.1.2.1.3).

While this fine-grained structure reflects both the author's wide-ranging expert knowledge and her well-wrought linguistic approach towards the KJB, the high number of subdivisions and the fact that a few of the subchapters are only one page long or even shorter (cf. e.g. 2.2.2, 2.2.3, 2.2.4, 2.3, 2.4, 3.6.2), do not only render the reading discontinuous at times, but also tend to undersell the contents. The text-coherent structure would have benefitted from putting the numerous individual phenomena into closer relation to each other rather than anatomizing and particularizing each of them. (In general, coherence and reader-friendliness could have been extensively enhanced by numbering and naming the (2 images and) 22 tables Lamb includes in her main text and by adding running heads).

The linguistic analysis of the text itself stretches over five of ten chapters, describing various aspects of typographical (ch. 4), morphological (ch. 5), syntactical (ch. 6), and lexico-semantic (chs. 7, 8) relevance. These core contents of the book are put into a broader context by two chapters presenting socio-historical cornerstones of the KJB's prehistory (33-47, ch. 2), its creation period as well as its paths of reception, adaptation and translation throughout the subsequent centuries (49-64, ch. 3), all preceded by a concise introductory chapter (21-32, ch. 1) that lays out the author's analytical objectives and approach.

The length and density of the core chapters is rather varied, ranging from as little as 16 pages (ch. 6) up to ca. 80 pages (chs. 5 and 7), essentially displaying a somewhat unbalanced array of analytical insights and sustaining examples. At the same time, however, the length of the individual chapters on the one hand and the depth of descriptive analysis presented therein on the other hand do not necessarily correlate: Chapter 4, for instance, provides a rich and valuable account of typographical and punctuational characteristics on 44 pages, while chapter 5, the longest section of the book, contains subchapters that are so particularized that the length of some of its sections, as already mentioned, hardly exceeds half a page.

Overall, Lamb's study lacks argumentative coherence as well as conceptual and terminological depth. The former is mainly curtailed by the fact that Lamb fails to consistently establish intratextual cross-references and relations between her observations and the claims she formulates in 1.4. It is only in chapter 9 (and chapter 10, a direct English rendition of chapter 9 respectively), titled "Summary and Outlook," that she finally picks them up and briefly works them through.

The issue of "conceptual and terminological depth" becomes particularly apparent in chapters 5 and 6, where Lamb neither adequately discusses her notional choices, nor brings them (or the phenomena she refers to, respectively) into the context of recent and relevant historio-linguistic research. The reader must thus infer that the terminology was adopted merely unquestioned from the course books that are repeatedly cited throughout the book (e.g. Brunner 1984; Crystal 2003; Görlach 1994; 2002; Graband 1965; Kisbye 1971-72)[1]. This and the aforementioned fact that the individual (sub)chapters stand isolated rather than interlocked and argumentatively coherent create a reading analogous to a perfunctorily encyclopaedic inventory, conventionally expected in an introduction to historical linguistics or, more specifically, Early Modern English, rather than in a linguistic research study.

As Lamb shifts her focus onto lexico-semantic issues including semantic change, lexical loss and expansion, her explanations and style take on a more confident and plausible tone. The author amends and adds to the findings presented by Crystal (2004) and complements the 2012 OED version's list of earliest recorded lexical material in chapter 7, while chapter 8 further explores phraseological and idiomatic influences the KJB has wielded on the Modern English lexico-syntactical inventory. While Lamb's itemization of idioms is thorough, again complementing Crystal's explications from 2010, this chapter, too, falls short of clear-cut terminological stance-taking and lexical coherence: the author's use of the German nouns 'Phraseologismus,' 'Phrase,' 'Idiom,' 'Redensart,' 'Redewendung,' 'Schlüsselwort,' and 'Zitat,' for instance, seems interchangeable, and remains, just like Lamb's classification of idioms in contrast to e.g. collocations (cf. list in 8.1.1.1: e.g. brotherly love, two mites, no small stir, great whore), uncommented and intransparent.[2]

Lamb's reasoning and roundup in chapter 9 is systematic and transparent – needless to say, however, that a study summary and outlook will inevitably leave open questions to be postponed to future works. It would have been intriguing to learn more about cross- and inter-genre implications deductible from her findings. After all, it has recently been claimed by e.g. Goodman that "[the KJB's] robust language [...] kept to a vocabulary less than a third the size of Shakespeare's, allowing it to fulfill Tyndale's dream, that one day the Bible's message would be open to the humblest speaker of English" (2013, 73)[3].

Overall, Lamb chose a clearly descriptive rather than an interpretively ambitious take on the KJB, which is why her analytical approach did not grant her much space for innovation or creativity in the first place. Consequently, the study's research outcome and contribution to the field and any adjacent disciplines cannot be regarded as particularly groundbreaking. *Die* Authorized Version of the Bible (1611) *und ihre Sprache* still comes off as a solid text-analytical and descriptive study, providing "a comprehensive and systematic analysis" of the complex linguistic layers treasured by the text (see above). In fact, the meticulous structure and particularization of these is a

---

1 Karl Brunner. *Die englische Sprache II*. Tübingen: Niemeyer, 1984 (reprint 1960-62); David Crystal. *The Cambridge Encyclopedia of the English Language*. Cambridge: UP, 2003 (2nd ed.); Manfred Görlach. *Einführung ins Frühneuenglische*. Heidelberg: Winter, 1994 (2nd ed.); Manfred Görlach. *Einführung in die englische Sprachgeschichte*. Heidelberg: Winter, 2002 (5th ed.); Gerhard Graband. *Die Entwicklung der frühneuenglischen Nominalflexion*. Tübingen: Niemeyer, 1965; Torben Kisbye. *An Historical Outline of English Syntax*. 2 volumes. Aarhus: Akademisk Boghandel, 1971-72.

2 The reader would have benefitted a lot from a much more systematic and comprehensive index containing the phrases Lamb identified in the KJB in their entirety.

3 Lenn Goodman. "The King James Bible at 401." *Society* 50 /1 (2013): 73-80.

clear strength of this book that can definitely serve as a valuable springboard into more specific studies on and in relation to the King James Bible.

MONIKA KIRNER-LUDWIG

Viveka Velupillai. *Pidgins, Creoles and Mixed Languages. An Introduction.* Amsterdam and Philadelphia: John Benjamins. 2015. viii + 599 pp.

There is a wide range of introduction books on pidgins and creole languages and they all have contributed considerably to the field starting with Hall (1966), Todd (1974), Romaine (1988), Arends et al. (1994)[1] among others. However this introduction offers more than an introduction.

The book consists of two parts. In Part I the first three chapters deal with definitions of pidgins, creole languages, and mixed languages with their respective linguistic features. The author introduces snapshots. These snapshots have more or less the same format and aim at giving the reader some brief socio-historical and sociolinguistic overview followed by some insights into the structures of the language concerned. A short text and some primary sources are also included.

The remaining chapters (4 to 8) handle the theoretical issues closely linked to these areas. Chapter 4 discusses the socio-historical background of pidgins and creole languages. While chapter 5 provides an overview on the major theories of genesis accounting for pidgins, chapter 6 concentrates on the theories of genesis that explain creole languages. Chapter 7 introduces crucial notions in language contact such as variation and change and relates them to the areas under discussion. Chapter 8 provides a stand on these languages in society. Issues such as language policy and planning, as well as some cultural issues are discussed.

Part II zooms into some typical features of these contact languages by checking them in both the pidgin and creole language samples. The author compares the distribution of these features in the samples with that in non-pidgins and non-creoles. The reader should note that such a systematic discussion of assumptions and testing has not been offered in any previous introductions. The distinction between the various samples (e.g. for creoles, extended pidgins) is very helpful to the beginner student. In chapter 9 the reader is introduced to consonants and vowel inventories, syllables and tones. Chapter 10 investigates some morphological processes such as synthesis and reduplication while chapter 11 focuses on nominal plurality and (in)definiteness. In chapter 12 tense, mood and aspect are discussed. Word order and passive constructions form the object of investigation in chapter 13. Chapter 14 analyses relative clauses and serial verb constructions. In chapter 15 the author discusses pragmatics, especially negation, polar questions and finally politeness.

This book provides a clear and accessible introduction to current work in the field of Contact Linguistics. One major achievement of the book is the integration of

1 See Jacques Arends et al., eds. *Pidgins and Creoles: An Introduction*. Amsterdam/ Philadelphia: John Benjamins, 1994; Robert Hall. *Pidgin and Creole Languages*. Ithaca: Cornell University Press, 1966; Suzanne Romaine. *Pidgin & Creole Languages*. London: Longman, 1988; and Loreto Todd. *Pidgins and Creoles*. London: Routledge & Paul, 1974.

extensive chapters on three well-established types of contact languages (pidgins (including extended pidgins), creole and mixed languages, given that mixed languages have seldom been included alongside with pidgins and creole languages in the discussion on contact languages. Two exceptions here are Arends et al. (1994) and Winford (2003)[1]. Further, the author successfully provides the reader with a global perspective on these languages, covering the Atlantic, the Indian Ocean and the Pacific worlds. Another achievement of this book lies in its pedagogical value. The author provides exercises, key points, snapshots, summaries and an extensive glossary, thus addressing the needs of students. Further, the book has maps, ample examples with interlinearized translations, extensive sources, and short texts.

All in all, the book is well written. This volume can certainly be highly recommended as a course book for students interested in Contact Languages. Scholars with extensive knowledge in the field will also appreciate the wealth of data that has been carefully compiled in this book.

DANY ADONE

Wolfgang Hallet and Carola Surkamp, eds. *Dramendidaktik und Dramenpädagogik im Fremdsprachenunterricht.* Trier: WVT, 2015. 345 pp.

Dramendidaktik, Dramenpädagogik, szenisch-dramatische Verfahren, szenische Interpretationsverfahren, Handlungs- und Produktionsorientierung, kritisches Inszenieren, performative Fremdsprachenkompetenz, and, finally, *Dramenanalyse* and *Drameninterpretation* – these key terms of the present volume cover the range of approaches specified therein. Being faced with the intricate task of having to translate these meaning-laden terms into English, the reviewer feels slightly at a loss. Clearly, the established German-language discourses on Teaching English as a Foreign Language (TEFL) and, more specifically, the teaching of literature(s) and culture(s) appears difficult to link to the international TEFL discourses, including their specific technical terms. And, indeed, the highly sophisticated and specialized terminology employed throughout this collection of seventeen contributions to drama pedagogy, acting out or performance-oriented approaches to TEFL may be indicative of the first of four distinct and interrelated insights to be gained from this volume.

First, there is a highly refined and high-brow discourse evolving in the field of teaching drama and performance, be it drama as a topic or genre *sui generis*, be it the broader concept of foregrounding elements of performance and acting out as integral elements of foreign language pedagogy.

A second insight gleaned from this volume is that the discourse on drama and performance is neatly ensconced in the established German TEFL discourse patterns shaping and forming what we understand by "teaching literature." This includes the – to some, futile – attempt to make the teaching of literature compatible with the current competence-orientation, including the demand for functional communicative competences that are of use in the 'real world out there.' It also embraces present-day preferences for student-, process- and action-orientation and the new perspective on teaching-learning scenarios that go beyond the classroom and expose learners to the foreign language in places outside the usual confines of institutionalized TEFL.

1 Donald Winford. *An Introduction to Contact Linguistics*. Oxford: Blackwell, 2003.

Third, although there are several contributions integrating analytical, text-focused and "desk-bound" interpretations of dramatic texts, with one article (by Carola Surkamp with Ansgar Nünning) focusing particularly on "Categories, Questions and Methods of Drama Analysis in the Context of Scenic Methods […]," the brunt of the argument developed in all articles combined is clearly a shift from analysis and interpretation to using and creating something 'off the page.' A strong plea for performative approaches to TEFL is paradigmatically brought forward in Wolfgang Hallet's programmatic article on "Performativity and Theatricality in Everyday Life: Performative Competence and Cultural Learning." The call for observing the performative elements in everyday communication is echoed in several contributions such as in Jenny Passon's survey article on approaches to theatre and drama pedagogy (a very useful contribution); Manfred Schewe delineates recent developments from drama pedagogy to a performance-oriented concept; Barbara Schmenk critically attempts to link drama pedagogy to the demands of the *Common European Framework of Reference for Languages*, national standards and competence issues; Almut Küppers explores issues of intercultural learning via drama and drama techniques; Lotta König adds an important angle by discussing ways and methods of "staging gender"; Jochen Baier, Jasmin Bührle and Melanie Gecius suggest ways of combining drama classes with digital media productions. In addition to several projects concerning acting out or staging a play (see the theoretical contribution by Christiane Lütge and the projects discussed by Britta Freitag-Hild on *A Raisin in the Sun*, Stephanie Sommerfeld and Mark Bischoff on *Trifles*), there are several articles on practical issues of theatre projects (Ingrid Stritzelsberger; Heike Wedel; Franziska Elis, Adrian Hack, Hannes Mehrer). Katharina Delius and Carola Surkamp add yet another extremely useful article on furthering aesthetic competences through visits to theatre productions, detailing possible tasks according to the pre-, during- and post-visit pattern.

A fourth and final insight remains with the reader: this volume takes up the discussion of the shift from text analysis to acting out to using texts as triggers for performance(s) of any kind.[1] This collection of articles forcefully underscores the paradigm shift from drama, theatre or performance studies as being still connected with a literary text to an approach which highlights elements of "performance" as an integral part of human interaction and communication, of intercultural or cultural learning. This is encapsulated in the title of Franziska Elis' contribution, "Using Methods of Drama Pedagogy to Develop Language and Communicative Competences." The bottom line is clearly that readers of this collection of articles will find both the traditional field of literary approaches to drama and performance and the currently favoured field of "performance as communication." The broad perspective of this volume offers multiple suggestions as to how to interrelate and integrate both areas of research and teaching/learning.

LAURENZ VOLKMANN

1 These publications should have at least been mentioned in the introduction to this volume; see Rüdiger Ahrens et al., ed. *Moderne Dramendidaktik für den Fremdsprachenunterricht*. Heidelberg: Winter, 2008; Almut Küppers, Torben Schmidt, Maik Walter, eds. *Inszenierungen im Fremdsprachenunterricht. Grundlagen, Formen, Perspektiven*. Braunschweig: Bildungshaus Schulbuchverlage, 2011; Susanne Peters et al., ed. *Drama*. 2 vols. Series Teaching Contemporary Literature and Culture. Trier: WVT, 2006.

LIST OF CONTRIBUTORS

ADONE, Dany, Professor Dr., Universität zu Köln, Englisches Seminar I, Albertus Magnus Platz, D-50923 Köln, Germany, d.adone@uni-koeln.de.

BARTOSCH, Roman, Dr., Universität zu Köln, Englisches Seminar II, Gronewaldstr. 2, D-50931 Köln, Germany, roman.bartosch@uni-koeln.de.

CHILDS, Peter, Professor Dr., Newman University, Genners Lane, Birmingham, B32 3NT, UK, p.childs@newman.ac.uk.

DI SCALA, Roberto, Via Nazionale Cisa, 48ter, 54016 Terrarossa - Licciana Nardi (MS), Italy, roberto.discala@belmesseri.it.

GANTEAU, Jean-Michel, Professor Dr., University Paul Valéry Montpellier 3, Département d'Etudes anglophones, Route de Mende, 34 199 Montpellier Cedex 5, France, jean-michel.ganteau@univ-montp3.fr.

GYMNICH, Marion, Professor Dr., Rheinische Friedrich-Wilhelms-Universität Bonn, Institut für Anglistik, Amerikanistik und Keltologie, Regina-Pacis-Weg 5, D-53113 Bonn, Germany, mgymnich@uni-bonn.de.

HOLTZ, Martin, Dr., Ernst-Moritz-Arndt-Universität Greifswald, Institut für Anglistik/ Amerikanistik, Steinbeckerstr. 15, D-17487 Greifswald, Germany, holtzm@uni-greifswald.de.

HOUSWITSCHKA, Christoph, Professor Dr., Universität Bamberg, Institut für Anglistik und Amerikanistik, Kapuzinerstr. 16, D-96047 Bamberg, Germany, christoph.houswitschka@uni-bamberg.de.

KÄCK, Elin, Dr., Linköping University, Department of Culture and Communication, SE-581 83 Linköping, Sweden, elin.kack@liu.se.

KARSCHAY, Stephan, Professor Dr., Universität Hamburg, Institut für Anglistik und Amerikanistik, Von-Melle-Park 6, D-20146 Hamburg, Germany, stephan.karschay@uni-hamburg.de.

KIRNER-LUDWIG, Monika, Dr., University at Albany, State University of New York, Department of Educational Theory & Practice, ED 113/350, 1400 Washington Avenue, Albany, NY 12222, USA, mkirner-ludwig@albany.edu.

LIESKE, Stephan, Dr., Humboldt-Universität zu Berlin, Institut für Anglistik und Amerikanistik, Unter den Linden 6, D-10099 Berlin, Germany, stephan.lieske@rz.hu-berlin.de.

LÖSCHNIGG, Martin, Professor Dr., Karl-Franzens-Universität Graz, Institut für Anglistik, Heinrichstr. 36/II, 8010 Graz, Austria, martin.loeschnigg@uni-graz.at.

MÜLLER, Sabine Lenore, Dr., Universität Leipzig, Institut für Anglistik, Beethovenstr. 15, D-04107 Leipzig, Germany, slmueller@uni-leipzig.de.

PETERS, Susanne, Professor Dr., Otto-von-Guericke-Universität Magdeburg, Fakultät für Humanwissenschaften, Universitätsplatz 2, D-39106 Magdeburg, Germany, susanne.peters@ovgu.de.

PUSCHMANN-NALENZ, Barbara, Dr. habil., Ruhr-Universität Bochum, Englisches Seminar, Universitätsstr. 150, D-44801 Bochum, Germany, puschbbc@gmail.com.

ROSTEK, Joanna, Dr., Universität Passau, Englische Literatur und Kultur, Innstr. 25, D-94032 Passau, Germany, joanna.rostek@uni-passau.de.

STEIN, Daniel, Professor Dr., Universität Siegen, Seminar für Anglistik, Adolf-Reichwein-Str. 2, D-57068 Siegen, Germany, stein@anglistik.uni-siegen.de.

TATE, Andrew, Dr., Department of English and Creative Writing, County College, Lancaster University, Lancaster LA1 4YD, UK, a.tate@lancaster.ac.uk.

TÖNNIES, Merle, Professor Dr., Universität Paderborn, Institut für Anglistik und Amerikanistik, Warburger Str. 100, D-33098 Paderborn, Germany, toennies@mail.uni-paderborn.de.

VERSTEEGEN, Heinrich, Dr., Ruhr-Universität Bochum, Englisches Seminar, Universitätsstr. 150, D-44801 Bochum, Germany, heinrich.versteegen@ruhr-uni-bochum.de.

VOLKMANN, Laurenz, Professor Dr., Friedrich-Schiller-Universität Jena, Institut für Anglistik/Amerikanistik, Ernst-Abbe-Platz 8, D-07743 Jena, Germany, l.volk@uni-jena.de.

ZIMMERMANN, Ulrike, Dr., Albert-Ludwigs-Universität Freiburg, Englisches Seminar, Rempartstr. 15, D-79085 Freiburg, Germany, ulrike.zimmermann@anglistik.uni-freiburg.de.

ZWIERLEIN, Anne-Julia, Professor Dr., Universität Regensburg, Institut für Anglistik und Amerikanistik, D-93040 Regensburg, Germany, anne.zwierlein@ur.de.

STYLE SHEET

1. Only contributions written in English will be published. Please stick to either British or American English. Non-native speakers are requested to have their manuscripts proof-read by native speakers before submitting them.
2. The font size should be Times New Roman 10 (TNR 8 for footnotes).
3. Text and footnotes should be single-spaced. Please use footnotes instead of endnotes, numbered consecutively throughout the whole manuscript. For **book reviews**, please keep footnotes to an absolute minimum.
4. Italics are used for foreign words in the English text, for titles of books, plays, etc. Articles in periodicals or books are enclosed in double quotation marks (no italics), titles of periodicals etc. are given in italics.
5. Please use "quotation marks" instead of (typographic) “inverted commas” for all quotations not separated from the context. Quotations of more than three lines should be separated from the context and indented on the left margin (1 cm) without quotation marks. Omissions should be marked with square brackets […].
6. Bibliographical references are included in the text and/or footnotes in shortened form and in round brackets, indicating author, publication date and page numbers. If a title has more than one author, please order their names alphabetically, separated by semicolons, e.g. (Frye 1957, 85; Rosier 1962, 4). Please provide full references in the Works Cited section at the end of your article (see examples). Please note that the MLA does no longer require URLs for electronic/web sources.
7. Please observe AE conventions for punctuation (i.e. place commas and periods/full stops before the closing quotation marks): "Henry," she said, "please take them out."
8. Please send the manuscript by e-mail to: redaktion-anglistik@uni-koeln.de.
9. Reviews should not exceed 800 to 1000 words.

Bibliographical References

Beowulf: A Student Edition. Ed. George Jack. Oxford: Clarendon, 1994.

Frye, Northrop. *Anatomy of Criticism: Four Essays*. Princeton: Princeton University Press, 1957.

—. *The Educated Imagination*. Bloomington: Indiana University Press, 1964.

Horwitz, Elaine K. "Preliminary Evidence for the Reliability and Validity of a Foreign Language Anxiety Scale." *TESOL Quarterly* 20 (1986): 559-562.

—, Michael B. Horwitz, and Joann Cope. "Foreign Language Classroom Anxiety." *The Modern Language Journal* 70 (1986): 125-132.

Lowi, Theodore, Benjamin Ginsberg, and Steve Jackson. *Analyzing American Government: American Government, Freedom and Power*. New York: Norton, 1994.

New, William H. "Panel." *Taking Stock: The Calgary Conference on the Canadian Novel*. Ed. Charles R. Steele. Downsview, ON: ECW Press, 1982. 34-37.

Schoeck, Eric. "An Interview with Ian McEwan." 1 January 1998. *Capitola Book Café*. Web. 31 May 2010.

Other bibliographical references should observe the conventions set out in the *MLA Handbook for Writers of Research Papers* (7th Edition).

CALL FOR DONATIONS

The German Association for English Studies has opened a special account for donations:

Sparkasse Paderborn
IBAN: DE37 4765 0130 0000 0911 40
BIC: WELADE3LXXX

In a period characterized by a growing number of foundations and by a communal and individual spirit of support for worthy causes, we ask each member of the German Association for English Studies to increase the Association's ability to further the cause of the study of English in all its variations.

On behalf of the association
Christoph Ehland, Treasurer